.50

American Indian Collectibles

D0168013

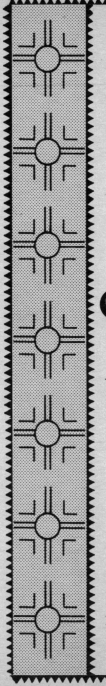

The
Official®
Identification
and
Price Guide
to

American
Indian
Collectibles

Dawn E. Reno

Photos by
Donald Vogt

FIRST EDITION

HOUSE OF COLLECTIBLES
NEW YORK

Important Notice. All of the information, including valuations, in this book has been compiled from the most reliable sources, and every effort has been made to eliminate errors and questionable data. Nevertheless, the possibility of error, in a work of such immense scope, always exists. The publisher will not be held responsible for losses which may occur in the purchase, sale, or other transaction of items because of information contained herein. Readers who feel they have discovered errors are invited to *write* and inform us, so they may be corrected in subsequent editions. Those seeking further information on the topics covered in this book are advised to refer to the complete line of *Official Price Guides* published by the House of Collectibles.

© 1988 Dawn Reno

All rights reserved under International and
Pan-American Copyright Conventions.

Published by: The House of Collectibles
              201 East 50th Street
              New York, New York 10022

Distributed by Ballantine Books, a division of Random House, Inc., New York, and simultaneously in Canada by Random House of Canada Limited, Toronto.

Manufactured in the United States of America

ISBN: 0-876-37752-5

10 9 8 7 6 5 4 3 2 1

*Dedicated to
my mother and father,
Donald and Elaine Brander,
for their support and love through the years.*

TABLE OF CONTENTS

▼▼▼▼▼▼▼▼▼▼▼

ACKNOWLEDGMENTS

▼▼▼▼▼▼▼▼▼▼▼▼

I would like to take this opportunity to extend my heartfelt gratitude to those people who helped my photographer, Donald Vogt, and I put this book together. Though my contributors are too many to mention, there are people throughout the Southwest who took us into their homes and shops, sometimes even providing us with lodging and food, that deserve medals for putting up with our whirlwind visit. The auctioneers, dealers, collectors, and museums who corresponded with me during my research period, lending copies of their catalogs and contributing photos and knowledge, are very special to me and without them this book would not have been possible.

Extra special thanks goes to my editor, Dorothy Harris, who lent a long-distance ear whenever I needed to discuss some quirk which had popped up during the writing of the manuscript; to my family, whose patience was often stretched to the limit; and to my photographer's partner-in-life, and my friend, Kristin Duval, who we missed having join us on our trip but whose support and appreciation transcended travel and time. My appreciation goes also to Bettie Curboy who provided the line drawings throughout the book. Most of all, thanks to my parents, to whom this book is dedicated and who were the first to make me feel that the sentences I strung together were worth reading.

INTRODUCTION

▼▼▼▼▼▼▼▼▼▼▼▼

When I began putting together a proposal for Indian collectibles, I turned my attention to what was going on in the antiques market. Much to my surprise, I discovered that decorating magazines were beginning to pick up on an interesting trend. Though New England saltbox houses and country antiques had not fallen from favor, items with a Southwestern influence and Indian arts and crafts were joining quilts and Bennington pottery as favored decorating pieces on the covers of the glossier magazines.

Predictions by major dealers and collectors were already being realized—Southwestern pieces such as weavings, pottery, and Indian arts would be strong for the next couple of years. Dealers have begun putting together investment portfolios that specialize in the acquisition of Amerind artifacts. Even retail gift shops all over the country are picking up on what they call "the Southwestern look." Shows, such as the annual San Francisco Antique American Indian Art Show and Sale, will also probably begin popping up in other parts of the country as interest in Indian items begins to "be revived" all over the United States.

The Smithsonian, known for its interest in native American items, as well as for its wonderful research facilities, incorporated a show of Indian arts in its "Lost and Found Traditions" series. The show focused on the continuing history of traditional art of the North American Indian and exhibited 382 of the best pieces made during the period 1965–1985.

When I traveled throughout the Southwest and other parts of the United States to obtain materials and photos for this project, I heard, more than once, that people were taking money out of the stock market and instead were investing in American Indian art/artifacts. That fact intrigued me because it meant the market for antiques would be strong—and that the Indian market was becoming even stronger.

"Be sure you tell your readers about connoisseurship," one of my contributors advised during a research trip through the Southwest. He made a good point. Connoisseurship is something of which we should all be aware, because even if we have only $100 to spend, we should buy the best item that $100 can buy. Not only will we be rewarded by owning something of which we can be proud, but we have probably made a good investment in the future.

Becoming a connoisseur of Indian items may not be easy. However, the knowledge one gains along the way is of a history rich in art appreciation, religion, and strength; a knowledge of lives so intertwined with Mother Earth that their involvement shows up in everything they do. The pride the American Indian feels for his people, religion, art, land, and life is something we can all experience without spending a cent.

Finally, a note of caution. As in most other areas of antique collection, copies and imitations abound. Factories in Japan produce cheap replicas of Indian jewelry, dolls, and pottery which we should not even allow into the United States. By developing a sense of connoisseurship, you can be sure that what you're collecting is truly an artifact made by native Americans.

American Indian Collectibles

ART

▼▼▼▼▼▼▼▼▼▼▼▼

INTRODUCTION

In compiling the information for this chapter, there was much deliberation about whether to focus only on Indian artists or also on those artists whose work includes scenes of Indian life. I have decided to include both of these categories. I believe without both, the collector will not see the full scope of American Indian art.

Publications such as *American Indian Art* and *Southwest Art* focus their attention on Indian art. They are the best sources for tracking what is happening today in the world of antiques—a resurgence of interest in art of and by the American Indian.

One recent development in the art world concerning artists who specialized in painting the American Indian was a major retrospective of the work of George de Forest Brush, held in 1985. Museums that held de Forest Brush's works loaned them to this widely shown exhibit, the first such show of his work since 1933.

Since that time, the field has opened even further. Many other galleries have spotlighted works of and by the American Indian. Antiques shows, such as the Indiana Antiques Show, recently featured Bodmer prints. This show is following the pattern formed in the past couple of years and it is predicted that more will pick up the trend. The Indian theme, once popular only in the Southwest, will soon rival New England antiques as the new "country look." The Smithsonian, grandfather of all museums in this country, also sponsored a recent exhibit in their "Lost and Found Traditions" series which highlighted Indian art. The show received a lot of press.

Suffice it to say, Indian art is part of the American heritage, and, should you own a piece of work in this category, you have an investment that will continue to grow.

In the Biographies section of this chapter, those artists who are Indian are denoted by tribe; those not so noted are either white or there was no tribal information uncovered during research.

AMERICAN INDIAN WOMEN ARTISTS

At this juncture, it is important to note that the first American women artists were Indian. During America's early years, Indian women used their sensitivity to texture and color to produce some of the most imaginative designs the world has seen. These designs are exemplified in their quilling, pottery, blanket weaving, beadwork, and painting scenes on walls, tepees, and clothing.

Their art was not taught to them in a classroom, but passed down to them by their mothers, sisters, aunts, and grandmothers. The geometry of forms they used, the interlocking of figures and space, are techniques which American Indian women have used for centuries, and which abstract painters now struggle for years to master.

SYMBOLS IN INDIAN ART

The Amerind artist did not paint just to see a pretty picture. He was often telling stories through his art, relaying family histories or tales of battle, or giving directions to another location.

Though most symbols used have a very clear, definitive meaning, that meaning can change if it is painted in a different color. A pipe tomahawk, for example, represents a peaceful council; if painted red, however, it could also denote a war council. Symbols also mean different things to different tribes. A triangle, for example, or a semicircle with straight lines descending from the base, is a raincloud and rain to one of the Pueblo tribes. It can mean a mountain with streams to a Plains Indian, however, or a bear (or bear claw) to other tribes.

The Southwest tribes use many different designs, as do the Pacific Coast, Northwest Coast, and Plains tribes. Southwestern Indians decorate pottery, rugs, sandpaintings, and kachinas with their symbols, while Northwest Coast tribes use symbols on house poles, boxes, rattles, clothing, and carvings. The Plains Indians use symbols on hides, blankets, and clothing. By learning to recognize some of these symbols and their meanings, you are learning a new language, and the work done by the Amerind will suddenly become more interesting . . . yet, more mystifying.

Some of the symbols used are depicted below:

Arrow = protection

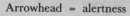

Arrowhead = alertness

Bear tracks = good omen

Big mountain = abundance

Bird = carefree

Butterfly = beauty

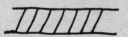

Cactus = sign of desert

Deer tracks = plenty of games

Enclosure = surrounded

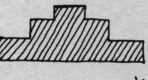

Hopi cloud = prayer for snow

Horse = journey

Lasso = captivity

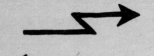

Lightning = swiftness

Lightning snake = swiftness

Rain clouds = good prospects

Raindrops = food

Rattlesnake jaw = strength

Running water = no thirst

Squash blossom = fertility

Summer bird = prayer for warmth

Sun symbol = happiness

Thunderbird = bearer of happiness

Thunderbird tracks = bright prospects

Watchful eye = caution

PLAINS INDIAN ART OF HORSE PAINTING

Though not something which can be kept on display, or which we can attribute to a certain artist, we must consider the Plains Indian art of painting their horses. The animals were painted to go into war and were camouflaged or decorated according to tribal ritual and ceremony.

Certain tribes used symbols and colors unique to that clan, but some markings were used by all. For example, when a warrior had led his people into battle, a rectangle was painted on his horse. If an enemy had been struck down or hand-to-hand combat had occurred, the symbol on the horse would be a handprint. The Sioux's mark of highest honor was a red handprint on the rump of the warrior's horse.

Other symbols include thick circles with red centers which meant a battle had been fought from behind logs or rocks and enemies had been killed. Small open circles in a row meant the warrior had been in a battle which had been fought in trenches. Circles around the horse's nose were thought to improve the animal's smell; if made around the eyes, it was believed eyesight would be improved; around other body parts, such circles could show that the animal had been wounded. Coup marks were signified by three or four short, straight lines, while arrowheads on the horse's hooves signified the surefootedness and fleetness of the horse.

Each marking had a different meaning and some markings meant different things to different tribes.

SOUTHWESTERN SAND PAINTING

Because they were not originally done as art, sand paintings were not collectible until recently. Although the general belief is that the Pueblo Indians taught the Navajos the art of sand painting, the Navajos insist that their art was taught to them by the "Holy Ones."

Sand painting has traditionally been used by the medicine man in an effort to maintain the delicate balance of the world. That balance can only be upset by man when he "causes" a disease or illness. The Shaman comes to the offender's hogan, designs his sand painting on clean white sand on the hogan's dirt floor, and incorporates an opening in the painting which faces east. This opening will make it difficult for evil to enter. Only five sacred sand colors are used in sand painting and each detail must be perfect. The slightest deviation in this ritual is believed to cause great trouble. The medicine man, in a deep trance, takes the design for the sand painting from his mind, never making two alike.

Once the painting is finished, the patient is brought to the center of the work. The medicine man then performs his ceremony to drive the evil away. When done, the sand painting is swept into a blanket. Before sunset, the blanket is carried outside and the sand is blown into the wind—to be returned to Mother Earth so that the evil forces trapped by the sand painting will not escape.

The sacred designs of sand painting were not viewed by outsiders until the late 1800s. By the early 1900s, historians and traders were reproducing the designs. However, sand paintings were not done in a permanent manner until a "How to Sand Paint" kit was developed by David Villasenor (ca. 1960). To craft a sand painting, only handground rocks, minerals, or sandstone are used. The work is a buildup of these materials with the finest sands being the best to use.

Though sand paintings have only been commercially available for approximately 25 years, one can sometimes find earlier examples. Today, Amerind artists developing sand paintings are beginning to garner some interest in the art world.

BIOGRAPHIES

General

As you might be able to tell by reading some of the biographies included in this chapter, American Indian art was influenced by such people as Olaf Nordmark, a muralist, who taught a cross-section of American Indian artists; Frederick Dockstader, the Director of the Museum of the American Indian in New York City and a man who has a large collection of the finest of American Indian art; and Dorothy Dunn, a young white woman who founded the first department of painting at the Santa Fe Indian School in 1932. Regarding the latter, this was the first important Indian school in the United States. Dunn taught in the traditional style and instructed her students to paint without using any shadows. Another influence on American Indian art occurred during the early days of the Southwest when an advertising man, W.H. Simpson, decided to use art to lure travelers to the exotic regions of Santa Fe and Taos. Indians learned to do murals and to enlarge their work to poster size.

Because of the availability of work and the encouragement which they felt, artists built colonies in the area. Those establishments flourished and gave us a rich tapestry of works done by such artists as Georgia O'Keefe. Since that time, Indian artists have no longer been restricted by cultural barriers. They have begun breaking with tradition to use new mediums and materials not originally associated with Indian art work.

The lack of well-kept records at Indian schools and the lack of communication about Indian artists often make it difficult to trace an artist's history. In fact, the only book I found that documented biographies of Indian artists was published by the Museum of the American Indian in 1968. It was compiled by Jeanne Snodgrass while she was curator of American Indian art at the Philbrook Art Center. Snodgrass's accumulated information, garnered from exhibits and competitions held by the Center since its first exhibition in 1946, was the basis for the directory. Though plans were originally made to update the directory, the task has not been undertaken at this writing.

This compilation, as well as a good smattering of newspaper and magazine articles and other listings of artists, served as the basis for the biographies detailed in this chapter. Along with a brief description of the artist and his/her work, I have tried to include an approximate range of what the artist's work is currently bringing in today's market.

Narciso Platero Abeyta (1918–)

Originally named Ascending (Ha So Deh), Abeyta began his artistic career drawing on canyon walls, yet was later published in *Art in America*, by Tanner in 1957, as well as by others. Abeyta received his Bachelor of Arts degree in 1953 from New Mexico University, served in the U.S. Army during World War II, and worked for the New Mexico State Employment Commission as a job placement interviewer after returning home.

Abeyta's work has been exhibited in such shows as the San Francisco World's Fair (1939–40). He has won 14 awards, including the ITIC Grand Award.

Drawings by Narciso Platero Abeyta have sold for approximately $1200.

Alice Asmar

Asmar works in all mediums, but colored inks have been her specialty. She received her Bachelor of Arts degree and graduated magna cum laude from Lewis and Clark College in Portland, Oregon, and received her Master of Fine Arts from the University of Washington.

Asmar paints Indians because she sees them "as America's real ecologists." Solo exhibitions of her work have been held at Gallerie de Fondation des Etas-Unis, Paris, the Minnesota Museum of Art, and the Western Association of Art Museums. Her work has also been shown in New York and Italy.

Harrison Begay (1917–)

This Navajo was born in White Cone, Arizona, and his Indian name was Warrior Who Walked Up to His Enemy (Haskay Yah Ne Yah). Begay studied at the Santa Fe Indian School (1939), at Black Mountain (1940–41), and at Phoenix Junior College (1941).

Internationally known, Begay's work has had a great influence on other Navajo artists. He has 13 awards to his credit. His works have been published by Frederick Dockstader (Director of the Museum of the American Indian, 1961) and have appeared in a number of issues of *Arizona Highways* magazine, as well as in many other publications. His work has also been exhibited in such shows as the First Annual American Indian Art Exhibition in 1964 at Wayne State University and the Philbrook Art Center.

Begay's paintings have recently sold for approximately $1300 and his drawings have brought in the $500 range.

Albert Bierstadt (1830–1902)

Born in New York City, Bierstadt is best known as a landscape painter. He studied in Germany and Rome, exhibited all over Europe, then came to live in New Bedford, Massachusetts, in 1831.

Bierstadt became a U.S. member of ANA in 1860, and his work is held in museums all over the United States. He was awarded many honors such as The Order of St. Stanislaus of Russia in 1869, and The Imperial Order of the Medjidi from the Sultan of Turkey in 1886.

His work depicting Indians resulted from trips out West. There he concentrated on recreating the landscapes of the American frontier. His paintings of the American Indian are finely done and much admired by collectors of American art.

Bierstadt's paintings average around $15,000, although some have gone as high as $792,000. Drawings range from $1500 to $6500.

Archie Blackowl (1911–)

Blackowl was born an Apache and a descendant of the Cheyenne, Roman Nose. His Indian name is Flying Hawk (Mis Ta Moo To Va).

Blackowl studied at the Segr Indian School, as well as at the Concho Indian School. He learned various painting techniques from Olaf Nordmark, a muralist.

During his artistic career, Blackowl was commissioned to do murals for quite a few institutions (including the Riverside Indian School). He has had his work published by various publications. Blackowl has also held exhibits throughout the United States at galleries and museums, such as the Agra Gallery in Washington, D.C., and has won numerous awards.

Archie Blackowl's work is held in public and private collections throughout the United States.

Acee Blue Eagle (1907–1959)

Born on the Wichita Reservation in Oklahoma, Blue Eagle was a Creek/ Pawnee who became orphaned before he was five. Adopted by his grandparents, Blue Eagle chose to take his paternal grandfather's name, though his given name was Alex C. McIntosh and his Indian name was Laughing Boy (Che Bon Ah Bu La).

Blue Eagle spent part of his childhood at the Nuyaka Mission in Oklahoma. He was educated there, as well as at Oxford University in England; Bacone College, Oklahoma; and through commercial art classes given at Oklahoma S.U./S.T. from 1951–52.

His career was full and colorful, sending him throughout the United States and Europe. Blue Eagle gave lectures and exhibits on "Life and the Character of the American Indian." He also started, then became head of, the Art Department at Bacone College and conducted a television program in Muskogee, Oklahoma.

Acee Blue Eagle received many honors during his lifetime, one of which included being named "Outstanding Indian of the United States" in 1958. In 1959 he was honored for service to the state of Oklahoma through a resolution passed by the Oklahoma Legislature.

Acee Blue Eagle was commissioned by such Oklahoma public buildings as the Oklahoma College for Women and the Muskogee Public Library, and has had works published by Jacobson and D'Ucel, as well as in *Indians of Oklahoma* in 1966. He has been exhibited at the American Indian Expositions, the Denver Art Museum, Grand Central Art Galleries, and many others. Among his other credits are one-man art shows at the Young Gallery in Chicago, Illinois, and at the Muskogee Public Library, to name just a few. He has won over 40 awards in his lifetime and has had the honor of having his work held in major public and private art collections all over the world, such as in those held by Hailie Selassie, Eleanor Roosevelt, and King Alfonso XIII of Spain.

Blue Eagle's paintings sell in the four- to five-figure range in today's market and there are prints being made of his work on a regular basis.

Parker Boyiddle, Jr. (1948–)

Boyiddle was born with a mixture of Indian blood; his mother was Wichita-Delaware-Chickasaw and his father was Kiowa.

The artist graduated from Classen High School in Oklahoma City in

1965 and was honored with an art scholarship at the Oklahoma Science and Art Foundation.

His work has been exhibited at Riverside Museum in New York.

George de Forest Brush (1855–1941)

Brush was born in Dublin, New Hampshire, on September 28, 1855. He studied in Paris and exhibited his art all over the world, winning a gold medal at the Paris Expo in 1900, as well as at the St. Louis Expo in 1904.

His Indian paintings were done while he lived in Indian villages during the period between 1882 and 1886. He died in Shelbyville, Tennessee, on April 24, 1941.

His paintings and drawings range from $500 to $30,000.

George Catlin (1796–1872)

Catlin is often credited with being the most prolific painter of the American Indian, but he was also an author, ethnographer, historian, showman, and traveler.

Catlin's love of Indian lore and interest in art went hand-in-hand from the time he was a youngster until his death at the age of 75. His paintings of members of the various Indian tribes which existed during that period of time are most accurate and complete, more so than any other artist who took the time to record with paints the personalities and characteristics of the Amerind.

Catlin's art education began after he sold his law books and bought artist brushes and paints with the proceeds. He moved from Litchfield, Connecticut, to Philadelphia and, without having been taught the art of painting, became fairly successful painting miniature portraits. In 1824, he was elected to the prestigious Pennsylvania Academy of the Fine Arts.

In 1830, he began his travels to the Far West. Meeting with the Sac and Fox tribes, he did portraits and wrote of his impressions of the treaty which allied the two tribes. After leaving them, he painted Northeastern woodland tribes, such as the Shawnees, Delawares, Kickapoos, and Potawatomis. The Konzas, of Kansas, were visited by Catlin later that same year and Catlin wrote about the tribe. He stated that they most certainly "sprung from the Osages, as their personal appearance, language, and traditions clearly prove."

Before the smallpox epidemic of 1832, Catlin painted Otoes, Missouris, Omahas, and Pawnees. His writings during that period also give us some of the only historical information available on these tribes, about half of which were wiped out by the epidemic. During that same year, the Plains Indians visited Catlin while he was in St. Louis and their portraits were done by the artist. Other tribes which Catlin recorded with his brush include the Arikara, Sioux, Teton Sioux, Cheyenne, Mandan, Osage, Kiowa, Comanche, Wichita, Choctaw, Cherokee, Creek, Seminole, and perhaps a Nez Perce. Catlin also had his share of adventures during the period when he painted Indians. For example, there was the time he and a companion were held prisoners by Sioux Indians who did not want to allow the pair to venture into a sacred place.

His attention to detail and the notes which he took during his travels served to be the background for his *Letters and Notes on the Manners, Customs and Conditions of the North American Indians* and for his "Indian Gallery," completed in 1837. The latter included some 507 portraits, all listed in his 1840 catalog. Exhibits were arranged to show Catlin's "Indian Gallery" to the public in various eastern cities including Pittsburgh, New York, Boston, Philadelphia, and Washington. He also took his gallery to the Louvre in Paris, at the invitation of King Louis Philippe, in 1845.

After his last year in London (1848), Catlin began having financial difficulties and turned to writing books, traveling, and trying to copy his works on cardboard. He had hoped to sell his collection of paintings to the government but died before that was accomplished.

Today, works of Catlin's are often sold to museums and wealthy private collectors, though prints often come on the market at fairly reasonable prices. However, portraits by Catlin are always expected to bring five- or six-figure knockdown prices when auctioned.

Pop Chalee (Marina Liyan) (1908–)

Born of an East Indian mother and a Taos Indian father, Chalee's childhood fostered the art career which she chose. Her style, a light, surrealistic fantasy world, shows the influence of both cultures.

Chalee was tutored by Dorothy Dunn at the Santa Fe Indian School during the 1930s.

Robert Chee (1938–)

A Navajo artist, Chee attended school in Billemont, Arizona. He is one of the few lucky Indian artists who has been able to devote his career strictly to his art.

Chee's works have been published by such magazines as *New Mexico* magazine and the *Inter-Tribal Indian Ceremonial Annual* magazine. His work has been exhibited at the Museum of New Mexico and the Philbrook Art Center.

Public collections of his work are held by the Museum of New Mexico, the Philbrook Art Center, the Bureau of Indian Affairs, and many others. Frederick Dockstader and Leland Wyman are just two of the private collectors who have works by Robert Chee in their collections.

Woodrow Wilson Crumbo (1912-)

Woody Crumbo was born a Creek-Potawatomi Indian in Lexington, Oklahoma. His most current address is in that state, although he spent some of his life in Texas.

Crumbo's career as an artist began at an early age when Susie Peters encouraged him and other Anadarko, Oklahoma, Indian boys to paint. He returned to formal schooling at the age of 17 to study art and anthropology.

As with other Indian artists of his day, Crumbo studied under the muralist Olaf Nordmark. He was also taught watercolor techniques by Clayton Henri Staples, and O.B. Jacobson trained him in painting and drawing.

His first painting, "Deer and Birds," was given to the Philbrook Art Center in 1939. The artist has made it a point during his career to accurately complete a pictorial record of the Indian way. Much of his fame rides squarely on the fact that he has accomplished this goal.

Woody's career is long and interesting. He held a variety of arts and crafts positions and even designed aircraft for Cessna Aircraft and Douglas Aircraft. Crumbo was the artist-in-residence at the Gilcrease Museum and also served as the Assistant Director of the El Paso Museum of Art (1962-).

He has won many honors, including the Julius Rosenwald Fellowship, and his work has been published by many publications including *Tulsa Sunday World* magazine and *New Mexico* magazine. Exhibitions of Crumbo's work have been held all over the United States, Europe, and North and South America (over 200 in all), and he has held many one-man shows. Collections of his work are held by the Philbrook Art Center, the Gilcrease Institute, the Southeast Museum of the North American Indian, and many others.

Today, Crumbo lives in semiretirement near Tulsa, Oklahoma.

Charles Deas (1818-1867)

Deas grew up in Philadelphia and was educated in the classics and art. By 1835 he had moved to Upstate New York with his widowed mother and began following his instinct for art.

He, as others had before him (most notably, George Catlin), headed West to seek adventure. He lived in St. Louis for eight years, following through with his career and exhibiting there, and then in New York and Philadelphia.

Deas had a fascination for the Indian way of life and shared the view with other artists, such as George Catlin and John Mix Stanley, that Indians were human beings whose way of life should be saved and preserved. Charles Deas painted members of the Winnebago tribe leisurely playing checkers in 1842, after a long trip through the Wisconsin Territory. He also painted the Sioux tribe playing ball in 1843 and other scenes of Indian life in the years following. Few of his paintings survived during a year-long trip which took Deas through the Wisconsin Territory, but he took advantage of that time to collect sketches of the Winnebago tribe while there. Deas also painted the Sioux tribe in the summer of 1841 while he was visiting Fort Snelling. Again, few of these paintings exist today. Fortunately, however, they have been documented by Deas' biographer, Henry Tuckerman, who wrote about the artist for *Godey's Lady's Book* in 1846. In the unofficial journal of a Lt. J. Henry Carleton, Deas was described as a "Rocky Mountains' free spirit" who was quite at home with the Indians and whose good humor helped him break the ice with whatever Indians he was painting at the time.

At the height of his career in the 1840s, Deas produced now lost works such as "The Last Shot" and "The Oregon Pioneers." His last major painting was exhibited at the 1847 Mechanics' Fair, whereupon he left St. Louis for good.

Once back in New York City in 1848, Deas was committed to an asylum for the insane. His career had ended before he was 30 years old. His last painting, "A Vision," now lost, was a horrific, yet delicately beautiful depiction of despair and death. He died of apoplexy on March 2, 1867, while hospitalized at the Bloomingdale Asylum for the Insane in New York.

Deas' paintings have been exhibited and sold at the American Art Union in New York, as well as at galleries in St. Louis and on the East Coast.

Louis Drood

Drood was an English painter whose works average around $500 to $7500.

Jack Glover

Half Cherokee, half cowboy, this contemporary sculptor is all American. He is the author of 14 books on Indian culture, as well as a sculptor of investment-quality bronzes, a collector of Indian artifacts, and owner of an Old West museum and trading post in Bowie, Texas.

Glover believes strongly in his Indian heritage and religion and those beliefs come through in the beautiful bronze figurines he crafts on a regular basis.

Visitors to Glover's Museum in Bowie, Texas, will be regaled by his stories, his collection of Indian artifacts, and his knowledge of the history of the American West.

Joe Grandee (1929–)

A contemporary painter of the highest regard, Grandee was the first official Texas state artist. He has won many awards (e.g., the Franklin Mint Gold Medal 1973, 1974), has attended White House receptions and been the special guest at many government functions, and is a television and radio personality. He also has the honor of having his work shown in many American museums, including the Montana Historical Society, the El Paso Museum of Fine Art, and the United States Marine Corps Museum.

Grandee's paintings of the American West and American Indians are extremely realistic. He is such a stickler for detail that he has been known to dress models in authentic period clothing and to stage his paintings before actually painting them. He is a respected authority on the historical details of the American West and houses an incredible collection of clothing, artifacts, and other items in his gallery outside of Dallas, Texas. His wife, Murlene, is Grandee's promoter, accountant, research assistant, critic, business manager, and staunchest supporter, and the person with whom contact is made before meeting with the artist.

Works done by Grandee include a portrait of Lynda Bird Johnson's wedding, and a painting of a Texas Ranger, given to President Nixon on behalf of the state of Texas.

Though Grandee's first painting only netted him $75, originals of his work now command $35,000 or more.

Helen Hardin (1943–)

Hardin is Pablita Velarde's daughter (see page 24) and her style is more modern and abstract than traditional Indian painting. She began building that style after winning an art contest at the age of six years old (her subject was a fire engine). Even then, she wasn't intimidated by the fact that the contest was for boys only.

At the University of New Mexico, Hardin studied art history and anthropology, later winning a painting scholarship to a special school for Indians at the University of Arizona.

Hardin's first art show, in Bogota, Colombia, was almost a sell-out, and she has repeatedly won prizes for her art since that time. Her work, by her own admission, is definitely not traditional or classic. Hardin uses her drafting training in creating abstract and geometric works, and her paintings often have an art deco quality.

Helen Hardin is not only a leading Indian artist, but a television panelist and actress as well.

John Hauser (1859–1913)

John Hauser was an American artist who was known for his Indian paintings.

His work has recently sold for $1000 to $20,000, depending on subject matter and quality of the painting.

Velino Shije Herrera (1902–1973)

This Zia artist, also known as Velino Shije, Ma Pe Wi or Oriole, was born on October 22, 1902, at the Zia Pueblo in New Mexico. His name, Oriole, was adopted by him and used as a pun because it meant "bad egg."

During Herrera's career, he owned a studio in Santa Fe, taught painting at the Albuquerque Indian School, and was a rancher. Herrera was commissioned to do murals for the Albuquerque Indian School and others, and illustrated books during the 1940s. He has had his work published in magazines such as *School Arts*, *American Magazine of Art*, and *Arizona Highways*, as well as in books such as *Compton's Pictured Encyclopedia*.

Some exhibits which included his work were held at the Heard Museum in Phoenix, at various tribal ceremonials, at the Museum of New Mexico, and at the Southwest Museum. Herrera's works are included in private and public collections such as the Dockstader and Rockefeller collections.

When his wife, Mary, was killed in an automobile accident in the 1950s, Herrera, who was with her, was injured for life and his art career ended.

His paintings bring $400 to $1000 at auction.

Edward Hicks (1780–1849)

Hicks' painting of William Penn's treaty with the Lenape Indians hung as a sign for Samuel West's Inn in Chester, Pennsylvania, until 1920. In 1987, it was bought by the Newtown Historical Association in Newtown, Pennsylvania, and now hangs in the Court Inn, near Hicks' first house in Newtown.

Allan C. Houser (1915–)

Born Pulling Roots in Apache, Oklahoma, on June 30, 1915, this Chiricahua Apache's parents were held prisoner with Geronimo's band.

Though the artist's formal schooling ended at the eighth-grade level, he was taught by the muralist, Olaf Nordmark, the same painter who had taken other Indian artists under his wing. Through Nordmark's tutelage, Houser's talent emerged and he won such honors as a scholarship for sculpture and painting from John Simon Guggenheim and a Certificate of Appreciation by the IACB in 1967.

Houser's skills as a painter are equally matched by his talent in sculpting. During his career, Houser was commissioned to paint a number of murals in Indian schools, such as Fort Sill, Riverside, and Jicarilla, and he sculpted the marble war memorial entitled "Comrades in Mourning" at the Haskell Institute in 1948. *Arizona Highways* and *Oklahoma Today* are just two of the publications which have found Houser's work interesting enough to grace their pages.

Exhibitions have included the 1937 National Exhibition of Indian Art in New York, where he was the only American Indian represented, and the New York World's Fair in 1939. Houser also gave one-man shows at the Chicago Art Institute, the Denver Art Museum, and others. Awards include three Grand Awards and a trophy for outstanding work in Indian art from the Santa Fe Indian School.

Houser's work is held today in many public and private collections.

Grace Carpenter Hudson

Hudson, born in 1865 in Ukiah, California, specialized in portraits of Indian children. She studied at the Mark Hopkins Institute in San Francisco and later exhibited there, as well as at the Columbian Expo in Chicago in 1893.

Her works range from below $1000 to upwards of $35,000, with the majority of her paintings selling in the high teens.

William Robinson Leigh (1866–1955)

William Robinson Leigh was an American artist who was born in West Virginia and studied in Maryland. After quite a few one-man shows and exhibits, he died leaving a legacy of 534 oils and 344 charcoals at the Gilcrease Institute in Oklahoma. He was the author/illustrator of *Frontiers of Enchantment* and contributed to *Scribner's Natural History* and *Collier's*.

His paintings have auctioned off at around $2000 for small still lifes and $150,000 for pieces such as his Zuni pottery.

Charles Loloma (1921–)

Loloma is a multi-talented Hopi Indian who was born in 1921 in Hote-villa, Arizona. Though he was first known as a painter, Loloma is better known for his pottery and silversmithing talents.

After graduating from high school in Phoenix in 1940, Loloma received mural instruction under Olaf Nordmark and ceramics instruction at Alfred University. He served in the Army in World War II, then returned home to operate an arts and crafts shop in Shungopovi, Arizona, in 1955, and one in Scottsdale from 1956–60. Loloma also instructed special classes at the University of Arizona and Arizona State. In 1955, Loloma received a John A. Whitney Fellowship for his work in the research of raw native materials which were used in the making of pottery.

He has won awards in national and state competitions and has exhibited at the Arizona State Fair, the Museum of Modern Art in New York City, and the New Mexico State Fair.

Richard Martinez (1904–)

Born on the San Ildefonso Pueblo, Martinez's Indian name was Opa Mu Nu.

Martinez was one of the original students at the Santa Fe Indian School and helped paint a series of murals there in 1936. Most of his work was done between 1920 and 1950 and his subjects were often mythological or ceremonial.

Martinez's work was exhibited with the Exposition of Indian Tribal Arts, Inc., in 1931. Collections of his work are held by the Denver Art Museum, the Museum of New Mexico, and the Chrysler Art Museum, among others.

Georgia Masayesva

This Hopi artist was the first female to be selected the poster artist for the Festival of Native American Art (1988). She attended the University of Arizona where she received her Bachelor of Arts and her Masters in Education. Masayesva's photographs are sepia-toned, black-and-white images which are handtinted as they were 100 years ago.

Marshall Mitchell (1917–)

Mitchell produces Old West sculptures that have been compared to those done by Frederic Remington. His work deals with Western themes such as Indians and cowboys, as well as with the animals associated with the area. The artist's philosophy is that the Indians have been treated disgracefully, and this philosophy is apparent in his work as well as in his speech.

At the age of 12, Mitchell was left on his own when his parents divorced, and he spent his time outside of school doing a variety of odd jobs. Teachers and employers saw Mitchell's talent and helped him through the last couple of years in school by teaching him what they knew about art—sometimes even taking him home and feeding him.

The sculptor's works are exclusively represented by a dealer in Florida and are made in limited editions by what his representative calls "the grandaddy of contemporary Western art."

Tonita Vigil Pena (1895–1949)

A San Ildefonso native, Pena's Indian name was Quah Ah. She was painting by the age of seven in the San Ildefonso Day School, and was later encouraged by archeologists Edgar Hewett and Kenneth Chapman to paint village scenes. At that time, Pena developed a realistic, serene, and joyful style that became truly her own. Pena's sense of form and design enabled her to break away from the stiff figures which had been the norm for traditional painters from the San Ildefonso Pueblo.

Later in life, Tonita married and moved to the Cochiti Pueblo. There she taught the women at the Santa Fe Indian School to paint in any way they wanted.

Charles Pratt

Charles Pratt was born on an Indian Agency in Concho, Oklahoma, and began his career in art when his grandfather taught him how to make figures out of clay. He creates large-scale and miniature creations in cast-bronze, metal sculpture, and stone carvings. Talents also include being an accomplished silversmith.

He is listed in the 14th edition of *Who's Who in American Art* and has won more than 250 awards. His works are held in the Heard Museum, the Philbrook Art Center, and in many other centers.

Ben Quintana (1923–1944)

This young Cochiti artist made quite an impression on the art world during his brief career. Quintana won first prize in a poster contest at the age of 15 and won another (over 50,000 entries) at 17 years old. His work has been published in *Arizona Highways* and is held in public and private collections. He has been exhibited in many shows, one of which was the National Gallery of Art's "Contemporary Indian Painting" (1953).

William Rabbit (Contemporary)

Bill Rabbit, of Cherokee ancestry, worked as a silversmith in the early years of his career before turning to produce the award-winning paintings for which he is well known.

He paints, he says, with the influence of Solomon McCombs, Fred Beaver, Blackbear Bosin, and Jerome Tiger, combining the styles to please him. Rabbit fought in the Vietnam War and claims the experience "taught me to appreciate the commonplace and to appreciate every day."

Awards won by this contemporary artist are many and include first place at the Five Civilized Tribes Museum in Muskogee, Oklahoma (1981), and a number of prizes at the 61st Annual Gallup Ceremonial (1982). Rabbit was chosen as the poster artist for the 1985 "Trail of Tears" art show and was chosen for an exhibit at the Smithsonian Institute.

Collections of his work are held all over the world and he is represented in galleries throughout the Southwest.

Jamie Tawodi Reason (1947–)

Reason is a self-taught Cherokee artist who began carving in 1976. He is keeping alive the Cherokee art of carving cedar boxes, which were used to hold sacred items such as gourd rattles and fans. He focuses on nature, using the eagle feather as a recurring theme in his work. Reason's work can be found in galleries throughout the United States and Great Britain.

He has won many awards for his work and his boxes are currently being priced from $200 to $2000 each.

Robert Redbird (ca. 1940–)

Redbird is a Southern Plains Indian who was raised in Gotebo, Oklahoma, where he married and had two children.

He won Best of Class in theme and first place in painting at the Colorado Indian Market in Denver, Colorado, during the summer of 1987. He has also been named to the top five of "Best Investments in Indian Art under $1000 for 1987." Redbird is an associate pastor at the Tabernacle of Deliverance Church in Anadarko, Oklahoma.

Collections of his work are held by Carnegie High School and private collectors, and the Susan Peters Gallery of Anadarko, Oklahoma, represents him.

Kevin Red Star (1943–)

Red Star is a Crow Indian who was born in Montana and graduated from the Institute in 1965.

The Museum of New Mexico gave him a special award in 1965. Red Star was exhibited at that museum as well as at the "First Annual Invitational Exhibition of American Indian Paintings" in 1965 and at the Riverside Museum exhibit (New York City) in 1966 entitled "Young American Indian Artists."

The Indian Arts and Crafts Board holds a collection of his work.

Frederick Remington (1861–1909)

Born in Canton, New York, Remington was an only child. His father owned the local newspaper and his mother's family ran the local hardware business.

Raised in upstate New York, he went to school at the Highland Military Academy in Worcester, Massachusetts, and the Vermont Episcopal Institute in Burlington, Vermont, where he had his first formal art lessons. He also attended Yale University, where, it is said, he played a good game of football and was built perfectly for the game—large and muscular.

At 21, Remington married Eva Caten and they took off for Kansas. She left him there when she found out he was not the man she thought he was, after which he promptly went further west.

In a little over a year, the artist established himself as a New York illustrator with *Harper's Weekly*. He also illustrated for *St. Nicholas*, *Outing*, *Country Illustrated* magazine, and others. His oils began bringing in good money during the late 1880s, and the money brought his wife, Eva, back to his side. Remington's artistic style developed so rapidly during this period that it is hard to associate his early works with those he produced at the turn of the century.

Though never a real cowboy, and often uncomfortable with Western life, Remington painted Indians and the life of the Old West as though he had lived it all his life. Some of his illustrations which depict Indians include: "A Dash for the Timber" (1889); "The Outlier" (1909); "The Scout—Friends or Enemies?" (1890); "Downing the Nigh Leader" (1907); and "Apache Scouts Listening" (1908).

Remington's paintings are held in private collections and museums all over the world. They often reach the five-figure mark when they are brought up to auction.

Kenneth Riley (Contemporary)

Born and raised in the Midwest, Riley was an illustrator when he was an adult living in the East.

Riley studied at the Kansas City Art Institute and was a combat artist in World War II. He worked as an illustrator during the 1950s and his illustrations appeared in *National Geographic*, *Life*, and *Saturday Evening Post*.

Riley works in oil on fairly large canvases and has moved away from realistic painting to a more impressionistic style. His paintings of American Indians have won him various awards such as the Stetson Award at the 1987 Cowboy Artists of America show at the Phoenix Art Museum. He has also won the gold medal and Best of Show award at CAA in 1984, and the purchase award from Phoenix Art Museum for Bodmer in 1986.

Bert D. Seabourn (1931–)

Seabourn was born in Iraan, Texas, and his father, James, was a Cherokee. Seabourn married Bonnie Jo Tompkins in 1950 and they had two children.

The artist received a certificate of art from Oklahoma C.U. in 1960 and studied on his own with the Famous Artists Correspondence Art School. Seabourn has participated in exhibitions throughout the Southwest, including one-man shows at Henson Gallery (Yukon, Oklahoma) and Chandler Galleries in Oklahoma. Awards include three from ITIC.

The Oklahoma Art Center holds a collection of Seabourn's work.

Lois Smoky (1907–)

Born Bou Ge Tah, this Kiowa was encouraged to pursue her talent by Susan Peters, a field worker at the Anadarko Indian Agency in Oklahoma.

Smoky was the only female of a group of Kiowa Indians who became world renowned for their bold, broad style and knowledge of American Indian tribes and traditions.

John Mix Stanley (1814–1872)

One of the most important painters of Indian and Western life, Stanley visited the Blackfoot Indians in 1850 while on a railroad survey.

Today his paintings sell in the four- to five-figure range.

Carl Sweezy (1879–1953)

Born an Arapaho on a Cheyenne-Arapaho reservation near Darlington, Oklahoma, Sweezy's Indian name was Wattan (Black). He did not become Carl Sweezy until his older brother took the name of Sweezy and named the other children in the family likewise.

Sweezy was given a box of paints while in school at the age of 14 and learned to use them well. He continued to work in watercolors or oils during the rest of his career (though much of his work is unsigned). He worked for James Mooney and learned to paint in what Sweezy called "the Mooney Way." (Mooney was a Smithsonian Institute anthropologist.) Sweezy's work career also included a variety of jobs such as a stint as an Indian police officer, a farmer, a professional baseball player, and, as aforementioned, assistant to James Mooney.

Sweezy's work has been exhibited in a number of shows including The American Indian Exhibition (annual), the Inter-Tribal Indian Ceremonies, and the Museum of the Plains Indian. Collections of Sweezy's work are held by the Gilcrease Museum, the Museum of the American Indian, and the Philbrook Art Center, among others.

Monroe Tsatoke (1904–1937)

Tsatoke, or Hunting Horse, was a Kiowa who never took any art lessons until a woman named Susie Peters organized a Fine Arts Club and taught those children who showed a talent for drawing and other native work. Tsatoke's creative ability sustained him through a bout with tuberculosis. His association with the Peyote faith and the Native American Church helped him to express his religious feelings through his art.

The University of Oklahoma Press honored Tsatoke in *Indians of Today* and his work was commissioned by the Anadarko Federal Building, as well as by others. Tsatoke's work was exhibited at the United Nations Conference in 1945, as well as at many other conferences, and his work is held in public and private collections.

Today his paintings sell in the vicinity of $1500.

Pablita Velarde (1918–)

Velarde, a well-known artist, paints in the "traditional" style of Santa Fe and does accurate portraits of Indian life and culture. She did murals for the Bandelier National Monument in New Mexico (1939–1948).

David Williams (1933–)

Williams was born in Oklahoma of a Kiowa mother and Tonkawa-Apache father. His Indian name is "Tosque" or Apache Man, and he is descended from the famous Kiowa chief, Sitting Bear.

Williams' art education was through Bacone College. He established his career as a painter through exhibits at such places as the Sporting Gallery in Williamsburg, Virginia, and Stouffer's Manor Gate House in Pittsburgh, Pennsylvania.

Today his paintings sell in the $1500 range.

ART LISTINGS

Acrylics

Jackie Tobaahe Gene; Navajo; entitled "Gathering of the Medicine Men"; framed, dated '83, and signed.   **$110–$170**

Dan Namingha; Hopi; entitled "Parrot Deity."   **$125–$175**

Acrylic on Canvas

Nelson Begay; Navajo; entitled "Hatathli" (Navajo for Changer/Sand Painting Chanter), 18″ × 24″; depicts male Hatathli performing Shooting Chant; dated '78 and signed.   **$125–$195**

Courtesy of Many Horses Gallery, Los Angeles. Photo by Donald Vogt.

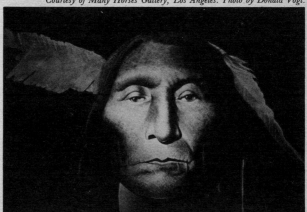

John Nieto; Quanah Parker (Comanche); 48″ × 60″.   **$12,000–$14,000**

Davis Ramos; 35″ × 47″.	**$3000–$5000**
Ben Wright; Peace Indian I; 48″ × 60″.	**$2500–$3000**
Ben Wright; Youth w/bow; 12″ × 86″.	**$2800–$3200**
Ben Wright; Return of the Buffalo; 48″ × 60″.	**$3000–$3400**
Ben Wright; Man From the East.	**$2500–$3000**

Bronzes

Courtesy of Jack Sellner, CAI.

Courtesy of Many Horses Gallery, Los Angeles. Photo by Donald Vogt.

Ernest Berke (1921–); entitled "Rallying His Warriors"; #59/200; 11½″ high; titled, numbered, signed, and dated 1979 (see above left).
$1200–$1800

Y.E. Cheno; A-Gi-Du-Da (grandfather) (see above right). **$5000–$7500**

Carl Kauba (1865–1922); Austrian; Seated Indian Chief on Horseback, 13″ high, 12½″ long. **$1200–$1450**

*Courtesy of Many Horses Gallery,
Los Angeles. Photo by Donald Vogt.*

Courtesy of Wanda Campbell, Indian Art Unlimited.

Jim Pasma; Prophecy of Sweet Medicine (see above left).

$8500–$10,000

Charles Pratt; bronze shield w/turquoise bear paw; 32″ × 18″ (see above right).

$2600–$3000

Bronze Sculptures

David Bradley (1954-); Chippewa; entitled "Little Big Woman."
$185-$275

Joe Halko, NWA, SAA (1940-); entitled "Chipmunk."   **$350-$475**

Bob Scriver, CAA (1914-); entitled "Paul's Bull"; #38/1000, 2⅜″ × 5″; mounted on walnut base; shows buffalo laying down; titled, numbered, dated (1968), and signed.   **$150-$225**

Courtesy of Jack Sellner, CAI.

Bob Scriver, CAA (1914-); entitled "Piegan Brave"; #34/35, 11″ × 11″; mounted on a walnut base; depicts an Indian warrior from the "Horn Society" mounted on a war pony; titled, dated, numbered, and signed.   **$2000-$2750**

Carvings

Tlingit; old fully carved Mountain Sheep horn w/many human and animal figures; 18″ × 5″; ca. 1870.   **$425–$650**

Turquoise; solid turquoise carving of a Pony Express rider on a horse; ca. 1980; 3½″ × 2″.   **$130–$160**

Drawings

Andy Tsinajinnie; unusual picture of man on a horse; ca. 1975; 9″ × 6″.
                    $20–$40

"Warrior"; colored "warrior" drawing showing several Indians on horses; 15″ × 10″.   **$25–$45**

Engravings

Courtesy of Susan Sheehan, Inc., New York.

After Karl Bodmer (1809–1893); "The Interior of the Hut of a Mandan Chief"; ca. 1840; engraving and aquatint w/handcoloring; 16⅜″ × 21¼″. Bodmer's drawings are currently selling in the $200 to $5000 range. Note that this engraving is "after Bodmer."   **$200–$5000**

Courtesy of Susan Sheehan, Inc., New York.

After Karl Bodmer (1809–1893); "The Travellers Meeting With the Mina-
tarre Indians/Near Fort Clark"; 1842; engraving and aquatint printed
in colors w/handcoloring.   **$200–$5000**

Courtesy of Susan Sheehan, Inc., New York.

Albert Bierstadt (1830–1902); "The Rocky Mountains"; 1866; engraving
and roulette; signed by the artist and engraver in pencil; 16¾" × 28";
proof before letters.   **$1500–$6500**

Karl Bodmer (1809–1893); ''Bison Dance''; 12″ × 17″; handcolored engraving. Bodmer's many paintings, drawings, and engravings of American Indian life range in price from $200 to $5000. **$200–$5000**

Etchings

Edward Borien; matted and framed etching from Borien estate depicting two mounted riders; ca. 1910. **$75–$100**

Ace Powell; framed limited edition (81/100) N.W. Coast etching; ca. 1975; 7″ × 5″ **$55–$80**

Hand-Tinted Lithographs (all of the following are by McKenney and Hall)

Entitled ''Ca-Ta-He-Cas-Sa-Black Hoof.'' **$150–$250**

Entitled ''O Che-Finceco.'' **$150–$250**

Entitled ''A Chippeway-Widow.'' **$150–$250**

Entitled ''Spring Frog.'' **$150–$250**

Entitled ''Okee-Makee Quid.'' **$150–$250**

Entitled ''Se-Loc-Ta.'' **$150–$250**

Entitled ''Ledagie.'' **$150–$250**

Entitled ''Red Jacket.'' **$150–$250**

Entitled ''Hayne-Hudjihini''; The Eagle of Delight; 21″ × 15″
 $135–$150

Entitled ''Chittee Yoholo''; A Seminole Chief; 21″ × 15″. **$135–$150**

Courtesy of Jack Sellner, CAI.

Entitled "Qua-Ta-Wa-Pea"; A Shawanoe Chief; 21″ × 15″.

$135–$150

Entitled "Apauly-Tustennuggee"; 21″ × 15″. $135–$150

Courtesy of Jack Sellner, CAI.

Entitled "Okee-Makee-Quid"; a Chippeway Chief; 21″ × 15″.

$400–$500

Entitled "War Dance."   **$275–$350**

Entitled "Pa-She-Pahaw."   **$125–$175**

Entitled "M'Intosh."   **$125–$175**

Entitled "John Ridge."   **$125–$175**

Entitled "Wat-Che-Mon-Ne."   **$125–$175**

Ledger Drawings

Cheyenne; ca. 1870; (C0043–05022).   **$3500–$4500**

Lee Joshua (1937–); Creek-Seminole; entitled "Coming on a Long Winter"; 20″ × 16″; shows blanketed warrior standing in snow; double matted, titled, dated '82, and signed.   **$175–$300**

Kiowa; ca. 1880; (C0021–02138).   **$5000–$6000**

Sioux; Short Bull; ca. 1880; (04288).   **$3900–$4200**

Lee Monette Tsa Toke (1929–); Kiowa; entitled "Shield Dancer" and "Eagle Dancer"; dated 10/15/59, titled, and signed.   **$300–$400**

Two colored ledger drawings showing Indians riding horseback; ca. 1885.
                                                         $100–$200

Limited Edition Prints

Jane Mauldin; No. 28/100; colored print of an Indian; ca. 1985; 9″ × 7″.
                                                         $10–$15

Ace Powell (1912–78); "Evening Prayer"; #99/1000; numbered, titled, and signed.   **$20–$55**

Ace Powell (1912–78); "The Last Hunt"; #236/1000, 11½″ × 22½″; depicts five Indian hunters on horseback in a winter scene w/buffalo in the background; numbered, titled, and signed.   **$20–$40**

Charles M. Russell (1864–1926); "Burning the Fort"; #385/1000, 17″ × 23″; famous picture showing mounted Indian warriors galloping away from the burning fort; matted, framed, numbered, and titled.   **$45–$80**

Charles M. Russell (1864–1926); entitled "Indian Stalking Elk"; double matted, framed, numbered, titled, and signed Museum of Native American Cultures.   **$90–$120**

Bert D. Seabourn (1931–); "Flight of the Phoenix"; #121/1006, 25″ × 25″; depicts a flying hawk superimposed over part of an old Indian man's face.   **$15–$25**

Bert D. Seabourn (1931–); Cherokee; entitled "Earth to Earth, Dust to Dust"; numbered and signed.   **$15–$30**

Quincy Tahoma; #421/1000; "The Last Struggle"; ca. 1945; 30″ × 18″.
                                                                              $55–$75

Lithographs

Parker Boyiddle (1947–); Kiowa–Delaware; entitled "Warrior"; #49/60, 30″ × 22″; shows the warrior wearing a buffalo headdress and holding a feather-decorated shield; signed and numbered.   **$100–$250**

Parker Boyiddle (1947–); Kiowa–Delaware; entitled "I've Touched My Enemy"; numbered and signed.   **$150–$250**

Courtesy of Zaplin-Lampert Gallery, Santa Fe, NM. Photo by Donald Vogt.

George Catlin; 1794–1872; "War Dance"; ca. 1844.

George Catlin; 1794–1872; "The Snow Shoe Dance"; 11¾″ × 17¾″; ca. 1844; hand-colored.

Jerry Ingram (1941–); Choctaw; entitled "Elk Woman"; #17/100; framed, numbered, and signed.   **$200–$250**

Contracted by the Millicent Rogers Museum, Taos, NM.
Courtesy of Jack Sellner, CAI.

Paula Pletka (1946–); signed, limited edition; entitled "Taos Turtle Dancer"; #59/80, 25″ × 19″; depicts the head and upper torso of the title in vivid red, yellow, white, blue, and brown colors against a black background; matted, numbered and signed.   **$600–$800**

Kevin Red Star (1943–); entitled "Abasole Camp"; #4/80, 24″ × 18″; depicts two northern Plains w/sunset-colored sky; numbered and signed.   **$225–$325**

Kevin Red Star (1943–); Crow; entitled "Mr. and Mrs. Chokecherry."
          $175–$225

Kevin Red Star (1943–); Crow; four lithographs; entitled Crow Res Cop I, II, III & IV; #10 of 60; depicts four different male Indians dressed in traditional Indian and nonIndian garments and accessories, all wearing a star (cop) badge; matted, numbered, titled, and signed.
          $550–$1000

Signed Day and Haghe (after George Catlin, 1796–1872); "Ball-Play Dance"; North American Indian Collection #22; 14″ × 18½″.   **$450–$550**

Signed Day and Haghe (after George Catlin, 1796–1872); "Catching the Wild Horse"; North American Indian Collection #4; 14″ × 18¾″.
          $425–$500

Signed Day and Haghe (after George Catlin, 1796–1872); "Wounded Buffalo Bull"; North American Indian Collection #16; 14″ × 18½″.
$475–$525

Two lithographs, Charles Loloma (1921–); Hopi; entitled "Quogole" and "Badger."
$200–$300

Oils

Courtesy of Zaplin-Lampert Gallery, Santa Fe, NM. Photo by Donald Vogt.

Albert Bierstadt; 1830–1902; oil on canvas; "Oregon Trail"; 30″ × 44″.
$10,000–$20,000

Carl Sweezy (1879–1953); Arapaho; entitled "Chief"; 18″ × 13″; depicts the title in a ¾ left head and torso view; matted, titled, and signed.
$400–$575

Ed Johnson; oil; painting of Navajo man by Navajo artist.
$100–$150

Carl Sweezy (1879–1953); Arapaho; oil on board; entitled "War Chief"; framed, titled, and signed.
$350–$500

Frederick W. Becker (1888–1953); oil on board; entitled "Desert Hot Wells"; #2; 9″ × 12″; framed, titled, dated 1966 (on back), and signed.
$200–$275

George Forbes; oil on canvas; Autumn Journey (Black Eagle); 18″ × 24″ framed. **$1900–$2200**

Grace Carpenter Hudson; oil; Pomo Indian children; ca. 1916.

Heinie Hartwig; oil painting; Tepee scene; ca. 1980; 13″ × 11″.
$475–$575

Louis Dood; born 1900; oil on panel; "Rendevous at Chimney Rock"; 14¼″ × 17¾″. **$500–$7500**

Louis Ship Shee (1900–1974); Potawatomi; oil on canvas; entitled "The Peace Pipe"; framed and signed. **$250–$500**

Paintings

Carol Prophet; ca. 1975; signed original art piece using some prehistoric pottery shards; framed; 16″ × 12″. **$45–$80**

Diane O'Leary (1986–); Choctaw; gouache landscape; 8″ × 6½″.
$45–$65

Ralph Tillman; signed, matted, and framed watercolor of an Indian on a horse; ca. 1940; 9″ × 7″. **$30–$60**

Robert Redbird; subject is Indian man; ca. 1975. **$110–$175**

Robert Redbird; winter tepee scene in oak frame; ca. 1975. **$235–$300**

Robert Redbird; "Vision" painting by Kiowa artist; ca. 1975. **$100–$200**

Robert Redbird; Indian face and other objects; ca. 1975. **$130–$200**

Signed "Richard Martinez"; Southwestern Pueblo, tempera; San Ildefonso depicting two eagle dancers. **$350–$450**

Signed "Wilson Dewey" (Sundust, b. 1915); Southwestern, tempera; San Carlos Apache, depicting a single figure Apache Gan Dancer; 8″ × 11″ excluding mat and frame. **$175–$250**

Signed "R. Chee" (Robert Chee, 1938–1971); two paintings; Navajo; tempera; one depicts a fawn closely inspecting an ant; the other shows three skunks emerging from an outcropping. **$300–$400**

Pen and Ink

Andrew Van Tsinajinnie; Navajo; entitled "Yeibichai Dancers"; 6″ × 9″; depicts 12 of the title in a circle in active positions; matted and signed. **$65–$95**

Charlie Bear; ca. 1975; drawing of an Indian girl; 8″ × 6″. **$15–$20**

Courtesy of Zaplin-Lampert Gallery, Santa Fe, NM. Photo by Donald Vogt.

George de Forest Brush (1855–1941); "Fremont's Address to Indians at Laramie"; ca. 1891; 17″ × 26″.　**$500–$30,000**

Olaf Wieghorst (1899–); entitled "Indian Profile"; 5″ × 4¼″; depicts the title in a right view; matted, framed, dated Christmas '71, and signed.　**$550–$725**

Pencil Drawings and Pastels

Parker Boyiddle (1947–); poster; "Great Pueblo Revolt, Tri-Centennial, 1680–1980"; 24″ × 16″; depicts three Pueblo Indians atop adobe buildings in left profile views.　**$10–$25**

Robert L. Knudson (1929–); pencil drawing entitled "Prehistoric Dwellings"; 11″ × 14″; double matted, signed, and dated '84.　**$80–$120**

Prints

Austin Deuel, AICA, WAI (1939–); "The Deer Slayer"; #198/375; 23¾″ × 17½″; depicts Indian hunter in a rocky snow-covered scene, holding bow with arrow at ready; numbered lower left, signed lower right.
　$20–$40

Parker Boyiddle (1947–); Kiowa-Delaware; entitled "Peyote Vision: Buffalo Skull"; 33″ × 24½″; depicts head of snarling grizzly bear superimposed over face of male Indian, superimposed over feathered buffalo skull.　**$20–$35**

Parker Boyiddle (1947–); Kiowa; entitled "Kiowa Warrior."　**$15–$25**

Winold Reiss; set of six colored Blackfoot prints; ca. 1915. **$35–$50**

Woody Crumbo; peyote bird. **$10–$15**

Sand Paintings

Courtesy of Broken Arrow Indian Arts and Crafts, Taos, NM. Photo by Donald Vogt.

Baatsoslanii; this artist signed his pieces E.B. Joe until 1974, then changed his signature to Baatsoslanii; this painting was done in 1988.

$3000–$3500

Francis Miller; Navajo; entitled "House of Many Paints." **$50–$100**

Judy Lewis; Navajo from Window Rock, Arizona; original sand painting; means "good luck." **$100–$150**

Signed Redgoat (Chenya Redgoat); Navajo; entitled "Lonewolf Pottery"; 12″ × 16″ framed. **$65–$95**

Sculpture

Brass sculpture depicting an Indian on a horse spearing a buffalo; ca. 1980; 9″ × 7″. **$55–$85**

Dennis Silvertooth; "Beneath a Dream Robe"; Silvertooth was 18 when he won a gold medal at Philbrook. **$3500–$3800**

E. Ashley; Zuni; stone sculpture w/three Zuni stone bear fetishes mounted on a lava rock and wood; signed; ca. 1985; 12″ × 7″. **$135–$165**

Jim Jackson; sand sculpture. **$1000–$1500**

Ken Camel; Flathead; large Indian bust; ca. 1982; 25″ × 9″. **$30–$50**

Northwest Coast; Northwest Coast head wearing a potlatch hat; ca. 1930; 11″ × 5″.   **$50–$75**

Signed Limited Edition Prints

Ace Powell (1912–1978); "Buffalo Hunt"; depicts two mounted Indian hunters on each side of the herd; numbered, titled, and signed.
                                                           $45–$75

Benjamin Harjo, Jr.; Southern Plains Indian; wood block print entitled "Many Beings Within the Four Seasons"; #3/32; 12″ × 10″; depicts surrealistic blanketed figures in right profile on views with five dark suns/moons overhead; matted, numbered, titled, and signed. **$35–$65**

Benjamin Harjo, Jr.; Southern Plains Indian; entitled "Medicine Lodge"; wood block print; matted, numbered, titled, dated '82, and signed.
                                                           $30–$60

Bert D. Seabourn (1931–); Cherokee; entitled "In the Beginning"; numbered and signed.   **$25–$45**

Harvey W. Johnson (1921–); entitled "Whitewater Keelboat"; #1/1000; 15″ × 26″; depicts the title with a total of eight hunters/trappers aboard; double matted, framed, numbered, and signed.   **$85–$145**

Howard Rees (1941–); entitled "Winter Sun"; #41/750; 17½″ × 24″; depicts three Indian hunters mounted on horseback crossing snow-covered ground; numbered and signed.   **$35–$65**

Howard Terpning, CAA, NAWA (1927–); entitled "Crossing Medicine Lodge Creek."   **$150–$200**

Jack Hines (1923–); entitled "Fort Laramie . . . The Gathering of the Tribes"; #31/1000; 20″ × 30″; depicts seven Indians on horseback; matted, framed, numbered, and signed.   **$85–$115**

Joe Beeler (1931–); Founding Member of CAA; Cherokee; entitled "The Warning"; matted, framed, numbered, and signed.   **$75–$125**

Ron Stewart (contemporary); entitled "Unknown Destiny"; #116/250; 18″ × 24″; depicts tepees in a snow-covered scene w/four mounted Indian riders preparing to cross a stream; numbered, titled, signed, and remarqued (small original sketch).   **$75–$125**

William Acheff (1947–); entitled "Tewa Lady"; #70/325; 11″ × 8″; depicts a historical-period, Southwest Indian pottery jar placed upon a banded Pueblo Indian weaving with a photograph of a Twea-Hopi maiden in the background; matted, framed, numbered, and signed.
                                                           $95–$135

Silkscreens

Three prints; Woody Big Bow (1914–); Kiowa; entitled "Flute Player"; "Eagle Dancer"; and "Feather Dancer."   **$25–$50**

Woody Crumbo (1912); Creek-Potawatomi; entitled "Baby with Fawn, Birds and Animals"; 16″ × 12″; matted and framed.   **$100–$150**

Tempera

Archie Blackowl (1911–deceased); Cheyenne; entitled "The Cheyenne Brave."   **$75–$200**

Ed Joshua, Jr.; Kiowa-Southern Plains; "Wolf Man"; 14½″ × 9″; left profile of two Indian men, one wearing wolf headdress w/large full moon in the background, dated '84 and signed.   **$35–$50**

Justino Herrera (1920–?); Southwestern Cochiti Pueblo; depicting five male dancers and two female drummers under a stylized sky.   **$300–$500**

Robert Montoya; San Juan Pueblo; depicts a single kachina dancer; signed "Soe-Kuwa-Pin '75."   **$100–$200**

Signed "Richard Martinez"; Southwestern Pueblo; San Ildefonso; depicting two eagle dancers; 10½″ × 12¾″.   **$350–$500**

Watercolors

Acee Blue Eagle (1907–59); entitled "Indian Maiden"; matted and signed.   **$1000–$1250**

Andy Tsinajinni, ca. 1980; shows many Indians dancing around a fire.
$35–$50

Beatien Yazz–Jimmy Toddy (1928–); Navajo; entitled "Yeibichai Dancers."   **$195–$265**

Bert D. Seabourn (1931–); "Cheyenne Girl"; 4″ × 3″; left profile of subject, matted and titled on reverse, signed LC, and dated '73.
$30–$75

David Stephens-Yona; Cherokee; entitled "Little People of the Cherokees"; dated '84 and signed.   **$25–$45**

David Stephens-Yona; Cherokee; entitled "Grannie's Stories"; depicts white-haired Indian woman, seated with needle, thread, and blanket in her lap, Indian youth beside her chair; dated '84 and signed. **$50–$75**

David Stephens-Yona; Cherokee; entitled "I Offer you Peace"; 12″ × 6″; showing spiritual Indian warrior extending peace pipe to realistic Indian warrior; dated '84 and signed.   **$30–$85**

David Stephens-Yona; Cherokee; entitled "Apache"; titled, dated, and signed.   **$40–$60**

David Stephens-Yona; Cherokee; two watercolors entitled "Apache" and "Society of the Ten Bravest," both depicting warriors standing beside their horses; both signed and dated '84.   **$100–$150**

David Stephens-Yona; Cherokee; two watercolors entitled "Question: Should you let your child pick their own pet" and "Ya got to stop and smell the roses"; both depict an Indian boy in various scenes; both dated '84 and signed.   **$85–$135**

Doc Tate Nevaquaya (1932–); Comanche; entitled "Black Legging Dancer"; double matted, framed, dated, and signed.   **$175–$225**

Duke W. Sine; Apache; entitled "Elder Statesman"; 15″ × 12″; bust portrait of white-haired Indian man w/shawl around shoulders; triple matted, signed, and dated '81.   **$65–$100**

Ed Joshua, Jr.; Kiowa–Southern Plains; entitled "Warriors"; matted, dated, and signed.   **$25–$55**

Ed Joshua, Jr.; Kiowa–Southern Plains; entitled "Kiowa Warrior"; 14″ × 18″; matted, dated '84, and signed.   **$35–$70**

From the Biltmore Galleries Collection, Biltmore Hotel, Los Angeles. Courtesy of Jack Sellner, CAI.

Hubert Wackerman (1945–); entitled "Sac and Fox—Minnesota 1815"; 18½″ × 14″; matted, framed, titled LC, signed and dated '74.
$175–$350

Jerry Lee-Hosteen Nez (1944–); Navajo; entitled "Fox Dance Yeibichai Dancer"; 10½″ × 7½″; matted, framed, and signed. **$85–$135**

Courtesy of Jack Sellner, CAI.

Joe Beeler (CAA 1931–); entitled "Mandan"; 8″ × 6½″; double matted, framed, titled LC; signed UC. **$750–$950**

Courtesy of Zaplin-Lampert Gallery, Santa Fe, NM. Photo by Donald Vogt.

John Hauser (1859–1913); "In the Enemy's Country"; 10″ × 18″.
$1000–$20,000

Jose (J.) D. Roybal (1922–deceased); San Ildefonso; entitled "Deer Dancer"; 5″ × 4″. **$175–$250**

Jose Encarnacion Pena (1902–1984); San Ildefonso Pueblo, "Koshare Dancer, Soqueen." **$250–$350**

Ken Longmore (contemporary); entitled "A Hard Watch"; 14" × 18"; Plains Indian campsite containing tepees, meat drying racks, and Indians against a high rock mesa background; matted, framed, dated, and signed. **$325–$475**

Lee Monette Tsa Toke (1929–); Kiowa; entitled "Pueblo Man" and "Pueblo Maiden." **$250–$400**

Michael Chiago-Tho-Hono (1946–); Papago; entitled "Still Life w/Pottery, Basket Corn and Sash"; double matted, dated '82, and signed. **$90–$120**

Mirac Creepingbear (1947–); Kiowa-Pawnee-Arapaho; entitled "Yesterday"; 19" × 14"; depicts face of male Indian with eyes closed superimposed over another of the same; only a left profile view with two riderless horses above; matted, framed, and signed. **$75–$125**

Paul Vigil; Tesuque; entitled "Tesuque Eagle Dancer"; matted, dated '67, and signed. **$200–$275**

Quincy Tahoma (1921–1956); Navajo; entitled "Grazing Horses— Monument Valley"; double matted, framed, dated '49, signed, and remarqued. **$200–$275**

Courtesy of Jack Sellner, CAI.

Rafael Medina; Zia; (1929–); entitled "Buffalo Dancer"; 14" × 10"; matted, framed, signed, and dated 1963 LR. **$475–$700**

Robert Redbird (1939–); Kiowa; entitled "Horse Thief"; titled and signed.   **$45–$65**

Shows Indian looking at the moon; ca. 1980; 15″ × 11″.   **$25–$50**

Courtesy of Jack Sellner, CAI.

Spencer Asah (1905–1954); Kiowa; entitled "Buffalo Hunter"; 13″ × 17″; triple matted, framed, and signed LC.   **$950–$1250**

Tonita Pena, Quah Ah (1895–1949); pair; "Male Cochiti Corn Dancer" and "Female Cochiti Corn Dancer"; matted, framed, and signed.
                                                                $850–$1250

Wood Block Prints

Benjamin Harjo, Jr.; Southern Plains; limited edition print; "Earth Mother"; #2/32, 11″ × 9″; Indian woman, completely covered w/shawl except for her face and one hand; matted, numbered, titled, dated '82, and signed.   **$20–$30**

Benjamin Harjo, Jr.; Southern Plains; "As long as"; #8/32, 14½″ × 9½″; depicts the right profile bust of a male Indian; matted, numbered, dated, and signed.   **$25–$45**

Jean Bales (1946–); Iowa; limited edition print; "Bear Mystery"; #19/60; shows bear in large proportions w/Zuni-like heartline; matted, numbered, titled, and signed.   **$30–$60**

Wood Carvings

Jamie Tawodi Reason (1947–); Cherokee; painted boxes; group of three award-winning carved cedar boxes.   **$200–$2000**

Tlingit; lot of three wood carvings; shark, grizzly bear, and whale; signed Abner Johnson, Tlingit.   **$55–$85**

Other

Acrylic on rice paper; Jean Bales (1946–) Iowa; entitled "Dancer," 13″ × 10″; depicts a male Indian facing left, body painted yellow, holding fur-wrapped lance in extended hand, round ring/circle in other; framed and signed.   **$300–$400**

Bust; classic plaster bust of elegant Indian warrior; ca. 1910; 18″ × 6″ × 12″.   **$50–$75**

Gouche on board; William R. Leigh (1866–1955); "At the Loom"; 29¹³⁄₁₆″ × 21⅝″. Leigh's paintings have auctioned off at around $2000 for small still lifes and $150,000 for pieces such as his Zuni pottery.

Graphic; signed Richard Skyhawk; ca. 1986; called "Hoop Dancer."
   $25–$50

Serigraph; Kevin Red Star (1943–); Crow; "Tranquility"; matted, framed, numbered, titled, and signed.   **$250–$450**

Totem pole; Haida; black argelite totem pole depicting a female shaman w/eagle on top; ca. 1920; 9½″ × 2″.   **$350–$500**

ARTIFACTS

▼▼▼▼▼▼▼▼▼▼▼▼

INTRODUCTION

Though the field of American Indian collectibles is a large and varied one, it can be safely stated that artifacts are the oldest form of collectibles in this area of the world of antiques. Some arrowheads or lanceheads found in Northern America have been thought to be more than 20,000 years old, yet such pieces of antiquity often sell for much less than more recent objects made by the Amerind. The categories listed in this chapter are only the tip of the iceberg. For instance, more than 500 types of projectile points exist and there are almost as many different kinds of knives.

For the novice, the field is vast and there is a lot to learn. For the professional, years of collecting may net only a few truly wonderful "finds," for knowledge is sometimes more crippling than uplifting.

Because the artifacts described herein are the products of ancient cultures from which the North American Indian came, I think it's best to give an overview of a couple of different ancient cultures before beginning our exploration of the types of artifacts found in North America.

THE ANASAZI TRIBE

The Anasazi lived in the southwestern United States, making a living growing corn, around the same time as Christ was living in the arid areas of Bethlehem and Nazareth. The buildings the Anasazi constructed were multi-family dwellings which were linked by well-constructed roads and served by futuristic water control devices and sewer systems. New Mexico holds 25,000 such Anasazi sites and many more are located in Arizona, Colorado, and Utah. Though there are thousands more waiting to be discovered, it is more than likely that modern man will pillage the land and dig under ancient ruins in order to find the riches of coal, natural gas, and uranium that are plentiful throughout the region where the Anasazi once roamed.

Scholars call these early people "Anasazi, the Basketmakers," because archeologists have discovered that these early settlers lacked pottery; their water vessels were tightly woven basketry ollas. However, pottery arrived around A.D. 500, the bow and arrow was obtained, and the hafted ax developed in the same era.

After A.D. 700, the Anasazi began living above ground and the kiva became the center for ceremonial life. Another important sociological change was that they began strapping their young to wooden cradleboards, causing the back of the baby's head to flatten.

Because the land they lived on was dry and drought was a constant companion, the Anasazi people were always on the move, looking for wetter lands and a more even temperature. Their main crop, corn, called for warm temperatures, but it also needed moisture to grow. After dealing with a fickle environment for another 100 years or so, the Anasazi decided to beat the system and, by A.D. 900, had learned to channel water to better suit their purposes.

They began to build pueblos from sandstone, and one of the finest examples of such architecture is Pueblo Bonito in Chaco Canyon. The area boomed and other communities blossomed in Chaco Canyon over the next 130 years. The main pueblo—Pueblo Bonito—contained some 650 rooms and was the largest building of its kind. Eleven other such structures in the canyon held another 2,000 rooms. You don't need much of an imagination to figure out how many people such buildings could house.

Craftspeople in this pueblo worked with turquoise and various metals. Laborers were kept busy enlarging the various buildings, loading and moving thousands of pounds of stone and timber—it was a busy community. Roads to and from the outlying pueblos were constructed with amazing engineering ability. These roads were still visible from the air as late as 1927 when Lindbergh made his famous flight. Even now, roads are still being identified. At this time, also, a most sophisticated astronomical device called the Chacoan "sun dagger" was constructed by these fascinating peoples.

Around 1150, a drought began which eventually brought a halt to the Anasazi community and Chaco ended up being a monument of sorts, void of any living civilization. The Anasazi abandoned the area. While Chaco was dying, however, the Anasazi culture on Mesa Verde was flourishing. By the end of the thirteenth century, the cliff dwellers began constructing an enormous temple to the gods, but it was never completed for they, too, gave up and abandoned their homeland.

The richness of this society—their tools, way of life, and talent for constructing large buildings—is still being uncovered by anthropologists and archeologists today.

THE MOUND BUILDERS

The mound builders were people who, just as their name implies, erected mounds in and around the central and southern states. They were the ancestors of Creeks, Cherokees, Natchez, and other tribes—the tribes who originally greeted the arrival of the white man.

Archeological research has uncovered stone pipes in Oklahoma which are believed to have been used in rituals by southern cult temple mound builders. Pieces of this culture have been found in Tennessee, Ohio, and Illinois as well.

Twelfth century Cahohia (north of the Rio Grande) was a community which supported 30,000 people. Farmers grew beans, squash, and corn; hunters found plenty of game; and craftsmen made ceramics and baskets which were carried by canoe to be traded with other establishments. Today Monk's Mound, part of Cahohia, remains in St. Louis and its base surpasses that of Egypt's Great Pyramid.

Mounds arise all over the Midwest. One, in southern Wisconsin, resembles a bird. In Ohio one resembles a dumbbell-shaped hilltop. The Newark Earthworks is the largest Hopewell mound complex in Ohio. South Carolina has the Fig Island Shell Ring, one of the oldest mounds in North America and, in Louisiana, a complex 3,000 years old is called the Poverty Point Mound. Huvasee Island in Tennessee is now partly submerged, but originally had temples on twin mounds.

Through study of these mounds, archeologists discovered that the dead were honored with material goods (Archaic Period burial grounds, Indian Knoll, Kentucky); that no pottery was made in the Illinois Valley by 1100 B.C.; and that the first pottery made in North America was made of clay strengthened by vegetable fiber (Stalling's Island, Georgia; Port Royal, South Carolina; and St. Johns River, Florida). The purpose of these mounds, whether made of shells, dirt or rocks, is not known, but they have enabled archeologists to assemble a history of each area, its arts and crafts, and its early Indian peoples.

At Poverty Point, a mound site in Louisiana, early artisans made ornaments of hard stone, such as red jaspar and hematite. Some pieces even resemble those made by the Olmeco, a people who lived across the Gulf of Mexico. The Hopewell Cult, appearing in the Ohio Valley by the second century B.C., left behind vestiges of its history, such as embossed breastplates, ear ornaments, ritual weapons, and scenes of the culture cut into silhouettes of hands, bird claws, animals, and headless men. It is thought that this culture was abandoned for fortified hilltop sites, though archeologists are not quite sure why.

Mounds changed around A.D. 700 and corn-growing communities seemed the mainstay of the Indian culture along the Mississippi. Monks Mound, in St. Louis, represents one of these communities and is, today, the largest ancient structure in the United States. By 1500, the mound-making communities along the Mississippi began to die. When the DeSoto expedition traveled through the area between 1539–42, they chronicled painfully little of the society. Today archeologists still struggle to piece together this chapter out of the North American Indian's past.

SOME TYPES OF INDIAN ARTIFACTS

Atl-Atl Weights

These weights are like bannerstones, only they do not have a large central hole as bannerstones do. Atl-atl weights are generally flat or concave on the bottom and most are long and narrow with square or round sides and tops.

Weights were functional as well as ornamental. Their function was to add weight to the lance, giving added impetus to the thrower. When well made, the atl-atl could be ornamental and some were even recognized as effigy forms.

The atl-atl was used for approximately 8,000 years throughout North America, from early Archaic times until A.D. 500.

Axes

The ax was a tool which was first made 6,000 years ago out of stone. Instead of using the chipping method which created projectile points, Indians learned to pound, grind, and polish larger stones. The ax became an integral part of their lives.

Grooves in the ax were used to secure the handle. It is also the way to tell the age of an ax, with the oldest being fully grooved, later axes being ¾ or ½ grooved, and the most recent being the celt (which came after the arrival of the white man). A celt was longer and narrower than the older axes and did not have a groove, but was instead mounted in a hole of a socket of a thick handle.

The Lakes area Indians made a fluted ax, while perforated mauls were unique to the Northwest Coast. The Southeastern Indians and Northwest Coast tribes made ceremonial monolithic axes—the Northwest Coast variety often having stonework shaped in the form of birds or other animals.

As with points, the value of an ax is determined by symmetry, workmanship, and balance. Damage to the ax should be slight or nonexistent if it is to retain a high value to a collector.

Bannerstones

The function of bannerstones is still a puzzle to many collectors. They are drilled from edge to edge with a hollow drill and are double-sided. They appear to be some sort of projectile (spear) point, yet it has been surmised that they were used as weights on early spears. Some bannerstones are sharp-edged, others are curved, and still others are made with an upward curve on each end.

Celts

Ungrooved axes or celts were found in early Southeast cultures. Celts with gouges in them were only found in the early cultures of Maine, while the Northwest Coast celts were long and double-edged (see Axes).

Drills

A drill can be almost any length and most have symmetrical bases. They were designed for hole making and are usually between 1–3″ long. Because of their use, drills were made of very strong rock materials or fossilized limestones, sometimes even of shells.

Some drills were used in the making of clothing or working with leather-like materials. A drill would be the tool, for example, to poke a hole in material so that a sewing tool or awl could follow through with sinew to keep the pieces together. Other drills were stronger and used to make holes in bannerstones or other mineral tools.

Knives

Knives made in prehistoric times have been found in many archeological sites throughout the United States. Some experts will tell you that it is often difficult to determine the difference between a point and a knife when collecting Indian artifacts. There are over 500 named chipped artifacts in this country, so this field of collecting requires serious study in order to be able to tell the origin of a knife, blade or point. For example, you will find an Ashtabula knife, distinguished by wide notches, a knife-like appearance, and offset tip, in Oneida County, New York. A cream-white, chert-type knife with basal strength, however, having wide and large notches, is typical of Pike County, Missouri, and is called Godar.

As scientists study artifacts, they determine the type names and the regions from which they came. It is a wonder that they can come to a decision about where these items originated when so many Indian tribes were nomadic, carrying their spears, knives, and arrowheads with them to use along the way. How confusing it must be for these geologists and historians when they find a Castroville knife, indigenous to Stone County, Missouri, and made of dark gray flint with white incisions, in Taney County, Missouri, where the Stanlee knife, an off-white chert, is said to have originated.

I certainly admire the collectors who are able to pick up a knife and immediately identify its age, its origin, and its name. However, I must reiterate something that always seems to ring true in the antiques business—if you are around collectibles long enough—touch them, study them, buy and sell them on a regular basis—you cannot help but learn more than you are aware.

The first and most important factor about knives is that prehistoric Indians used them for more than just cutting up game for food. A good knife was the most important tool an Indian could own. Of course different size knives were made for different purposes, and the shape of a knife's blade can often tell you its original use. Knives are generally split into three categories: scrapers, shapers, and drills (each category is additionally identified in other parts of this chapter).

Knives such as folsom points have been found north of Fort Collins, Colorado, at the Lindenmeir site. Microlithic flint blades have been found on Santa Rosa Island, off the coast of California. These bladelets are thought to have been used to drill shell beads. Paleo knife forms, found at the Williamson site in Virginia, were larger than fluted points and lacked grinding of the base bottom and lower sides.

In Illinois, at the Koster site (a 4000-year-old temporary hunting camp), it was proved that knives were part of the Indian's hunting tool kit since the hunters dressed the slain animal on site instead of bringing it back to the camp. Even in Vermont, at the Reagan site just south of the Canadian border, knives have been found which resembled projectile points.

To determine the value of prehistoric blades, collectors keep in mind the symmetry of the knife, what material was used (glossy, fine-grained flint is more desirable than dull, large-grained chert), the type of knife, its configuration, the workmanship put into it, and, above all, its condition.

Projectile Points

This category includes both arrowheads and lanceheads, and it is often difficult to tell the difference between the two. The easiest guide is by measuring the piece. The average length of a lancehead is about 2″, while the space between basal notches is approximately ½″. Arrowheads are between 1-1½″ long and the space between basal notches is approximately ¼″; they are also thinner and lighter in weight. The atl-atl (covered previously in this chapter) was the most widely used North American weapon before A.D. 500 and was a hand-held lance thrower, which is very rare today. The atl-atl had a feather-vaned main shaft, which was retrieved, while the thin, short foreshaft was left in the animal.

Points were made by chipping processes and the makers of such points were highly regarded by their tribes. To make a fine grade point was a skill which is appreciated even today in regard to the value of such a point in the collectibles market. Workmanship and quality is determined by the thinness of the point, the regularity of pressure-chipping scars, the point's size (larger being more valuable), and the grade of material used. There should be visual ''balance'' in a point, meaning that both sides should be symmetrical. Though collectors may choose such a point because it is more pleasing to the eye, however, one must keep in mind that the original purpose for such symmetry was that a blade would fly straighter and farther if it was as evenly made as possible.

Each tribe had a different style of point. Some arrowheads are jagged edged, while others have sharp tips and rather rounded bodies. Hopewell points (ca. 300 B.C. to A.D. 300) are rather curved, the point itself being artistic with rounded edges. Hohokam points (A.D. 600–1400), on the other hand, are tall and thin with jagged edges. The two points, though used for basically the same purpose, look nothing alike. The most amazing part of studying Indian projectile points is that no two tribes made exactly the same *type* of point, yet they were all making points at the same time.

The different parts of a projectile point are illustrated as follows:

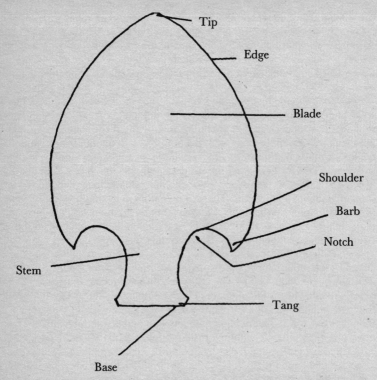

Blades were set into a slot to fit the size of the base and were then tied onto the wood with wet sinew which tightened as it dried.

Some cultures, such as some northern California tribes, judged a person's wealth by the amount of obsidian blades he had. Such blades were used in ceremonies, as in the White Deer Dance.

Scrapers

Scrapers look the same as their name implies. Those of prehistoric age are less interesting and much cruder than later examples, and tribes, such as the Plains Indians, used them to scrape and prepare animal hides for tanning. The Yurok tribe used scrapers or adzes with stone handles. Because the short, strong edges of scrapers often had to be repolished, they show heavy wear.

Though prices are low for these artifacts (usually under $5 each) there are not many collectors who hunt for these items.

Shapers

A hafted shaper has a base which remains mostly intact and either a single or double working edge. Shapers are not chipped, but rather ground down, giving the edge a smooth face and a sharp cut.

Shells

Early Indians used shells to make a variety of artifacts including jewelry, fish hooks, ornaments, gardening tools, and dippers or spoons.

"Wampam," the beads used in trade, was often made from shells such as bivalve halves. They were treated by the Hohokam tribe with pitch and saguaro cactus acid to create the first etchings.

Spades

Spades are usually heavier than a digging blade, with a squared and blunted bottom edge. The better the polish on the blade edge (a sign of use), the more valuable the spade to a collector.

Slate Artifacts

Slate articles are beautiful and they required simple methods to execute. However, condition is an important factor in the determination of collectibility and pricing of slate artifacts. Breakage, scratches, and dull surfaces are some of the things to consider when buying an artifact made from slate. The collector should also be aware of the importance of proper drilling in slate pendants and gorgets. The holes should be strategically, as well as artistically, placed.

Because of the difficulty in finding pieces of slate in collectible condition, as well as the beauty of slate pendants, birdstones, and gorgets, the value of slate artifacts is higher than the projectile point-type artifacts of which we spoke earlier. However, with a lot of diligence and a little luck it is still possible to put together a collection of pieces for $50 (or less) each.

ARTIFACT LISTINGS

Arrows and Arrowheads

Arrowhead coffee table; two-tiered, wooden coffee table w/over 600 arrowheads and spear points mounted under glass; 18″ × 16″ × 39″.

$500–$700

Arrowheads; Riker mount containing three choice Oregon gem points; prehistoric.   **$75–$100**

Arrowheads; two large choice Columbia River arrowheads, prehistoric.
                                                                    $35–$50

Arrows; Plains; two feathered Plains arrows w/stone points; ca. 1870.
                                                                   $100–$150

Copper arrowheads; old native copper (cleaned) hunting arrow tips from Alaska; ca. 1700; 5 pcs.   **$35–$50**

Axes and Ax Head

Ax head; large mottled black ¾ grooved ax head; prehistoric; 7″ × 4½″.
                                                                   $100–$125

Ax, stone; fully grooved black stone ax head from the Columbia River; prehistoric; 6″ × 3″.   **$40–$60**

Stone ax; choice greenish ¾ grooved jadeite ax head; prehistoric.
                                                                   $150–$200

Stone ax; gray ¾ grooved stone ax head; prehistoric.   **$65–$85**

Stone ax; large brown Ho Ho Kam stone ax head from Arizona; prehistoric; 7″ × 3½″.   **$20–$50**

Stone ax; choice greenish ¾ grooved jadeite ax head; prehistoric.
                                                                   $100–$125

Stone ax; Ho Ho Kam; ¾ grooved stone ax head; 4½″ × 2″; prehistoric.   **$45–$75**

War ax; heavy iron head w/tacks, file marks, and w/bead- and wire-wrapped handle; ca. 1880; 22″ × 7″.   **$450–$550**

Bows

Northwest Coast; wide, carved wooden bow w/rawhide hand-hold; ca. 1870; 52″ × 1″.   **$250–$200**

Northwest Coast; long, wide carved wooden big game bow; ca. 1910; 53″ × 2″.   **$35–$50**

Northwest Coast; large wooden bow w/sinew string and sealskin wrap; ca. 1890; 50″ × 1½″.   **$75–$100**

Plains; very early, long red and yellow ochre-painted Plains bow; ca. 1870; 60″ × 1½″.   **$75–$100**

Plains; classic narrow wooden Northern Plains bow; ca. 1870; 55″ × 1″.
                                                                    $45–$70

Plains; beautiful old recurved wooden short bow; ca. 1860; 32″ × 1½″.
$100–$150

Sioux; recurved wooden bow w/sinew string; ca. 1900; 18″ × 1½″.
$150–$200

Sioux; recurved wooden bow w/sinew string; ca. 1900; 48″ × 1½″.
$150–$200

Clubs

Plains; Northern Plains "Flop knob" war club w/fully beaded handle and horsehair suspensions; 29″ × 1″. $300–$400

Sioux; egg-shaped stone club w/beaded handle; ca. 1890; 19″ × 2″.
$100–$130

Sioux; painted wooden war club w/metal blades w/hair suspensions; ca. 1870; 31″ × 5″. $175–$225

Sioux; egg-shaped brown stone head on a fully beaded wooden handle; ca. 1860; 18″ × 2″ $100–$150

Sioux; large gray egg-shaped stone head attached to a hide-covered wooden handle; ca. 1870; 30″ × 5″ $115–$175

Sioux; red stone egg-shaped club on long, fully beaded handle; 28″ × 5″.
$250–$350

Collections

Bag containing 14 arrowheads and other miscellaneous items; prehistoric.
$20–$40

Fantastic glassed frame containing 1500 points laid in the form of two deer and the sun; 48″ × 53″ $600–$1000

Frame containing 13 large points and beads from Missouri; prehistoric.
$55–$75

Frame of 25 large points and beads from Missouri; prehistoric. $35–$55

Frame containing 15 assorted arrow and spear points; prehistoric. $30–$50

Frame containing nine stone salmon cleaning knives; prehistoric. $15–$35

Frame containing 40 white stone points; prehistoric. $40–$60

Frame containing over 50 choice arrowheads; prehistoric; 11″ × 9″.
$75–$150

Glassed frame containing 50 very unusual pink choice arrow points; prehistoric.
$25–$50

Glassed frame containing 66 fine Columbia River arrowheads; 12″ × 10″; prehistoric. $35–$50

Glassed frame containing 52 arrowheads and points; prehistoric. **$85–$100**

Glassed frame containing 55 Columbia River points; prehistoric; 12″ × 10″. **$60–$80**

Glassed frame containing 54 Columbia River points and some trade beads; prehistoric; 12″ × 10″. **$125–$175**

Glassed frame containing rare Columbia River gem points, trade beads, and an old coin; 11″ × 9″; ca. 1820. **$75–$100**

Glassed frame containing 60 Oregon points; prehistoric; 12″ × 10″. **$50–$75**

Glassed frame containing 56 Oregon arrowheads; prehistoric; 12″ × 10″. **$50–$75**

Glassed frame containing seven arrowheads and many rare trade beads; ca. 1870; 11″ × 9″. **$85–$100**

Glassed frame containing 39 pipes, net sinkers, and other artifacts; prehistoric; 23″ × 18″. **$75–$100**

Glassed frame containing four rare Phoenix buttons, old Chinese coins, beads, etc., from the Columbia River; 12″ × 10″; ca. 1840. **$175–$225**

Glassed frame containing 50 very unusual and ornate projectile points; prehistoric; 10″ × 12″. **$175–$225**

Glassed frame containing 37 Columbia River cogs, pestles, balls, and sinkers; prehistoric. **$375–$425**

Glassed frame containing 53 Oregon points; prehistoric; 11″ × 9″. **$60–$80**

Glassed frame containing 51 choice arrows and spear points; prehistoric; 12″ × 9″. **$155–$180**

Glassed frame containing 61 Oregon arrowheads; prehistoric; 12″ × 10″. **$60–$80**

Glassed frame containing nine arrowheads and many rare trade beads; ca. 1900; 11″ × 9″. **$95–$140**

Glassed frame containing 75 black and brown obsidian arrow and spear points. **$200–$350**

Group; Southern Plains; including a beaded hide awl case and a "strike-a-light" pouch, each trimmed w/tin cones, a beaded hide belt pouch, a woven beadwork strap w/pouch, a bone "hairpipe" necklace w/brass and translucent red glass beads, and a doll w/model cradleboard, wearing a cloth costume, red painted details; provenance: "Captured from Apaches in 1878 by Mrs. R. Der. Hoyle." **$1650–$2000**

1500 choice points mounted in Northwest Coast bear design; 48″ × 52″; prehistoric. **$600–$1000**

Huge glassed frame containing 1500 projectile points inlaid in prehistoric animal designs; 53″ × 48″.   **$700–$1000**

Large frame; excavated Columbia River artifacts including points, fossils, beads, etc.; prehistoric.   **$100–$200**

Large glassed frame containing over 55 bone artifacts from the Columbia River; 23″ × 18″; prehistoric.   **$160–$200**

Large glassed frame containing 268 similar points; prehistoric.   **$75–$100**

Riker mount containing three Oregon gem points, all three having serrated edges; prehistoric.   **$135–$170**

Riker mount containing 25 obsidian arrowheads and other pieces; prehistoric.
                                                    $60–$80

Riker mount containing 24 arrowheads along w/elk antler hide scraper.   **$115–$130**

Riker mount containing 15 pieces of Mimbres material; prehistoric.   **$45–$75**

Riker mount containing 21 choice stone arrowheads; prehistoric.   **$100–$150**

Riker mount containing 22 large stone arrowheads.   **$70–$125**

Riker mount containing seven prehistoric pottery pieces; prehistoric.   **$25–$50**

Riker mount containing 16 pieces, including arrowheads, bones, and beads; prehistoric.   **$35–$50**

Riker mount containing 43 pieces of material excavated from the Columbia River; prehistoric.   **$30–$50**

Riker mount containing four choice Rogue River points; prehistoric.   **$75–$125**

Riker mount containing 22 stone arrowheads; prehistoric.   **$20–$40**

Two mounts containing eight choice Oregon and Washington gem mounts; prehistoric.   **$60–$80**

Two Riker mounts containing a total of 21 arrowheads and spear heads; prehistoric.   **$45–$70**

Two small Riker mounts, each containing five gem arrowheads; prehistoric.
                                                    $60–$85

Wooden frame containing nine rare ceremonial and effigy points; prehistoric.
                                                    $75–$100

Fetishes

Sioux; small beaded hide umbilical cord fetish in lizard form; 4″ × 2″.
                                                    $55–$80

Zuni; snake fetish carved from elk antler; ca. 1950s; the fetish is adorned w/tin mudheads and is signed "J. Boone—Zuni." The Boone family is noted for jewelry and other works.   **$600–$800**

Courtesy of Jack Sellner, CAI.

Zuni; antler, shell, hide, and feathered fetish; 12½″ long; serpent/dragon/ horned sea monster w/two protruding (v-shaped) horns and tongue.

$225–$450

Jade

Adze; rare old Columbia River jade adze; prehistoric; 3½″.   **$50–$75**

Celt; prehistoric; large, finely worked jade celt from the Columbia River.   **$200–$300**

Celt; prehistoric; highly polished, finely worked jade celt from the Columbia River.   **$135–$175**

Knives and Knife Cases

Choice dark gray, stone ceremonial knife from the Columbia River; prehistoric; 14″ × 4″.   **$250–$300**

Large knife case w/paint and tacks and containing an old knife; 18″ × 3½″.   **$85–$100**

Northwest Coast; choice handmade knife w/carved animal head handle and painted wooden sheath; ca. 1975; 15″ × 4″.   **$95–$125**

Plains; hide sheath w/geometric beadwork and containing an old knife; ca. 1910; 11½″ × 3½″.   **$100–$150**

Plains; lazy stitch knife sheath, ca. 1880s–1890s.   **$150–$250**

Plains; old handmade knife and painted rawhide sheath; ca. 1880.

$55–$80

Unusual carved bone knife or awl; ca. 1900; 10″ × 1″.   **$15–$20**

Yurok; long, double-pointed, black obsidian ceremonial knife; prehistoric; 11″ × 1½″.   **$100–$150**

Mortar and Pestle

Black stone phallic pestle found on the Columbia River in 1960; prehistoric; 8″ × 3″.   **$100–$150**

Choice black stone bell pestle from the Columbia River; prehistoric; 4½″ × 7″.
                                                                       $120–$160

Choice gray stone mortar and matching bell pestle from the Columbia River; prehistoric; 14″ × 7″.   **$150–$175**

Gray stone mortar and pestle from the Columbia River; prehistoric; 10″ × 9″.
                                                                        $35–$70

Wasco; rare stone mortar and pestle excavated near Celilo Falls on the Columbia River; ca. 1700; 11″ × 4¾″.   **$115–$150**

Pipes

Hopewell; very large and unusual human sacrificial idol pipe from Illinois; prehistoric; 8″ × 6½″.   **$275–$375**

Sioux; black stone "T" bowl w/red stone and pewter inlay and long beaded stem; 28″ × 2″ × 6″.   **$300–$400**

Sioux; black stone "T" bowl w/red stone and pewter inlay; dated 1888; 21″ × 2″ × 7″.   **$125–$175**

Sioux; huge black stone "T" bowl w/pewter and red stone inlays and w/a huge beaded and tacked stem; 40″ × 2″ × 6″.   **$275–$350**

Sioux; small fine red catlinite "T" bowl w/carved wooden stem; ca. 1890; 19″ × 2″.   **$135–$150**

Wasco; rare excavated green stone "cloud blower" pipe w/lizard effigy (could be lower Klamath River); prehistoric; 6½″ × 1″.   **$300–$400**

Points

Agate; fantastic, large finely chipped Oregon agate point; prehistoric.
                                                                        $65–$95

Bird; bag containing approximately 50 tiny bird points; prehistoric.
                                                                        $45–$65

Folsom; classic chipped stone folsom point in Riker mount; prehistoric.
                                                                        $35–$50

Two points; one large, tan, notched spear point and one smaller gray, fluted spear point; prehistoric; 9″ × 5½″.   **$85–$100**

Yuma; fine large Yuma (Paleo) point from Texas; prehistoric; 4½″ × ¾″.
                                                                       $125–$140

Spear Heads

Black obsidian spear point; prehistoric.   **$20–$40**

Huge gray spear head in a large Riker mount; prehistoric; 16″ × 2½″.
                                                                         $125–$200

Stone Items

Discoidal; round flecked gray stone Mound Builder discoidal; prehistoric.   **$50–$75**

Items; five assorted arrowheads, eccentrics, etc.; prehistoric. **$35–$50**

Tool; choice black carved stone Mound Builder tool; prehistoric; 13″ × 3″.   **$150–$200**

Tepee Rests

Cheyenne; willow tepee rest all put together in the old style; ca. 1930; 86″ × 35″.   **$215–$275**

Northern Plains; old willow tepee rest w/canvas trim; ca. 1900; 78″ × 40″.
                                                                         $250–$300

Tomahawks/Pipes

Tomahawk; Crow; original iron head w/cross cutout and bead-wrapped handle which was added later; ca. 1870; 22″ × 11″ × 5″.
                                                                         $200–$300

Tomahawk, pipe; all original Plains pipe tomahawk w/traces of paint and w/file-burned handle; ca. 1870; 17½″ × 8″.   **$200–$275**

Tomahawk, pipe; narrow pipe head w/tacked and file-burned wooden handle; ca. 1870; 21″ × 8″.   **$150–$200**

Tomahawk; Plains; iron head w/heart cutout and w/tacked and decorated handle; ca. 1880; 22″ × 6½″.   **$80–$120**

Other

Carving, Wasco; rare basalt carving of an unusual-looking human head; prehistoric; 5″ × 4″.   **$125–$150**

Ceremonial wand, Northern Plains; buffalo horn dance wand w/fully beaded handle; 29″ × 1″.   **$300–$400**

Fossil; prehistoric Alaskan ivory.   **$20–$40**

Medicine items; five old Navajo sacred medicine items in a box; ca. 1880.   **$65–$90**

Quiver and arrows; pitched covered wooden quiver w/seven old arrows; ca. 1870; 24″ × 3″.   **$350–$400**

Tool; Hopewell; bonded gray slate tool from a mound; prehistoric.
                                                                                    $25–$45

Trade beads; strand of large cobalt blue trade beads; ca. 1890; 24″.
                                                                                  $75–$100

BASKETS

▼▼▼▼▼▼▼▼▼▼▼▼

INTRODUCTION

Indian baskets were made for a variety of uses. Some, like the Apache water jars, were made to carry liquids, while others were woven for a much gentler reason—to carry babies. Baskets were made to carry loads of fruit, corn or wheat. Some were made as bowls for eating food, for shelling beans or for mixing herbs. Trays and plaques were made for ceremonial or, even, gambling purposes. Baskets were made to hold trinkets, clothes, and other belongings. Sifters were made for those Indians who grew wheat or corn. Indian fisherman wove fish weirs in a basketry fashion, while those owning horses wove saddle bags.

All baskets were meant to fill some kind of working role in everyday Indian life, yet some were made as gifts, such as those miniature baskets made by the Pomo Indians of California. They are considered some of the finest baskets in the world, woven so tightly that there are 60 stitches to the inch. Baskets have also been part of Indian ceremonies and in each tribe the basket has its place and use. Navajo medicine men use baskets in their healing rites, as part of the wedding ceremony, and in religious ceremonies.

Most basketmakers remain anonymous, but when white people began to trade with Indians some weavers came to prominence [i.e., Mary Benson (Pomo), Mrs. Hickox (Karok), and Dat-So-La-Lee (Great Basin), whose biography appears later in this chapter].

There are many legends which surround the art of basketry. The Navajos have a myth about the Bat Woman and the strength of her baskets. The Pueblo Indians tell a story of a young man being lowered over a cliff in a basket—in an effort to obtain eagle feathers—and how he learned the eagle's secrets and lived with them. The Hopis tell the legend of Tiyo, the mythical snake hero.

Geometric designs on baskets have evolved as many other designs have. Simple and square-edged at first, Greek key designs evolved into scrollwork that was eventually integrated into pottery designs. Other geometric designs mean different things to different tribes (i.e., one tribe may say an hourglass shape is distinctive of a bird, while another may call two opposite triangles their bird design). A cross means different things to different tribes. For example, to the Thompson Indians the cross depicts the crossing of trails; to the Yokuts, it represents a battle; and the Wallapais and Havasupais see the cross as a phallic symbol.

Each tribe uses the materials available to them in their area. Each has a different style of weaving and uses different colors and different symbols in their basketmaking. We will discuss a variety of tribes and their basketry later in the chapter.

As with other types of baskets, condition is of the utmost importance. If the edges are broken or there are holes in any portion of the basket, your investment is not something of which you can be proud. Once you have decided on the condition of your basket, you should pay attention to the tightness of the weave. Fifteen stitches to the inch is considered a fine weave, 28 to the inch is an art; then the rest of the factors will fall into place (the design, the colors, the workmanship, etc.).

SOME MATERIALS USED IN BASKETMAKING

Tribe	*Material*
Nez Perces, Wascos (Plains)	Split corn husks and wild hemp.
Hopi (Southwest)	Yucca and fine grass.
Klickitat (Northwest)	Roots of young spruce and cedar trees, squaw grass.
Mono (California)	Tender shoots, roots and fibres.
Panamint (California)	Young shoots of tough willow, sumac shoots, horns on pods of unicorn plants, and yucca roots.
Paiute and Havasupai (Southwest)	Martynia (cat's claw), yucca, and amole.
Pima and Maricopa (Southwest)	Sisal willow, squaw weed, skunk weed, tule root and martynia.
Poma	Roots of slough grass.
Southern California	Tule toot and squaw weed.
Tlingit	Spruce root, split and soaked in water.

COLORS USED IN BASKETRY

Color in basketry, as well as in other crafts, is symbolic to the Amerind. For instance, the Cherokees believe that red is synonymous with success or triumph, blue signifies defeat or trouble, black is death, and white (what else?) is peace and happiness. Red is generally considered sacred to almost all tribes. During the Ghost Dance period, performers wore designs painted in red, yellow, green, and blue—colors meant to sharpen the performers' spiritual perceptions.

Tribe	*Use of Colors*
Cahuilla (California)	Only used yellow, white, black, and brown. The only one of these colors that is not natural is black, and it was made by taking a pot of mud from the sulphur springs near their home, boiling it, and stirring the mud and water together. Once the mud settled, the liquid was poured off and used to color the splints.
Havasupai (Southwest)	Use the peeled pod of the martynia, which is black, and do not dye the willow they use.
Hopi (Southwest)	Use plants, flowers, and roots as dyes, though much of their modern basketry uses aniline dyes.
Klickitat (Northwest)	Natural color of squaw grass, used in Klickitat basketry, is white. When soaked in water, it becomes yellow; if soaked in hot water, it becomes brown. Urine is often used to dye the materials used to make blankets.
Navajo (Southwest)	Use colors for everything, even when planting corn. For example, white goes first because it is the color of the east and has most importance; blue, the color of the south, goes next; yellow, the next color in the sunwise movement, is planted after blue; and black is last.
Poma (Southwest)	Dyed their basketry materials by a process using charcoal paste, willow ashes, and dirt. The process took nearly 80 hours to produce what the Pomas considered a perfect dye.

Potawatomi (North Central U.S.)	Their baskets are the color of gold sunset clouds.
Shasta (California)	Dye the white grass they use brown by adding an extract of alder bark. Maidenhair fern stem is used for the black details in their basketry.
Yakima (California)	See white, blue, and yellow as their spiritual colors.
Zuni (Southwest)	Yellow is north, west is blue, south is red, and east is white.

BASKETMAKERS

The most famous North American basketmaker was Dat So La Lee (or Mrs. Louisa Kayser), who lived from approximately 1850 to 1924. Kayser was born into the Washo tribe that lived around Lake Tahoe and it was there that she learned to make baskets with her people. After her tribe's land was stolen by settlers and polluted by miners, Dat So La Lee worked at odd jobs such as washing clothes and being a maid.

When she was 60, her talent was recognized by Abe Cohn, who owned an emporium in Carson City, Nevada. He became her business agent, providing her and her husband with a home, food, clothing, and payment for medical bills, and she provided him with all of her baskets.

Dat So La Lee's weaving was tight and even, and her baskets are classics. Her triangular and flame-shaped motifs are perfectly spaced to the field on which they are placed. Some of her baskets have symbols on them which represent sunrise or the midday ascending heat waves.

Though she could not sign her name, she used a handprint as her signature. Cohn listed, numbered, and titled Dat So La Lee's baskets according to his conversations with her, and his efforts make it easier to study her development as an artist. When Dat So La Lee brought her work to the St. Louis Exposition in 1919, she was one of its stars.

Other basketmakers are known to exist, though biographies of them are rare. It is not common for basketmakers to put their signatures on their work, thus the work of the researcher is made even more difficult. It is my hope that someday biographies will exist for these artisans and, perhaps, we can begin with those who have won awards for their work.

This is one of the reasons why it is important to document the antiques you buy, and to be certain that you obtain as much information about the makers of your Indian pieces as possible! Documentation could mean an easier time selling your collection in the future and it could also mean that your collection will be worth much more.

DIFFERENT TRIBES AND THEIR BASKETMAKING

Aleut (Northwest)

Aleut baskets are among the finest woven baskets of all North American Indian baskets. The weaving is extremely delicate and, though they stand the test of time well, they always give the impression that they will fall apart the moment you touch them.

Apache (Southwest)

Since this tribe is split into different denominations, I will give the general information first, then a few details on the different variations of this Southwestern tribe.

Apache basketry's main components are their water jugs (tuus) and burden baskets. The jugs are made of sumac or strawberry twigs, which are twined and woven over each other. Juniper leaves and red ochre are used to fill in the cracks and the jar is waterproofed with pinon pitch, applied with a brush made of cow's hair. The Apache burden basket is made of willow, cottonwood or wild mulberry, and decorated with strips of buckskin which end in tin cones that "tinkle" when the baskets move. These pendants are typical of Apache work. Other tribes, such as some in California, hang bits of shells or beads as decorative accents on their baskets, and even decorate them with feathers.

The swastika design is one common to Apache (as well as Pima) basketry and is said to represent water, an important item to most Indian tribes. The design may also be called "whirling logs." The "swirling" line represents the source of the water supply and the geometric lines leading away from the center of the design depict winding streams.

JICARILLA APACHES

Jicarilla Apaches are located in the northwestern part of New Mexico. They use a five-rod coiling method and sew their coils together with gold sumac. No plaited work has been found that was made by the Jicarilla tribe.

Though coiled baskets were made for the tourist trade, wicker baskets were the type the Indians made for personal use.

MESCALERO APACHES

The Mescalero Apaches (south central New Mexico) use a three-rod stacked coiling method to weave their baskets.

Early attempts at basketry proved that their use was completely utilitarian. Their weaving was coarse and their colors and designs rather boring. Once the Mescalero Apache began to make commercial baskets, however, their style improved, though their weaving, in general, is still not as fine as that of other tribes.

SAN CARLOS AND WHITE MOUNTAIN APACHES

The San Carlos and White Mountain Apaches are expert weavers who incorporate intricate designs in their work. Most of their basketry work is coiled and they use willow or twigs in weaving. Water bottles (ollas), bowls, saucers, trinket baskets, cradles, etc., are made by these Apaches.

SOUTHERN APACHES

The finishing stitch used by Southern Apaches is simple coiling around the splint.

California Mission Tribes

The California Indians came under the control of Spanish religious leaders when the Spaniards took the land from the Indians. The Spaniards built missions and attempted to help the Indians by introducing Christianity. The military bought the Indians and forced them to work as slaves. Eventually, the Indians took Spanish names, learned how to speak the language, and thus began communicating with the mission fathers.

The basketry considered to be that of the Mission Indian covers a broad category which includes the weaving of the many tribes and subtribes that were under the control of the Spanish missions (beginning in 1769). The basketry has a similar structure and style, though there was a wide difference in the language of the tribes which made them.

Normally more peaceful and calm than their Southwestern Indian brothers, California tribes such as the Modoks, Karoks, and Yuroks wove fine baskets from the reeds and vegetation common to their home. The Mission Indians used three main types of vegetation in weaving their baskets, though many types were available throughout the regions where they lived, some of which would have been easier to use.

Juncus grass, which grows beneath mountain oak trees, allowed a variety of color combinations in design because of its variegated stem. Sumac provided a white color for backgrounds and for outlining dark patterns. The Indians often dyed juncus a dark brown to accent patterns woven into their baskets. Deer grass, found commonly in Southern California, was the gradd-bundle foundation material.

Geometric patterns, as well as pictures of animals such as doves, burros, camels, fish, rats, mice, butterflies, lizards, and rattlesnakes, decorate baskets made by Missionary Indians. Though designs were similar, no weaver ever copied another's design exactly (except for the rattlesnake and, even then, the maker took special care to add his own identifying features).

Their baskets were closely stitched and fine, some comparable to the intricacies of Pomo basketweaving. Eighteen to 30 wrappings per inch is the average stitch count for most Mission Indian baskets and one can find all sizes, shapes, and designs.

They were never decorated with beads and only occasionally were they decorated with feathers—the decorating done during the weaving itself was where the weaver expressed his/her art. The materials used included sedge root, willow, bullrush root, and redbud bark. The most common design in all California basketry is the rattlesnake design. Also commonly used among these Indians is the "quail" design—distinctive because of its plume, which resembles an upside-down golf club. They also incorporated flower and fern designs into their basketry.

The Mission Indian rattlesnake baskets were rare during the late 1800s because they bore a stigma of evil. But when the baskets were made for the tourist trade, there were two distinct types of rattlesnake baskets. One was an abstract design found in the Chumash, Monache, Panamint, Shoshone, Tejon, Kawaiisu, Yokut, and Tubatalabal territories. The other was a realistic version of the reptile, produced in the late nineteenth century, and these later baskets were the ones made "for sale." Indians always respected the rattlesnake and its power, and they believed that blindness, untimely death, and other misfortunes that plagued the weavers of rattlesnake baskets were directly associated with the power of the snake. Because of this belief, production of the baskets came to a halt around 1920.

Maria Antonia, a Dieguene, is credited with first designing the rattlesnake basket in 1898, although others before her may have made cruder versions of the same design. Mary Snyder, a Chemeheuvi Indian, was well known throughout Arizona for making the same type of basket and design, using a unique combination of Chemeheuvi and Cahuilla materials. Though her baskets look like those made by Southern California Indians, different materials were most likely used. Chemeheuvi basketmakers almost always used willow for white stitches and devil's claw for black; true Mission weavers never used these materials.

Chemeheuvi (California) See also California Mission Tribes.

Basketry by this Indian tribe is not as available as others. The tribe is a small Shoshoni band that was originally Californian but later "moved in" with the much larger Mohave tribe when their own reservation proved uninhabitable.

Chemeheuvi basketry is refined yet sprightly. Their designs—animals, butterflies or animal tracks—are considered the property of the weaver and are not supposed to be copied by other artisans.

Creek (South Central U.S.)

The Creek's technique of plaiting was to twist the ends of the warp into a false braid. Often the colors in a Creek basket will be oranges and browns.

Cherokee (South)

Indians of the Cherokee nation used the plaiting technique to weave baskets, bending their warps over a hoop.

Haidas (Northwest)

As with everything else they make, the Haida Indians cover their basketry with totemic symbols and drawings.

Havasupai (Southwest)

Havasupai baskets are masterful and were made most frequently during the period from 1900 to 1925. The Havasupai Indians made about the same amount of money from their best baskets as they did from the most poorly made. In the early 1970s, the art was dying out and less than half a dozen weavers were left.

Many ethnologists believe that pottery and basketry share much the same history. Early reports of life among the Havasupai of Arizona (there is a portion of the tribe left, living on the floor of the Grand Canyon) showed that the base of a basket would be lined with clay, the pottery piece would be formed within the basket, and then it would be removed to stand on its own as a vessel. Baskets, or basketry vessels, had originally been used to transport water. The talent of those early basketmakers must have been great for them to be able to weave so tightly that their baskets could hold liquid!

Hidatsa (Northwest)

The Hidatsa Indians wove their baskets from box elder and willow bark. The pieces would be dyed before being woven together to form geometrically patterned baskets.

Hopi (Southwest)

The Hopi Indians are considered the greatest basket producers of the Pueblo Indians. They practiced all three types of weaving and are characterized by the great variety in their basket shapes and designs. Because baskets were used in trade, occasionally a Navajo design will show up on a Hopi basket, or vice versa.

Supposedly Hopi basketry degenerated when they began to use aniline dyes in the late 1800s and early 1900s. By 1906, the Hopis had shifted from Old Oraibi to Hotevilla and had gone back to using natural dyes. They were also still using large coils. By the late 1920s and 1930s, they reduced the size of their coils and improved their designs, and by the early 1960s they had much improved their work overall. Higher and higher peaks of artistic perfection in Hopi basketry continue to be reached and more elaborate designs are being used.

Traditionally, Hopi baskets have been made only on the second mesa of the Hopi Reservation in Arizona. The materials generally used by Hopi basketweavers are galetta grass and yucca.

Designs were less generalized and coordinated in earlier baskets than they are now. Patterns were basically geometric or in a sunburst style, with rays going out to the edge of the basket, though other themes (including clouds with or without rain and kachinas) have been used.

Between 1930–60, patterns became more elaborate and structured. Wedding trays became established and the pattern would not necessarily go out to the rim of the basket as it had earlier. When the 1960–80 period arrived, Hopi baskets were serving the needs of those interested in Indian crafts and their values climbed to a new peak.

Plaques are the most abundant form of Hopi basketry and designs have changed in the past 100 years. Kachinas and mudheads have often been incorporated into the new designs. There is symbolism in the way Hopi women weave plaques: if the inner grass is left to "flow out," having an unfinished appearance, its maker is an unmarried virgin (this is called the "flowing gate"); married women of childbearing age leave the ends of the grass flowing, but the grass is cut off approximately one inch from the last stitch (called the "open gate"); widows or women who are incapable of bearing children finish off their work completely (the "closed gate").

It is always important to know what types of material the Indians use in their basketry. The Hopis use sumac for warps and several types of rabbit brush for wefts. Their plaiting is also distinctive because they tie the yucca splints of ring baskets over a sumac withe.

Hopi designs are geometric and extremely colorful—sometimes incorporating seven to nine colors in a single piece of basketry. The Hopis use more color in their basketry than any other Southwestern tribe. The most common designs in Hopi basketry are the lightning symbol and the rain clouds, as well as mountain and valley symbols. Butterflies, eagles, and kachinas may be woven into basketry pieces, making the overall effect even more striking than a geometric design ablaze with color.

The difference between a Hopi wicker bowl and tray goes further than just the depth of the piece; the bowl has straighter sides and a larger, flatter bottom. Most Hopi basket/bowls are decorated in bands. Though these bands may consist of two or three natural colors (or many colors, as in plaques), the banding of colors is fairly normal.

Peach baskets (or trays) are not as flat as piki trays, nor as deep as peach gathering baskets, and they are always woven in plain wicker weave. A piki tray is flat and rectangular and used for serving piki (cornmeal bread served for ceremonial purposes). The main area of the piki tray is plaited by weaving bundles of split elements over other bundles of the same. The trays are used by Hopis in ceremonies and are usually made of wrapped coils. Some of these trays are wonderfully decorative and colorful, incorporating such patterns as the spider web.

Hopi burden baskets have often been called peach gathering baskets (as opposed to peach *trays*). These baskets were used by the men to gather peaches and corn and were woven by the women. It is the same type of basket used in the Bean Dance.

The Hopis made snake charm liquid in a basket. This ritual began with the medicine man pouring liquid into a basket from the six sacred directions of the Hopi (north, south, east, west, up, and down). He went through some incantations and the ceremony ended with the medicine man mixing white paint from the earth with the liquid in the basket, then rubbing the paint on the body of the chief priest.

The Hopis also wove a basket which imitates a spider's web and used this basket in dances and offerings in honor of the spider woman (Kokyan-wuh-ti). Sacred meal trays also often bear this spider web design.

Baskets are so intrinsic to the Hopi culture that they even have basket dances (La-la-kon-ti or Rain Dance; Owakult and Kohonino basket dances). In the Kohonino dance, only baskets made by the Havasupai Indians (who traded regularly with the Hopis) are used.

Hopi baskets often win first prize at ceremonials and markets throughout the Southwest, and there are new weavers, some as young as 12 or 13, competing for first place every year.

Iroquois (Northeast)

The basketmakers of the Iroquois tribe used the plaiting technique in making baskets, using two splints to make a double hoop, then using the hoop to hold the upper ends of the warps.

Jemez (Southwest)

The Jemez Pueblo is the only one of the Rio Grande pueblos still active in the art of basketmaking today. Men and women have pursued this art and still produce plaited baskets. Jemez baskets were made for winnowing, washing wheat, shelling corn, and other purposes, and one weaver might make three to five baskets per week.

Jemez weavers use yucca as their main material because it is readily available and can be harvested at any time during the year. Sumac is also used. Most Jemez baskets are round because almost all of the mats are woven in squares.

Navajo (Southwest)

Basketry of the Navajo tribe, as in many others, serves a purpose, whether it be utilitarian or ceremonial.

The Navajo basketry water bottle (tus jeh) was an ingenious way of carrying water a great distance. It could be easily fastened to a saddle or a belt by a rawhide thong, and if dropped, kicked or bumped, it would not break or dump the precious fluid it carried.

The basket used in the Navajo wedding ceremony is a highly collectible piece. To know the history of the ceremony in which this basket is involved makes the wedding basket even more desirable. The bride's family prepares a corn meal porridge, carried in the basket, then a male relative sprinkles pollen in a design over the meal. When the bridegroom enters the bride's hogan, the basket of porridge is placed between them, with the bride's male relative still in the room. With great ceremony, the bride and groom perform small services for each other, then he takes a pinch of porridge from where the lines of the design, which were sprinkled on the meal earlier, meet. Once his bride matches his actions, the bowl is passed to the other younger guests while the elders give the wedding couple sage advice.

Northwest Coast

Northwest Coast tribes often wove their twined baskets upside down and depict fish in their basketmaking.

Papago (California)

Early Papago baskets, sturdy black trays of martynia (devil's claw), were used for parching corn with live coals. Modern baskets are made of yucca leaves, coiled over bear grass, or yule stem foundations.

Today, Papago weavers make baskets that are in tune with commercial needs (i.e., wastebaskets, hampers, and covered baskets). Papagos now make miniature horsehair baskets as well.

Paiutes (Southwest)

The Paiute tribe has three distinct styles of basketmaking. They use aromatic sumac, yucca, and martynia in creating their baskets. The Paiute bowls, known as "Navajo Wedding Baskets/Apache Medicine Baskets," are the most sought after of all Paiute baskets.

They weave the border in a diagonal whip stitch, often called the "herringbone," and the stitch is the distinguishing mark of Paiute, Navajo, and Havasupai weaving. The Navajos, however, claim this stitch to be their own and even tell a legend of how a Navajo basket-weaving woman was given the idea for the stitch from the god Qastceyelci. It is said that Qastceyelci tore a piece of juniper off a tree and threw it into the woman's half-made basket, causing her to imitate the juniper leaves' peculiar folds in her work. Since then, if the margin of a basket is broken through or torn, it is considered unfit for sacred use and must be given away.

The Paiutes incorporate into their basket designs their belief that the Paiute came from an underworld (or "lower" world), which corresponds to the hills and valleys of the upper world. The communication link between the two (Shipapu) is represented by the basket's opening. If the opening is closed, the basketmaker would make it impossible for any more of her people to be born into the upper world.

Pima/Maricopa (California)

The Pima and Maricopa baskets are similar to the Paiute, Havasupai, and Apache, though their work is coarser. The border stitch these tribes use is also different (a forward and backward kind of stitch). The Pima tribe makes shallow, medium-size bowls, closely woven of cattail, over which the basketmaker sews strips of willow shoots and devil's claw. The Pima bowls are made with such well-known designs as the fret, star, butterfly, squash blossom, swastika, and whirlwind.

The Pima also make miniatures of their creations, some of which are held in museums. A good example of a Pima miniature basket might take as long as three months to make.

Pomo (California)

According to early experts, the Pomas used nine distinct weaves in their basketry (ca. 1880–1920) and there were five other weaves found in baskets earlier than that era. The weaves are described in detail in many books on basketry.

The first weave to produce patterns was the "bam-tush." The weave process, a one-rod coiling method, was an increasing spiral and the basket would eventually show spaces which required extra ribs. These were filled in with stitches made by a bone awl. A change of thread would be required to make the pattern and we often find rings of "ti" stitches worked into the pattern. ("Ti" in the Poma language means ponderous, stable, and unyielding, and this describes the Poma double weave which is actually twined weaving.)

The weave of the basket can also tell us its usage. Seed baskets were of a fine weave, while water baskets were finer still. Gathering baskets could be a looser weave depending on whether the basket was being used to gather acorns or a larger substance.

The shape of the basket also dictated its use. For example, ovoid-shaped baskets held sugar, trinkets, or clothing, while conical baskets were used to transport items, being hung by a headband that was placed over the carrier's brow. Plain baskets held food, while fanciful ones were given as gifts.

Southwest

The Indians of the Southwest not only made baskets through the art of weaving natural fibers, but also used that art to make baby cradles, water bottles, and hats, just to name a few.

Yavapai (Southwest)

There is much discussion about whether the Yavapai taught the Apaches to weave or vice versa. Whatever the case, Yavapai baskets are strong enough so that food can be boiled in them. Burden baskets were made in abundance because the Yavapai did not have horses.

The materials used by the Yavapai in making baskets today include willow twigs (for coiling), split willow, and devil's claw for sewing. Yavapai designs are interesting—they combine geometric designs with animal and human figures, and the same designs are not often used more than once.

Zuni (Southwest)

Baskets were made by the Zuni people for everyday use as well as for ceremonial purposes. They made plaited and wicker baskets, but are *not* known for making coiled baskets.

It is noted that plaited baskets were made by the Zuni at the turn of the century and were still being made during the 1930s; however, wicker baskets are more readily available.

Zuni workmanship is not as good as Hopi—the finish is not as tight and the sewing is not as regular. Little decoration was done on Zuni baskets and it appears that they were made more often to fulfill a purpose than to serve as decoration.

BASKET LISTINGS

Aleut

Carrying basket; large, finely twined w/native cord and w/rim loops; red and blue geometric designs; 10″ × 5″; ca. 1880.   **$160–$200**

Classic fine-twined basket w/lid and w/red wool floral designs; ca. 1890.

$275–$350

Apache

Bowl; 13″ diameter, 4″ deep; ca. 1900; belonged to a woman whose cousin sent it back to her from the Southwest.   **$850–$1050**

Bowl; 12″ fine-weave bowl decorated w/figures of men.   **$800–$1000**

Courtesy of C. E. Guarino, Denmark, ME.

Burden; woven with the "Ti" band upright warps w/three bands of dark brown designs, the bottom w/rawhide support skin and hide bands stretched at the top rim, other rawhide fringe at sides, the top w/rawhide binding rubbed w/"sacred" yellow pigment; ca. 1900s; 18″ diameter opening, 14″ high. **$700–$800**

Burden; San Carlos; excellent condition; ca. 1920; 21″ × 3″.
$1500–$1750

Burden; twined basket, flaring cylindrical form decorated w/panels of fringed hide. **$500–$750**

Coiled basketry tray; woven in willow and devil's claw w/concentric geometric bands; 19″ diameter. **$800–$1000**

Coiled basketry olla; rounded neck, woven in willow and devil's claw w/human figures, tepee-type structures, and geometric devices; 20½″ high (rim and stitch damage). **$675–$975**

Coiled basketry bowl; tapering sides, woven in willow and devil's claw w/bands of checkered designs; 9″ diameter. **$375–$500**

Coiled basketry tray; woven w/flat base, flaring sides; woven in willow and dark brown devil's claw; spoked pattern radiating from the solid tondo, radiating joined diamond motif; 16¾" diameter.   **$1500–$1700**

Coiled basketry olla; woven in "bottleneck" form, slightly flaring body, well shouldered, bands of concentric meandering linear motif; 9" high.   **$700–$900**

Coiled basketry tray, woven in willow and devil's claw w/standing human figures and dogs contained by elongated "dagger" devices; 10¼" diameter.

$500–$700

Coiled basketry tray; flat base and low flaring sides, woven in willow and black devil's claw w/radiating rosette pattern enclosing horses, deer, and human figures; 16¼" diameter.   **$2400–$2700**

Coiled polychrome; 3½" × 12¾"; positive (natural), negative (black), and red (light rose) five-pointed star/flower designs; ca. 1900.   **$500–$750**

Dark arrowpoint designs woven into sides; good condition; 9".   **$310–$375**

Figural; ca. 1900; 10" diameter, 3½" deep; figures around perimeter.

$1200–$1600

Gathering basket; 9" × 12"; made of split bark and bound w/deerskin; deerskin fringe around base; fine condition.   **$60–$90**

Large (15" × 13") basket; traces of pine resin; human hair carrying loops; complete and in good condition.   **$165–$225**

Large coiled 5" × 16" w/black three-petal star/flower design radiating from the tondo to rim, interspersed w/alternating men (9) and cross designs (3); ca. 1900.

$1500–$2000

Miniature; contemporary tray made by "Tu".   **$100–$150**

Miniature; burden basket.   **$10–$15**

Old coiled; 3" × 10"; decorated w/alternating cross and dog designs near the rim and a six-pointed star/flower radiating from the black tondo; ca. 1900; mint condition.   **$550–$750**

Olla; w/flaring body rounding at the shoulder, tapering to a cylindrical neck; woven in willow and devil's claw with concentric interlocking step-terraced diamonds which enclose piggybacked triangle design motifs; 21" wide, 21½" high.   **$2200–$2500**

From the William R. Nash Collection. Photo by Donald Vogt.

Olla; coiled; w/small, slightly indented base, squat body, and flaring rim; woven in willow and devil's claw w/meander bands flanking a row of human figures, alternating w/crosses, geometric devices in the fields above and below; 11″ high; an old label attached reading "Dan R. Williamson Collection."   **$1600–$2000**

Tall; coiled basket w/striking dogs, birds, swastikas, and arrowheads; ca. 1935; 10″ × 7″.   **$500–$700**

Tray; round, coiled basketry tray w/simple black line design; 12″ × 1½″; ca. 1920.   **$150–$250**

Tray (2); pair of coiled basketry trays; left—flat base, low flaring sides; woven in willow and black devil's claw w/radiating rosette pattern enclosing horses, deer, and human figures; 16¼″; right—woven w/flat base, flaring sides; in willow and dark brown devil's claw; spoked pattern radiating from the solid tondo, radiating joined diamond motif; 16¾″ diameter.   **$1500–$3000 ea.**

Water jar; 10″ × 8″ diameter; bought from Creek Council House Museum; ca. 1900.   **$150–$200**

Water; large pitched water basket or tus; 12″ × 8″; ca. 1890.
                                                         $260–$300

California

Bowl; shallow bowl measuring 15″ × 3½″; ca. 1900.   **$800–$1000**

Coiled basketry bowl; Maidu; flaring form, decorated w/band of joined, elongated triangles in dark red-brown on dark golden field; diameter 11″ (rim damage).   **$450–$650**

Coiled basketry bowl; Pomo; tapering globular form, woven in bracked fern root and willow w/joined wedge and other geometric devices; 6¼" diameter. **$425–$475**

Coiled basketry bowls (four) and tray; Maidu and Pomo; diameter 6½", 7", 10¼" and 14½" (rim damage to group); provenance: collected by a teacher in the service of the Department of Interior, Office of Indian Affairs, stationed at Carson, Nevada, Indian School from 1895 to 1910. **$700–$800**

California Mission

Coiled; 2½" × 10½"; polychrome w/gold, tan, and natural colors; ca. 1900–1940. **$225–$325**

Coiled polychrome basketry bowl; deep flaring form; woven with expanding columns flanked by triangles; diameter 16¼". **$550–$650**

Chehailis

Lidded; large oval lidded basket w/green and black geometric design; 8" × 7"; ca. 1920. **$60–$110**

Twined; round twined basket w/rim loops and green line design; ca. 1920; 6" × 3". **$40–$60**

Courtesy of Jack Sellner, CAI.

Twined; 14½" × 14"; fish-type; has braided drawstring like rim; ca. turn of the century. **$350–$500**

Cherokee

Contemporary 9″ × 9¹/₂″ basket; ca. 1970; by Diana Scott.   **$125–$250**

From the collection of Joyce Williams.
Photo by Donald Vogt.

Storage; North Carolina Cherokee museum quality splint basket; 12¹/₂″ diameter × 16″.   **$400–$600**

Chilkotin

Rare; smaller, rectangular embricated storage basket; 13″ × 7″; ca. 1880.   **$250–$350**

Very large; rare, embricated storage basket w/classic wire reinforcement top; 25″ × 12″ × 12″; ca. 1880.   **$300–$500**

Choctaw

Double weave river cane; rare; ca. 1900s; 5¹/₂″.   **$200–$300**

From the collection of Joyce Williams. Photo by Donald Vogt.

Handled; typical group of baskets w/ handles; ca. 1900–1910.

$100–$200 ea.

Cowlitz

Berry; embricated conical hard berry basket w/fine weave; ca. 1860; 9″ × 7½″. **$95–$150**

Coiled; huge, hard coiled basket w/polychrome geometric designs; 14″ × 10″; ca. 1920. **. $600–$800**

Huge, classic, embricated basket w/finger-woven trumpline from "Abe" Lincoln's personal collection; ca. 1880; 18½″ × 18″. **$2900–$3500**

Rectangular; rectangular embricated basket w/rim loops and lines of cross design; ca. 1900; 10″ × 5¼″ × 8″. **$275–$325**

Round; hard coiled w/rim loops and embricated design by Mary Kioma; ca. 1920; 8″ × 3½″. **$175–$250**

Groups of Baskets

From the collection of Joyce Williams. Photo by Donald Vogt.

Apache; group of Apache baskets; ca. 1920; three are western Apache; one is Jicarilla and was woven to be used as waste basket; some are as is. $150-$200 ea.

California Mission, miscellaneous; group of Mission baskets including one decorated w/red and one decorated w/black utility baskets; the one in red measures 8½" × 9" and the one decorated in black measures 6¼" × 6". $250-$300 ea.

Choctaw, storage; 20" × 19"; ca. 1910. $250-$350

Small one is 3" × 3". $125-$175

Creek, work; used for chafing and winnowing; ca. 1920. $100-$200

Miscellaneous; one is Pima, typical design, measuring 7½" × 3½".
                                                            $300-$400

Pima, measuring 3½" × 9". $200-$400

Maricopa, coiled, measuring 5½" × 5". $175-$250

Miscellaneous; one is damaged Hopi basket. $45-$65

Zia example from the 1920s. $200-$300

Santo Domingo basket ca. 1920s. $55-$85

Jemez. $35-$55

Contemporary Jemez. $45-$75

Courtesy of Robert W. Skinner, Inc., Bolton, MA.

Miscellaneous; one is Aleut twined swing basket of cylindrical form, finely woven in golden rye grass w/silk-embroidered sawtooth banding in red and green, braided openwork edging and handle; diameter 3½″.

$400–$500

Northwest Coast twined rattle top basket; Tlingit; polychromed cylindrical body and top decorated in polychrome, twined false embroidery designs of linear and concentric wedge motifs; attached old label on lid—"rare tlingit, 1859 or earlier, British Columbia"; 6⅝″ diameter. **$450–$600**

Southeastern twill plaited baskets; Chitimacha/Choctaw; blown out square forms in natural, yellow, black, and red. **$150–$200 ea.**

California coiled basketry gift basket; Pomo; shallow bowl form decorated in radiating step/terrace pattern motif, with attached quail's topknots and red feather decoration; 3″. **$175–$250**

From the collection of Joyce Williams. Photo by Donald Vogt.

Miscellaneous, Koasati; Southeast tribe; ca. 1920. **$25–$50 ea.**

Miscellaneous, Wyandotte. **$35–$100 ea.**

From the collection of Joyce Williams. Photo by Donald Vogt.

Northern California; large one is a Pit River, ca. 1900; smaller one is Thomson River.   **$90–$150**

Papago, miniature; made of horsehair and used to hold thimbles.

$35–$50

From the collection of Joyce Williams. Photo by Donald Vogt.

Papago; these baskets are still being made and are not as collectible as older examples; one is decorated w/figures and measures 6″ × 3¼″; ca. 1900.   **$200–$300**

Large coiled example, measuring 14½″ × 6″.   **$400–$500**

Tray, which measures 9" diameter and is ca. 1920s. **$75–$125**

An unusual latticework basket which came from Kansas and measures 8" × 5¼".
$100–$175

Pima; group of six; 9" squash blossom design; pre–1900. **$600–$800**

8" –1940s. **$250–$450**

7½"; lightning design; 1890–1900. **$550–$800**

1930s, Greek key design. **$500–$550**

contemporary. **$450–$550**

twirling logs, 1930s-40s. **$200–$400**

Pomo; group of miniature Pomo horsehair baskets.

Seminole, pair; pine needle-covered basket and wall hanging basket; ca. 1910. **$25–$75 ea.**

Haida

Plaited; oval plaited basket w/two bands of line designs; ca. 1920; 8" × 3". **$75–$100**

Rare; round twined bowl w/openwork and a shoulder; 6" × 4"; ca. 1920. **$125–$250**

Hopi

Coiled basketry storage bowl; decorated overall w/"smiling" dark red and brown deer on a natural ground; coiled loop handles; diameter 16" (minor stitch damage). **$250–$350**

Coiled; done by Mary Jane Batala for the New Mexico State Fair in 1978; won second prize; miniatures at the Kiva/Steve Cowgill.

Coiled; 6" × 10¾"; polychrome w/black, brown, yellow, and natural colors in terraced cross within large rectangular panel designs; ca. 1930–1940. **$225–$325**

Dish; coiled; woven; circular; 11¼" diameter. **$85–$95**

Doll; Shalako doll in basketry; done by Bertha Wardsworth for the 1987 SWAIA Indian Market; won first place and best in division; miniatures at the Kiva/Steve Cowgill.

Fancy coiled tray; 12" diameter; polychrome w/black, sienna, yellow, green, and white colors in a Kachina maiden design by Ramona Lenahema. **$175–$250**

From the collection of Joyce Williams. Photo by Donald Vogt.

Handled; 17½" × 11½" × 5"; coiled; ca. 1910.   **$300–$500**

Plaited; unusually shaped; 11¼" square; in yellow and natural colors.
                                                            $40–$70

Plaited; sifting or winnowing basket.   **$45–$60**

Plaited; 3" × 14½"; used for winnowing/sifting.   **$20–$40**

Plaque; wicker basketry plaque; 12" diameter; polychrome (faded colors); 1920s.   **$45–$100**

From the collection of Joyce Williams. Photo by Donald Vogt.

Plaques; group of wicker plaques from different mesas; there are some contemporary looking ones in the group that are actually old and very colorful; one in back is coiled, other four are wicker weave; ca. 1900–1910.   **$100–$300 ea.**

Pot; yucca coil done by Joyce Saufke, ca. 1974; woven in the shape of a pot.

Storage; coiled; 12″ × 12″.   **$400–$500**

Wicker basketry plaque; 10¾″ diameter; polychrome w/orange, red, black, green, and white.   **$95–$140**

Wicker; 12″ × 14½″ diameter; polychrome; ca. 1900–1930.

$250–$375

Hupa

Choice miniature twined basketry bowl; slanted brown geometric designs; ca. 1940; 3″ × 2″.   **$65–$100**

Cooking; large twined mush cooking basket w/unusual fret design; ca. 1890; 9″ × 4½″.   **$75–$125**

Hat; classic twined woman's basketry hat w/geometric designs; ca. 1910; 6″ × 3″.   **$225–$275**

From the collection of Joyce Williams. Photo by Donald Vogt.

Hat; 7½″ diameter, 3″ high; fairly common, ca. 1930.   **$350–$500**

Courtesy of Jack Sellner, CAI.

Hupa-Karok; large, old twined burden basket; 15″ × 13″ diameter at rim; excellent condition. **$300–$500**

Miniature; woven. **$65–$105**

Klamath

Bowl; round twined bowl w/brown and yellow porcupine quill design; ca. 1910; 8½″ × 4″. **$120–$150**

Classic fine twined basketry hat; diagonal stair/step design; ca. 1910. **$175–$225**

Gambling tray; rare, old, twined gambling tray; ca. 1870; 9″. **$35–$50**

Gambling tray; very rare, round, twined gambling tray w/very crisp designs; 13½″ diameter; ca. 1880. **$450–$650**

Seed; unusual twined seed basket w/geometric design; ca. 1900; 6″ × 5″. **$35–$50**

Twined; 5″ × 8½″ polychrome with red, yellow, and natural colors in banded designs; ca. 1900–1930. **$110–$160**

Twined; unusual large round twined basket w/lid and carrying handle; ca. 1910; 11″ × 7½″. **$175–$225**

Twined; extremely fine twined basket w/yellow porcupine quill and brown hourglass motif; 8″ × 4″; ca. 1900. **$175–$225**

Twined; fine, small polychrome twined basket w/green arrows and beaded top; ca. 1900; 4″ × 2½″. **$70–$100**

Klickitat

Conical; classic conical hard basket w/rim loops and geometric embrication; 9" × 7½"; ca. 1890. **$100-$200**

Conical; classic conical hard basket w/rim loops and geometric embrication; ca. 1930; 9" × 7½". **$250-$300**

Embricated; rare small embricated basket w/rim loops; 6" × 5½"; ca. 1890. **$105-$150**

Hard coiled and embricated huckleberry basket; ca. 1870; 8" × 7½".
$55-$75

Large rectangular embricated storage basket w/rim loops (some damage) and geometric designs; ca. 1890; 16" × 10". **$200-$300**

Miniature; unusual miniature-figured coiled basket; ca. 1970; 1½" × 1".
$35-$50

Miniature; classic design; hard coiled; 1" × 1"; ca. 1970. **$35-$50**

Old figure embricated basket w/animal and human figures; top damage; 14½" × 12"; ca. 1870. **$100-$200**

Small conical embricated hard basket w/rim loops; ca. 1890; 6" × 5".
$70-$100

Tiny embricated basket w/rim loops and polychrome geometric design; by Nettie Kunecki; ca. 1980; 1½" × 1". **$40-$60**

Maidu

Coiled basketry tray; decorated w/plumed triangular motifs in reddish-brown on a golden ground; diameter 16" (rim damage); provenance: collected by a teacher in the service of the Department of the Interior, Office of Indian Affairs, stationed at Carson, Nevada, Indian School from 1895-1910. **$275-$350**

Coiled basketry utility bowl; deep open form, decorated w/radiating concentric step devices in reddish-brown on a golden field; 13½" diameter (rim damage); provenance: collected by a teacher in the service of the Department of the Interior, Office of Indian Affairs, stationed at Carson, Nevada, Indian School from 1895-1910. **$425-$500**

Made from dark redbud; ca. 1900. **$150-$200**

Makah

Bottle; superfine basketry-covered bottle covered w/figures; ca. 1890; 5" × 2". **$55-$75**

Carrying; miniature twined carrying basket w/whale on each side; ca. 1980; 2″ × 2″.   **$20–$40**

Carrying; rectangular carrying basket w/unusual pictorial schoolhouse design; 12″ × 8″ × 3″; ca. 1920.   **$60–$100**

Finely woven, miniature lidded basket w/boat, whale, and duck; ca. 1986.
                                                              $30–$50

Finely twined, large lidded basket w/birds and geometrics; ca. 1920; 6″ × 5″.
                                                           $175–$225

Large basketry-covered abalone shell; ca. 1920; 6″ × 5″ × 2″.   **$45–$65**

Lidded; oval, twined lidded basket w/row of geometric designs; ca. 1900; 4″ × 3″.   **$30–$50**

Lidded; round, fine, twined lidded basket w/swastikas all around; ca. 1910; 5″ × 2½″.   **$38–$48**

Lidded; large, round, twined lidded basket w/whales, boats, and ducks all around; ca. 1935; 7″ × 5″.   **$35–$50**

Lidded; fine little lidded twined basket w/ducks all around; ca. 1980; 2¾″ × 2″.   **$20–$40**

Lidded; round, twined lidded basket w/birds all around; ca. 1940; 4½″ × 3″.   **$65–$85**

Lidded; small, twined lidded basket w/birds and boats all around; ca. 1940; 3″ × 2″.   **$35–$50**

Lidded; large, round lidded basket w/multicolored sea monsters all around; ca. 1930; 7″ × 4″.   **$150–$200**

Oblong; oblong twined basket w/lid and a band of bear grass figures all around; ca. 1930; 4″ × 2½″.   **$35–$50**

Old bottle and lid; covered w/twined basketry; ca. 1920; 9″ × 3″.
                                                              $55–$85

Small twined basket w/lid and a boat and whale decoration; ca. 1986; 3″ × 3″.
                                                              $30–$50

Small twined basket w/lid and eagle design; 2½″ × 2¼″; ca. 1986.
                                                              $30–$50

Twined and plaited; round, twined, and plaited basket w/whaling boats and ducks all around; 8″ × 7″; ca. 1920.   **$60–$100**

Twined; round twined basket w/whaling boat and ducks all around; ca. 1920; 5″ × 3″.   **$25–$50**

Twined; very fine twined basket w/lid and with arrows and ducks as designs; ca. 1920; 3″ × 2″.   **$40–$70**

Twined; round twined basket w/lid and steamboat designs; ca. 1910; 3½″ × 2½″.   **$50–$75**

Unusual basketry-covered shell w/whale figures all around; ca. 1986; 4″ × 3″.
$60–$80

Mescalero Apache

Typical design; ca. 1920–30. **$200–$300**

Tray; shallow bowl measuring 22″ in diameter; ca. 1870. **$600–$1000**

Water jar or storage basket; braided hair trumpline loops, very tightly woven; once may have had pine pitch covering; good condition. **$60–$75**

Mission

Bowl; large, round coiled bowl w/line and geometric designs; ca. 1890; 13″ × 5″. **$100–$150**

Bowl; round, coiled basketry bowl w/yellowish star designs all around; 7″ × 4″; ca. 1920. **$175–$225**

Coiled storage basket; banded flaring body woven in dark brown triangular motif, w/faded yellowish-brown designs near rim; 15″ deep, 6½″ high. **$375–$425**

Mission/Maidu, coiled basketry bowl; woven w/black- and red-winged design motifs; 6½″ wide. **$125–$175**

Round, deep coiled bowl w/unusual stair design; ca. 1920; 11″ × 4″.
$110–$150

Round, coiled basketry bowl w/connecting square designs; 5″ × 3″, ca. 1900.
$140–$200

Tray; miniature, coiled basketry tray; ca. 1940; 3″ diameter. **$15–$30**

Mono

Bowl; western Mono, coiled flared bowl w/striking black arrow and stair/step design; 9″ × 5″; ca. 1840. **$400–$500**

Utility; coiled utility basket measuring 20¼″ × 8¾″. **$1000–$1250**

Navajo

Coiled (rare); 3¾″ × 14″; polychrome w/black, dark green, brown, and natural colors, ca. 1900–1940. **$250–$375**

Dish; coiled; diameter 13½″. **$65–$85**

Rare; old; coiled; 3″ × 14½″; black and natural colors in concentric circle and triangle designs; ca. 1930s. **$275–$350**

Courtesy of Gunther Adams, Rangeley, ME. Photo by Dawn Reno.

Shallow bowl; basket is decorated w/figures and lightning designs.
$4500–$5000

Wedding; contemporary wedding basket given to medicine man for performing the ceremony. **$25–$35**

From the collection of Joyce Williams. Photo by Donald Vogt.

Wedding; coiled sumac splints over three-ring construction; finish is herringbone weave; measures 13″ diameter; ca. 1920. **$300–$350**

Wedding; classic coiled Navajo wedding basket w/spirit release line; ca. 1935; 11″ × 3″. **$175–$225**

Navajo/Ute

Coiled basketry tray; 3¼″ × 17″ diameter; polychrome; ''wedding'' style; excellent condition.   **$150–$185**

Coiled; 3″ diameter; polychrome; ''wedding'' type; natural, black, and red.   **$45–$85**

Coiled; 3″ × 15½″; polychrome; ''wedding'' style w/black, sienna, and natural colors; ca. 1940s.   **$65–$95**

Coiled; 2½″ × 11½″; polychrome; ''wedding'' style w/black, dark orange, and natural colors; mint condition.   **$55–$75**

Coiled; 3½″ × 15″; polychrome; ''wedding'' style w/black, red, and natural colors; shows use and age.   **$65–$100**

Coiled; 2½″ × 12½″; polychrome; ''wedding'' type w/black, red, and natural colors.   **$45–$75**

Coiled; 3½″ × 14¼″; polychrome; ''wedding'' style w/black, red, and natural colors.   **$75–$125**

Coiled; 2″ × 13¾″; polychrome; ''wedding'' style w/black, sienna, and natural colors.   **$75–$125**

Nootka

Bottle; unusual basketry-covered bottle; ca. 1920; 8½″ × 3″. **$45–$75**

Large lidded basket; colorful whaling scenes all around; 11″ × 9″; ca. 1910.   **$225–$300**

Twine; round twined basket w/rim loops and colored line designs; ca. 1935; 7″ × 4″.   **$70–$125**

Nootka/Makah; twined; 2″ × 3½″; lidded; polychrome w/dark red, natural, and dark brown colors; ca. 1900.   **$45–$70**

Northern California

Jar; possibly Mono; geometric design; ca. 1870s.   **$500–$600**

Three (3) baskets; Hupa/Karok/Klamath; twined bowl forms w/dark brown geometric designs over a yellow field; 3½″, 8¾″, and 12″ (roughness to group).   **$350–$400**

Northwest Coast

Lidded; circular; woven; Makah, miniature.   **$55–$100**

Lidded; Makah; woven.   **$55–$75**

Twined and plaited; 5″ × 5½″; Nootka; polychrome w/red, natural, brown, and tan colors, ca. 1925.   **$45–$75**

Paiute

Burden basket; rare, openwork, twined, conical burden basket w/red line design; 12″ × 10″; ca. 1900.   **$200–$300**

From the collection of Joyce Williams. Photo by Donald Vogt.

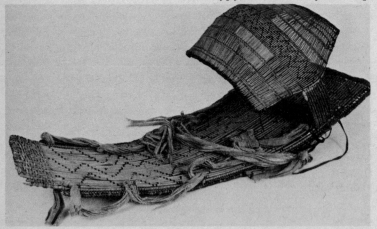

Cradleboard; basketwork cradleboard w/original strappings; decorated in the zigzag pattern which indicates that the baby it was made for was male; measures 27″ × 12″   **$500–$750**

From the collection of N. A. McKinney. Photo by Donald Vogt.

Medicine jar; ca. late 1800s; 4¾″ tall; horsehair handle; sealed w/pinon pitch; rare.   **$200–$300**

Polychrome coiled basketry tray; "Navajo Wedding Basket"; 14" diameter.
$120-$150

Seed jar; 8" × 11" twined seed jar; ca. 1890. **$250-$300**

Papago

Basketry plaque, 11" diameter; green- and natural-colored yucca w/"man in the maze" design. **$50-$85**

Bowl; round, coiled basketry bowl w/slanted stair/step design; ca. 1935; 5½" × 3¼". **$35-$50**

Coiled basketry tray; 1½" × 10" × 11½" oval of beargrass, devil's claw, and yucca materials. **$30-$50**

Coiled beargrass; 1½" × 4¾"; bowl-shaped. **$15-$25**

Coiled novelty; 2" high cup w/handle; ca. mid-twentieth century.
$20-$30

Coiled basketry tray; 13¼" diameter w/large black five-pointed star/flower and triangle designs; mint condition. **$90-$130**

Coiled; 3½" (inc. lid) × 3½"; beargrass and yucca construction.
$30-$45

Coiled; 1¼" × 7¼" tray; buffalo head-like designs. **$25-$45**

Coiled; 6" × 9¼"; two horizontal parallel lines of black serrated designs. **$70-$115**

Coiled; 6" including lid × 6½"; beargrass and yucca construction.
$30-$65

Coiled; 2½" × 11½"; polychrome w/black, green, and natural colors in a five-pointed star/flower design. **$65-$105**

Coiled; 5" (including handle) × 6" × 8" oval w/black terraced designs. **$30-$60**

Coiled; 2" × 11" tray; Pima-like fret designs. **$85-$135**

Coiled; 4" × 8"; tapering sides in bowl shape. **$15-$25**

Coiled; 6¼" × 9"; double horizontal row of terraced designs. **$50-$95**

Coiled; 1½" × 9½" tray; black rectangular designs. **$20-$35**

Coiled; polychrome with green, black, and natural colors. **$55-$85**

Coiled; 1⅜" × 8"; beargrass and yucca tray w/green terraced designs.
$30-$50

Coiled; 3" × 5½" × 6¾"; oval with horizontal connected terraced design. **$30-$55**

Coiled; 3" × 6¾"; black rectangular designs. **$25-$55**

Coiled; 1½″ × 8½″; polychrome w/black, green, and natural colors.
$20–$40

Coiled; 3¾″ × 7¾″ × 11¼″; oval w/handles and black "coyote track" designs.
$40–$80

Coiled; 1¼″ × 12″ × 16″; oval tray w/connected rectangular designs; ca. 1940s.
$50–$75

Coiled; 2¾″ × 7¼″ bowl shape w/handles.
$10–$25

Dish; round, coiled basketry dish w/handle; 6¾″ × 6″; ca. 1945.
$20–$40

Courtesy of Jack Sellner, CAI.

Figure; pair of rare, coiled basketry figures; one woman w/removable hat holding mandolin; one woman w/removable hat carrying purse.
$200–$300 ea.

Large coiled; 3½″ × 13½″; black rectangular terraced designs; by Sophie Sara Ficio.
$75–$125

Miniature; coiled "wheat stitch" whirlwind bowl; 2¼″ diameter; ca. 1970.
$15–$30

Old coiled; 3⅜″ × 6¾″; polychrome w/black, yellow, and natural colors in rectangular-shaped vertical designs; ca. 1940s.
$30–$60

Older coiled, 5″ × 10½″.   **$65–$120**

Papago/Pima; coiled; 3″ × 9″ with connected, black, slanted triangle designs; ca. 1900.   **$45–$95**

Tray; coiled; ⅞″ × 4½″.   **$15–$25**

Two (2) coiled baskets; a bowl, 8″ tall, and an eagle-decorated tray, 12″ diameter.   **$150–$200**

Pima

Bowl; round coiled bowl w/classic Pima fret design; ca. 1935; 8″ × 2″.
                                                        $85–$115

From the collection of Joyce Williams. Photo by Donald Vogt.

Classic example; 17″ diameter, 5″ deep; came from Arizona at turn of the century.   **$650–$850**

Coiled basketry tray; shallow form, woven w/flaring sides; solid tondo w/rabbit ears meander pattern, 10¼″ diameter.   **$425–$500**

Coiled basketry tray; small flat base w/flaring sides; solid tondo w/radiating linear devices and human figures; 14¼″ diameter.   **$375–$500**

Coiled; 3½″ × 11¼″ tray; ca. 1900.   **$175–$250**

Coiled; 4⅜″ × 7½″ w/three horizontal rows of black terraced designs; ca. 1900.   **$250–$350**

Coiled; 3″ × 7½″ w/black "coyote track" designs; ca. 1900. **$85–$125**

Coiled; 3½″ × 9″ bowl w/radiating black terraced designs from the center; ca. 1920.   **$140–$240**

Decorated w/human figures; 3½″ × 9″.   **$200–$400**

Fine weave; 9″ diameter; ca. 1920.   **$185–$200**

Horsehair; miniature coiled horsehair basket; ca. 1940; 2″ diameter.
                                                             $45–$75

Large old coiled; 4″ × 19½″ tray with black fret designs, ca. 1900.
                                                             $375–$500

From the Two Star Collection, Houston. Photo by Donald Vogt.

Large; 22″ basket w/twirling logs design; 1910–20.   **$1600–$2000**

Large, old, coiled basketry bowl; 6½″ × 15″; used for native wine/cooking/food; ca. 1900.   **$350–$550**

Miniature; horsehair basket w/lid; 2″ × 1″; ca. 1920.   **$15–$30**

Miniature; extremely fine coiled miniature horsehair basket w/lid; 2″ × 1″; ca. 1970.   **$20–$30**

Miniature; coiled basket w/whirlwind design; 2″ diameter; ca. 1940.
                                                             $20–$30

Old coiled; 3¼″ × 9½″ w/black tondo and two horizontal rows of "winged" whirling logs/swastika-like designs; ca. 1900.   **$175–$250**

Oval tray; very finely coiled oval tray w/two rows of rattlesnake design; 7″ × 4½″; ca. 1930.   **$130–$160**

Small horsehair basketry olla; ½″ × ½″; ca. 1960.   **$20–$35**

Wheat straw; rare wheat straw basket measuring 10″ diameter and 8″ high, with a 6″ neck opening and 3¼″ base; ca. 1900. **$250–$350**

Woven coiled; 15″ diameter; ca. 1900.   **$195–$200**

Pima/Papago

Horsehair; ⅞″ × 2¼″; black mouse w/white bead eyes, ears, tail, and whiskers.   **$30–$50**

Horsehair, ¼″ × 1″ diameter; black and white w/black stitches.

$15–$25

Horsehair; ½″ × 1″; white w/black stitches.   **$15–$30**

Horsehair; ½″ × ½″; white w/brown stitches.   **$15–$25**

Horsehair; ⅜″ × 1½″; black w/black stitches.   **$15–$20**

Horsehair; ⅜″ × 1″; black with white stitches.   **$20–$30**

Horsehair; ⁵⁄₁₆″ × 1¹⁄₁₆″; black w/white stitches.   **$15–$25**

Horsehair; 1¼″ diameter; plaque white w/black fret designs and stitches.   **$25–$40**

Pit River

Basketry-covered brown whiskey bottle; ca. 1900; 10″ × 4″.   **$100–$125**

Bowl; rare miniature twined basketry bowl; ca. 1910; 4″ × 8″ × 4″.
$225–$275

Twined bowl; striking red, graduated, connecting arrowhead designs, 7″ × 4″, ca. 1890.   **$100–$185**

Pomo

Coiled basketry gift basket; shallow bowl form, decorated in radiating step/ terrace pattern motif, with attached quail's topknots and red feather decoration; 3″.   **$175–$225**

Miniature; coiled basket; ca. 1930; 1″ diameter.   **$25–$45**

Three (3) miniature coiled gift baskets; of squat globular form, each decorated on exterior surface w/multicolored bird feathers; 2¾″ diameter, 1½″ diameter, and ¾″ diameter (minor feather loss to group). **$500–$650**

Quinault

Coiled; large coiled basket w/handles and red and green geometric design; ca. 1920; 17″ × 8″.   **$70–$100**

Raffia; oval coiled raffia basket w/handle and geometric designs; ca. 1930; 16″ × 12″. **$35–$50**

Twined; round twined basket w/simple line design; ca. 1920; 8″ × 5″. **$55–$80**

Salish

Embricated; rectangular embricated basket w/rim loops and geometric designs; ca. 1900; 8″ × 4″. **$80–$120**

Miniature; woven. **$90–$125**

Rectangular; embricated basket w/geometric designs; ca. 1890. **$110–$175**

Round; round embricated basket w/lid; ca. 1910. **$105–$175**

Tray; rectangular embricated tray w/handles and geometric designs; ca. 1910; 21″ × 2″. **$160–$225**

Tray; huge round embricated tray w/handles and polychrome star design; 20″ × 2″; ca. 1910. **$200–$300**

Trunk; very fine, small, rectangular lidded trunk w/embricated geometric designs; ca. 1910; 4″ × 8″ × 4″. **$225–$275**

Trunk; large embricated storage trunk w/lid and polychromed diamond designs; 18″ × 12″; ca. 1910. **$175–$250**

Rectangular lidded basket w/handles and embricated six-point star designs; ca. 1935; 9½″ × 4″. **$110–$150**

Siletz

Clamming; large, old, openwork clamming basket; ca. 1900; 22″ × 12″. **$55–$75**

Round, twined carrying basket w/handle; ca. 1920; 7″ × 5″. **$50–$75**

Storage; large, twined storage basket w/simple brown line design; ca. 1930; 14″ × 11″. **$75–$100**

Skokomish

Bowl; classic twined bowl w/rim loops and a row of dogs around the top; ca. 1920; 10″ × 7½″. **$150–$200**

Choice twined basket w/gold zigzag design; ca. 1890; 18″ × ½″. **$175–$225**

Oblong; unusual oblong basket w/embricated quail plume design; ca. 1910; 13″ × 7″ × 3″. **$50–$75**

Rectangular; rectangular embricated semi-hard basket w/purple and yellow original designs; 7″ × 7″ × 10″; ca. 1930. **$80–$120**

Twined; classic twined basket w/brown and black triangular designs and a row of dogs all around the top; ca. 1910; 5″ × 4″. **$35–$50**

Utility; huge cedar bark-plaited utility basket w/rim loops; ca. 1900; 15″ × 12″. **$175–$225**

Southeastern

Large; older; coiled; 1½″ × 13½″ × 17″; oval sweetgrass tray w/handles. **$75–$125**

Three twill plaited; Chitimacha/Choctaw; of blown-out square form; in natural, yellow, black, and red; sizes 2½″, 4″ and 5″. **$375–$425**

Southwestern

Coiled polychrome basketry tray; shallow flaring form; woven in willow, devil's claw, and red-dyed willow w/whirling and linear geometric devices, waving human figures, and dogs; 15½″ diameter. **$475–$675**

Coiled trays; one—Apache; finely woven in willow and black devil's claw w/whorling pattern interlocking near rim w/band of triangular motifs; 14½″ diameter; the other—Jicarilla; 15″ diameter. **$425–$525**

Coiled tray; Pima; deep circular form; woven in willow and devil's claw w/spiraling pattern of step/terraced lines; 19″ diameter. **$650–$750**

Coiled basketry olla; rounded body tapering to a small cylindrical neck; woven in willow and devil's claw with a pattern of longitudinal zigzags; high 11¾″; minor stitch damage. **$400–$600**

Tillamook

Jar; round twined basketry jar w/banded designs; ca. 1930; 6″ × 5″. **$65–$90**

Rare Tillamook basket; made after the tribe moved to Grande Ronde; 8″ × 7″; ca. 1880. **$135–$150**

Tlingit

Bowl; round, twined basketry bowl w/striking brown, gold, and orange designs; ca. 1910; 10″ × 3½″. **$250–$300**

Carrying; large and unusual oblong carrying basket w/handle and geometric designs; ca. 1910; 13½″ × 6″. **$60–$80**

Glass bottle covered w/twined basketry; ca. 1920; 4½″. **$185–$200**

Large unusual twined storage basket w/lid and gold geometric designs; ca. 1910; 8″ × 6″.   **$250–$350**

Lid; rattle top basketry lid or disc; ca. 1910; 5½″ × 1¹/₁₄″.   **$65–$75**

Oval, twined basketry mat; ca. 1910; 10″ × 6″.   **$95–$125**

Oval basketry mat w/circular designs; 11″ × 8″; ca. 1890.   **$115–$160**

Polychrome; large old basket w/polychrome geometrics; ca. 1900; 11½″ × 16½″.   **$100–$150**

From the collection of David L. Atteberry.
Photo by Donald Vogt.

Rattle; ca. 1900.   **$500–$600**

Rattle top; polychromed cylindrical body and top decorated in polychrome-twined false embroidery designs of linear and concentric wedge motifs; attached is old label on lid: "rare tlingit, 1859 or earlier, British Columbia"; 6⁶/₈″ diameter.   **$450–$600**

Rattle top; superfine twined rattle top basket w/outstanding brown and orange geometric motif; ca. 1920; 6″ × 5½″.   **$300–$500**

Rattletop; choice finely twined rattletop basket w/outstanding brown fret design; ca. 1910; 5″ × 3½″.   **$325–$375**

Root; round, brown spruce root basket w/gold Chevron designs; ca. 1910; 7″ × 4″.   **$175–$250**

Root; brown, terraced spruce root basket w/lid and gold geometric design; ca. 1910; 12″ × 1½″.   **$25–$50**

Straight-sided; old straight-sided basket w/striking orange and black fret designs; ca. 1880; 6″ × 4″. **$100–$150**

Superfine, small twined basket w/bright pink and brown diamond edges; ca. 1910; 4″ × 3″. **$275–$325**

Twined spruce; Northwest Coast; root basket. **$45–$85**

Very fine weave pedestal basket w/colorful floral and geometric motif, 4″ × 4″; ca. 1910. **$275–$300**

Washo

Bowl; single-rod coiled bowl w/red butterflies all around; ca. 1920; 8″ × 4″. **$145–$175**

Coiled basketry bowl; squat globular body decorated in bracken fern and willow; 5⅞″ diameter; 3″ high. **$450–$550**

Old coiled; 4¼″ × 6″; polychrome (painted) w/dark green, red, and natural colors in terraced vertical and diamond designs; ca. 1920s.
$85–$125

Yurok

Burden; rare, large conical burden basket w/brown designs all around; mint condition; 7″ × 4″; ca. 1890. **$500–$700**

Fine miniature basketry bowl; brown and black designs; ca. 1920; 3″ × 2″.
$85–$140

Openwork twined basket; bands of cross design; ca. 1910. **$275–$325**

Tall openwork twined basketry-covered glass; ca. 1920; 11″ × 9″. **$85–$115**

Other

Athabascan; oval birch bark basket w/embricated rim; ca. 1910; 6″ × 2″.
$15–$30

Chimehauvi; spitoon shape; 10½″ × 9″; ca. 1900. **$400–$500**

Chippewa; older coiled grass and birch bark; 3½″ (inc. lid) × 6″; sweetgrass w/yellow, green, and white porcupine quill-decorated lid in a leaf design. **$50–$75**

Great Lakes; older birch bark; 4″ × 8¼″ × 9¼″ oval w/connecting diamond designs. **$40–$80**

From the collection of Joyce Williams. Photo by Donald Vogt.

Havasupai; double bowl; measures 15½" × 8"; ca. 1920s. **$500–$800**

Iroquois; old plaited; 22½" ash splint construction w/sweetgrass handles and remnants of blue dye color on certain strips used for contrast; ca. 1910–1915. **$175–$250**

Jemez; plaited; 5" × 12½" winnowing and sifting basket. **$30–$60**

Micmac; round basket w/lid and quilled top; ca. 1910; 4" × 3". **$45–$75**

Modoc; finely twined miniature Modoc basket; ca. 1920; 4" × 2½". **$70–$100**

Oneida; covered splint basket w/black water-base paint decoration; 15¼" high, 14" diameter; accompanying period note: "Mary (Hopkins) Cornell when she lived at Eaton, NY, or near there, on about 1824" (hole on one bottom corner). **$150–$250**

Panamint; woven wicker; cylindrical with recessed flaring neck; woven with a frieze of vertical lizard images in dark brown on light ground beneath a frieze of opposed birds in light brown; dark brown bottom treatment of triple-spoked wheel; 14½" high. **$375–$425**

Payute; utility, woven, diameter 9". **$65–$75**

Powatan; utility; large plaited ash splint utility basket w/painted designs; ca. 1910; 19" × 11". **$60–$80**

Queets; round twined basketry bowl w/line design; ca. 1935; 7" × 4½". **$35–$50**

From the collection of Lahoma Haddock Goldsmith. Photo by Donald Vogt.

Seminole; pine needle and raffia turtle basket made by Leia Battise.
$10–$15

Seri; large coiled; 4½" × 16½"; w/brown and natural colors in an 11-pointed terraced star/flower design.   **$150–$250**

Southwest Pima; woven; coiled; ca. 1900; 15" diameter.   **$195–$200**

Tsimshian; very fine and rare plaited basket; ca. 1910; 4" × 4½".
$150–$175

Tulare; fine coiled shoulder basket w/bands of rattlesnake designs; rare; ca. 1920; 8" × 5½".   **$600–$800**

From the collection of Joyce Williams. Photo by Donald Vogt.

Tulare–Yokut; 6½" × 11¾"; ca. 1920.   **$500–$750**

From the collection of David L. Atteberry. Photo by Donald Vogt.

Western Apache; the dark material is called "devil's claw"; 9½" tall; ca. 1880–1890. **$600–$700**

Western California; Burden; possibly Mono or Yucca. **$500–$750**

From the collection of Joyce Williams. Photo by Donald Vogt.

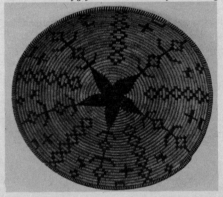

White Mountain Apache; tray; 15½" diameter; bought in 1875 from trader on Gila River; excellent condition. **$800–$1000**

Woven; eagle and geometric decoration measuring 3'11" × 7'11".
$415–$460

Yokut; coiled basketry bowl; squat-shouldered form, woven in yellow willow w/finely woven dark brown square, circle, triangle, and "bowtie" design motifs; 7½" diameter. **$300–$400**

BLANKETS/RUGS

▼▼▼▼▼▼▼▼▼▼▼▼

INTRODUCTION

Human beings have a natural need to keep warm and dry because of our lack of body hair. Because of this fact, the native American had to learn to make blankets and coverings to keep him warm.

Some New England and Northeast tribes used weaving of plant and tree materials to make cloaks or blankets for themselves. Other tribes simply used the skins of the animals who were common in their area, and still others weaved the feathers of local birds into capes and blankets. Then there were the Indians who *learned* to weave, and it is those tribes in whom we are most particularly interested in this chapter.

Because of the gradual transition from blankets to rugs, I have chosen to blend the two subjects into one chapter, although I have kept the pricing index separate and have attempted to keep as much of the information categorized as possible. This, however, is a bit difficult when speaking of Navajo weavers because so many collectors have used the early blankets as rugs. Keeping this in mind, remember also that the Navajo tribe, though the most accomplished at the art of weaving, was not the only tribe to make decorative and warm blankets/rugs.

Recognized today as masterpieces of abstract art, Navajo blankets are the domain of women. Early blankets, dating from 1800, were simple and came in dull colors of natural wool, such as brown and white. Later, the "chief" blankets used bold colors and strong designs. Boxes and diamonds were used; red bayeta wool and indigo blue were used most freely. "Eye dazzlers" came even later, which used many colors and complex designs that resulted in wonderful optic effects.

Different patterns and styles of blankets were made during different periods. By knowing these facts, one is often able to date the blankets one buys. For instance, shoulder blankets with stripes running across the width were made from 1875 to 1890; women's shoulder blankets, which have three bands of repeated designs but are smaller than men's blankets, were made around 1885, while the men's versions were made approximately 20 years earlier. Navajo Indian weavings for the tourist trade were considered garish until they were encouraged to go back to using vegetable dyes (around 1920).

A staple in Indian blanket/rug making was trade cloth or stroud cloth (because it came from Stroud, England) and it was used by almost all

Indian tribes. Introduced in the seventeenth century, its use spread rapidly because of its appearance and warmth.

The tribes in the southwest used tradecloth less than other North American tribes, possibly because the Southwestern tribes were already capable of making their own fabrics. The cloth was red, black, navy blue, and green, and was made into shawls, blankets, and other garments. Because of its use, much of the other weaving done by the Amerinds (other than those in the southwest) was outdated.

TRIBES AND THEIR BLANKETS

Acoma (Southwest)

The Acoma, though not well known for their weaving, made blankets which were used as squaw dresses. The body of the blanket was often black and it would be decorated with embroidered border designs.

Chilkat (Northwest)

Though Chilkat women wove the blankets, as did the Navajo women, the blanket patterns were designed by the men of the tribe, and any deviation from those designs was forbidden.

Aristocratic leaders wore the Chilkat robes in tribal ceremonies. The robes displayed the animal totem of the clan.

The blankets were made of mountain goat wool, which was tightly woven with yellow cedar bark. The Tlingit tribe produced most of them and they are considered the robes of Northwest Coast Indian nobility, as we mentioned before.

Their abstract representations of crest animals were woven into the fabric and usually three edges of the blanket dripped with thick fringe. Ravens, salmon, and whale's heads were commonly depicted on these nineteenth-century blankets. The "diving whale" blankets are the most common, and, at first glance, all appear to be the same. Fineness of yarn and quality of weave, however, differ in each blanket. Early and mid–nineteenth-century examples are finer than later ones.

The blankets were woven on a bar loom which resembled the letter "H." The horizontal bar on this type of loom could be set at a level which was comfortable for the weaver. The warp was suspended from the loom in lengths which followed the form of the blanket—the "warp weighted loom" technique. The threads, which were yet unwoven, were kept wrapped in bags because it took six months to a year to make a blanket and there was less chance that they would become soiled this way. The actual weaving was done in a tapestry-twined technique and the long fringed sections were filled in with goat wool when the weaving was completed. Though these blankets could be as large as 72″ × 38″, the more normal dance apron size was 18″ × 38″.

Button blankets evolved when the Northwest Coast tribes began trading with the white Europeans and Americans who visited them during the latter part of the eighteenth century. These blankets were usually made from blue Hudson's Bay Company blankets which were bordered on three sides with red trade material. An applique crest would be sewn to the blanket and outlined with mother-of-pearl buttons. Haida, Tlingit, and Kwakiutl tribes made these blankets in the late nineteenth and early twentieth centuries.

Chumash (California)

The Chumash Indians of California made blankets out of feathers. The narrow pieces of bird skin were entwined with a cord to strengthen them, then they were woven in a warp and woof technique.

Hopi (Southwest)

Pueblo blankets are traditionally woven by the men. The blankets may be white or cream-colored wool with blue, brown, or black horizontal stripes. The "Moki" blanket, one of the oldest Hopi styles, is woven with dark blue or black stripes and shoulder blankets often have checkered or tartan patterns.

All blankets woven by the Hopi have a looser weave than those textiles woven by Navajos, and embroidery weaving is used by the Pueblo weavers to decorate their textiles.

Maidu (California)

Maidu blankets are made of rabbit skins, which are common animals in California. Strips of skin were left uncured, then knotted into one long line. The strips were wound back and forth between two stakes horizontally, then the same type of strips were twined up and down, making a blanket which was thick, incredibly soft, and warm.

Navajo (Southwest)

Red Turkish woolen cloth was called "bayeta" and was first acquired by the Navajo from Mexicans and, later, from trading posts who sold bolts of it. The Indians would buy the cloth and unravel it to use the thread for their blankets.

Even when the Navajo first began making bayeta blankets, their durability, warmth, and quality of weaving was noticed and appreciated by potential buyers. The price was high back then for a fine bayeta blanket ($200 in the early 1900s) and has risen accordingly over the years. The work on these blankets takes a Navajo woman many months to complete, but, once accomplished, the blanket can literally hold water.

Most of the early blankets were made to be worn on the chief's shoulders and might have had a slit in the center for the chief's head, allowing the blanket to be worn as a poncho. The finest of these blankets were worn only on festive occasions or at ceremonies.

The Navajo learned about dying wool from Mexicans and Pueblo Indians, whose skills were limited; thus, the color selection the Navajo had was limited as well. Blue was made from indigo; the bayeta wool was made in reds, black, blues, greens, pinks, oranges, and yellows.

One can tell a bayeta blanket by seeing if a thread shows a single strand when pulled to pieces. If it is three strands, then the yarn is Germantown. Other experts argue, however, that one can only tell a true bayeta if it burns or if it has a rough and fuzzy feel.

Regardless of how you try to verify a true bayeta, I believe the surest way is to "learn by doing." By attending auctions, going to shows, and visiting shops that specialize in Indian material you will be able to place your hands on old Indian blankets and learn their names and how they feel from the experts. Pretty soon you, too, will become an expert and be able to tell a blanket by the feel of it under your fingers—even with your eyes closed!

CHIEF'S BLANKETS

Blankets which are woven crosswise, instead of lengthwise, are called "chief's blankets." The Navajo term for these blankets is Honal-Kladi or Honal-Chodi. Chief's blankets were meant to be wrapped broadside around the body and the stripes are shown off better in this fashion.

While it is almost impossible to stretch the stitches of the weft so that you may see the warp, the blanket would most likely hold water. Blankets of this quality are the most collectible and are the ones that bring the highest auction prices. Such blankets are few and far between now, although the quality of today's Navajo blankets is still extremely high and will never be touched by blankets woven any other way. Perhaps that is one of the most amazing things about Navajo weaving—they are still weaving by hand, without the benefit of machines, and their products are far superior to anything that is machine made.

Chief's blankets have gone through three phases. The first phase was a blanket that was a favored trade item among the Ute and Sioux. This version had a black "streak" or belt in the center and was popular with the Shoshoni and Ute tribes. The second-phase blanket had small red rectangles woven into the ends and middles of the blue stripes. This created a 12-block pattern. In the 1860s, the third-phase chief's blanket emerged with a full diamond in the middle, quarter diamonds on each corner, and half diamonds in the center of each edge. After this phase and during the 1880s, weavers began incorporating pictorial elements and cross motifs into their textiles.

Though it was originally noted that chief's blankets belonged to the chiefs (men) of the tribe, there are many documents which show women wearing the blankets (i.e., Brule Sioux women wore them on special occasions).

Germantown yarns were introduced to the Navajo by 1850, and the Indians, not satisfied with the yarn, twisted it to make it firmer and tighter. These yarns were dyed with vegetable dye which made their colors reliable and resistant. Though it was felt by some that the introduction of Germantown yarns produced a deterioration in the Navajo blankets, other weavers did their best work with these yarns and continued to produce weavings which would hold water.

Certain trade posts, such as Hubbell's in Ganado, Arizona, began to take these blankets into their posts to sell. The first Navajo blankets that Mr. John Lorenzo Hubbell put up for sale were marked to sell at $2 each. Little by little, Hubbell and his partner, C.N. Cotton, urged Navajo blanket weavers to produce more of their weavings. The Indians saw a growth in their income and were pleased with it. Hubbell and Cotton saw a way to make money and they were pleased. Commercialism had arrived.

More trading posts jumped on the bandwagon, and aniline dyes were soon introduced to the Navajo women who lived around Fort Defiance. The cotton warp was then sold for a low price to Indian weavers and a demand for cheap blankets was created. The Navajo women were now urged to make more blankets in a shorter period of time and they began to take less care in cleaning their wool. The result was that the wool would not take a proper dye and the colors were uneven. All these factors combined to make a blanket of lesser quality, looser weave, and harsher fabric—the ultimate result being a lower scale of pay for the weaver.

The art of weaving deteriorated quickly, but, thankfully, there were those in the business who were determined to build the art back up to its original form and to bring the quality back into the Navajo's products. Dealers who understood what was happening, and knew that poor quality articles could only result in little (or no) sales, decided to take it upon themselves to refuse to trade in any blankets which were not of the highest quality.

J.B. Moore, whose trading post was near what is now Crystal, New Mexico, took it upon himself to take the raw wool the Navajos produced and to ship it East for cleaning. Once the cleaning process had been performed, the wool was shipped back to New Mexico and the Indians were free to card, spin, and dye the yarn in the manner they chose. The weavers who had proven themselves to be proficient were given specific amounts of wool—enough for a particular size blanket—and only given more when the first batch produced a blanket. As a result, Moore's mail-order business was successful and the quality of the rugs produced by the people working for him was much higher. Through Moore's original efforts, the Navajo improved their weaving once again and the quality soon came back to a standard that was pretty close to what it had been in years past.

Once the market for blankets and rugs made from the wool of their sheep became demanding, the Navajo then had to be taught more scientific ways of raising their sheep so that they produced the most for the weavers. In 1911, the government put together a plan for breeding the sheep and taught the Indian how to increase the size of their sheep and improve the quality of its mutton and wool. The suggestions were carried out and, by 1912, four times as many blankets were produced.

The Navajos have used colors as symbols in their weaving since the advent of the art. Green is the color which symbolizes youth, while yellow, blue, orange, and red represent maturity or harvest time. Brown and gray mean death and decay, and black is symbolic of mourning. It was not sheer folly which showed the Indian the symbolism of these colors, but nature, and, if one takes the time, the reasoning behind the symbolism is quite easy to understand. It is also easy to understand why red, the color associated with the life-giving sun, is the favorite of the Navajo weavers.

The dyes to make the colors for Navajo rugs were made from natural ingredients which the Indians found near their homes. Sumac, yellow ochre, and pinion gum were boiled together to make black dye; yellow was from the flowering tops of Bigelovia graveolens; red came from the bark of Alnus incana var. virescens (black alder) and juniper twigs, mixed with a few other ingredients; and blue came from a native blue clay which was boiled with sumac leaves.

As there is symbolism connected with the colors which are used in Navajo blankets/rugs, so is there symbolism in the design elements incorporated into the weaving. It must be said that each weaver incorporates some of her own thoughts and interpretation of designs (influenced, perhaps, by the person for whom she weaves) into her weaving, but the origin of the designs reaches far back into the Navajo's history. Some designs were borrowed from the Mexicans, others from the Pueblo tribes, some from the sacred sand paintings of the medicine man, and still others from nature itself.

Into each design is built an "escape hatch" of sorts—an exit for the weaver's spirit so it does not get trapped in her work. This "escape hatch" takes the form of an error made in the work to declare the weaver's knowledge of the small place a human holds in this universe.

Some of the designs medicine men used, and which were copied by weavers, featured the Navajo gods—the "yei." Divine characters, the yei were both male and female and are shown in these depictions as extremely long and thin beings who wear masks. A male yei wears a helmet-like mask and is known by the eagle plumes/owl feathers attached to the mask. He is also known by the fact that he holds a spruce twig in the left hand and a gourd in the right. A female yei, usually dressed in white, is indicated by her rectangular mask, yellow arms, and chest (females were created of yellow corn, males of white), and the spruce wand held in each hand. Each yei figure represents a different god. There are Ganaskidi, which are mountain sheep or bighorn gods; Hastseyalti, or the Talking God; and Hastsehogan. Usually bordering each depiction is the rainbow goddess.

Corn is one of the most important foods to the Navajo, so it represents a vital part of their ceremonies. Its symbol is used all the time in paintings, on masks, and in the designs for rugs and blankets.

Sunbeams are made of parallel straight lines in a scarlet color. They are often depicted in sand paintings, on masks, and in designs on blankets and rugs.

The queue symbol, representing the scalps of their enemies, is painted on depictions of the god Tobadzistsini, or Child of the Water. Sometimes the queue symbol is open and, at other times, it is closed—each has a different significance.

Lightning is represented by zigzag lines, and Navajo myths say gods use lightning as ropes. When painted in white on a black background, the lines represent lightning on the face of a cloud.

Geometric designs used by weavers incorporate parallel lines, zigzags, triangles, spurs, quadrilaterals, hourglass figures, rectangles, double triangles, terraced edges, s-forms, crooks, feathers, stars, key patterns, bird forms, mosaic patterns, and any combination of the aforementioned.

The trading post owner, Lorenzo Hubbell, had a group of blanket designs painted in oil and hung them on his office walls. "Modern" Navajo blankets appeared with designs that had names such as Tsin alnazoid (Roman cross), Kos Yischin (cloud image), Be 'ndastlago noltizh (cornered zigzag), and Nahokhos (swastika cross). They were used in conjunction with the old designs or on their own, depending on the weaver's preference.

When weavers first began interpreting yei figures or kachina figures in their blankets/rugs, it upset the Indian population greatly. Any dealer who had such a piece for sale in his trading post would consider his life to be in jeopardy. After the initial arguments, dissension was still strong and the tribe still believed the sacred yei figure should not be represented on anything more lasting than a sand painting. However, the weavers still made a few here and there and today the figures are commonly seen as part of rug/blanket designs. The older versions, however, are still rare and considered highly collectible.

Nootka (Northwest)

Because mountain goat wool was highly prized, often the only blankets in a Nootka tribe were owned by the chiefs of the tribe, and these blankets were only worn on ceremonial occasions. The blankets were decorated with bold designs of the region.

Salish (Northwest)

Salish blankets, sometimes fingerwoven like the Tlingit but often twill-plaited, were usually white. The materials used included mountain goat wool, down, cattail fluff, and hair from white dogs.

The mountain goat wool was cleaned and the coarser outer hairs removed. The finer hairs were beaten to straighten them, and other fibers may have been added to increase the thickness of the weave (i.e., bear, raccoon, squirrel fur). The fibers were worked onto spindles with rods which were often 3'-4' long. A small, white-haired domesticated dog was bred by these people for its wool and some have proposed that the animal may have been in the pomeranian or spitz family.

The designs used in these early blankets were complicated and colorful, but we do not know the actual colors they used because none have survived. The ones which have been sketched show us that there were three types of blankets: a plain diagonal weave; a twined weave "nobility blanket"; and the decorative twined weave.

The white blankets were brightened with clay and were cleaned by being beaten. Many were used as shrouds and buried with the bodies of members of the tribe, leaving us few examples of this type of weaving.

In more modern times, the Salish used commercial yarns and a weaving frame and produced finer, more decorative textiles.

Zuni (Southwest)

The Zuni style of weaving differs from the Navajo mainly in quality (the Navajo being the superior weaver) and also in the fact that their materials are usually black or dark blue wool woven in a diagonal style.

Squaw dresses were basically blankets, woven diagonally, and were worn wrapped around the wearer under the right arm and fastened over the left shoulder.

RUGS

At an exhibit held at the Museum of Our National Heritage in Lexington, Massachusetts (February–July, 1988), the symbolism of Navajo rug designs was explored. Through this exhibition, anthropologists showed that three Navajo deities—Changing Woman, Born for the Water, and Monster Slayer—show up in nearly every Navajo rug ever woven. The symbols are also evident in other areas of Navajo culture (i.e., on petroglyphs and objects used in certain ceremonies). The idea that weaving patterns have cultural meanings has ruffled a few feathers among historians and anthropologists. Up until this exhibit, the theory had not been so thoroughly researched.

Navajo appear to be the last of the rug-making Indians in North America, and their work sells for very high prices because the common assumption is that if it was woven by a Navajo, it will last forever.

The Chilkat weavers of the Northwest Coast have almost become extinct. There are fewer women alive who retain this knowledge with each passing year and the Eastern weavers have been even less interested in preserving what rug weaving skills they once had.

Navajo rugs, as blankets, are woven completely by hand, and one rug may take the weaver many months to complete. The finest Navajo rugs are woven in Two Grey Hills, New Mexico, an area between Shiprock and Gallup, New Mexico, but rugs from Crystal, Wide Ruin, Teec Nos Pas, and Ganado are also well known. (The typical black, gray, and red Navajo rugs are indicative of the ones made in Klagetoh and Ganado.) Wide Ruin rugs were made of subtler colors—in beiges, light pinks, and whites—and designs were often simple geometric figures separated by varying width stripes. The deep red backgrounds and simple designs of Ganado rugs are often revivals of earlier patterns.

Navajo are weaving less rugs than they once did, and, because they are scarce, the prices are affected. One rug, 3' × 5', could take the maker 400 hours to weave. The Navajo women weave the fibers of their rugs so tightly that some rugs will hold water. A good rug may have 30 threads to the inch; the better ones have 90, some even more.

Navajo "eye dazzler" rugs, made with commercial Germantown yarns from Pennsylvania, were made from 1880–1910. The sand painting rugs, which depict the sacred yei figures, always have a mistake incorporated into their design and their borders are never closed because the weaver does not want to trap his spirit in the piece. Perhaps one of the most difficult designs for a weaver to accomplish is two-faced weaving—each side of the rug has a different design. Zigzags and rectangles are the basic patterns of storm design rugs, which have been made since 1900 in the area near Tuba City, Arizona.

Contemporary New Lands weavers are being encouraged to switch from aniline-dyed wool to vegetable-dyed wool. The design they use is still Teec Nos Pas, but the rugs have a three-dimensional look. The new style has given weavers a boost because the soft pastel colors of the rugs, combined with their visual impact, has opened up a new retail field for them. The colors and styles of these new weavings are adaptable to styles other than the traditional Southwestern style into which they have heretofore been paired.

BLANKET LISTINGS

Chimayo

Central bird design w/storm design interior, stripes, and whirling log design; multicolors on gray background; minute amount of color bleeding; ca. 1930; 47″ × 84″.   **$125–$175**

Wall hanging; heavy yarn in green, red, and tan design with red fringe at bottom; two small soil spots; 30″ × 72″.   **$45–$65**

Wool; ca. 1900, tightly handwoven w/100% wool yarns w/gray field, large stylized diamond pattern in black, white with broad and narrow bands in a deep wine red; 4′ × 7′; very good condition.   **$200–$250**

Germantown

Saddle; diamond design w/red, blue, gray, white, and green; 21″ × 21″.   **$140–$200**

Weaving; fragmentary weaving; ca. 1880; 62″ × 43″.   **$210–$250**

Weaving; choice fringed weaving w/geometric and cross designs; ca. 1900; 40″ × 22″.   **$125–$175**

Haida

Button; blue trade cloth button blanket w/killer whale design; pearl buttons and red trade cloth trim; 65″ × 6″.   **$750–$1000**

Large, fine button blanket w/large bear and trim in old pearl buttons; 56″ × 56″; ca. 1920.   **$600–$800**

Hudson Bay

Four points; 66″ × 81″.   **$45–$85**

Large, striped, unusually colored Indian blanket; ca. 1920; 84″ × 69″.   **$50–$100**

Navajo

CHIEF'S

Rare; small, chief's-style, striped saddle blanket; ca. 1890; 30″ × 30″.
$110–$150

Third-phase; ca. 1880; handspun wool on wool warp; red, dark brown, faded indigo blue, and natural; 50″ × 67″. **$5200–$5800**

From the William R. Nash Collection. Photo by Donald Vogt.

Third-phase; bayeta and indigo weave; ca. 1875; 53″ × 76″; one of the finest 19th-century blankets ever handled by dealers in the Southwest.
$25,000–$35,000

Very early; vegetable dye, chief's pattern saddle blanket; ca. 1910; 33″ × 26″. **$100–$150**

CHILD'S

Courtesy of Morning Star Gallery, Santa Fe, NM. Photo by Donald Vogt.

Classic child's blanket; ca. 1865; 32″ × 47″; (01493). **$9500–$10,000**

Courtesy of Morning Star Gallery, Santa Fe, NM. Photo by Donald Vogt.

Classic child's blanket; ca. 1860; 31″ × 52″; (C0031–01694).

$30,000–$35,000

Classic child's blanket; ca. 1860; (01590). **$21,000–$23,000**

Germantown

Fringed weaving; woven on a red ground in mustard, gold, olive, rust, and dark red, with serrated joined diamonds, bound at top w/dark red wool, fringed at bottom; 58 × 33″; minor roughness. **$325–$500**

Storm pattern w/red, yellow, blue-gray, maroon, white, purple, and light gray; ca. 1900s; 64″ × 85″. **$3725–$5250**

"Sunday saddle" type with black, white, and green colors in banded and vertical zigzag (serrated) columns; 27½″ × 35″; ca. 1900. **$1150–$1400**

Transitional blanket/rug; 65″ × 84″; bold black, red-orange, and white colors; ca. 1900. **$2500–$3500**

Woven on a bright red ground w/natural white, teal green, and lavender-gray Germantown yarns in a pattern of zigzag chevrons in counterpoint; 30″ × 50″; tightly woven, fine condition. **$1650–$2000**

Woven on a bright red ground w/natural white, teal green, and lavender-gray Germantown yarns in a pattern of zigzag chevrons in counterpoint; 30″ × 50″. **$1750–$1900**

Woven in celery, red, gold, white, black, dark green, and light pink with an "eye dazzler" pattern composed of rows of serrated wedges and diamonds; remnant wool fringe on both ends; 38″ × 59″. **$850–$950**

MANTA

From the William R. Nash Collection. Photo by Donald Vogt.

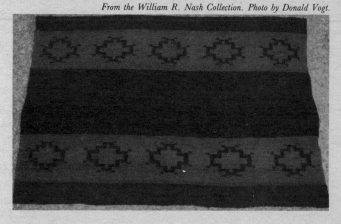

Woman's manta; twill woven w/natural-shaded dark brown center flanked by two rows of terraced diamonds in indigo blue against broad-ravelled red bands, the long borders in indigo blue; 55½″ × 36¾″.

$5000–$5500

From the William R. Nash Collection. Photo by Donald Vogt.

Woman's manta; twill woven in commercial yarn w/central dark brown panel flanked by two rows of terraced crosses against red bands, the blue side borders each w/zigzag pattern; 55″ × 48″.   **$5000–$5500**

Saddle

Classic, handwoven, striped saddle blanket; 30″ × 30″; ca. 1940. **$20–$40**

Early, handwoven, natural wool saddle blanket; 28″ × 15″; ca. 1920.
                                                                $30–$50

Ganado double-dyed; red, gray, black, and natural diamond design; 33″ × 61″.   **$90–$150**

Handwoven saddle blanket w/stars in the corners; ca. 1940; 23″ × 22″.
                                                                $35–$50

Nineteenth century; extra long staple wool w/marvelous sheen; wear at ends and salvage; 30″ × 48″.   **$85–$135**

Rare "pulled warp" diagonal-weave saddle blanket; ca. 1900; 46″ × 30″.
                                                                $50–$75

Woven w/100% handspun wool and some Germantown yarns; ca. 1880s; in bright crimson red, deep and pale Germantown violet yarns, beige, natural gray w/three groups of stripes w/embattled edges; some soiling and yarn pulls; 32″ × 53″.   **$250–$350**

Serape

From the William R. Nash Collection. Photo by Donald Vogt.

Transitional serape; woven on a shaded red handspun ground w/pattern of crosses and terraced lozenges; in blue, green, yellow, and pale pink commercial yarn, and natural white handspun; 69″ × 54½″.
                                                                $8000–$8500

From the William R. Nash Collection. Photo by Donald Vogt.

Transitional serape; woven on an orange-red ground in white and two shades of indigo blue and blue-green w/pattern of terraced zigzigs centering a row of crosses down the back; parallel bars and short serrated columns on the sides.   **$9000–$9800**

TRANSITIONAL

Blanket/rug; 60″ × 86″; dark brown, creme-white, and medium brown colors in "floating" trapezoidlike-shaped designs; ca. 1900.

$375–$575

Blanket/rug; 60″ × 80″; NE Reservation area; dark brown, mottled brown, gray-brown, and white colors in banded designs; ca. 1900; mint condition.   **$525–$750**

Blanket/rug; 57½″ × 77″; dark brown, red-orange, mottled brown, and white colors; ca. 1900; excellent condition.   **$850–$1000**

Blanket/rug; 43″ × 86″; NE Reservation area Pound blanket; dark brown, gray-brown, and white colors in a large serrated "X" and whirling logs/swastikalike designs; ca. 1900.   **$550–$750**

Twill weave weaving; ca. 1900; 34″ × 44″; red background, black and orange stripes.   **$800–$1000**

Blanket/rug; 56″ × 83″; dark gray, red-orange, white, and gray-brown colors; ca. 1900s.   **$750–$950**

WEAVING

Choice little double-faced weaving w/yei figures on one side and stripes on the other; ca. 1970; 22″ × 17″.   **$80–$125**

Weaving in dark brown, white, and purple crosses and serrated saw-toothed designs on a shaded red ground; 31″ × 46″; edge damage.   **$600–$800**

Weaving in style of woman's wearing blanket; woven on shaded brownish-black ground w/three red panels, two w/stepped zigzag and cross motifs, twill woven on one side; 48″ × 70″.   **$1000–$1200**

Northwest Coast

Button; contemporary frog design; blue trade cloth w/red trim; 60″ × 77″.   **$200–$250**

Button; ceremonial blanket; wonderful graphic owl figure in red trade cloth outlined in mother-of-pearl buttons on purple; late 19th or early 20th century; two nailhead-size moth holes; 53″ × 58″. **$875–$1000**

Button; eagle design; blue trade cloth w/red trim; 36″ × 51″.

$60–$80

Pendleton

All wool; large; ca. 1940.   **$85–$100**

Blue-background wool Indian blanket w/geometric designs; ca. 1940. **$65–$100**

Classic striped wool; large; ca. 1930.   **$35–$50**

Fine old striped blanket measuring 60″ × 55″; ca. 1920.   **$35–$50**

Line design in black, green, red, blue, and white w/green fringe; 71″ × 60″.
$30–$50

Old wool Indian blanket; ca. 1920; 58″ × 36″.   **$100–$150**

Striped wool trade blanket; ca. 1940; 88″ × 56″.   **$60–$80**

Striped "Beaver State" Indian blanket; ca. 1935; 19″ × 2″.   **$50–$75**

Striped "Beaver State" Indian blanket; ca. 1950; 76″ × 64″.   **$75–$100**

Trade; double-faced geometric design; ca. 1920; 70″ × 63″.
$60–$100

Wool double weave; in golds shading to red and green on brown background; reverse diamond design in same colors; original felted binding worn off and label gone; minute wear to blanket; 60″ × 80″.
$75–$150

Yarn fringe on all four sides; 61″ × 58″; brown.   **$50–$75**

Yarn fringe on all four sides; 62″ × 54″; green.   **$50–$75**

Rio Grande

Courtesy of C. E. Guarino, Denmark, ME.

Germantown; "Vallero" wearing blanket; ca. 1880; woven w/two panels joined at the center in an eye-dazzling pattern of diamond forms, repeated chevrons, and two "Vallero stars" of eight points placed at the tips of the central figures; side borders of serrated, indented lines, and eight-pointed geometrics in deep red, crimson, teal green, dark blue, ochre, and white; warps are two-ply handspun wool; all colored areas in four-ply Germantown wool yarns; the white elements are single-ply homespun wool; this wearing blanket is a classic example of Vallero weavers active from 1860 to the 1890s, a subgroup of the Rio Grande people; Vallero stars are always eight-pointed; 50″ × 89″; one side with a slight faded area, but in overall excellent condition with vibrant colors. **$3100–$3500**

Serape; ca. 1800s; Chimayo; joined in center; blue on white background; black and red design elements. **$1500–$2000**

Wedding or utility; ca. 1885; tightly woven in single-ply handspun Rambouillet-Merino fleece wool on a four-ply cotton warp in two widths seamed at the center; forms a traditional pattern of broad and narrow stripes in deep indigo blue, natural undyed white, and a yellow ochre (gold) from rabbit brush dyes; the striped pattern has been over-embroidered with wool yarn geometrics, giving an overall design disguising the stripes; 86″ long, 45⅕″ wide; condition very good w/embroidery overlay worn in spots, the fringe worn but knotted and intact, the basic woven body without impairments. **$600–$700**

Sioux

Beaded hide blanket strip; stitched in lime green, greasy yellow, blue and white heart reds on a white beaded ground; sinew sewn; 64″ long; minor bead loss. **$700–$900**

Large classic hide saddle blanket w/sinew geometric beadwork and fringe; ca. 1940; 75″ × 28″. **$1250–$1800**

Other

Courtesy of Jack Glover, Sunset, TX. Photo by Donald Vogt.

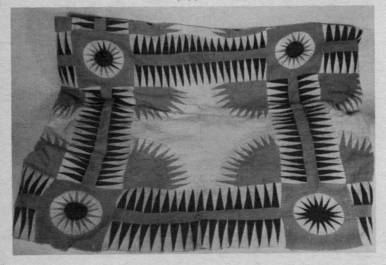

Giveaway; giveaway blanket of Wounded Knee Massacre in Dakota Territory; extremely rare; the red star means a death and three red triangles indicate wounds.

Indian; large twill-weave blanket w/fringe; ca. 1930; 86″ × 56″.
$200–$250

Kwakiutl; trade cloth button blanket w/beautiful white pearl button designs; ca. 1920. **$450–$650**

Lap, Rio Grande; colorful small-figure lap blanket; ca. 1935; 44″ × 22″.
$30–$50

Navajo; old classic bayeta; 45″ × 66½″ w/bayeta; re-carded and homespun wool in indigo blue, lilac, bayeta red, vegetable green, re-carded pink, gray-brown, and white colors; ca. 1865–75. **$6500–$8500**

Plateau, Horse; floral-beaded black w/red trim; Nez Perce horse blanket; 33″ × 54″; some damage. **$350–$400**

Prairie tribe cloth; decorated shawl 43″ × 65″; Oto, Osage, Winnebago, Illinois, Omaha; dark blue with sky blue and fuchsia satin-like decoration. **$70–$110**

Salish, wool; rare handwoven Frazer River wool blanket; ca. 1965; 40″ × 21″. **$55–$75**

Trade, Pendleton; double-faced geometric design; ca. 1920; 70″ × 63″. **$60–$100**

RUG LISTINGS

Chimayo

Sampler; red, gray, aqua, and white colors in large Thunderbird and banded designs; 14½″ × 15″; ca. 1st 3rd of 20th century. **$15–$20**

Woven fringed wool; 14″ × 17″ (inc. fringe); blue, red, green, and white colors. **$15–$25**

Woven fringed wool; 9½″ × 23″ (inc. fringe); blue, gray, red, black, and white colors. **$15–$25**

Woven fringed wool; 14″ × 16″ (inc. fringe); gray, black, red, and white colors. **$15–$20**

Woven fringed wool; 7″ × 12″ (inc. fringe); blue, gray, red, and white colors. **$15–$25**

Woven fringed; 7″ × 11″; in black, white, blue, aqua, green, and red. **$20–$35**

Navajo

Fancy

Klagetoh area with Teec Nos Pas influence; 54½″ × 87½″ w/black, taupe, gray, gold, white, and rust colors; ca. 1950s–60s. **$850–$1100**

Older 24½″ × 34″; "American Flag" with red, white, and purple colors; has fifty "stars". **$225–$325**

Old 51½″ × 65″; Teec Nos Pas/Red Mesa outline w/red, maroon, orange, green, yellow, blue, black, gray, tan, and white colors; ca. 1925; excellent condition. **$1800–$2500**

Six-figured yei, w/three yeis, two cornstalk symbols and a rainbow god/guardian in red, green, white, black, blue, yellow, and cocoa colors; 35″ × 37″.

$95–$125

Whirling Logs/Tsil-Ol-Ni sand painting; gray, chili red, yellow, black, green, raspberry, aqua, gold, blue, and white colors; mint condition; 52½″ × 54½″. **$1250–$1600**

GERMANTOWN

Dark blue, gray, yellow, orange, red-orange, and white colors in diamonds within a large, serrated diamond design; 56″ × 84″; ca. 1900. **$1200–$1800**

Fringed; fancy old rug which measures 36″ × 39″ (inc. fringe); aqua, red, gray, black, and white colors; ca. 1900. **$450–$650**

Maroon, green, and white colors; 19″ × 20¾″; ca. 1900; mint condition. **$85–$125**

Maroon, green, and white colors; 19″ × 20¾″; ca. 1900; mint condition. **$85–$125**

Old 17½″ × 18″ sampler; red, yellow, gray, maroon, and white colors; ca. 1900. **$45–$85**

Old 19″ × 20″ sampler; red, white, green, and black colors; ca. 1900. **$75–$125**

Sampler; 14″ × 21″ orange, burgundy, red, white, and green colors; ca. 1900–10. **$65–$95**

NATURAL WOOL

Courtesy of W. J. Arbuckle, collector. Photo by Donald Vogt.

Dyed wool; 19″ × 40″; colors are mustard, white, tan, black, and brown; contemporary. **$100–$150**

Floor rug; brown, gray, and white geometric designs; ca. 1935; 50″ × 26″. **$70–$100**

Handwoven Navajo saddle blanket; 29″ × 27″; ca. 1940. **$35–$50**

OLD

Eastern Reservation; 42½″ × 70″; dark brown, rust, gray-brown, and white colors in vertically connected, serrated diamond designs; ca. 1940s; excellent condition. **$300–$500**

Pictorial; 43″ × 86″; Eastern Reservation area; dark brown, mottled brown, and white colors in whirling log/swastika-like, large terraced diamond and man with hat designs; ca. 1920s. **$600–$750**

Red, black, light gray, and white colors in vertical rows of connected, serrated diamonds and zipper-like designs; 43½″ × 66½″; excellent condition. **$190–$275**

Rug-fringed pillow; 15½″ × 17½″ (incl. fringe) sampler; dark brown, red, white, and gray-brown colors in diamond designs; ca. 1960s. **$35–$50**

Tapestry quality; 37½″ × 62½″, Two Grey Hills; black, gray, white, brown, and taupe colors; ca. 1950s–60s. **$850–$1100**

PICTORIAL

Won award in 1980 at the New Mexico State Fair. **$1100–$1400**

Woven on a cream ground; gray, red, and dark brown border encompassing a central design of turquoise, red, dark brown, black, khaki, and pumpkin chickens, horses, cattle, ant-people figures, buckets, feathers, and cowboys holding branding irons; 52″ × 84″; minor dye runs and edge roughness. **$3600–$4000**

SAMPLERS

1910 Germantown sampler on loom; 13″ diameter x 19″ high. **$250–$350**

Sampler; dark brown, white, and orange colors in serrated diamond and half-cross designs; 18″ × 20½″ ca. 2nd quarter 20th century. **$25–$45**

Sampler; black, white, red, and gray colors in a large, serrated diamond design; 19½″ × 20½″ ca. 1930s–40s. **$20–$45**

Sampler; orange, black, and white colors in serrated designs, 19½″ × 20½″ ca. 1940s. **$35–$65**

Teec Nos Pas

From the Two Star Collection, Houston. Photo by Donald Vogt.

All handspun and natural dyes; ca. 1910.   **$2400–$2600**

From the Hadden/Saylor Collection. Photo by Donald Vogt.

By Gloria Cambridge; 20″ × 28½″.   **$800–$1000**

Circle of cottonwoods; ca. 1900–1910; natural and aniline dyes; homespun
typical design of transitional period.   **$1400–$1600**

Eye dazzler; all native homespun wool w/use of aniline dyes and natural wool colors; the blue is from blue jean dyes; ca. 1920s; 43″ × 85″.
$9000–$9800

Teec Nos Pas outline w/black, dark gray, white, green, light gray, cocoa, medium brown, and gold colors; 42″ × 50″.　　**$300–$400**

THROW

Colorful small Gallup throw rug; ca. 1950; 37″ × 19″.　　**$20–$40**

Gallup throw; 19¾″ × 38″; red, gray, black, and white colors in serrated diamond design; ca. 1960s.　　**$40–$80**

Throw; 21½″ × 42″; black, white, gold, and gray colors in serrated diamond designs.　　**$45–$75**

Throw; 16½″ × 36″; mottled gray, yellow, brown, white, and orange colors in banded and serrated designs; ca. 3rd quarter 20th century.
$25–$40

Throw; 16″ × 34″; dark brown, gray, red, white, orange, and blue colors in serrated diamond designs.　　**$25–$50**

Throw; 18½″ × 35″; black, red, white, and mottled green colors in serrated designs.　　**$25–$50**

TRANSITIONAL

Dark brown, red-orange, mottled brown, and white; 57″ × 84″; 1925.
$1000–$1500

North Eastern Reservation area; 54″ × 100″; black, dark brown, dark gray, and white colors; ca. 1900; near mint condition.　　**$800–$1200**

Serape; 75″ × 52″; ca. 1800.　　**$9500–$10,000**

TWO GREY HILLS

Black, brown, gray, light brown, and white colors; 43½″ × 71″; ca. 1930–50.　　**$700–$1000**

Classic natural wool weaving; ca. 1950; 58″ × 38″.　　**$525–$700**

Courtesy of Naranjo's, Houston. Photo by Donald Vogt.

Typical style in natural wool; ca. 1930; colors are tan, gray, and black.

$4000–$5000

Woven in red, white, and shades of brown on a gray field; bordered central geometric devices; excellent condition, ca. 1930s; 48″ × 82″.

$700–$900

WESTERN RESERVATION

Floor rug with multicolored sawtooth motif; ca. 1935; 65″ × 62″. $85–$100

Geometric handwoven rug; 36″ × 64″; ca. 1950. $65–$115

WOVEN

Black, cream, and mustard geometric motifs, with meandering sawtooth-line border around a shaded brownish-gray field; 45″ × 72″. $450–$600

Black, shaded brown, red, and white; 54″ × 69″. $350–$500

Black, sand, red, and white geometric devices on a shaded gray field; 69½″ × 42″.

$375–$425

Black, red, and white serrated diamond motifs on a shaded gray ground; 67½″ × 45½″. $250–$300

Brown, tan, red, and cream diamond and cross design; 7′8″ × 4′2″.

$415–$450

Brown, tan, cream, and red geometric square and rectangle design; 5′3″ × 3′3″.

$275–$315

Brown, cream, pumpkin, tan, and gray diamond arrow design; 5′1″ × 3′8″.
$385–$425

Dark brown, white, sand, and red geometric motifs on a shaded gray ground; 29″ × 52″.
$300–$450

Fine Gap "storm pattern" in soft brown shades; ca. 1965; 36″ × 22″.
$40–$80

Light brown, dark brown, cream, jagged diamond pattern; 7′ x 4′3″.
$380–$410

Red ground in pink, light blue, white, brown, and black w/large central double-hooked motif bordered by concentric-stepped rectangles; 44″ × 76″; minor staining.
$325–$500

Red, black, and white on a shaded gray field bordered central design of stepped lozenge motif; 53″ × 77″.
$425–$525

Shaded gray ground in red, black, white, and dark brown w/elaborate geometric and pictorial motifs; 88″ × 54″; minor edge roughness and staining.
$550–$650

Two; woven in red, black, white, and shaded brown; 32″ × 52″; and 24″ × 60″.
$425–$550

Yei

Woven w/row of skirted Yeibachi figures with numerous feathers interspersed; brownish-black and red encompassing border woven in violet, teal, red, orange, white, yellow, dark brown, and pale green; 43″ × 69″.
$600–$700

Woven w/100 wool yarns in multicolors on a mottled-gray background; the border in a rich brown w/elaborate serrated pattern in black, teal blue, and white; five yei figures predominate the design with the end two wearing headpieces w/three feathers, in contrast to the central three w/four feathers and different pendants; 7′ × 4′3″; very good condition.
$2100–$2500

OTHER

From the Hadden/Saylor Collection. Photo by Donald Vogt.

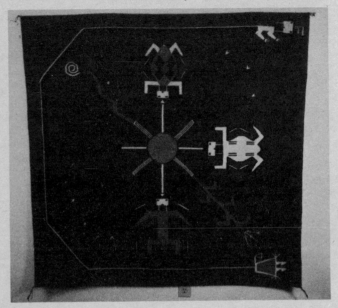

Beauty Way/Water Creatures; done in 1974 by Desbah Tutt Nez; handspun, vegetable, and aniline dye; 1st prize at 1975 Scottsdale. **$8000–$9000**

Choice, large, early storm pattern w/crisp colors in the geometric design; ca. 1930; 96″ × 58″. **$900–$1200**

Choice old Crystal weaving w/central lozenge and fishhook motif; ca. 1930; 81″ × 53″. **$600–$800**

Crystal area vegetable dye; 60″ × 105″; dark brown, gold, light gray-brown, white, and medium brown colors in narrow and wide-banded arrowhead and hourglass designs; ca. 1950s. **$850–$1350**

Dark brown, red, gray-brown, and white colors; 77″ × 120″; ca. 1930–50. **$2250–$3250**

Defiance area Klagetoh-like; 3′3/4″ × 4′3/8″; black, red, gray, and red colors; by Louise Yazzie. **$100–$150**

Fine old Ganado Red w/"railroad track" lozenge and diamond motif; ca. 1930; 76″ × 42″. **$250–$350**

From the Hadden/Saylor Collection. Photo by Donald Vogt.

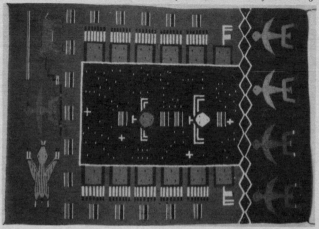

Hail Way/Night Sky; by Albert Jackson; 41½″ × 59¾″. **$3500–$4000**
Klagetoh area rug with red, gray, black, and white colors; 38″ × 53″;
ca. 1930s.   **$200–$300**
Large, old, floor-type; 82″ × 126″; Eastern Reservation; dark brown,
gray-brown, and white colors; ca. 1930s; excellent condition.
                                                            $1200–$1600

From the Hadden/Saylor Collection. Photo by Donald Vogt.

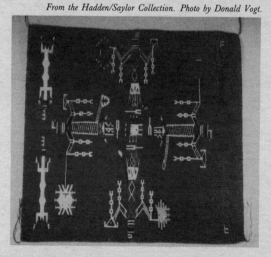

Male Shooting Chant; done in 1980 by Zonnie Gilmore; handspun, vegetable dyes, and measuring 38″ × 40″.   **$3500–$4000**

Mat; white and red geometrics on black ground; 18″ × 18½″.

$55–$75

Miniature rug and loom; 13¾″ × 11″; containing a partially finished weaving in black, orange, yellow, and white colors. **$20–$40**

Northeast Reservation area; 52″ × 89″; dark brown, red, light brown, and white colors in serrated diamond designs; ca. 1930s **$625–$775**

Red, gray, black, and white colors in three vertical rows of serrated diamonds; 30″ × 50″. **$55–$75**

Red and black w/terraced designs; ca. 1935; 50″ × 28″. **$175–$225**

Small rug w/Waterbird design; ca. 1965; 39″ × 18″. **$50–$75**

Storm w/rainbow yei; by Marita Gould; measures 42½″ × 62″.

$1500–$1700

From the Hadden/Saylor Collection. Photo by Donald Vogt.

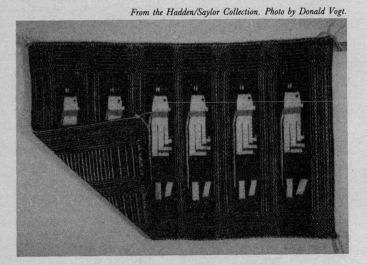

Two-faced yeibechai; by Harriet Smiley; won 2nd place at 1987 Navajo Nation Fair; 21½″ × 33½″. **$395–$450**

Western reservation; red, white, black, and gray floor rug; ca. 1935; 60″ × 30″. **$70–$100**

Wide Ruins area; tan, burgundy, white, orange, gold, gray, and dark green colors in banded, terraced, and serrated diamond designs.

$225–$375

Yevishai; 20″ × 29″; different color skirts on the woman is unusual; contemporary. **$300–$400**

CLOTHING

▼▼▼▼▼▼▼▼▼▼▼▼

INTRODUCTION

Many people just think of the Plains Indians when they picture an Indian and his/her clothing, but there are scores of other tribes and their ways of dress are as different from the tribes of the Plains as the rest of their lifestyles.

Most of the tribes wore breechcloths as a primary garment, as well as moccasins. Breechcloths, worn only by men, provided an equally long apron in both front and back. Leggings were also worn by a variety of tribes. They were often trimmed down the flap, which ran down the side of the leg, with quillwork or beads. The flap was also frequently fringed. The hip portion of the leggings was cut higher for men so that they would fit better and the outer part of the legging waist was tied to a belt to keep them up around the waist. Shirts and/or capes were also common. Hats or bonnets, though accepted pieces of clothing, differ greatly, even among those Indians who belong to the same tribe. Footwear was adapted to the climate that each particular Indian tribe endured, though most went barefoot for at least part of the time.

Snowshoes were used by Eastern, as well as Western, Indians. The frames for snowshoes made by the Eastern tribes were usually oval, while the Western snowshoes were narrow.

The Northern tribes, such as Algonquins and Athabaskans, used rawhide strips to make the netting for their snowshoes.

Maidu snowshoes are similar to those worn by other California Indians. One or two thongs cross over the width and two to four crisscross those. The hoop is a small oval with no netting, no tailpiece, and no provision.

DECORATION OF CLOTHING

Quillwork

The Plains Indians used quills in decoration and their art reached its peak just prior to their acquisition of the horse. Before they acquired horses, the Plains tribes stayed in one place for long periods of time.

This gave the women a chance to take their time with the artwork they produced by weaving quills into fabric and leather.

Their skill at the craft was a subject of pride and there were very definite levels of skill among the women in the tribes. The most artistic of them perfected dyes, designs, and stitches, which the other women willingly followed. It was an honor for a woman of great skill to pass her secrets along to another. The patterns which they used were mostly geometric before 1880. After that time, some tribes began using floral designs.

With the use of trade beads becoming more widespread in the early 1880s, quillwork began to be threatened as a decorative art. It did not start to disappear, however, until seed beads were readily available (after 1840). Today, the Sioux tribe is the one that produces most of the quillwork.

Sewing the quills of a porcupine onto a soft hide was an ancient Blackfoot (as well as other tribes) way of decorating clothing. Before the quills were sewn down onto the fabric, the quillmaker soaked them in her mouth to soften them. They would sew the quills so that they would form patterns and designs. Quills could be used in their natural colors or dyed. The old basic colors were red, yellow, and green. The dye that was used on quills was made from plants. The plants were first wetted, covered by the quills, then wrapped until dry. When dry, the plant color had permanently soaked into the quills. Tools used in quill decorating included a piece of hide upon which to work, an awl, a smooth object used to flatten the quills once they were sewn down, and strands of rolled sinew.

Quills were kept in special bags fashioned out of buffalo bladders. A slit was made in the bag, through which the quills were inserted, and the bag was usually stiff enough so that the quills inside would be kept straight. The thin quills were the ones a quillworker preferred to work with because they didn't split as easily as the larger, older ones did.

Blackfoot quillmakers go through a traditional initiation and have to follow rules such as not eating porcupine meat and not allowing anyone to pass in front of them while they are quilling. An older woman will initiate a younger woman into the art.

Because of the advent of beadwork and the lack of knowledge of the art of quilling among the older women, there are few quillworkers left among the Blackfoot women today. It is said that one of the reasons quillworkers died was that the substance in porcupine quills made them hemorrhage.

Beadwork

TRADE BEADS

Glassmaking secrets were closely guarded in the early history of the art. Egyptians were one of the earliest producers of glass beads, although much of the early glassmaking as we know it was done in Soviet-held countries. Factories were started in Lebanon thousands of years ago and still produce today, although Venice, Italy, now bears the privilege of being known as "The Mother of Modern Beads." The process of glassmaking is an interesting one and one which has changed through the years, coming through such stages as "winding," "blowing," and "drawing."

We can credit Christopher Columbus with being the first person to introduce beads to the Indians; he gave a string of red beads to the natives of San Salvador. As other early explorers arrived in America, they, too, brought beads. The way we can determine the age of trade beads is to first determine where the beads were made, then find out when that country's people arrived in America. Though this method will not always give you an accurate age of the beads, it at least will give you a starting point from which to proceed.

The first beads used freely in trading were Spanish. Quickly on the Spaniard's heels came Dutch, French, English, and Russian settlers, and, in 1622, Jamestown, Virginia, became home to the country's first glass factory. Explorers spread the use of glass trade beads until they finally reached Alaska, the other side of the country.

The bead "Russian blue" became the most popular bead in Alaska and it was soon dubbed the "chief" bead. Other popular beads include the "Hudson Bay" bead, used in Canadian trade—it was a red bead with a translucent center; the "vaseline" or "cave agate" bead, which was made in a variety of colors, and was faceted and transparent with a hole through its center; and the "Hubbell" bead, which was made in Czechoslovakia between 1915 and 1920 and sold by the Hubbell Trading Post in Ganado, Arizona, located on the Navajo Reservation.

Different patterns are used in beading techniques, such as weft and warp combinations; the bias-diagonal stitches, which are very difficult to perfect and which were most often used throughout the Great Lakes region; and oblique weaving. Other patterns involve concentric circling; bead wrapping; spot or overlay stitching; spiral stitching, found in native American coiled basketry and used by the Midwestern Musquakiis; the spoked pattern, used by the Indians of Oklahoma; scalloped bead winding, used by the Utes and Comanches; and the lazy stitch, used by most Indians west of the Mississippi, which was the most commonly used stitch.

Plains Indian beadwork began when Europeans introduced the beads as trading material. The Plains women immediately put them to use as decorative accents on most of their leather garments. The beads were fashioned into geometric patterns or animal/human figures, which were intricate parts of the designs created by this artistic group of people. Their garments reflected light and movement, as well as their feeling of being one with the Earth.

After 1910, the beadwork made by the Plains tribes declined in quality. Many believe the reason to be that the Indians were no longer hunting; they did not have cause to use animal skins, which had been readily available, as clothing. Another reason is that being confined to the reservations left the Indian with a lack of interest in the old crafts, which had once reflected their happiness.

Because of the interaction between the tribes occupying the Plains area, certain crafts of one tribe bear close resemblance to those of another—Cheyenne and Arapaho artwork is quite similar, for instance. The beadwork on the clothing of the Kiowa, Comanche, and Plains Apache is sparse—their beadwork talents were displayed on borders or in isolated figures instead. The Sioux uses the lazy stitch when sewing their beads, which leaves the beads in loose rows. They do not lie flat, but have a bumpy appearance. Blackfoot beading is done with the applique stitch, requiring the simultaneous use of two threads—one thread strings the beads, the other stitches them down.

Bead colors that were popular with the Blackfoot tribe included blue, "greasy" yellow, "Cheyenne" pink, green, and rose. Seed beads were often Italian and were a good glass with soft subtle colors. New beads, however, came with each shipment, and we see Venetian glass beads, Russian cobalt, and Czechoslovakian as well.

The geometric beadwork of the Blackfoot consists of large figures made up of other smaller ones (i.e., squares, triangles, rectangles). Common designs such as the "feather design" and "mountain design" are used, but there are no tribal meanings to the designs a beadmaker invents.

Some trade beads may have reached the Blackfoot as early as the beginning of the 1700s through trade with other tribes who had direct contact with merchants. The pony beads, however, were being widely used on Blackfoot garments beginning around 1830. The most common color combination was white and sky blue. Beads were used to trade for a good buffalo robe or horse—eight shanks being the equivalent of a buffalo robe in 1870.

During the 1870s, when seed beads were introduced, Blackfoot beadworkers turned to the style of beadwork most common today. Once the smaller beads were available, whole articles were beaded, instead of just the edges, and flower and leaf designs became popular.

Though beading is considered a native American art, it would never have begun if the Indian had not traded with the white man.

WAMPUM

Along the East Coast, North American Indians called their beads "wampum" and made them from quahog shells (hard shell clams). Their color arrangement on a string was used to send messages between tribes, and, when woven into belts, wampum was used in ratifying treaties. Wampum was used as a form of money until 1792 when the United States government brought silver dollars, coins, and ten dollar gold pieces into use.

CLOTHING OF THE VARIOUS TRIBES

Algonquin (Northeast)

This Northeast tribe cut and used rabbit skins for capes, mantles, and other garments, and used beaver pelts for robes and fur hats. Shirts were made by taking two skins of approximately the same size and shape and piecing them together. Leggings were made from single-folded and trimmed skins.

Apache (Southwest)

A young Apache girl wore a two-piece, white buckskin, beadwork-decorated dress during her "coming out" ceremony. (For further information see "Plains Tribes".)

Athapaskans (Northwest)

This tribe habitually used beaver pelts for hats and robes. They also made a unique kind of trouser which was attached, in one piece, to their moccasins. During the winter, these warm pants/moccasins worked well with snowshoes, which the Athapaskans found useful when tracking their prey through deep snow drifts.

Blackfoot (Plains)

The Blackfoot women of the 1910–20s era wore long trade-cloth dresses with bands of different colors (perhaps ribbons) around the bottom. Often the blouse part was decorated with quillwork and/or beading. Children generally dressed in miniature versions of what the adults wore, including the fancier headdresses and buckskin outfits. Women's buckskin dresses decorated with shells and fanciful beadwork were used for special occasions/ceremonies only, and often lasted a lifetime. Usually the women would be buried in this clothing. Wrinkled clothing was worn by the women as a sign of grief when someone close to them had died. They would also hack off their hair or leave it unbraided, gash their arms and legs or, if the one who died had been deeply loved, cut off one of their fingers.

Blackfoot clothing generally was made of white hides, and the designs followed basic patterns which were easy to recognize by members of the other tribes.

Robes were the Indians' replacement for outer clothing (i.e., jackets or coats) and, for most men, were indispensable as they often wore only a breechcloth and moccasins underneath. Buffalo or elk robes were decorated with stripes, which were either painted, quilled, or beaded. These robes were reserved for special occasions. Men would decorate their clothing with symbols of their war triumphs or religious strengths.

Though blankets were given to the Indians (Pendleton and Hudson Bay) by the government or were traded to the Indians in exchange for the Indians' arts and crafts (i.e., beadwork, quillwork, basketry, or jewelry) after the 1920s and were used for clothing, the elk-hide robes were still used during that period and are still worn by holy women during the Sun Dance ceremony.

Summer and winter clothes were basically the same styles, either elongated to cover more of the body or worn in layers to add extra warmth during the winter. Hides, heavy and often not conducive to easy washing, were readily exchanged for the wool trade cloth of the early settlers and traders. Though the wool was just as heavy and warm as the hides, it washed easier. Indian women began to wear calico print blouses under their cotton dresses once trade-cloth dresses became popular. They also wore something on their heads and became quite fond of peasant-style scarves.

The Blackfoot made two different styles of moccasins. The oldest (the "real moccasin," according to Blackfoot language) was soft, but wore out quickly and was hard to repair. It was constructed from a single soft hide which was folded in half, then sewn. "Extras," like tongues and ankle flaps, would be added separately. Two-piece moccasin construction began in the early 1900s. The bottom of this moccasin was made separately, then sewn to the sides. The bottom, therefore, could be easily replaced or patched when it was worn. For winter, the moccasins would be made of shearling sheep hide instead of the usual buckskin.

If a woman was adept at making moccasins, she was also wise to keep a set of foot patterns for all of the people for whom she had made moccasins in the past. Though the old women always used sinew to sew up moccasins, some of the modern makers use thread or "imitation sinew."

A notable characteristic of a Blackfoot moccasin is the small fringed trailer which sticks out from the moccasin's heel. Also, red wool was usually sewn into the seam between moccasins and high ankle flaps. The majority of Blackfoot moccasins are decorated with small designs between the toe and instep. Few have been found that are fully covered with quillwork and beadwork. These forms of decoration are more often found on moccasins made by other tribes.

Some Blackfoot moccasin designs are sketched below:

"Crooked Nose"

"Round"

"Striped"

"Three Finger Beadwork"
(most definitely Blackfoot design)

"Basic Floral Design"

The common and traditional style of Blackfoot women's dresses began to be seen around 1800 and were also worn by neighboring tribes. The style for today's Indian women (who may wear such a dress to special occasions) has a cape sewn to the main body, whereas the traditional style resembled a slip and did not cover the arms and shoulders.

The bottoms of dresses made out of hides are wavy because the hides were left in their natural shape. The skins that were made into dresses were sewn with the flesh side out, making it easier to apply beadwork designs. If the skin from which the dress was made was deerskin, the tail was often used as decoration to hang down the center of the chest.

Characteristics of Blackfoot dresses include: (1) a curve in the beaded breastband that mimics the shape of a deer's back end; (2) a triangular symbol on the lower front of the dress, symbolizing womanhood; and (3) two more symbols on the lower part of the dress which are said to represent kidneys.

Pony beads were used in early beadwork. These beads are what some call "real beads." Two colors of beads were normally used for the breastband and dark and light colors were combined for contrast. Though geometric sections were used to break up the colored stripes, as a rule no other designs were used. Shoulder bands, however, were decorated with smaller beads, new colors, and designs.

Red, black, and blue trade cloth was often used as patches on the bottom of most dresses, with one color backing the other. These pieces of trade cloth were also trimmed with beads.

Before the introduction of trade beads to the Indian culture, quillwork was the form of decoration used (see Leather chapter for further information). Dresses made of red or blue trade wool were known to ravel, so the white edge of the cloth was often used for the bottom edge. Again, that edge would be decorated with beadwork.

Another style of beadwork was to alternate the rows of beads with cowrie shells or elk's teeth. This particular style was popular during the

Victorian Age and through the 1920s. "Basket beads" (large, tubular beads) were used with this kind of beadwork. Full, colorful skirts trimmed with rows of bright ribbons completed the dress.

The induction of trade cloth and cotton changed the Blackfoot way of life considerably, and even the style of women's clothing began to look different. Capes became popular and were used over calico dresses, and some dresses were even made from velvet.

Cheyenne and Arapaho (Plains)

Clothing made by these two tribes was characterized by a long fringe of buckskin trimming the majority of their garments.

Crow (Plains)

In the Crow tribe, women's dresses were made of red wool trade cloth (red was of the highest value). They were often decorated with many elk teeth, which some Indians called "the diamonds of our ancestors."

Eastern Tribes

The tribes in the Eastern part of the United States wore robes of animal skins which were sewn together and fringed. If the hair was left on, they were considered to be the finest of robes. These pieces were decorated according to the maker's individuality.

Summer clothing was often woven from natural grasses and light barks. The robes and mats woven were not rough, as we would imagine them to be, but sweet-smelling and light enough to be worn on hot summer nights. Unfortunately, few have endured the test of time and are not truly collectible because of their rarity.

Eastern Woodland

Moccasins worn by Eastern Woodland tribes were usually decorated single pieces of leather, the cuffs of which were often added later.

Erie and Susquehannock (Lakes Area)

These two tribes wore animal heads, such as panthers and bears, as hats.

Forest Tribes (Northwest)

Skirts made by some of the Forest tribes were of a single skin, wrapped around the waist, and secured with a belt. Though simple, these skirts were often tailored, decorated, and fringed and were beautiful garments.

Shirts worn by the women of these tribes were shorter than the ones that men wore and were poncho-shaped. Short leggings worn by these women came just above the knee and their moccasins were cut differently than the men's. Belts and sashes were worn to support or tailor their clothing as well as to decorate it.

Hidatsa

The Hidatsa tribe favored many brilliant shades in their quillwork which is also known for its distinctive plaiting. Examples of this type of quillwork can be seen at the American Museum of Natural History's Department of Anthropology.

At turn of the century powwows, a Hidatsa headress would often be made from a gray felt cap decorated with beads, ribbon, ermine strips, feathers (dyed to suit the maker), a bison horn, horsehair, and a red tail decorated with eagle feathers. A beautiful bonnet was not necessarily the mark of an honorable man; however, the man who wore such a bonnet in battle had to be brave because his enemy would want to kill him just to win the bonnet!

After 1885, the Hidatsa tribe underwent some changes and became, in many respects, pretty modernized. Clothes were made of calico and wool. Quilts made from cotton replaced painted buffalo robes. They made their beadwork for the tourist trade and their style was the same as other Plains and Woodland tribes. Though the Hidatsa were being pressured by European life, however, they held tightly to their identity.

Hupa (Southwest)

Hupa women wore basketry skull caps (see Basket chapter for further information).

Iroquois (Northeast)

The Iroquois, who lived in the Northeast and endured harsh winters, wore peaked fur caps to keep their heads warm.

Iroquois (Northeast) and Pueblo (Southwest)

The men of these two tribes, though not close in miles, wore kilts. Iroquois kilts were made of doeskin, while Pueblo kilts were of woven fabric.

Kutchin (Northwest)

The Kutchin Indians of western Alaska made finely tanned caribou outfits. The skirts hang below the knees and are v-shaped, decorated with beadwork, and fringed. The trousers are attached to moccasins, even on summer outfits.

Lenape or Delaware (Northeast)

These tribes wore robes made of bark or hemp fibers. Feathers would be twisted into the robe to completely cover the outside and the weaving was done in such a way that the feathers lay flat.

Mandan (Plains)

In the Mandan society, only the men who had won honor marks were permitted to paint such marks on their clothing and other objects.

Menomini and Omaha (Plains)

These two tribes were known to wear turbans as headgear.

Naskapi (Plains)

The Naskapi Indians removed the hair from caribou skins, then painted complex designs on them.

Navajo and Pueblo (Southwest)

The men's moccasins made by these tribes are ankle height and can be tied or strapped, but women's moccasins are white and have a wide strip that is wound around the leg until it reaches the knee.

Women's clothing usually consists of mid-calf velvet skirts in deep burgundy colors, and they wear loose, peasant-type blouses with them.

The Southwestern Indians' dress is always accented by wonderful turquoise and silver jewelry. Squash blossom necklaces are worn by both sexes, as are concha belts and bracelets (for more information, see Jewelry chapter).

Northeast

In the Northeast, the northern Plains and Lakes areas, women's dresses resembled jumpers and were made with separate sleeves. This style lasted until the jumper was replaced by skirts and blouses.

Northwest Coast

Hats worn by Indians of the Northwest Coast tribes are often made of finely woven basketry materials. Their conical forms appear to be similar to hats worn by immigrant Chinese workers in the late 1700s. These hats are often painted with decorations or decorations can be woven into the hat during the making. Sometimes the hats are used to display lineage emblems. Cedar bark, spruce root, and grass were used to make these basketry hats.

The tribes of the Northwest Coast made their own cloth, often out of mountain goat wool, for their garments. These garments were decorated in much the same way as their blankets, with stylized figures of humans, birds, and animals, and were extremely complicated in design, though warm and soft to the touch. Animal skins were used as clothing during the long, extremely cold winters, and often boots or footgear would be tempered with the oil from seals or whales in order to make them warmer and waterproof.

Omaha (South Central U.S.) and Osage (Plains)

The Omaha and Osage tribes wore otter fur hats that were brimless. These hats would be decorated with quill and beadwork, shells, large beads, and jinglers, and sometimes the backs of the hats would have streamers or feathers.

Osage wedding hats looked like bowlers and were gaily decorated in feathers. Their favorite colors appeared to be red, white, and blue, maybe influenced by the colors of the American flag.

Plains Tribes

The Plains tribes are know to be the ones who initiated the clothing worn during the Ghost Dance period during the 1890s, at the peak of their frustration with the white man. Created by Wovoka or "The Cutter," son of Tavibo, the Prophet, the Ghost Dance religion promised the Indians their Messiah.

Though painted clothing was fairly common among the Plains Indians, clothing made during the Ghost Dance period was distinctive in that it was decorated with supernatural designs that were painted in unusual colors. This type of clothing is highly collectible and usually very expensive. Once you see and feel Ghost Dance clothing you will automatically know it the next time you have the opportunity to study it. The feeling it conveys grabs a person and pulls him into the design and the significance of what was happening at that time in Indian history.

Normally, however, skirts worn by Plains women were shaped like short-sleeved nightgowns and they were combined with a waist. Plains, Prairie, Eastern Apache, and some Basin and Plateau tribeswomen wore skin dresses of a very simple design. Two elk hides would be needed for a woman's dress and would be attached at the shoulders by a yoke. The natural curve of the hide would form the uneven, graceful hem of the dress and, more often than not, the animal's tail would remain on the hide and would act as natural decoration for the dress.

Because most Plains warriors went naked to the waist or wore robes, shirts were worn only for ceremonies or special occasions. Older shirts are like ponchos with open sides. Decorations on warrior's shirts included beading, quillwork, tassels or fringe, painting, and hair or ermine.

Both male and female Plains Indians wore leggings, though the female version only came to the knee while the male version extended to the hip. The leggings, plain or decorated, were basic tubes made out of buckskin and slid over the legs like pants, but without the waist and crotch. The leggings were attached to the owner's belt.

Plains moccasins were one piece, soft soled, and held on by a drawstring. Decoration included beading on the toe and painting—sometimes even a combination of both—and quillwork.

Pueblo (Southwest)

Clothing worn by women of the Pueblo tribes has undergone some changes. Dresses, traditionally black with a black- or brown-woven, diagonal twill center, were embroidered in blue by the Zuni and in red by the Acomas and other Pueblos. An apron, gingham underdress and shawl were combined with the plain, one-shouldered black dress, and, for fiesta, a manta was hung from the shoulders by ornate silver pins. Maiden's shawls and buckskin leggings were worn by unmarried women and their hair was done in the "butterfly" style.

The Hopi wedding robe is a plain, white, cotton weave whitened with chalk and is the largest cotton fabric woven by the Hopis. It is woven by the groom's male relatives and worn by the bride. A reed case is made to carry the bride's wedding sash and other garments. The case has long tassels (symbols of fertility) which hang from the corners. After the wedding, the robe is embroidered with colorful yarn and is used during major Hopi ceremonies. The needlework is done by men and usually utilizes traditional symbols such as rain clouds, butterflies, and birds.

Salish (Northwest)

The Salish tribe wear tall, fancy sombrero-type hats. At each potlatch (a feast in which the giver of the feast gives away most of his/her property), the wearer of such a hat receives a ringed constriction on its peak. The number of rings the wearer has on his hat indicates his generosity.

Seminole (Southeast)

Seminole men's clothing consisted of turban, breechcloth, calico shirt, and neckerchief. When visiting town, the Seminole would add some brooches, pantaloons or leggings, watch chains, and safety pins to their normal attire (though few Seminoles actually owned watches).

Women wore cotton or calico skirts and long shirts, which left a portion of their waists bare. Calico patches of different colors were sewn on as ornamentation and no moccasins were worn. They wore a great many necklaces made of beads and silver around their necks.

This tribe does not use beadwork on their clothing as other tribes do, but instead weave the beads into belts, fobs, and garters.

CLOTHING LISTINGS

Apache

Cape; woman's hide cape, fringed and scalloped around the bottom w/row of coiled red, white, and blue beads around the edges; the neck opening is surrounded by a large circle of tin cones in a double row; also, a smaller circle of brass medallions and of blue and white seed beads in rope pattern; across the bottom is a row of tin cones and a row of large medal medallions.   **$750–$1000**

Dress; two-piece woman's dress w/ribbon work and bells; ca. 1930.
$75–$100

Fringed hide and trade cloth shirt and leggings; a red fringed cotton shirt w/ribbon trim and pair of trade cloth applique-decorated leggings.
$50–$100

Hat band; braided leather band w/bead and horsehair decoration; ca. 1985; 32".   **$35–$70**

Moccasins; hide soles and toe guard, tall yellow muslin tops; ca. 1890; 32" × 6½".   **$60–$100**

Arapaho

Moccasins; classic full beaded moccasins w/buffalo hide soles and sinew sewn; ca. 1880; 11" × 4".   **$600–$800**

Moccasins; three pair, each w/bead stitched uppers, all sinew sewn, all with hard soles; 10", 10¼", and 10¼"; inside one pair: "Made by Arapaho Indians at Ethete, Wyoming—1935".   **$175–$275**

Assinoboin

Dress; unusual green velvet dress w/brass snap and bead decoration; ca. 1900; 52" × 49".   **$500–$700**

Dress; large trade-cloth dress w/full basket beaded top; ca. 1900; 50" × 48".   **$650–$850**

Athabascan

Boots; high-top moosehide moccasins w/beaded toe; fur and red cloth trim; ca. 1975; 16" × 9".   **$70–$100**

Chief's coat; soft tanned buckskin jacket w/fringe and floral beadwork on shoulders and front; 26" × 22"; ca. 1900.   **$250–$500**

Coat; rare hide chief's coat w/beaded floral designs and w/fringe; 29" × 19"; ca. 1890.   **$225–$275**

Moccasins; large moosehide moccasins w/fur trim; flag and eagle beaded on felt toe; 11" × 4"; ca. 1935.   **$40–$80**

Moccasins; rare, large, plaited birch bark moccasins; ca. 1910; 10½" × 4".   **$45–$70**

Moccasins; buckskin moccasins w/floral beaded toes and fur trim; ca. 1920; 9" × 5".   **$40–$75**

Moccasins; large, moosehide puckered-toe moccasins w/floral beadwork on toes; ca. 1910; 10½" × 3".   **$35–$50**

Mukluks; moosehide moccasins w/seal fur and wolf trim; ca. 1920; 9" × 3½".   **$40–$80**

Belts

Five full-beaded leather belts w/loomstrung beadwork. **$50–$75**

Loomstrung w/red, yellow, and blue designs on white; 1½″ × 36″; plus
1½″ × 32″ belt w/same colors. **$10–$15**

Blackfoot

Leggings; trade-cloth leggings w/colorful beaded strip; 36″ × 18″;
ca. 1940. **$125–$175**

Moccasins; beaded hide; beaded tops and heels; red and blue trade stroud
cloth around on the cutwork cuffs; bead colors: greasy yellow, turquoise,
sky blue, pink, black, and white; 10¼″ long. **$800–$900**

Cheyenne

From the William R. Nash Collection. Photo by Donald Vogt.

Leggings; blue trade-cloth leggings, edged w/red silk; a beaded panel
featuring crosses and diamonds extends from top to bottom; the outside
edges contain tin cones w/locks of human hair; ca. 1890. **$600–$800**

Moccasins; child's moccasins w/geometric beadwork; 7″ × 3″;
ca. 1880. **$100–$125**

Moccasins; full beaded, sinew-sewn, hard-sole moccasins w/geometric
designs; ca. 1920; 10″ × 4″. **$130–$150**

Moccasins; full beaded, hard-sole moccasins w/geometric designs;
ca. 1940; 10″ × 4″. **$140–$160**

Moccasins; hide moccasins w/rawhide soles and full beaded uppers in geometric designs; ca. 1900; 10″ × 4″. **$160–$200**

Moccasins; contemporary beaded moccasins; ca. late 1970s. **$350–$450**

Dress

Great Lakes; beaded and sequined, possibly Winnebago; aqua trim on dark blue background decorated w/red beads and red, copper, and black sequins; ca. 1930–40s. **$200–$325**

Large beaded and fringed deerskin dress; beadwork around neck and sleeves; fair condition. **$90–$125**

Warm Springs; girl's buckskin dress w/fully beaded black, white, and orange geometric yoke; ca. 1940; 38″ × 34″. **$350–$500**

Comanche; beaded and fringed hide man's leggings; they are edged w/rows of metal studs and beads; ca. turn of the century; descended through family. **$6250–$8500**

Men's full-length, beaded buckskin leggings; ca. 1940; large. **$50–$80**

Kiowa

From the collection of David Atteberry. Photo by Donald Vogt.

Leggings; red trade-cloth lining; red, green, and white beading down the side of the leg; ca. 1880–1900. **$1000–$1200**

Shirt; fringed buckskin shirt w/many painted Ghost Dance symbols; ca. 1890; 42″ × 18″. **$675–$800**

Leggings

Blue trade cloth decorated w/ribbons and a beaded breechclout; the clout is badly damaged by moths, but the beaded areas are intact. **$65–$85**

Child's; beaded deerskin; 4″ wide band of red, blue, green, and pink geometric designs on white field; sinew sewn. **$70–$100**

Moccasins

Iroquois; choice pair of beaded child's moccasins w/fine pony beaded designs; ca. 1880; 5½″ × 3″. **$90–$120**

Kootenai; high-top buckskin moccasins w/geometric beaded designs; ca. 1935; 9″ × 4″ × 9″. **$45–$75**

Large; trimmed w/narrow beaded panels; orange, blue, green, black, and white designs; good condition. **$30–$50**

Ojibway; soft buckskin moccasins w/rows of beaded decoration; ca. 1940; 8″ × 3½″. **$40–$80**

Pair of deerskin, 1″ × 4″ beaded panels on instep; green, orange, blue, red, and white design; good condition. **$45–$75**

Plains Cree; choice, hard-sole, white buckskin moccasins with multicolored floral beadwork; ca. 1890; 10½″ × 4″. **$175–$225**

Courtesy of Jack Sellner, CAI.

Pueblo; ocher-dyed, coin-button, high-top moccasins; 16″ high w/six Washington quarter buttons. **$150–$250**

Roughly tanned, rawhide looking; red, white, and blue beaded design.
$20–$40

Santee Sioux; ladies soft buckskin moccasins w/hard sole and floral bead-work; ca. 1890; 9″ × 3½″. **$125–$175**

Sinew sewn w/multicolored beadwork borders and toe designs; good condition.
$45–$70

Tlingit; sealskin low-top moccasins w/beaded geometric designs on the toe; 10″ × 4″; ca. 1935. **$40–$75**

Navajo

Blouse; squaw's traditional "plush" in rust color, decorated w/25 fluted, round, and repousse butterfly ornaments. **$100–$150**

Courtesy of Robert W. Skinner, Inc., Bolton, MA.

Dress; women's; one panel, finely woven w/dark brownish-black center flanked by two rows of stepped terrace and linear designs in indigo blue against red panels; fine narrow stripes in green; cotton warp; 45″ × 33″. **$1000–$1200**

Man's rug vest; rust, aqua, black, gold, and gray in serrated diamond designs. **$75–$125**

Sash; handmade orange, white, and pink sash; often used in birthing.
$30–$40

Sash; small handwoven child's sash belt; ca. 1940; 31″ × 1½″.
$10–$15

Nez Perce

Beaded hide baby moccasins; 4¼″ long; sinew sewn and decorated w/cobalt blue, lavender, red w/white centers, and white beads in a narrow "T" design; ca. 1900; mint condition. **$45–$100**

Gauntlets; high-top buckskin gloves w/bow and arrow beaded on them; ca. 1935; 11″ × 7″. **$45–$80**

Moccasins; soft sole, full beaded moccasins w/geometric designs; ca. 1900; 10″ × 4″. **$150–$200**

Vest; buckskin vest w/classic multicolored floral beaded designs; ca. 1920; large. **$350–$500**

Vest; full beaded "Dreamer Society" contour beaded vest w/floral designs; ca. 1900. **$800–$1000**

Northern Plains

Beaded hide child's moccasins; 4¾″; fully decorated across the vamp, toe, sides, and around back w/cobalt blue, chili red, clear red, yellow, and white beads; mint condition. **$70–$95**

Beaded cloth vest; decorated w/cobalt blue, sky blue, red, clear green, and faceted brass beads; ca. 1900–1930. **$350–$550**

Courtesy of Jack Sellner, CAI.

Moccasins; fully beaded hide moccasins; 9″ long; decorated w/clear red, lime, cobalt blue, orange, sky blue, chili red, metallic, and white beads; excellent condition. **$285–$385**

Osage

Courtesy of Morning Star Gallery, Santa Fe, NM. Photo by Donald Vogt.

Leggings; women's leggings; ca. 1900; (04651).   **$750–$850**

Shirt; ribbon-work shirt in mint green, pink, and purple panels; ca. 1860; made of Chinese silk; construction technique is reverse applique.   **$4000–$5000**

Courtesy of Morning Star Gallery, Santa Fe, NM. Photo by Donald Vogt.

Wedding hat; woman's wedding hat; ca. 1920; set w/coat; (04250 and 04251).   **$1200–$1500**

Plains

Dress; beaded and fringed hide girl's dress, w/translucent blue beaded yolk containing crosses and triangle motifs in white, dark blue, bright green, translucent red, and faceted silver, and white beaded panels containing rows of crosses in similar colors; tiny beaded rectangles on the skirt; large glass beads on the fringe; 38″ long.   **$4500–$5000**

Moccasins; beaded.   **$55–$85**

Moccasins; rare old Southern Plains beaded hide moccasins; 10″ long; sinew sewn, decorated w/cobalt blue, lavender, waxy yellow, pony trader blue, green, black, white, and clear red beads; excellent–near mint condition.   **$400–$600**

Moccasins; beaded hide moccasins, hard soled w/triangles in light and dark blue and translucent red against similar grounds; translucent, green beaded panels on the fronts and ankles; 10″ long.   **$600–$800**

From the William R. Nash Collection. Photo by Donald Vogt.

Moccasins; three pairs beaded hide moccasins, w/geometric devices; one pair each for child, youth, and adult; provenance: Cephas Buttes, Dakota Territory, 1885.   **$750–$850**

From the William R. Nash Collection. Photo by Donald Vogt.

Moccasins; beaded hide moccasins; hard soled; decorated w/thunderbirds in yellow, blue, and translucent red against white beaded ground; 10″ long. **$600–$800**

Pouch; beaded. **$45–$95**

Pouch; small; beaded; with geometric decoration. **$45–$100**

Pueblo

Sash; 2½″ × 51½″ long (incl. fringe); red, white, and green colors in geometric designs. **$20–$40**

Sash; colorful handwoven sash belt w/fringe; ca. 1950; 50″ × 4″.

$25–$50

Shawl; woven wool manta; 39″ × 56″; black with ties and tassels; type used in Pueblo Indian ceremonies by Kachinas, dancers, and women. **$100–$195**

Seminole

Dress; cape dress w/wedding collar and earrings (cape is black, jewelry is black and red). **$50–$100**

From the collection of Lahoma Haddock Goldsmith. Photo by Donald Vogt.

Life jacket; contemporary life jacket made of Seminole patchwork with no seams; paired w/old Seminole earrings and necklace made of bone, brass, and old cut glass.   **$300–$500 ea.**

Sioux

Cape; child's cape in black velvet w/beaded eagle and cowrie shell trim; ca. 1910; 18″ × 13″.   **$35–$70**

Girl's boots; decorated w/fine beadwork and brass spots; 14″; designs in red, blue, greasy yellow, and white; sinew sewn, good condition.
                     $100–$150

Leggings; each beaded w/geometric patterns against a white ground; bead colors: apple green, bright blue, and white heart reds; sinew sewn; 18″ long.   **$550–$700**

Leggings; large, beaded, buffalo-hide women's leggings w/classic beaded geometric designs; ca. 1880; 18″ × 7″.   **$650–$900**

Courtesy of Canfield Gallery, Santa Fe, NM. Photo by Donald Vogt.

Moccasins; beaded hide; 9″ long; green back; figured white bands w/red, blue, yellow, and black accents; ca. 1890. **$600–$900**

Moccasins; fine, old, full-beaded, sinew-sewn, hard-sole moccasins; ca. 1890; 11″ × 4″. **$190–$225**

Moccasins; pair of full beaded; green, white, red, and blue on white; sinew sewn. **$65–$95**

Moccasins; old buffalo hide moccasins w/geometric designs on the toes; ca. 1880; 9″ × 3½″. **$75–$140**

Old beaded, quilled and fringed hide pipe bag; 36½″ long (including fringe) × 11″ wide decorated on both sides w/dark blue, green, waxy yellow and red w/white center beads and red, purple, and gray-green quillwork; ca. 1900. **$1000–$1500.**

Shirt; fringed and painted muslin shirt, used for Ghost Dance; decorated on one side w/sun and star, a spreadwinged eagle w/lightning bolts surmounted by a sun, star, and crescent moon on the reverse; feather suspensions; 36½″ long. **$1500–$1750**

From the William R. Nash Collection. Photo by Donald Vogt.

Shirt; beaded and fringed hide shirt, stitched across the shoulders and along the arms w/white beaded panels of diamond and arrowfeather motifs alternating w/rectangles in yellow, bright green, pale orange, shades of blue, and translucent red; a triangular bib on the front and back, each beaded in similar colors; 31⅓″.   **$4000–$4500**

From the William R. Nash Collection. Photo by Donald Vogt.

Vest; beaded hide man's vest; lined w/blue and white cotton cloth and trimmed along the edges in maroon silk (?); the front stitched in yellow, bright green, dark blue, and translucent red and blue against a white beaded ground w/two stylized dragonflies (?) and angular devices, a tracked line surmounted by similar devices on the back; 18¼″.

$1200–$1500

Southern Plains

Moccasins; each hard-soled, beaded on the front and sides w/tapering column between rows of parallelograms and diamonds in white, pink, dark blue, and translucent red, yellow, and green against a cobalt blue ground; decorated w/rectangular ankle flaps, each w/red trade cloth and beaded trim; thick panels of hide fringe on the heels; ochre pigment; 10½″.   **$1200–$1500**

From the William R. Nash Collection. Photo by Donald Vogt.

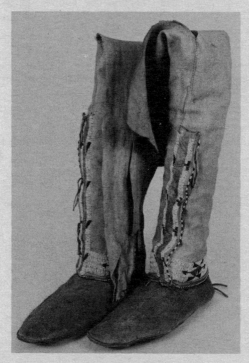

Moccasins; boot moccasins w/yellow and red pigment and white beaded panels of blue and translucent red geometric motifs around the ankles and up the calves; provenance: Cephas Buttes, Dakota Territory, 1885.   **$600–$800**

Painted buffalo robe; native tanned hide decorated w/"black bonnet" or "feathered circle" design in black and red; central decoration of four circles encompassed by wavy line; native sinew sewn repair; 92″ long, 67″ wide.   **$800–$1200**

Woodland

Courtesy of Jack Sellner, CAI.

Moccasins; beaded hide moccasins, 8½" long × 9½" high; decorated w/dark red, lime, blue, faceted clear purple, and white beads; excellent condition. **$165–$245**

Purse; small, bead trimmed, blue cloth; 3½". **$10–$15**

Sash; beaded, cross and geometric motif. **$65–$100**

Yakima

Leggings; pair of beaded cloth child's leggings w/geometric designs; ca. 1940; 11" × 8". **$45–$70**

Moccasins; soft-sole, beaded hide moccasins w/colorful geometrics; ca. 1930; 9" × 4". **$95–$125**

Purse; fully beaded w/floral designs and with a metal top and latch; ca. 1925; 10" × 6½". **$175–$200**

Other

Arm bands; porcupine quilled and feather decorated hide armbands; 16½" long; decorated w/red, yellow, purple, gray, and white quillwork; ca. 1900. **$200–$250**

Blouse; ladies sleeveless deerskin; fringed, beaded, and embroidered; embroidered silk flowers accented w/beadwork scrolls; long fringe at shoulders (10"); fringe down sides and at hem; very good condition. **$110–$175**

Boots; little girls' beaded doeskin; geometric designs in orange, blue, yellow, and red on white panels; white and orange border design around sole edges; row of brass spots up outside of leg; 15″ fringed top; old but not worn. **$170–$210**

Chimayo, jacket; wool; ladies; 28½″ long w/red, gray, black, white, and aqua colors; has double pockets and three buttons. **$25–$50**

Chippewa, bandolier bag; beaded; green, blue, and red flower designs on white beadwork field; trimmed w/black satin; sewn on old feed sack material; much of beadwork fringe missing. **$50–$75**

Choctaw, sash; beaded of typical white/beaded scroll design on brick-colored stroud cloth; blue-black braided wool accents; minor bead and wool loss. **$1100–$1500**

Flathead, beaded cloth and hide fringed vest; 27″ long (incl. fringe); decorated w/faceted clear dark red, yellow, clear green, iridescent, chili red, and clear beads in large floral and foliate designs on a white beaded background; ca. 1920s–30s. **$350–$500**

Haida, apron; cloth apron decorated w/miniature coppers and shells; 34″ × 22″; ca. 1930. **$125–$200**

Hat band; wide geometric design loom-beaded hat band; ca. 1980; 14″ × 2″. **$30–$50**

Headband; beaded; red and white on green. **$30–$40**

Courtesy of Canfield Gallery, Santa Fe, NM. Photo by Donald Vogt.

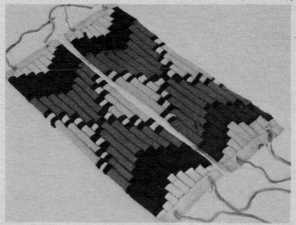

Hopi, armbands; ca. 1940; constructed of yarn-wrapped pieces in red, yellow, and green, trimmed in black. **$200–$300**

Jacket and trousers; tassel trim; bronze buttons decorated with assorted wildlife.   **$440-$500**

Klamath, twined basketry hat; 4³/₄″ × 7¹/₂″ diameter; in dark brown and mottled brown colors; ca. 1900–1925.   **$125-$225**

Miscellaneous Indian beadwork; incl. 1¹/₂″ × 30″ beaded loomstrung belt w/red, yellow, and blue geometric designs on white; 1¹/₂″ × 24″ beaded belt w/orange, black, red, blue, and yellow thunderbird design on white.   **$10-$15**

Modoc, cap; rare twined woman's cap w/purple and green diamond designs; ca. 1880; 7¹/₂″ × 4″.   **$115-$130**

Northwest Coast, headdress; polychrome; 20th century; in the form of an elongated wolf's head w/hinged lower jaw, flaring nostrils, abalone inlaid eyes and snout, horsehair tufting on ears, applied bone teeth, tacked copper strips forming eyebrows; paint colors: black, red, and turquoise.   **$900-$1200**

Pants; man's buckskin; fringed and beaded; floral beadwork designs of green, brown, blue, pink, yellow, and white; button fly; good condition.   **$160-$200**

Plateau, beaded hide gauntlets; 13″ long elk/moose; decorated w/sky blue, lavender, faceted black, brass metallic cut, clear lime, clear gray, and light blue beads in floral and foliate designs; ca. 1920–1930.

$110-$150

Shawl, Pendleton; double-faced and fringed; ca. 1965; 64″ × 44″.

$45-$70

Snowshoes; child/youth; 36¹/₂″ long and 11″ wide with high strung webbing, leather foot straps and tufts of red bayeta/Germantown yarn along the sides; the name Irene Farnham is carved into the tail of each.

$65-$105

DOLLS, GAMES, AND SPORTS

▼▼▼▼▼▼▼▼▼▼▼

INTRODUCTION

Every culture has its share of recreational activities and the Indians were no slouches when it came to thinking of ways to fill their leisure time. Before the Europeans even set foot on this continent, the Indians had invented enough games to fill a decent-sized reference book, and each tribe had its own version of certain games.

They were responsible for some of the sports that are so vital to week-end activities in today's American families—football, for instance, and lacrosse. Even the "yuppie" game of racquet ball has its origins in Indian history.

Their dolls are among the finest and most imaginative created. They used the tools available to them, but never shirked the opportunity to decorate the most miniature of toys or dolls.

If you, as a collector, have chosen to collect strictly Indian dolls, toys, and games, you have a wide and interesting field from which to choose. Above all else, you should have a wonderful time adding to your collection.

DOLLS

Hopi (Southwest)

The Hopi artisans have contributed quite a bit to the field of Indian collectibles, but perhaps their most noted contribution is that of Hopi Kachina dolls.

The Kachina cult is probably the most important part of the Hopi religion and has received more attention than the religions of other Pueblo cultures. The Hopis believe it is extremely important to preserve harmony with the world and nature, and the Kachinas provide the Hopi guidance to seek this peaceful way of life. Because of their holy place in Hopi society, Kachinas may never be photographed. In fact, most Hopi villages maintain their privacy by forbidding the use of cameras, tape recorders, and sketching.

Kachinas are benevolent Hopi spirits which are said to exist in the

San Francisco Peaks. It is told that they rehearse in those peaks and prepare themselves for their main function: the making of snow or rain.

The Kachinas are extremely important to Hopi society, thus the San Francisco Peaks are considered sacred. When developers built a ski lift several hundred feet below a sacred site in these peaks, the Hopis objected strenuously and their Navajo neighbors, to whom the peaks are also sacred, joined them in their protestations. However, another permit to build a ski lodge and another lift was granted, and it has seriously endangered the religion the Hopis practice.

The Kachinas traditionally begin to appear in villages after the winter solstice and join with the men there to dance in the kiva and pray for the new year. Until late July, the Kachinas dance in one of the twelve Hopi villages until the villages host Niman ceremonies (home dances) for the Kachinas to return to their homes in the mountains. This dance is the time when Hopi brides, dressed in white cotton robes traditionally woven by their husbands' uncles, are presented to the Kachinas.

During the planting season, gifts of Kachinas are given and the distributors of these gifts are able to select whatever Kachina they desire to be, and also to name their successor for the next year.

The young children are given the dolls, which have been made by their male relatives, and are allowed to play with them in the ensuing days. Most Hopi children have no toys other than those they receive from the Kachinas or make for themselves. Sprouts are wrapped around the Kachinas that are given as gifts for the newborn children, and some sprouts are also left as a gift for the Kachina impersonator who will distribute the gifts.

Hopi children have, apparently, learned a valuable lesson from receiving Kachina dolls as gifts. Because the times when a Hopi child receives presents are few and far between, the number of children who love money or get a thrill from possessing items is low. Instead, they give to those who give to them—mainly by returning good thoughts and behavior.

Kachina initiation for the Hopi children begins around the age of eight. Before their initiation, the children receive close haircuts (the girls having a tuft left in the front). The initiation takes place every fourth February as part of the Powamu ("Bean Dance"). The ceremony introduces the child to his ancestors, the Kachinas, as his birth introduced him to his father, the Sun.

In Third Mesa initiations, the affiliation of the godfather with the Kachinas determines whether or not the child goes through the whipping ordeal (reserved for discipline problems). In this training procedure, the Mother of the Kachinas holds a bunch of yucca switches while the Whipper Kachina applies them to the nude boy or clothed girl, who is supported by his/her godfather and the godfather's sister. The initiation is meant to teach the child the difference between the supernatural and reality, and what their role is in the scheme of things. After the ritual, the boy joins one or more of the secret societies and the girl joins those of her ceremonial aunt.

During the season when the Kachinas take part in the dances and festivals held in the Hopi villages, the Hopis are reacquainted with the approximately 500 Kachinas who exist in their religion. There are approximately 300 currently active Kachinas and another 20 who make infrequent appearances. The Chief Kachinas are the most important and have jurisdiction over other Kachinas, as well as over village life. They appear at every ceremony, and dolls are not usually made in their likeness. The Warriors or Police Kachinas are another important group. It is their job to see that the public does not interfere with the dancers or venture into the wrong area. The Mudhead Kachinas are the clowns of the group. They function to lighten the atmosphere and to tease some of the other more serious Kachinas.

Though Hopi men are traditionally the Kachina carvers, Oraibi women have been known to make Kachinas, thus intruding on what has traditionally been a male occupation. Old Kachinas were carved from cottonwood (ba'ko) and painted with natural colors. They were usually decorated with real feathers and pieces of leather were used as skirts or tops. Fabric was also used to make other accessories.

The Kachinas that are currently being made are extremely beautiful and carved out of a single piece of wood. Instead of being completely painted, as the old ones are, these new Kachinas are only partially painted and there is no other material used to decorate them—they are strictly sculptures made from wood.

Doll dances, once too secret to be discussed, were held by the Hopi and may even continue to be held at Hotevilla. The dolls were worked by strings and would represent corn-grinding Maidens (Gnumamantu), Shalako girl (Shalakmana), or water-drinking girl (Palhikmana). They were worked much the same as puppets.

Some of the Kachinas one might see are as follows:

1) Bear Kachinas have red nakwakwosi ("prayer feathers") placed on their heads because the bear is a warrior and all warriors have red feathers.

2) Eototo appears every year on each of the three mesas. He is the equivalent of the village chief and the "father" of the Kachinas.

3) Aholi appears in the company of Eototo, but only on the Third Mesa during the Powamu ceremony.

4) One of the oldest recorded Kachinas is Kokosori, who is always portrayed by a boy.

5) One of the police or guards who protects the ceremonies is the angry-looking Wuyak-kuita. He is often at the rear of the Bean Dance Procession and his appearance terrifies the clowns.

6) Tsitoto appears on all mesas and is a well-known ancient Kachina. He is a very colorful figure with a brightly colored, bird-like helmet mask. He carries a bunch of yucca leaves and often appears at the Bean Dance.

7) Talavai Kachinas used to wake the people in the village by singing on the rooftops in pairs. They are no longer used.

8) The only masked Kachina who is truly a woman is Pachavuin Mana. She brings bean sprouts into the village during the Pachavu Ceremony.

9) The Eagle Kachina or Kwahu dances during one of the March night ceremonies or during the Powamu. The dancer imitates the eagle as closely as possible.

10) The Buffalo Kachina is always masked and dances for the life and population of the buffalo. He usually holds a lightning stick and rattle.

11) Tawa Kachina or Sun Kachina appears with a spruce tree in his left hand and a bell in his right. He is not often impersonated.

12) The Deer Kachina is very popular in the Plaza Kachina dances. He prays for an increase in the deer population and has power over the rain.

13) One of the best known Kachinas is the Hemis Kachina. He is said to come from the Jemez Pueblo and dances a stately dance in the final dance of the ceremonies.

14) Kokopele is the humpbacked Kachina who plays a flute.

There are hundreds more and everyone has his favorite. There are a few books which list some of the Kachinas and their designated duties, but none which detail each and every one.

Seminole (Southeast)

Seminole dolls are made in all shapes and sizes, though the look of them is generally the same. They are cloth dolls dressed as the Seminole women themselves—in bright-striped, long cotton shirts with matching full blouses, a number of beaded necklaces around the throat, and black felt hats. Dolls are the Seminole's major craft and some are made for decoration, while others are made to be used as doorstops.

Yuma and Mohave (Southwest)

The Yuma and Mohave tribes of the Colorado River designed and decorated pottery dolls for the tourist trade. These dolls were embellished with beads and cloth.

Biographies of Some Known Doll Makers

JOHNSON ANTONIO

Antonio is a Navajo who carves dolls from wood. They are folk art in design and are now becoming collector's items. He began trying his hand at carving dolls in order to make more money to send his children to school. Antonio's carvings capture the Navajo spirit and culture, and are authentic in their clothing and costumes.

His work has been shown at the Wheelwright Museum of the American Indian in a one-man show, and other museums and galleries have also begun to show his work.

CECIL CALNIMPTEWA

A Kachina carver of high regard, Calnimptewa is well known for his true Kachinas, as well as for his understanding of draping materials. Calnimptewa learned his carving from Muriel Navasie and has passed that knowledge on to his own students, such as Dennis Tewa, winner of the 1983 Gallup Inter-Tribal Ceremonial. The artist's innovations have given new nuances of artistic rendering to his Kachina carvings. Calnimptewa has won top awards at ceremonials such as the one in Gallup, NM.

NEIL DAVID, SR.

David is a Hopi from the First Mesa who is also an excellent artist versed in other medias. He belongs to the Artist Hopid, a group of Hopi artists, and may have been the first to convert the painted Kachina into a three-dimensional being. David is prolific and versatile and brings to his figures a feeling of reality which makes them appear truly alive.

WALTER HOWATO

One of the first Kachina carvers to partially paint his figures, Howato entered his Kachina in the Santa Fe Indian Market in the early 1970s.

BRIAN HONYOUTI

Honyouti carved a Crow Mother emerging from the kiva, which is said to be one of the first wood Kachinas only partially painted (Howato did the other).

RONALD HONYOUTI

Ronald, Brian's brother, began carving after Brian, and his Butterfly Girl won Best of Class at the Gallup Inter-Tribal Ceremonial in 1983.

ALVIN JAMES MAKYA

This Kachina artist was born in Old Oraibi and attended high school in Carson City, Nevada, where he learned carpentry. He was in the Marine Corps from 1957–60 and lived as a carpenter after returning home.

Makya studied Peter Shelton's Kachinas and vowed to make Kachinas as good, or better, than those he studied. Makya considered his Kachinas something which "makes my living worthwhile." During the early 1970s, Makya Kachinas were not on the market, but those which had been sold earlier brought four-figure prices.

HENRY SHELTON

Shelton was first persuaded to carve a raw wood Ho-ote about 40 years ago and proceeded to term it "very difficult," but during the mid-1960s, he went on to carve two Snake Dancers and an Eagle Dancer, both of which were eventually cast in bronze. It was his Kachina figures which caused a change in the carving of the beloved dolls.

LOWELL TALASHOMA

A well-known carver, Talashoma creates small traditional dolls in a contemporary style. His carved wooden Kachinas are now being cast in bronze, copies of which Talashoma's agent markets and sells to galleries and collectors.

WILFRED TEWAWINA

Tewawina carved several plain wood Hopi figures during the period from 1965–70.

TYPES OF TOYS

Apache Playing Cards

Though card playing was known to exist as a social custom in other North American tribes, there are no tribes which were known to make playing cards other than the Apaches. No one really knows when the Apache began making playing cards, and it is argued whether the game was introduced to them by white men or by Spanish-Mexican traders. The cards the Apache designed were often named with words of Spanish derivation and their suit terms were identical to the Spanish versions. The Apache playing cards were usually larger than Anglo ones, but they included suits and picture cards as did the Anglo version. A full deck consisted of anywhere from 32 to 52 cards and did not reflect the mathematical parallel which served as the foundation of the playing cards of the white men. The cards averaged 9 cm. × 6.5 cm. in size, and only the faces of the cards were painted and decorated.

The Apache cards were usually made out of rawhide and all decoration was handpainted by the best of their artisans. They were produced in limited quantity, thus increasing their value because of their scarcity. The red color used on the cards was produced by mixing a combination of barks, roots, and ashes, while rabbit brush blossoms made yellow and purple amaranth made purple. Green was from turquoise, and black from yucca juice and charcoal. Brown was derived from walnuts, and cactus juice served as a fixative.

Natural phenomenon, special events, places, and people, as well as items associated with soldiers and pioneers, were symbolized in playing cards. The early round version of cards had suits represented by fish and shells, while others had flowers or coins as symbols.

In the latter part of the 1800s, cards made by the Apache went through an evolution, and the cards began sporting designs such as rifles, swords, and soldiers. The Indian painted what most influenced his life and, at that point, the American soldier was upsetting the normal cycle of Indian life.

The games of chance were played by men, women, and children, with all having an equal chance at losing everything they possessed. Everything that was "bettable" was anted-up in a card game (i.e., money, horses, blankets, etc.). As a result, the Apaches were professional card players and would take on anyone—including soldiers—at the game.

Though the details of actual games played with these cards are vague and basically unknown, it *is* known that the Yavapai and Mohave tribes often used the cards as blame-pointing clues, leaving them scattered on the ground after a holdup or wagon attack, when they wanted the settlers to believe that the Yavapai and Mohave's enemy, the Apache, were the attackers.

Boys' Toys

Boys' toys included child-size bows and arrows, tops, drums, whips, and horse gear. Also common were boy or warrior dolls.

Cutout Figures

Cutout figures made from birch bark were designed by Indian women of the North, Northeast, Subarctic, and Lakes areas. Some forms were human, while others were of animals and birds. The Athabaskans sewed such figures onto their birch bark containers, while others were used as toys.

Girls' Toys

Young girls often had miniature tepees with miniature furnishings to play with, or the older members of the tribe would make child-sized tepees for the girls to play in.

Girls would fashion their own dolls out of available materials and dress them, Indian style, with leftover skins discarded by their mothers or other members of the tribe. If the girl was extremely ambitious, she might talk one of the boys into hunting a squirrel or some other small animal to use that hide as doll clothing material. The small tepees and furnishings were often just as elaborately decorated as the adult versions.

The girls with the longest hair would donate some hair for the dolls and sometimes fathers from well-off families would make special toys for their favorite daughters. Miniature pipe bundles, small play horses or small travois packs in which the girls could put their dolls were "special" toys which not all of the girls would have.

Wooden Animals

Wooden animal toys were fashioned by the Plains Indians for their children. Bears, buffalo, and horses are probably the most common toys which they carved.

Willow branches were used by the Northern Plains Indians to make horses. One piece could be split to form the neck and ears; the other half of the same piece could be split to make the forelegs, and the tail and back legs were made the same way. Examples of these toy horses are held by the Montana Historical Society.

Dice, used by the Plains Indians as gaming pieces, were often carved in the shape of small animals. Some examples of these pieces, carved of wood or bone, can be found in the American Museum of Natural History.

GAMES/SPORTS

Archery

Under the umbrella of archery came any game where an arrow or dart was shot at a mark or object. Grass or bark targets were used by some tribes (i.e., Crow, Zuni, Potawatomi), while a yucca ball was shot at by the Navajo and kelp was used by the Makah. The Omaha tribe would shoot other arrows lodged in a tree or cacti.

Bull-Roarer

A thin piece of wood to which a thong with a piece of wood on the end was attached was called a bull-roarer. A youngster in the Ogala, Teton or Omaha tribe would grasp the end of the stick and whirl the thong around his head. The piece of wood on the end of the thong would whip through the air making a whizzing noise.

Buzz

Another whirling toy common to the Indian children was the "buzz." It was made of a flat piece of shell, bone, pottery, or gourd with cords tied to both sides. The cords were held out straight and the piece in the middle circled a couple of times, then the cords were pulled tight and the board/piece in the center would "buzz."

Cat's Cradle

Common to quite a few Indian tribes, the cat's cradle game has its roots in mythology. The Zuni say the game was taught by their grandmother, the Spider, and the Navajo say they were also taught by the Spider people.

The game is played with a simple piece of string which is wound through the fingers, making various designs. Such tribes as the Sak and Fox, Apache, Hupa, and Navajo have histories of playing this game.

Chunkee

Chunkee was the Southeastern Indian version of the hoop-and-stick game. It was played with a stone disk and the object of the game was to come as close as possible to where a player's rolling disk would stop with your tossed pole.

The artist, George Catlin, well known for his intense studies of the American Indian, painted members of the Mandan tribe playing the game, which was also enjoyed by Creek men.

Dice

Games played with dice were common to approximately 130 Indian tribes and all North American tribes had some kind of knowledge of dice. To play the game, one needed dice and counting tools. These counting tools could be as simple as sticks or could be something like an abacus. Some museums attribute beaver teeth dice to the Karok

Indians. The game, originally known to have come from Oregon, may have only come to the Karoks since occupation by the white men.

Arapahos and other tribes made a basket which was used in their dice games. The basket, flat with slanted sides, was usually not fanciful. The dice were made from very different materials, though Arapaho were known to use bone or plum stones. Dice made of bone have even been found in archeological diggings done in the Southwest.

The dice were tossed in the air, landing in the basket, and points were scored on the way the dice landed. The game of dice was very detailed and, more often than not, serious gambling was employed on the part of the players. Though both men and women played dice games, the ceremonial games were played strictly by men. The game of dice was considered sacred to the Zuni war god and cane dice were sacrificed to him.

Football

The National Football League did not invent football as many couch potatoes have been led to believe. The game was first played by Indians in the Algonquin tribes (Massachusetts, MicMac, Narragansett, and Powhatan, with the MicMacs being the predominant ones), which probably explains why the great Indian football player, Jim Thorpe, had no trouble comprehending, as well as mastering, the game. Other tribes have also been known to play some form of the game.

The balls were made of buckskin or stone and the goals were two erect sticks, or lines, at the ends of the playing field.

The Indians would play "county against county" and the goals were often a mile apart. Before playing, they would put on war-type paint and their weapons would be put to the side so that all would play in good humor.

Four-Stick Game

Played by the Klamath, Modoc, Achomaivi, Paiute, Washo, and possibly Chinook tribes, the four sticks in this game may be referred to as the war gods and their bows. The players sit opposite each other, with one player in possession of the four sticks. This player's hands are covered with a mat as he rearranges the sticks under the mat, out of sight of the other players. Each player is then required to guess how the sticks are arranged, and the player who guesses correctly gets a point and the game is handed to him, and so on. The game is accompanied, as are many others, by the harmonious singing of the players.

Hoop and Pole

Hoop and pole games were popular during all seasons with the Indian tribes who lived along the American-Canadian border. The Plains tribes played this game by throwing spears at webbed hoops which were rolled along the ground.

Lacrosse

The game of lacrosse was originally Indian, though borrowed by the whites and now played by them with equal fervor. Lacrosse was played by most Eastern tribes. The Iroquois tribe used a racquet which closely resembled the ones modern lacrosse players use. Southeastern tribes used smaller sticks with round nets on the end, and single sticks were used by the Lakes area tribes. The game was also played by the Chippewa, Huron, Miami, Penobscot, Sauk and Fox, Shawnee, Skokomish, and Winnebago tribes.

Racquet Ball

Racquet ball was distinctly a male game for the Indians who played it. The game was played by many tribes, and only one that we know of (Santee) allowed men and women to play the game together. Though it was played by a number of different Eastern, Northern, and Great Lakes tribes, the game is not recorded as having been played in the Southwest.

The ball used in the game was made of wood or buckskin which was stuffed with hair. The racquet was a stick with a round net on its end. The field used was much the same as a football field setup.

Ring and Pin

Quite a few Indian tribes played the game known as ring and pin. Perhaps you did not need another player to engage in playing the game.

The ring was attached to a thong and swung into the air. The object of the game was to catch the ring on a pin or dart which was fastened to the other end of the thong. The game was played by Indians all over North America, and to this day there are games which resemble this ancient favorite.

Shinny

Most tribes from the Plains area to the Pacific Coast played a game called shinny, which resembled baseball. A stick and ball were used, but the stick had a curved end, like a hockey stick.

Snowshoes

Snowshoes were used by Eastern, as well as Western, Indians. The frames for snowshoes made by the Eastern tribes were usually oval, while the Western snowshoes were narrow. The Northern tribes such as Algonquins and Athabaskans used rawhide strips to make the netting for their snowshoes.

Maidu snowshoes are similar to those worn by other California Indians. One or two thongs cross over the width and two to four crisscross those. The hoop is a small oval with no netting, no tailpiece, and no provision for heel play.

Snow Snake

A stick called a snow snake was flung, then the distance measured, by Western tribes as well as the Iroquois. This game appears to be the predecessor of the javelin toss, now so prominently favored in the Olympic games.

Toboggans

The Northern Indian tribes used wooden toboggans for many different reasons (i.e., to carry belongings from one place to another, to transfer people who couldn't walk, and just for the sport of riding the flat piece of wood with one curved end down the hill).

MUSICAL INSTRUMENTS

Simple rhythm instruments or musical rasps were made from the shoulder blades of deer. A stick was rattled along the notches of the bone to create a rhythmic sound.

Instruments, such as the flutes made by the Hupas or the dance whistles of the Plains Indians, were made from tubular bones. Some were decorated or engraved. The Yurok flute was an open tube of elder wood with three or four holes which were evenly spaced. To get a noise, one would blow diagonally across an end. Though the flute was usually played by a young man during courtship, older people would often play the flute for meditation.

The Pomo whistle could be made of bone or reed, single or double, and could be tied, pierced or cut off. Cahuilla whistles were made of huikish, Elymus cane, and were played by men who sang and danced about the young men who underwent the ordeal of the ants.

Yavapai miniature basket, olla polychrome, ca. 1890. (*Courtesy of Morning Star Gallery, Santa Fe, New Mexico. Photo by Rita Rivera*)

Panamint bottleneck basket with zoomorphic design, made by Mary Pinkle, ca. 1930, valued between $8500 and $9000. (*Anonymous collector*)

Klickitat berry basket, ca. 1870, valued between $3500 and $4000. (*Anonymous collector*)

Atsuwegi basket. Note that the design on the basket on the left matches the eye design in the face on the basket on the right, valued between $7500 and $9500. (*Anonymous collector*)

Zia pottery olla, ca. 1875, valued between $2000 and $2500. (*Courtesy of Adobe Gallery, Albuquerque, New Mexico. Photo by Donald Vogt*)

Acoma pottery, olla polychrome, ca. 1900, valued between $5000 and $6000. (*Courtesy of Adobe Gallery, Albuquerque, New Mexico. Photo by Donald Vogt*)

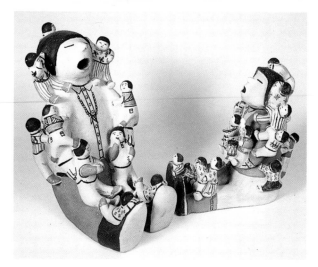

The piece of pottery on the right is by the master potter
of storyteller figures, Helen Cordero, ca. 1965, valued between $7500 and $8000. On the left is a storyteller made
by Buffy Cordero, Helen's 17-year-old granddaughter, ca.
1988, valued between $750 and $800. (*Courtesy of Adobe
Gallery, Albuquerque, New Mexico. Photo by Donald Vogt*)

Zuni pottery, kiva bowl, ca. 1880, valued between $5500
and $6500. (*Courtesy of Morning Star Gallery, Santa Fe, New
Mexico. Photo by Donald Vogt*)

Comanche chief's headdress, made of eagle feathers, ca. 1916–1917. (*Courtesy of Jack Glover, Sunset, Texas. Photo by Donald Vogt*)

Peyote painting by Zuni medicine man to show people what cycle of the moon to hold ceremonies. (*Courtesy of Jack Glover, Sunset, Texas. Photo by Donald Vogt*)

Southern Plains moccasins, estimated value between $1200 and $1500. (*Courtesy of William R. Nash Collection. Photo by Donald Vogt*)

Painted cedar box used to hold Cherokee sacred items. Carved and painted by Jamie Tawodi Reason. (*Courtesy of artist. Photo by Ospray Graphics*)

Navajo Germantown Eyedazzler, ca. 1890, estimated value between $10,000 and $11,000. (*Courtesy of Morning Star Gallery, Santa Fe, New Mexico*)

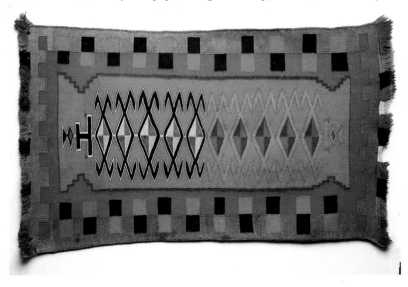

Sioux shirt used for Ghost Dance, valued between $1500 and $1750. (*Courtesy of William R. Nash Collection. Photo by Donald Vogt*)

Apache woman's hide cape, estimated value between $750 and $1000. (*Courtesy of William R. Nash Collection. Photo by Donald Vogt*)

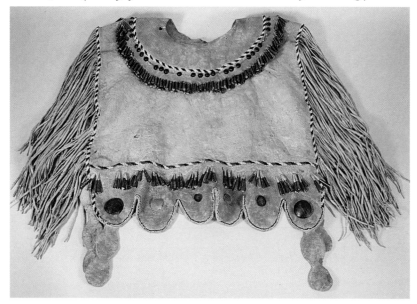

Hopi contemporary Kachinas done by Manuel Kooyahoema of the Hopi Third Mesa, estimated value between $800 and $1000 each. (*Courtesy of Adobe Gallery, Albuquerque, New Mexico. Photo by Donald Vogt*)

Beaded ceremonial horn used in buffalo dance. (*Courtesy of Jack Glover, Sunset, Texas. Photo by Donald Vogt*)

Fetish necklace, ca. 1980s, estimated value between $300 and $400. (*From the collection of N. A. McKinney. Photo by Donald Vogt*)

Navajo necklace, ca. 1920, estimated value between $3000 and $3500. (*Courtesy of Adobe Gallery, Albuquerque, New Mexico. Photo by Donald Vogt*)

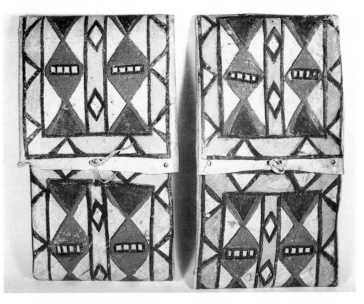

Above: Northern Plains leather parfleches, ca. 1875, estimated value between $1000 and $3000. (*Courtesy of Canfield Gallery, Santa Fe, New Mexico. Photo by Donald Vogt*) Below: San Felipe leather shield, ca. 1860, value estimated between $9500 and $10,000. (*Courtesy of Morning Star Gallery, Santa Fe, New Mexico. Photo by Donald Vogt*)

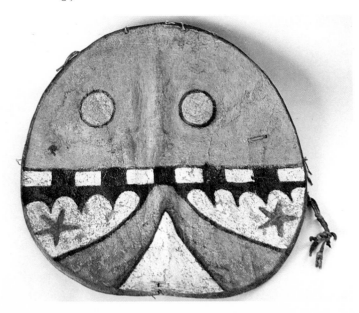

DOLLS, GAMES, AND SPORTS LISTINGS

Cheyenne

Courtesy of Canfield Gallery, Santa Fe, NM. Photo by Donald Vogt.

Cradle; ca. 1890; beaded hide on wood frame w/brass tack decoration; overall length 14½". **$2500–$3500**

Moccasins; tiny, full-beaded, hide toy moccasins, ca. 1920; 2" × 1". **$65–$85**

Cree

Fine buckskin costume w/beading around yoke and fur trim; felt face; papoose on back; 11½" high. **$155–$175**

Stone face; 12" high; ca. 1950. **$250–$300**

Groups/Collections

Collection; glass case containing 37 assorted Indian dolls; ca. 1920; 37" × 22". **$500–$700**

Collection; glassed case containing 32 Indian and Eskimo dolls, including three w/ivory faces; ca. 1920. **$500–$700**

Cradleboards, Apache; miniature cradleboards made of silver and wood materials. **$10–$15 ea.**

Dresses; bead-decorated blue trade cloth and black cloth dresses; beaded w/lace sleeves. **$50–$75**

Miniatures at the Kiva/Steve Cowgill. Photo by Donald Vogt.

Hopi, Kachina; contemporary Kachinas by award winning carver Cecil Calimptewa.   **$7000–$9000 ea.**

Hopi, Kachinas; group of contemporary Kachinas; one is female ogre Kachina by Neal Kayourptowa.   **$145–$200**

Whipper's Uncle by Finkle Sahmu, Hopi Tewa, Pulacca, Arizona. **$145–$200**

Telauai Kachina (Morning Kachina), by Bear Dance.   **$195–$250**

Wolf Kachina.   **$45–$75**

Hopi, contemporary Kachinas; 12″ Eototo (white mask) and 13½″ Aholi (turquoise mask); two of the Chief Kachinas; always travel in a pair; done by Manuel Kooyahoema of the Hopi Third Mesa.
$800–$1000 ea.

Courtesy of Broken Arrow Indian Arts and Crafts, Taos, NM. Photo by Donald Vogt.

Hopi, Snake Dance set; done by Cecil Calnimptewa; one of the most famous single sets of Kachinas carved to date; the Snake Dance is rare; a lot of carvers won't even attempt to carve something as intricate as this.   **$15,000–$18,000**

Courtesy of W. J. Arbuckle. Photo by Donald Vogt.

Hopi, Kachina; group of Hopi Kachinas; made by Lucy Dougi, Chinle, Arizona; contemporary; one is Sundancer; one is White Wolf; one is Eagle Dancer; one is Black Buffalo; one is Angry Kachina.

$25–$50 ea.

Hopi, Kachinas; done by Henry and Mary Sheldon (husband and wife carvers); Mary does miniatures and Henry does large Kachinas; Mary's work averages $400 to $600.   **$400–$600**

The Cumulus Cloud Kachina (with the ribbon).   **$2000–$2500**

Indian, four various Indian dolls; all stuffed with cloth with various costumes; all have wear; 8″ to 10″ in height.   **$80–$100**

Lot of eleven; including polychromed, carved, wood ceremonial figures, fabric dolls, rope doll, and carved bone doll (largest 17½″).
                                                        $385– $500

Miscellaneous; group of Skookum and other dolls; ca. 1930s.
                                                        $20–$65 ea.

Navajo, pair of 19″ china dolls; dressed in Navajo costumes; woman's costume is red velvet w/brocade sash and turquoise bead buttons; man wearing white velvet trousers and red velvet shirt w/silver and turquoise buttons.   **$140–$180**

Navajo, pair; handmade man and woman; 18″ high; traditional dress; Rose Hadley.   **$75–$115**

Navajo, five small Navajo dolls; handmade costumes of velour and other fabrics, with metal concho belts, beaded necklaces on the females, painted ragfaces; each approximately 3″ more or less; pre–1900.
                                                        $55–$85

Pair handcarved; man and woman dressed in blankets and handmade clothing; wooden faces, straw-filled bodies; good condition. **$130–$160**

Pueblo, pottery; two early handmade pottery dolls; ca. 1935.   **$60–$80**

Courtesy of private collector. Photo by Donald Vogt.

Seminole, group of dolls; all approximately 6″ high and dressed in traditional Seminole clothing; a couple (man and woman) are unusual in that they have molded noses.   **$15–$200**

Skookum, pair; one 11″ high and the other 12½″ high.   **$40–$65**

Skookum; pair; dolls in finely detailed blanket costume; pristine condition; male 16¾″ tall; female 16″.   **$130–$160**

Hopi, Kachina

Avachoya-QA-O; 15″ high; 1940s.   **$235–$350**

Black Buffalo Dancer.   **$135–$165**

Courtesy of Broken Arrow Indian Arts and Crafts, Taos, NM. Photo by Donald Vogt.

By Cecil Calnimptewa and Muriel Navasie; husband and wife award-winning carvers (wife taught husband to carve):

One is Muriel's Crow Mother.	**$4200–$5000**
Cecil's Ram.	**$4200–$4500**
White Buffalo.	**$6000–$6400**

Carved wooden; decorated with hand-ground pigments; 9¼". **$90–$125**

Carved and painted miniature Hopi Mudhead Kachina; ca. 1970; 3½" × 3".
$35–$50

Ca. 1900; painted cottonwood root; polychrome; 11" high.
$2500–$3000

Carved and painted corn Kachina w/hoop and dance rattle. **$60–$85**

Chakwaina; 10¼" high; signed John Martin. **$110–$140**

Chop/sowi-ing (antelope); 12"; signed Pat Sauphe. **$110–$160**

Contemporary Kachina done in wood; stained; all one piece; 12" high; Sio Hemis Kachina by Lauren Honyoti from Hopi Third Mesa.
$1800–$2000

Courtesy of Adobe Gallery, Albuquerque, NM. Photo by Donald Vogt.

Contemporary Squash Kachina; carved by Malcolm Fred; Hopi Third Mesa; 10″ high.   **$800–$1000**

"Crow Mother"; 9¾″ high; standing figure on wood base.   **$90–$150**

Dancing figure w/mask and fur cape, wearing kilt; 13″ high.   **$150–$200**

Dancing figure w/tableta headdress and fur cape; 14″ high.   **$165–$190**

Dancing figure with "paralyzed Kachina" mask and fur cape; 9″ high.
                                                                 $55–$85

Done by Warren Phillips; Prickly Pear Kachina.   **$5500–$6000**

Finely carved and painted Crow mother Kachina w/basket; 8½″ × 4½″.
                                                                 $60–$85

"Hon Bear"; 10½″ high; action figure on wood stand.   **$80–$140**

I'She (mustard green); 7″ high; signed Wiefred Huma.   **$35–$75**

"Kau-a"; 10″ figure on base.   **$100–$150**

Kocha Mosairu (White Buffalo); 7¼″; signed Taiz.   **$65–$85**

Kokopelli (Assassin Fly); 3½″ high; signed Silas Roy.   **$115–$175**

Kwikwilyaka (mocking); 3½″; signed Silas Roy.   **$175–$225**

Large carved and painted wooden "warrior"; 20″ × 9″; ca. 1986.
                                                                $125–$250

Large (12¹/₂") older Kachina; H. Hano Clown made by Tino Youvella; has a "surprise" under his breech cloth.   **$250–$350**

"Left Hander"; 11" high; action figure on wood base.   **$110–$160**

"Mastof"; 11" high; standing on wood base.   **$90–$150**

Miniatures at the Kiva/Steve Cowgill. Photo by Donald Vogt.

Miniature Kachina by Dwayne Dwahough; ca. 1984.   **$1200–$1500**

Mongwu (Great Horned Owl); 7¹/₂" high; signed Taiz.   **$45–$75**

Mudhead Kachina w/drum; bun missing at back of head and feathers on head worn off; crack at joint of right arm; 16" high.   **$150–$200**

Mudhead; 11¹/₂" high.   **$65–$115**

Mudhead w/shaker and feather in hands; signed Sanfard Honyamtowa.
                                                             $120–$160

Mudhead w/fur ruff and drum and stick in hand; signed Edison Brown.
                                                             $100–$150

Older 7¹/₂" high Sipikne (Zuni warrior god); ca. 1930s–40s. **$90–$150**

Older type; 8³/₄"; Ota/Kwasa-itaqa (Skirt Man—Third Mesa type).
                                                             $75–$110

Older Polik Mana (Butterfly Maiden); 12³/₄" high.   **$110–$180**

Courtesy of Jack Sellner, CAI.

One is signed Mocktima; 15″ high; Hemis (Jemez, Ripened Corn).
$150–$275

Talavai (Morning Singer); 12″ high signed W. Maktima. $175–$275

Palhik Mana (Butterfly Girl); 24¾″ by Walter Hawato. $325–$425

Pong (Mt. Sheep); 13½″. $125–$195

From the William R. Nash Collection. Photo by Donald Vogt.

Probably representing Tawa, the Sun Kachina; w/deep red-painted body and yellow legs, forearms, and shoulders; the helmet mask w/pale blue face; rainbow decoration along the chin; triangular mouth, rectangular eyes, warrior marks on the cheeks, and a concentric wedge of spotted rainbow decoration on each temple; wearing a tall crown of feathers; 13⅝" high; an old label remaining on the underside reading "Kachina doll, Grand Canyon, Arizona, 1939."   **$1200–$1500**

"Rainbow Dancer"; not Kachina, but social figure; 14¾" with feathers.
                                                            $60–$100

Signed Silas Roy; 3⅞" high.   **$110–$165**

"Sipikne"; 11¾" high; action figure on wood base.   **$70–$150**

"Snake Dancer"; 10" high; standing figure on wood base.   **$100–$150**

Snake Kachina dancer; painted leather, horsehair fringe on mask; one of the finest of contemporary work; 18" high.   **$575–$700**

"Squash"; 10¾" high; on wood base.   **$130–$160**

"Sun Kachina"; figure standing on wood base; 14½" high.   **$90–$160**

Tema left-hand hunter; 8½" high.   **$90–$150**

Courtesy of Naranjo's, Houston. Photo by Donald Vogt.

Traditional style "Corn Maiden"; made by contemporary artist J. Michael Bear (Acoma/Sioux).   **$800–$1000**

Two-piece Kachina "Koshare"; made by Dawa, Hopi Kachina carver; certificate of authenticity included.   **$1000–$1250**

From the William R. Nash Collection. Photo by Donald Vogt.

Wearing a terraced tableta w/raincloud and phallic symbols, his body painted black; 15¾"; Jemez or Ripened Corn Kachina; Hopi name is Hemis Kachina.   **$500–$750**

Wolf Kachina in action position; 15″ high; some damage.　　$120–$150

Wooden Coyote Kachina; yellow body w/black spotting and white kilt; accompanying mount inscribed "Kachina Doll from Hopi Indian, Oraibi Mesa, Painted Desert, Arizona, August 1, 1932″; 6¾″ high; missing one ear.　　$225–$400

Wood Kachina; painted overall in white, w/tubular snout, concentric rectangular eyes, and tall tableta w/terracing across the top painted w/corn and butterflies; called Butterfly Kachina or Poli Sio Hemis Kachina; 16½″ tall.　　$500–$750

Yapa; w/white head, large red ears; signed Leo Barber.　　$70–$150

Navajo

Carved and painted; 12½″; Yeibichai (Navajo deity); signed Tom W. Yazzi.　　$100–$130

Female figure; sewn dress, velour shirt, bead necklace, painted rag face, body, tin metal concho belt; 8″ high; lacking bandana; ca. 1900.
　　$35–$50

Figure of a woman working at a loom; 17″ × 15″.　　$30–$50

Handmade doll pin cushion; ca. 1935; 6″ × 4″.　　$15–$25

Handmade female doll; ca. 1975.　　$10–$20

Healing; wood-carved doll w/traces of paint; 5½″ × 1¾″.　　$100–$150

From the collection of Joyce Williams.
Photo by Donald Vogt.

Signed on leg 'Naz Bah''; and dressed in traditional wine-colored dress.
　　$100–$125

Squaw; 19½" high; traditionally dressed w/plush blouse, real hair tied in native "bun" style, full-length pleated skirt, authentic sash around waist, and miniature jewelry.   **$200–$250**

Plains

Courtesy of Donna McMenamin, private collector.
Photo by Donald Vogt.

Buckskin doll w/beaded belt; 12"; ca. 1930s.   **$150–$200**

Doll form on wood cradle board; 13½" × 5".   **$25–$50**

Made of leather and horsehair.   **$210–$300**

Polychrome hide doll/charm; small stuffed figure; red linear and circle designs over yellow pigment ground w/blue pigments along seams; human hair coiffure; rawhide suspension at back of featureless head; 4¼" tall.
                                                              $650–$800

Skookum

16" high.   **$25–$45**

Large and early doll; 14" × 5".   **$100–$150**

Original blanket and paper label on bottom (Pat. Feb. 17, 1914).   **$60–80**

Toys

Athabascan, snowshoes; fine and fancy painted; ca. 1880; 80" × 46".
                                                              $475–$525

Canoe; birch bark toy canoe; 25" × 8".   **$25–$45**

Cards, ten birch bark cards. **$30–$60**

Chess set; metal-sculptured chess set of cowboys and Indians w/wood and metal board by Charles Pratt. **$550–$750**

Cradle; miniature hide-covered cradle w/round top, some beadwork; 9″ × 5″. **$40–$60**

Sioux, dress; miniature woman's dress; yoke beaded in blues and red on a white ground on buffalo hide backing; rest of dress is homespun from cloth; stenciled inside dress: ''U.S. Indian Agency''; beaded and fringed decoration on dress skirt; all beading sinew sewn; 12″ wide × 13½″ long. **$745–$1000**

Snowshoes; large, handmade ''True Temper'' snowshoes, ca. 1930; 61″ × 10″. **$55–$75**

Snowshoes, MicMac; 42½″ long. **$65–$85**

Snowshoes; pair of rawhide and bentwood snowshoes. **$30–$60**

Snowshoes; pair of toy snowshoes; handmade; 13″ × 13½″. **$40–$50**

Sioux, game; old pin and bone child's game w/traces of paint; ca. 1870; 5″ × ¾″. **$70–$100**

Other

Courtesy of Robert W. Skinner, Inc., Bolton, MA.

Beaded hide doll; Sioux; wearing a fringed hide dress with a fully beaded yoke; body of dress w/dyed red-plaited quillwork and beaded ornamentation; fully beaded high boots; long horsehair coiffure; beaded earrings on edge of face; bead colors: white heart reds, light blue, clear and greasy yellow, white, and royal blue; 17¼″ tall. **$1400–$1800**

Buckskin, Northern Plains; beaded clothing, 12" tall.　　**$400–$600**

Clown Kachina; Santa Clara; signed miniature clown Kachina by Margaret and Luther; ca. 1965; 1½" × 1½".　　**$40–$60**

Diorama, Navajo; Navajo woman weaving rug diorama; she's wearing maroon dress and child is dressed in same fabric and color.　　**$50–$75**

From the collection of Joyce Williams. Photo by Donald Vogt.

Euchee; large doll made by Milo Yellowhead of Euchee tribe of Oklahoma; small one made by Hattie Harris.　　**$40–$80 ea.**

Great Lakes style; carved wood and birch bark wrapped; 6" × 2½".

$15–$30

Indian; woman w/child and wool blanket.　　**$50–$75**

Northwest Coast; dancer doll in full costume by Erla Graham; ca. 1975; 30" × 6".　　**$375–$500**

Pueblo, Kachina; 8" Katoch Ang-ak-china (barefoot, long-haired Kachina).　　**$100–$135**

Seminole; palm fiber w/banded cloth costume; small tear in cloth, 4" high.　　**$15–$25**

Southwest Indian; mother and papoose in leather and cloth, seated in front of a loom; in glass case measuring 19" × 14" × 11".　　**$55–$125**

Courtesy of Naranjo's, Houston. Photo by Donald Vogt.

Spirit; Hank Orr (Cherokee); handcarved and masked fox dancer; 14½″; 1984. **$1000–$1250**

EPHEMERA AND ADVERTISING

▼▼▼▼▼▼▼▼▼▼▼

INTRODUCTION

Ephemera

General information about the Amerind has been produced since white people got their first glimpse of native Americans. Such information, whether fiction or nonfiction, or symbols used to advertise various products, is a side of American Indian collecting which few collectors of Indian arts and crafts even consider to be Amerind "collectibles." However, the newspapers, magazines, and books which have highlighted the Amerind, or which have been written by American Indians, are, indeed, collectible; they constitute a rich well of knowledge for those more interested in the written word rather than tangible items which bespeak the Indian heritage. Writers are just as much a part of the arts as are the potters, jewelry makers, and artists mentioned in other chapters of this book.

Because almost every publication in the United States has mentioned American Indians at one point or another during its publishing lifetime, I have not attempted to detail those who have taken a special interest in the subject. I will say, however, that such magazines and newspapers, such as *Harper's* and *Leslie's*, chronicled Indian events with much relish in the early days of U. S. publishing history, and articles published in their pages were often embellished with engravings or sketches done of the various tribes. Interest in the "red man" was extremely high during that period in our history and the mixture of curiosity and fear which journalists had toward their subject often colored the articles unfavorably.

In later periods, the various tribes began publishing their own periodicals which, though often scarce, are collectible. Also collectible are current magazines/newspapers, such as *The Indian Trader* newspaper, *American Indian Art* magazine, and the beautiful, new, glossy magazine put out by the Heard Museum entitled *Native Peoples*. Books written about the various tribes are also plentiful and some may be found to date back to the early beginnings of the United States. Being a lover of the written word (as well as the owner of a very small house), this is where my interest lies, and I have found many interesting and well-illustrated books on the American Indian which were published in the early nineteenth and late eighteenth centuries. Though much of the information related in these early tomes has been proven incorrect, there are some (such as Catlin's *Letters and Notes on the Manners, Customs and Conditions of the North American Indians*) which have survived the test of time to tell a very accurate tale of the habits and lifestyles of the original owners of this country.

American Indians have also told their own story for hundreds of years, but it was not until recent times (the last hundred years or so) that the Amerind's story was written and printed by him/her because most stories and family/tribal history were passed on verbally. Indian writers have still not received their just due; and, when pressed to name a famous Amerind author, most cannot; I'm sure that with time, however, this fact will also change.

Advertising

The Amerind has long been a favored figure in the advertising world. Perhaps the earliest use was the cigar store Indian, but the use of an Indian in a headdress or sitting regally on top of a horse continues to be the logo of advertising firms today.

With the help of some general information about various tribes and specific information about authors, photographers, and uses of advertising in this chapter, we hope to give you a view of the written word and the documentation of (and by) the American Indian.

General Information

Because of the many years of propaganda, both by the government as well as by missionaries, the Indian people have been forced away from their traditional ways. Though there is a resurgence of interest in Indian tradition now, and even the reservation schools are encouraging children to learn the old ways, it is still difficult for people to choose the way they want their lives to go. And everytime one of the elders in the tribe dies, some portion of Indian knowledge goes with him.

Just as all our forefathers suffered discomforts and had harder lives than we've had, so it has been among the Amerind tribes. Though women did hard work, often waiting on husbands who wanted to be treated like kings, men also left their warm tepees in the dead of winter to hunt for food for their family.

The Indian reservations have diminished in the hundred years between 1880 and 1980 and have moved their locations. Today, the largest reservation in the United States is the Navajo reservation, which is located in northwestern Arizona, northeastern Nevada, and southern Colorado and Utah.

It is hard for us, so used to modernized living—microwaves, VCR, color TVs, and fast cars—to slow down enough to learn the ancient ways of the Indian culture. Yet, if the younger Indians are not allowed to feel proud of their heritage and to learn all they can from the elders of their tribes, the knowledge built from thousands of years could disappear. The Amerind has valuable information to pass on—his/her religion, medicine, arts, and crafts—and it is something we should *all* be careful enough to preserve . . . not in museums, but in the hearts, minds, and hands of those still alive to pass on the traditions.

GENERAL TRIBAL INFORMATION

Abenaki (Northeast)

The Abenaki Indians call the white ash the snowshoe tree "because Indians make snowshoes from it." This tribe has recently been receiving attention in New England newspapers because of land disputes and their concern with the ecology of their land—something which their white brothers have to be reminded is important.

Sky City of Acoma (Southwest)

The Sky City of Acoma is on a mesa because of attacks by Spaniards, who did not succeed in driving Indians from their Pueblo. The Acomas still live there and it is one of the oldest continuously occupied villages in the United States.

Alaskan Tribes

The Athabascan, Haida, Flingit, and Tsimshian tribes have a rich and dazzling heritage of craftsmanship. Though we think of totems and dance poles as being their exclusive reign, they are also responsible for wonderful baskets, carved wooden pieces, decorated clothing, and unique utensils (covered in other chapters).

Blackfoot (Plains)

At one time during the 1800s, the Blackfoot had a cure for cancer (which they called "big boil" or "big pimple"). Through the years, the cure has been lost, but the old women of the tribe have told younger members that the cure came from a root. It has often been noted that the tribes did not experience a great deal of sickness in the early days, except for the diseases passed on to them by traders. Once schools were set up and reservations established, the Indians' natural immunity system was broken down and diseases ran rampant.

With reference to family life, the Blackfoot man often had more than one wife. Sometimes that wife would be procured when the original wife had become pregnant and needed more help. If the man did not choose to have another wife, he would bring in a younger sister or his mother, but not the wife's mother, as the mother-in-law was not allowed to be in his company.

There were many superstitions about what a pregnant woman should or should not do (i.e., she should not stand in the doorway of her home; she should be either in or out). The Blackfoot believed if she didn't go all the way out she would have hard labor. The pregnant woman stayed out of her own home while someone took care of her (no one stayed in their own home while ill). During this period of time, the woman's mother, if she was alive and able, cared for her.

After birth, the baby and its mother would be dressed in rags for 30 days (the mother used her pregnancy clothes). Every four days the young mother would be given a cleansing ceremony and, in addition to massages, the woman was given a girdle in order to get her body back into shape. These first 30 days were a period of trial—a way of seeing whether everyone would survive the birth. At the end of the 30-day trial, they would move camp, the mother would go through one more cleansing ceremony, both baby and mother would get dressed in new clothes, and the baby would finally get a name.

The naming ceremony was held by the father, if he was an important or holy man, or by one of the elders. It was important for the child to have a good name in order to give it a good start in life. The ceremony consisted of blessings and prayers, after which the father or elder announced the name he was giving to the child. Though the mother was not active in the name-making ceremony, she would often give her children nicknames during their young days. Men often carried an inherited name, while, surprisingly, women were named for famous war deeds.

It was common for grandparents to raise one of their grandchildren. The closeness between the two generations has always been fostered and, as a result, traditions have been passed on. Widows who were alone were given an orphaned child to take care of. That act solved *two* problems—the loneliness of both parties and the problem of who would take care of each of them if they had remained alone.

Hopi (Southwest)

The Hopi call themselves "Hopitu Skinumu"—the peaceful people. They live on three mesas in central Arizona and occupy a dozen small towns there. Their reservation occupies a portion of the much larger

Navajo nation. The Hopi people live much as their ancestors did; in fact, Oraibi is one of the oldest continuously occupied towns in North America. Their buildings resemble ancient "apartment houses" where people shared open fires and prayed to their gods (Kachinas) to give them the rain necessary to bring their crops to fruition.

The tribe has survived such catastrophes as a wave of smallpox in 1775, which took most of the population; the arrival of white men into their otherwise isolated existence in 1826; and the continuing presence of people who wanted to modernize their culture from the 1850s onward. During this continuous onslaught, the Hopi people have fought to retain their independence and their isolated mesas in the arid eastern region of Arizona.

Today, state highways cut their way through the villages and mesas of Hopi land, but the Hopi still try to keep some of the privacy for which they've had an uphill battle. Signs at the roads leading to the mesas on which they've built the majority of their communities advise visitors to check in, not use cameras, and, mostly, to just have respect for the Hopi way of life.

The Hopi arts and crafts are highly regarded in the Indian collectibles field. Hopi Kachinas, baskets, jewelry, and pottery help to ease some of the economic hardships of the Hopi nation.

The ceremonial life which the Hopi have kept as close to the original as possible is as far from the Anglo regions as a cow is from an eagle. The Hopi Kachinas (gods) are fascinating and many, and are subjects for the Kachina dolls covered in the "Dolls, Games, and Sports" chapter.

Iroquois (Northeast)

The Iroquois nation, now known as the Six Nations, is considered the most completely evolved of all North American tribes. The Iroquois Constitution not only includes the majority of "freedom" statements as found in the U.S. Constitution, but "one-ups" the U.S. Government by giving women and children rights, and by pledging a certain responsibility to the environment. The Iroquois have believed, since they founded their League, that they would be responsible for bringing peace to all nations.

IROQUOIS NATION

Tadodaho is the title which means speaker of the house for the Grand Council of Six Nations Iroquois Confederacy. The ceremonial staff of office is an eagle-headed cane with a pictograph of each of the original peace chiefs carved into it. The Iroquois Six Nations consists of the Mohawk, Oneida, Onondaga, Cayuga, Seneca, and Tuscarora. They consider themselves a nation separate from the United States and even issue their own passports. They call themselves Haudenosaunee or the People of the Longhouse.

The Nation is located in central and western New York State (Onondaga Indian Reservation) and is not part of the United States. Once someone is inside the reservation, federal and state officials have no rights on the reservation and Indian law is followed.

The Iroquois world consists of 17 separate and distinct communities, ranging from Quebec and Ontario in Canada, to New York, Wisconsin, and Oklahoma settlements.

The Iroquois women play a strong role in their society. Clan mothers select and depose chiefs, and the line of inheritance is carried by the women of the tribe.

Mandan and Hidatsa (Plains)

Often studied in the early days of westward exploration by people such as George Catlin, Prince Maximilian, and Karl Bodmer, the Mandan and Hidatsa tribes of North Dakota fell prey to smallpox in 1837–38. The disease killed almost the whole combined population of both tribes. However, the people who survived pulled together and the two tribes moved to a spot in McLean County, on the Missouri River, that they named "Like-a-Fishhook."

There they started a new village, and, once again, began growing corn, squash, beans, and sunflowers, and practicing the domestic crafts of pottery, basketweaving, quillwork, and hide painting. When the Arikara tribe joined them in 1862, they came to be known as The Three Tribes.

Natchez, Choctaws, and Chickasaws (South Central U.S.)

Natchez, Choctaws, and Chickasaws originally lived along the Natchez Trail and welcomed travelers at Indian stands from the early 1800s until the Treaty of Dancing Rabbit Creek forced the Choctaws to Oklahoma. Some Choctaws still remained in the area, talking of building an Indian village and museum.

Navajos (Southwest)

Navajos call themselves the Dineh, the "People"; their land is called Dinetah, the People's Country. They arrived from the north, anthropologists say, and settled around Gobernador Canyon. Both Navajos and Apaches speak Athapaskan languages, which are closely related to the Indian languages of the Pacific Northwest, Alaska, and Canada. Navajo legend has a different way of looking at their appearance in New

Mexico—they say the "People" emerged from underworld regions about 75 miles north of the Gobernador Canyon, through a hole near Silverton, Colorado.

The "People" have 75 clans. Marriage within the clan is considered incestuous. They are the largest tribe in the United States and own about 14,000,000 acres in Arizona, New Mexico, and Utah.

The Hopis and Navajos are constantly squabbling and settle their differences in court; Hopis claim Navajos are "borrowers" of Hopi culture and white culture.

In 1972, the United States offered the Navajo nation the opportunity to run their own reservation. It would be the first time in more than a century that the tribe would control its own future, as well as the $110,000,000 operation which had been run by the Department of Interior's Bureau of Indian Affairs. The tribe has its own legislature, police, and courts, and only answers to the federal government on traffic regulations and major crimes, such as murder, rape, and robbery.

In the Navajo tribe, property is traditionally passed through a wife's clan. The husband lives with her people and does not own anything except his clothes, jewelry, and saddle. In the old days, a man would consider himself divorced if his wife put his saddle outside the door.

Seminoles (Southeast)

Wewoka, the Seminole nation's capital, was put up for sale somewhere around 1900. It was located halfway between Oklahoma City and South McAlester, and was an enviable piece of property. Its virtues were propounded during the period of time that the territory was sold. At that time, the people of Wewoka received $15 a year for every man, woman, and child who was a citizen of the Seminole nation.

The countryside surrounding Wewoka was used for growing wheat, corn, and other cereals. It also produced a sizeable crop of cotton—sizeable enough that The Wewoka Trading Company owned a large cotton gin.

Taos Pueblos (Southwest)

Indians built their pueblos (villages) as high as five stories with no ground-level openings, which was a protection against enemies. Now pueblos in Taos have openings for windows and doors, but little else has changed—no electricity or running water for approximately 1000 Indians.

Zunis (Southwest)

The Zunis own a lot of horses and consider them a mark of wealth. They are among the most prosperous of the Indian tribes. The first jewelry makers of the tribe learned to work silver from the Spanish.

VARIOUS MISCELLANEOUS ITEMS

Apache Corn—Medal and Book

Apache Corn—medal and book—was issued in 1971 to mark the 100th anniversary of the White Mountain Indian Reservation. The book and medal were placed in a time capsule on the reservation, to be reopened in another 100 years. One side shows a "Gan" Dancer (the official symbol of the tribe), while the other depicts an Apache scout astride his horse. Thirty-eight coin medals and accompanying books were issued, depicting the 38 representative American Indian tribes.

Calumet Baking Powder

Calumet Baking Powder has used an Indian as their advertising symbol for many years. The company, located in Chicago, Illinois, has made three or four different sizes (1 lb., 8 oz., etc.), and the original red, black, and yellow label has changed little since the beginning of its rise. Large cans are valued at $20–$25 and small cans are valued at $15–$20.

Cigar Store Indians

Cigar store Indians originated with Sir Walter Raleigh, the Englishman who introduced tobacco to America. Though these figures are called "Indians," they are actually a combination of the Indians who smoked the "weed" (as Raleigh termed the tobacco plant), the plantation owners who grew it, and the Negro slaves who worked the fields. The carved "Indians," placed at the front door of a tobacco shop, were an early form of advertising.

The people who made their living carving these figures were often shipcarvers who had turned away from carving figureheads when American's shipping industry was in a decline. Master carvers such as Charles Robb, Gustav Hentzel (also known for his carousel figures), Wilhelm Schimmel, John Bellamy, and Louis Jobin (a Canadian carver who had done ship figureheads and religious figureheads before attempting to carve cigar store Indians) are represented in collections such as the superb one held by the Shelburne Museum in Shelburne, Vermont.

The carvers depicted their wooden Indians with full headdresses, whether the figures were male or female. Female figures often wore skirts much shorter than the accepted style of the day, or had breasts which were exposed—a shocking sight in the mid–1800s.

"Seneca John," an Indian who was a well-known personality, was carved for the purpose of selling tobacco and was completely recognizable, right down to his headdress, rifle, and deerskin leggings. Other cigar store figures included an Indian trapper, Indian princesses, and a large variety of chieftains.

The National Museum of American Art in Washington, D.C., acquired a pair of cigar store Indians in 1987 entitled "Indian Squaw" and "Indian Brave." Carved of wood, painted, and stained, and having some metal accessories, this pair is thought to have been made around 1870 in New Jersey because they are similar to a figure which has been owned by a New Jersey family since the late nineteenth century.

Ojibwa

Ojibwa fine cut tobacco was packaged in a yellow tin with red and black lettering. Made by the Scotten Dillion Company of Detroit, Michigan, the flat round tin featured an Indian with one hand outstretched and the other holding some tobacco leaves. The round tins are valued at $85–$115.

Round Oak

Round Oak made stoves, ranges, and furnaces. They used an Indian chief, wearing three red feathers in his hair and a bear claw necklace around his throat, as their advertising symbol on a round cardboard sign. The sign was trimmed with oak leaves. The Indian's face was in the center with the words "Round Oak" in a semi-circle around his head. Below the Indian's face were the words "Doe-wah-Jack" and "Stoves, Ranges and Furnaces." The signs are valued at $275–$300 and the trade cards at $30–$35.

Sleepy Eye Flour

Sleepy Eye Flour's trademark was a profile of an older Indian whose name was (appropriately) "Old Sleepy Eye." Flour and cereal products were made by the Sleepy Eye Milling Company in Sleepy Eye, Minnesota, and the Massachusetts-based company offered their customers a large assortment of premiums, all adorned with their Indian trademark.

Metal signs, stoneware pitchers, and paper or canvas banners were made by the company and are now increasingly difficult to find. The sign is valued at $800–$1000.

Sure Shot

Sure Shot chewing tobacco was displayed on country store counters in its own metal display case depicting an Indian with an arrow pulled at the ready. Their slogan was "Sure Shot Chewing Tobacco—It Touches the Spot." The metal case held individual paper packages of the tobacco. The metal container is valued at $250–$300 and the packages at $15–$18.

INDIAN WOMEN IN ADVERTISING

From 1915–40s, Indian maidens were used for various types of advertising, including gracing calendar covers, playing cards, postcards, and almanacs.

Companies such as Brown and Bigelow of St. Paul, Minnesota, hired Caucasian women to pose as Indian maidens, picturing them in seductive ways against the backdrop of a blue mountain or a clear moonlit lake. American Art Works of Coshocton, Ohio, Hayes Litho of Buffalo, New York, Arthur B. Cotas, the Fairman Company and Knapp Company joined Brown and Bigelow in zealously producing the calendars which were in vogue. The Flemish Art Company captured the female Indian image, Gibson girl-style, on wooden boxes, mirrors, and trinkets, burning the image onto the cover of the box.

Illustrators known for their Indian maiden images included Walker, Burrich, McKenzue, Arthur, F. J. Harper and J. Knowles Hare (who also did covers for the popular magazine *Saturday Evening Post*), Henry H. Intermeister (who worked for the Knapp Company), and Zula Kenyon, the only female artist to illustrate Indian women.

PHOTOGRAPHY

Photographers who worked during that early period of ground breaking to capture the elusive society of various Indian tribes (1850–1900) often reflected the attitudes of the white race toward the original Americans. Because they were the first to record that presence, they dealt with Indian reluctance to use the sacred sun to make images which neither moved nor spoke. They also dealt with their own drive to take photographs which would preserve the new knowledge they had uncovered and leave a legacy for history. Early photographers such as Jean-Jaques Rousseau, John Mix Stanley, John Wesley Jones, and Robert Vance produced images which served to form valuable archives of information.

These early contacts were, for the most part, healthy and gratifying for both parties. White people were learning about the other occupants of the continent and, if they had studied harder, they may even have learned to understand why the tribes grew threatened when the lands of their ancestors were invaded with wagon trains full of new settlers. The "noble savage" the early photographers had encountered was now feared and fought against.

A different group of photographers began taking photos of those tribes not yet in conflict with the American military. Government photographers, whose work would be part of a survey of the land, included William Henry Jackson, Jack Hillers, and Timothy O'Sullivan. Army photographers, like Will Soule and Ben Wittick, produced worthy collections of images for the military. In Washington, Alexander Gardner and Zeno Schindler used their talents to capture Indian delegates in formal and dignified poses.

During the first two decades after the Civil War, tensions between the U.S. Government and the Indians were so volatile that few photographers got the chance to photograph them in a natural setting. The anti-Indian feeling that "the only good Indian is a dead Indian" colored photographers' abilities to portray the Amerind with any kind of humanity. The photos of this period were "safe" romanticized views of Indians, not portraits of successful Indian leaders. It was the age of Queen Victoria, the dime store novel was popular, and Indians were stars in Wild West shows, such as the one put together by the legendary Buffalo Bill Cody. The Indian was made into a circus figure; someone who could be watched from a distance and degraded because Americans knew little, and did not care to know more, about Indian civilizations.

Biographies

EDWARD S. CURTIS

Edward S. Curtis invested years of his life to photograph Indians. He believed the life they led before the invasion of the white man was an idyllic one and he approached them with this type of view. This philosophy is reflected in the many views he captured of the people other photographers turned away from.

Curtis spent time learning the Indians' ways, traveling with them, and sharing his respect for their culture. He posed his Indians so that he could photograph them in powerful, deeply moving compositions.

Shan Goshorn

Shan Goshorn was a Cherokee who was born in Baltimore, Maryland. Her Cherokee name is Noon de Da Lon a ga el, "Yellow Moon."

Goshorn majored in silversmithing, after high school at the Cleveland Institute of Art, Cleveland, and changed her major to photography in her third year. She then transferred to Atlanta College of Art in Atlanta, Georgia. Her work has been shown at Southern Plains Indian Museum.

Timothy O'Sullivan and William Bell

Timothy O'Sullivan and William Bell were responsible for taking documentary photographs of the American West. The photos were taken during 1871, 1872, 1873, and assembled during 1875 by First Lt. George Montague Wheeler of the Army Corps of Engineers. The photos were taken during expeditions through areas of the United States which are now the states of Utah, California, Arizona, New Mexico, and Arizona.

During the 1871 expedition, O'Sullivan photographed areas of the Southwest which included part of the Grand Canyon, Death Valley, and the Apache territory. In 1872, Bell swung north to photograph more of the areas in and around the Grand Canyon, parts of Utah and Nevada, and the Colorado River. In 1873, O'Sullivan went back to work and this time chronicled sights in Arizona and New Mexico. He traveled in a crescent shape through what is now the Navajo reservation in the northern parts of the states, the south through the center of both states.

Wheeler, the leader of the survey and born in 1842, was a Hopkinton, Massachusetts, native and was a topographical engineer. The photos were used, as Wheeler proposed, to chart "astronomical, geographical, and topographical observations, artificial and economic features, the geologic and natural history branches being treated as incidental to the main purpose." The photos ended up not only being used for topographical reference, but also to help the U.S. Army gather and exterminate the tribes of Indians who lived throughout the Southwest. Pah-Ute, Apache, Zuni, and Navajo lifestyles and people were photographed during the expedition.

O'Sullivan was chosen by Wheeler because of the recommendation of William Henry Jackson, a famous frontier photographer. He claimed that Timothy O'Sullivan, an Irishman born in 1840, was "one of the best of the government photographers." O'Sullivan was apprenticed to Matthew Brady during the early part of his career and later joined Brady's semi-official corps of photographers during the Civil War. Many of his pictures are included in *Photographic Sketchbook of the Civil War*, by Alexander Gardner, even though Brady and Gardner took credit for many of them. He was later hired to be the official photographer for the expedition through the Isthmus of Darien, which resulted in the eventual building of the Panama Canal.

During the O'Sullivan treks, O'Sullivan nearly drowned, one man died in the desert, and two civilian guides disappeared, but the photographs survived a perilous journey down the white water rapids of the Colorado River. The expedition drew to a close with the onslaught of winter, and Wheeler, as director of the dangerous journey, sent a group back to Congress with the photos that had been taken. Unfortunately, some of the photos that had survived the rough ride down the Colorado were lost when the stagecoach was ambushed and one of the party was killed.

William Bell replaced O'Sullivan during 1872 with the Wheeler survey. Bell was a Philadelphian who used a dry photographic process, which was unusual for other photographers who worked with the same subject matter.

In 1873, O'Sullivan returned to complete the survey and produced some of his more memorable works. His works showing the Zuni Indians and their ancient pueblo were some of the first photos to document that lifestyle.

The expedition produced a variety of documents and photographic data which remain powerfully historic.

JULIUS VANNERSON

Julius Vannerson, the manager of a studio in Washington, D.C., photographed Indian delegations in 1858 and treated them as he would any other type of delegation. He was not concerned whether one Indian was more important than another; he just did the best work he could, for a rather uncaring client—the American government.

ADAM CLARK VROMAN

Adam Clark Vroman had a clear, realistic vision of the Indian and chronicled the Hopi life with an empathy few have been able to match either before or after. His work, during the late 1890s, chronicled his anger at the conditions under which the Indians were forced to live, as well as his determination to do something about it. The photos which he took were aimed at "raising the consciousness" of others.

He photographed the Hopi, Taoseno, Navaho, and Zuni tribes, but not with full war bonnets and memorabilia as Curtis did, nor in a room which was foreign to them as Vannerson did. Instead, he showed them as human beings who were struggling to eke out an existence on the arid plains and mesas of the Southwest. His photos clearly showed the Indians' strong religious characters, the depths of their beliefs, and exposed the truth of the Indians' lives as no white man ever had before.

THE INDIAN IN FICTION

Many popular magazines that had a wide distribution at the turn of the century were publishing short stories about the American Indian. Though some were stereotypical, an amazing portion of fictionalized Indians were realistically depicted. When movies and TV drew visual portraits of Indian characters, those Indians were, more often than not, stereotyped more than their earlier literary counterparts.

In reading what has been written by, as well as about, the American Indian, you can decide what, if any, stereotypes have been carried through the ages regarding various tribes, their habits and customs, and what the Indian's popular image was at that time and what speech patterns were used. Remember, though, that we are speaking of *fiction*, and writers of fiction are bound to treat the subject of Indians far differently than writers who are attempting to accurately portray the native American and his/her place in society.

One fine collection of Indian stories is *Indians, Indians, Indians*, edited by Phyllis R. Fenner and published by Franklin Watts in 1950. This anthology features a story called "The Second Race," by Merritt P. Allen.

BIOGRAPHIES OF INDIAN WRITERS AND THOSE WHO SPECIALIZED IN INDIAN STORIES

Frank Applegate

Native Tales of New Mexico (Lippincott, 1932) featured Frank Applegate's stories "The Apache Kid," "The Buried Treasure of Cochiti," "The Founding of Hano," and "Hopi Susanna Corn Blossom." His stories were also featured in *Indian Stories From the Pueblos* (Rio Grande Press, 1929).

Mary Austin

Another Indian story anthology, *One Smoke Stories* (Houghton, Mifflin, 1934), featured stories about many different tribes which appear to have realistic overtones about the culture of the various tribes they depict. The prolific writer for this and other publications of that time was Mary Austin.

George A. Boyce

In the anthology *Some People are Indians*, it appears the editors were trying to convince white people that the native American was a human being. George A. Boyce was an author published by then on a regular basis.

Robert J. Conley

Robert J. Conley was a Cherokee Indian who wrote for *Indian Voice*. His short stories were about Indians who tried to make their way into the white man's world.

Adelina Defender

Adelina Defender, a Pueblo Indian, wrote "No Time for Tears" for *An American Indian Anthology* (Blue Cloud Abbey, 1971). It is a story of the way a woman was treated in the mission school and how they forced her to turn her back on her Indian ways.

Charles A. Eastman

Charles A. Eastman, a popular Santee Sioux short story writer, was published in *Old Indian Days*, *Harper's*, *Sunset*, *Craftsman*, and *Ladies' Home Journal*. His stories, written in the early 1900s, are a combination of realistic Indian stories and tales of how various Indians coped with the ways of the white men.

William Faulkner

A well-known writer who wrote many short stories about the American Indian was William Faulkner. His short stories appeared in such publications as *Go Down, Moses*, *The Saturday Evening Post*, and *Collected Stories of William Faulkner*.

Hamlin Garland

Hamlin Garland, a prolific short story writer, published a good number of stories where the plot focused on the American Indian and his/her conflicts with white men. *The Book of the American Indian* made use of quite a few of his stories, as did *Prairie Son and Western Story*.

Richard G. Green

An Oneida Indian, Richard G. Green was actively writing in the early 1970s and was featured in such publications as *Indian Voice*. Green's stories are realistic depictions of everyday matters in Indian life and are clearly shown from the Indian's viewpoint.

George Bird Grinnell

Stories about Indian and animal mythology were created by George Bird Grinnell during the early 1900s for *Harper's*.

Ernest Hemingway

Even literary luminary Ernest Hemingway used his pen to create tales of Indian lore. Such short stories as "Indian Camp," Ten Indians," and "Fathers and Sons" were included in *The Short Stories of Ernest Hemingway*, published by Scribner's in 1935.

The stories, featuring Hemingway's character Nick Adams, have Hemingway's distinctive trademark of showing us the underside of people's characters and are not understanding to the ways of the Indians.

Dorothy M. Johnson

"A Man Called Horse," now well known as the film epic which starred Richard Harris, was originally a short story written by Dorothy M. Johnson and published in 1953 in *Indian Country* (Ballantine Books). The original short story was first published by Collier's. Johnson was a prolific writer of Indian stories.

Martha Kosanke

Romances about Indians were the focus of Exposition Press's 1954 publication called *Indian Romances of the Western Frontier*. It appears that most, if not all, of the stories published in this book were written by Martha Kosanke.

Jack London

Jack London, well known for his tales of the Northwest Territory, devoted a good deal of time to writing stories about Indians, which are included in collections such as *The God of His Fathers and Other Stories* and *The Best Short Stories of Jack London*.

N. Scott Momaday

N. Scott Momaday (1934–), a contemporary Indian author, won a Pulitzer Prize for *House Made of Dawn* (1968), a story about a Tanoan Indian World War II veteran who reenters society. He also wrote *The Way to Rainy Mountain* (1969), which was illustrated by his father and is about Kiowas visiting his grandmother's house.

Momaday's father was Kiowa and his mother was part Cherokee. He was raised on Navajo, Pueblo, and Apache reservations in Oklahoma. Momaday received his Ph.D. in literature from Stanford University and taught at the University of California at Berkley and Stanford, as well as at others.

He lives in Tucson, where he teaches at the University of Arizona. Also written by him are two volumes of poetry, a memoir, and a coffee table book called *Colorado: Summer, Fall, Winter, Spring* (1973).

Simon J. Ortz

From the Acoma Pueblo, famous for its pottery makers, came the writer Simon J. Ortz. Ortz, whose work was published in the late 1970s in such publications as *Howbah Indians* and *The Man to Send Rain Clouds: Contemporary Stories by American Indians*, wrote short stories about modern problems with Indians as the main characters. The stories are realistic and their characters could be any average American. Some deal with war and some with a character's reaction to life's turmoils, yet all are believable and true to life.

Verner Z. Reed

During the turn of the century, Verner Z. Reed was producing fiction about the American Indian for anthologies such as *Tales of the Sun-land* (Continental, 1897) and *Adobeland Stories* (Badger, 1898), and for periodicals such as *Overland Monthly*. Using true Indian names, Reed's characters were often Pueblo Indians who dealt with religious problems or related legends of their culture.

Frederic Remington

Frederic Remington, the artist/sculptor, exercised his literary talents by doing short stories about the Amerind for *Harper's* during the turn of the century. His main characters are usually whites or half-breeds who relate the Indians' tale through their own eyes, though often repeating the Indians' words.

Leslie Siko

Leslie Siko (Laguna Pueblo) published a number of stories in the 1974 Viking book *The Man to Send Rain Clouds: Contemporary Stories by American Indians*, including the title story. Her work is diversified and includes tales which give a fictional recounting of historical facts, as well as contemporary stories of families and their everyday conflicts.

William Joseph Snelling

In the early 1800s, William Joseph Snelling wrote of the Northwest Indian. He must have been intimidated by the public's view of the "noble savage" because much of his work was done anonymously in *Tales of the Northwest: Or, Sketches of Indian Life and Character*.

John Steinbeck

John Steinbeck, another literary giant, wrote stories about the Amerind which were published in *The Long Valley* in 1938 (Viking).

Cy Warman

Cy Warman, another turn-of-the-century author, was featured in a number of periodicals and anthologies in *Frontier Stories* (Scribner's 1918) and *Weiga of Temagami and Other Indian Tales* (McLeod and Allen, 1908). His stories relate tales of Indians and their relations to French-Canadian settlers, often centering on half-breed characters.

Frank Waters

Frank Waters, born in 1902 in Colorado Springs, is the author of stories about American Indians. He wrote 22 books including *Fever Pitch* (1930), *Masked Gods* (1950), *Book of the Hopi* (1963), *Pumpkin Seed Point* (1969), *Mexico Mystique: The Coming Sixth World of Consciousness* (1975), and *Flight from Fiesta*. His book, *The Man Who Killed the Deer*, was in print for more than 40 years and is about a young Taos Indian caught between two cultures.

Waters' father was part Indian, so he spent some of his childhood at trading posts on Indian reservations. He was familiar with Utes who moved into his hometown with whom he visited with his father. He attended Colorado College and majored in engineering, but dropped out to take a laborer's job in the Salt Creek, Wyoming, oil fields.

OTHER

Dance Group

The American Indian Dance Theatre, formed in the spring of 1986, travels through the West giving performances to enthusiastic crowds. Performers are dancers and musicians from the most important American Indian dance festivals and ceremonials in the region. Future projects include travel throughout the country, Europe, and the Far East, as well as a TV special and film appearance.

Will Sampson (Actor)

Will Sampson (died 6/3/87) was a Creek actor and artist as well as a member of the Screen Actors Guild. He promoted the Indian in acting, directing, writing, and producing.

As an artist, Sampson sold his first painting at the age of three. He did landscapes, western, and Indian scenes in the style of Charles Russell, and won the Philbrook Art Center (Tulsa) art award in 1951, as well as many others. Sampson exhibited at the Smithsonian, Library of Congress, Amon Carter Museum, and the Creek Council House Museum. He played the role of Chief Bromden in "One Flew Over the Cuckoo's Nest."

EPHEMERA AND ADVERTISING LISTINGS

Advertising

Cigar tin, Kennebec; ca. 1915; depicts Indian in side view; $2\frac{1}{2}$″ × $8\frac{1}{2}$″ × 4″.   **$40–$60**

Dispenser, Indian Rock Ginger Ale; pump dispenser; ca. 1913–19; pump may not be original.   **$3600–$4000**

Courtesy of Donna McMenamin, private collector. Photo by Donald Vogt.

Dolls; Skookum dolls made by Tammen Mfg. Company of Colorado during 1910–15 (they used to promote Skookum apples); earliest are handmade, dried apple heads; all in excellent condition.   **$25–$250**

Sign, Mail Pouch Tobacco; ca. 1905; thin cardboard litho under glass; extremely rare; shows Indian papoose hanging in pouch on tree; 14½″ × 19½″.   **$1600–$1800**

Sign, Sleepy Eye; lithographed on tin; self-framed; 24¼″ × 20″; depicts "Old Sleepy Eye," Indian chief; ca. 1895.   **$375–$450**

Tin, Mohawk Chief Tobacco; 4″ × 6″ tobacco container; won best award at 1985 Convention, Allentown, PA.   **$750–$1100**

Ephemera

Advertising

Old ax advertisement showing an Indian; ca. 1920; 9″ × 6″.   **$10–$20**

Books

Complete set of Henry R. Schoolcraft's *Information Respecting the History, Conditions, and Prospects of the Indian Tribes of the United States;* Philadelphia, Lippincott, Grambo and Co.., 1853–1857; six volumes; large quarto; rebound in modern cloth; various degrees of waterstaining; many plates, maps, and engravings; two volumes inscribed by Commissioner of Indian Affairs, J.W. Denver. **$850–$1000**

Crooked Beak of Heaven and *Indian Artifacts of Northwest Coast;* ca. 1975.
$45–$75

Dictionary of American Indian and *Voices from Wounded Knee;* ca. 1978.
$25–$35

Five North American Indian-related Books; titles include; Gladys A. Reichard, *Navajo Shephard and Weaver*, First Edition, Nov. 1936; G. Moon, *Indian Legends in Rhyme*, 1917, illustrated by Karl Moon; Fr. J.K. Dixon, *The Vanishing Race*, plates by R. Wanamaker; H. Whitney, *Hunting With the Eskimos*, 1910, embossed frontis "Presentation Copy"; and L. Spence *Myths and Legends of the North American Indians*, 1914.
$150–$200

Group of American Indian-related books; nine volumes; includes Rev. J.G. Wood, *The Natural History of Man*, London, 1870; and George Mills, *Navajo Art and Culture*, Colorado, 1959. **$125–$175**

Group of Northwest Coast Indian and Eskimo reference books.
$425–$500

League of the Ho-De-No-Sau-Nee (or Iroquois), by Lewis H. Morgan; Dodd and Mead and Co., 1904. **$40–$60**

Lot; On the Border With Crook (1891); *Heroes and Hunters of the West* (1858); *Life of Sitting Bull; History of the Indian War of 1890–1891.* **$50–$75**

Lot; lot of associated pieces for Chief Shunatona, Director of the U.S. Indian Band; includes 8″ × 10″ photo w/lengthy inscription and signature; a piece of sheet music entitled "The Trail to Long Ago" w/photo of Chief Shunatona along w/signature and inscription; several poems, letters, dated 1930 from the "Land of the Ojibways," Minneapolis; another from a Pittsburgh hotel. **$30–$50**

Lot of 11; books and pamphlets relating to American Indians; includes *Pawnee Bill's Trading Post Catalog.* **$45–$75**

North American Indian-related books; volumes; includes F. Dellenbaugh, *The North Americans of Yesterday*, New York, 1906; L. Frank and F. Harlow, *Historic Pottery of the Pueblo Indians*, Boston, 1974; and G. Wharton James, *Indian Basketry*, Pasadena, 1902. **$150–$200**

Primitive Industry or Illustrations of the Handwork in Stone, Bone and Clay of the Native Races of the North Atlantic Seaboard of America; George Bates; Salem; 1881. **$30–$50**

Rinehart's Indians; by F.A. Rinehart; 1899; Omaha, Nebraska.
$70–$110

The American Indian in the United States 1850–1914; by W.K. Moorehead; Andover Press; 1914. **$25–$35**

The Blanket Indians of the Northwest; by Col. G.O. Shields; Vechten Waring Co.; 1921.   **$40–$60**

Totem Tales, Indians of Ohio, and a handmade bark book; ca. 1930.
                                                                          $25–$35

Two books; The Tlingit Indians and *Primitive Heritage;* ca. 1965.   **$25–$50**

Two books; The Washo and *The Cheyenne;* ca. 1965.   **$15–$30**

Who's Who in Indian Relics.   **$15–$25**

PHOTOGRAPHS

Artifact photos; large box full of black-and-white Indian artifact photos;
ca. 1985.   **$15–$30**

Curtis Goldtone; miniature Curtis Goldtone on glass in original frame;
ca. 1910; 3″ × 2½″.   **$70–$125**

Curtis; signed E.S. Curtis; photo of a nude Indian maiden from the
back; matted and framed; 6″ × 4″ image; ca. 1910.   **$65–$85**

Curtis; signed E.S. Curtis; photo of an Indian man; matted and framed;
ca. 1910; 6″ × 4″ image.   **$60–$100**

Curtis; signed E.S. Curtis; photo of a nude Indian maiden from the
back; matted and framed, 10″ × 8″ image; ca. 1910.   **$150–$200**

E.S. Curtis; matted sepia tone of "Old Person—Peigan"; ca. 1911;
24″ × 16″.   **$120–$150**

E.S. Curtis; platinum print; 6″ × 8″; 1904; "Canyon de Chelly."
                                                                    $1400–$1600

Courtesy of J. J. Brookings Gallery, San Jose, CA.

E. S. Curtis; 7″ × 5″; 1904; "Portrait of an Indian Brave."
$1500–$1700

Courtesy of J. J. Brookings Gallery, San Jose, CA.

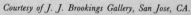

E.S. Curtis; crotone; 9″ × 7″; ca. 1904; "Vanishing Race—Navajo.
$3900–$4300

E. S. Curtis; two photos—one titled "Sioux Appeal," the other "The Vanishing Race"; mounted on brown paper, with embossed copyright legend "L.L.A."; both signed by the photographer ("Curtis") in ink.
$275–$350

F.A. Rinehart; Broken Arm—Ogalla Sioux; 1898 platinum print photo with original color tinting; 9″ × 7″. **$140–$160**

F.A. Rinehart; Chief Wolf Robe (Cheyenne); 1898 platinum print photo with original color tinting; 9″ × 7″; very good condition. **$130–$160**

Five framed, assorted Indian photos; ca. 1935. **$20–$40**

Hand-tinted; framed picture of head and upper torso of male Indian wearing feathered headdress and hair pipe bone breastplate; dated 9/23/27 on back. **$100–$150**

Indian; large original photograph of a very well-dressed Nez Perce lady w/Pendleton blanket; ca. 1910; 15″ × 10″. **$45–$80**

Nez Perce; hand-tinted photo of an Indian in a stand-up bonnet; ca. 1900; 7″ × 4″. **$25–$40**

Original Hileman photograph of Two Guns White Calf signed by both people; ca. 1927; 12″ × 15″. **$85–$125**

Three; frame of three old Indian photos; ca. 1900. **$70–$85**

Three original Indian photographs of different Indians; ca. 1900 **$30–$50**

Two; American Indian Cabinet Carte de Visite; 19th century; each inscribed on reverse: the first, "A Victoria B.C. young Indian with his Hudson Bay blanket around him," 2½″ × 3¼″; the other, "Crowfoot, Chief of the Blackfeet, taken at Regina . . . when in route . . . July 7, 1884," 4″ × 8¼″. **$125–$150**

PHOTOGRAVURE

E. S. Curtis; large browntone from the original folio "On the Shore at Nooka"; Plate 366. **$80–$100**

E.S. Curtis; large browntone from the original photo "The Piki Maker"; Plate 432; ca. 1906; 11″ × 15″. **$90–$120**

E.S. Curtis; large browntone from the original folio "Counting the Record"; Plate 413; ca. 1921; 11″ × 15″. **$80–$100**

E.S. Curtis; large browntone from the original folio "A Serrano Woman of Tejon"; Plate 512; 11″ × 15″; ca. 1924. **$60–$80**

E.S. Curtis; large browntone from the original folio "West Coast of Vancouver Island"; Plate 391. **$80–$100**

E.S. Curtis; large browntone from the original folio "Fishing Platform—Hupa"; Plate 465; ca. 1923; 11″ × 15″. **$60–$80**

E.S. Curtis; large browntone from the original folio "Women's Dress—Tolowa"; Plate 464; ca. 1923; 11″ × 15″.   **$130–$150**

E. S. Curtis; large browntone from the original folio "Yurok Drummer"; Plate 457; ca. 1923; 11″ × 15″.   **$100–$150**

E. S. Curtis; large browntone (with onionskin) from the original folio "Ceremonial Bathing"; Plate 376; ca. 1924; 15″ × 11″.   **$80–$100**

E.S. Curtis; large browntone (with onionskin) from the original folio "The Fishing Pool—So. Miwok"; ca. 1924; Plate 494; 15″ × 11″.
$130–$150

E.S. Curtis; large browntone (with onionskin) from the original folio "Depositing a Prayer Stick"; ca. 1924; 15″ × 11″.   **$70–$100**

E.S. Curtis; large browntone (with onionskin) from the original folio "On the Shores of Clear Lake"; Plate 477; ca. 1924; 15″ × 11″.
$80–$100

E.S. Curtis; large browntone (w/onionskin) from the original folio "The Berry Picker—Clayoquat"; Plate 368; ca. 1915; 15″ × 11″. **$50–$75**

E.S. Curtis; large browntone (with onionskin) from the original folio "Principal Female Shaman of the Hupa"; ca. 1924; Plate 467; 15″ × 11″.   **$75–$100**

E.S. Curtis; large browntone (with onionskin) from the original folio "Wild Grapes"; Plate 480; ca. 1924; 15″ × 11″.   **$50–$75**

E.S. Curtis; sepia photogravures; six; 20th century; Plate 232, "Flathead Camp on Jocko River," copyright 1910; Plate 44, "The Pima Woman," copyright 1907; "A Piegan Dandy," copyright 1900; Plate 187, "Tearing Lodge-Piegan," copyright 1910; all marked "Photogravure John Andrew and Son"; also, Plate 592, "Offering to the Sun-San Ildefonso," copyright 1925; Plate 426, "The Potter," copyright 1906; both marked "Photogravure, Suffolk Eng. Company, Cambridge, Mass."
$800–$950

E.S. Curtis; large browntone from the original folio "Hupa Woman"; Plate 468; ca. 1923.   **$60–$80**

E.S. Curtis; large browntone from the original folio "Lucero–Santo Domingo"; Plate 557; matted and framed; ca. 1925; 22″ × 18″.
$75–$100

E.S. Curtis; large browntone from the original folio "Wife of Modoc Henry—Klamath"; Plate 445; matted and framed; 22″ × 18″; ca. 1923.   **$75–$100**

220 *AMERICAN INDIAN COLLECTIBLES*

REPORT, BUREAU OF AMERICAN ETHNOLOGY, WASHINGTON

1878–80 (1881); Annual Report; good condition, spine shaky; comprehensive report on "Evolution of Languages" by Powell; "Study of Mortuary Customs of North American Indians"; "Central American Picture Writing" by E.S. Holden; "Cessions of Land by Indian Tribes to the U.S." by C.C. Royce; "Sign Language Among the North American Tribes" by Mallery. **$27–$40**

1885–86 (1891); 7th Annual Report; good condition; report on "Grand Medicine Society of the Ojibwa"; "Linguistic Families of North America." **$27–$35**

1886–87 (1891); 8th Annual Report; very good condition; reports on "Pueblo Architecture" by Mindeleff; "Ceremonial and Mythical Sand Painting of the Navajo Indians" by J. Stevenson. **$25–$35**

1887–88 (1892); 9th Annual Report; very good condition; with detailed reports on the "Point Barrow Expedition" by J. Murdoch; report on the "Medicine Men of the Apaches" by Capt. John Bourke. **$50–$75**

1888–89 (1893); 10th Annual Report; very good condition; complete report on "Picture Writing of the American Indian" by G. Mallery. **$27–$35**

1889–90 (1894); 11th Annual Report; very good condition; study of the culture and living customs of "The Sia" by M. Stevenson; report on "Ethnology of the (Eskimo) Ungara Distr."; comprehensive report on "Sioux Cults, Myths, Beliefs." **$25–$35**

1890–91 (1894); 12th Annual Report; very good condition; "U.S. Mound Explorations" by Cyrus Thomas; report on mounds in Manitoba, Dakota, Minnesota, Wisconsin, Iowa, Illinois, Missouri, Arkansas, Louisiana, Mississippi, East and West Tennessee, Kentucky, Alabama, Georgia, South Carolina, Florida, West Virginia, Ohio, Pennsylvania, New York, and Minnesota. **$30–$40**

1898–99 (1903); 20th Annual Report; very fine condition; report on the "Aboriginal Pottery of the Eastern United States" by W. Holmes. **$30–$50**

OTHER

Glass negative; showing couple in Ghost Dance dress.

Postcards; 56 old Indian and Old West-related. **$75–$110**

Postcards; L. Peterson; 14 postcards of Indians which include Minnehaha, Chief Big Feather, Chief Yellow Hawk, Chief Sitting Bull, Chief Eagle Feather, Chief Geronimo, Chief High Horse, Starlight, Fighting Wolf, Red Cloud, Hiawatha, White Swan and Papoose, Sunshine, Eagle Feather, and Squaw. **$75–$110**

Poster; 20″ × 30″ of Indians of North America and two pairs of Osage Indians with engraved metal arm bands. $10–$15

Sioux Indian painting portfolio, volumes I and II; C. Szwedzicki; rare and complete two-volume set entitled "Volume I: Paintings of The Sioux and Other Tribes of the Great Plains"; "Volume II: The Art of Amos Bad Heart Buffalo." $3000–$4000

From the collection of Lahoma Haddock Goldsmith. Photo by Donald Vogt.

Stamps; first-day covers featuring Indian history. $15–$25

Stereoviews; lot of seven of the Indians and the West; Feast Dance at Crow Reservation; Graves at Little Big Horn; Giant Ten Ox Team dragging Logs at Boulder Creek Camp; Unloading Reindeer at Seattle; Herd of Wild Buffalo near Flathead Lake; Ute Indian and Family; Cattle Roundup. $50–$75

Stereoviews; lot of three cards on the Southwest Indian tribes; Chief of Kachinas Dance at Moki Village; Moki Cliffs of the Middle Mesa, Arizona; Wolpi—a Chief Pueblo of the Mysterious Moki Race (Cliff Dwellers), Arizona. $65–$85

JEWELRY

▼▼▼▼▼▼▼▼▼▼▼

BUYING INFORMATION

When buying any antique item, it is always important to know the tricks of the trade. Since quite a bit of what is being sold as Indian jewelry is being imported from the Philippines or Taiwan, it is imperative that the "buyer beware." For this reason, as well as to educate those who are interested in pursuing the idea of building a collection of Indian jewelry, I have detailed a few ways to evaluate your jewelry before buying it.

Breaks in Stones

Turquoise often has breaks in the stone, which is acceptable if you are buying a piece of jewelry for personal use. If you are buying for investment purposes, however, it is important to check the piece carefully.

Do not replace a broken stone. Instead, have it mended by a reputable smith—preferably one familiar with turquoise and its markings.

If a stone has a hole plugged with a silver spike, this proves that the piece was made before 1900 because that is the way the pieces were repaired at that time.

Hollow Silver Beads

Silver beads were made three different ways: by hand, bench, or machine. Machine-made beads have no flaws and are all alike. Handmade beads may have flaws, and, though the sizes will be close, each will be a little different. Silver beads which are extremely shiny are not old, and old silver beads should not be taken apart and polished.

Pawn

Pawn jewelry began in the 1870s when Indians traded at posts. They traded their jewelry during the winter when they needed income to get through the season. They redeemed it when their sheep were sheared, and payments for the wool gave the Navajo the cash they needed to feed and support themselves.

The pieces which were pawned were secondary, expendable pieces that the Navajo could afford to lose—they usually did not pawn their best pieces. Only if the Indian did not retrieve his jewelry within a specified time could the dealer sell it, and, because of regulations imposed by the Bureau of Indian Affairs (that the jewelry could only be sold for what the dealer paid plus 10%), the pawn jewelry which came on the market was a bargain.

Though there is still some pawn jewelry on the market, it is not as plentiful, nor as inexpensive, as it was before World War II. Again, the buyer should beware because there are people making phony squash blossom necklaces of 1941 dimes and others who print pawn tickets to put on "junk" jewelry in order to sell it as true pawn.

Signatures

Most Indian jewelers do not sign their work as a normal practice, though it is becoming more common than it once was on the earlier work done by the Navajo and Zuni smiths. If you find a signature, it does not have the meaning it would if you were holding a fine piece of china.

Before the white man influenced Indian style, he could tell his work or the work of others by the style and the craftsmanship—it was not necessary to place another type of symbol on the work in order to announce its make. During the 1930s, the Hopis began a regular use of hallmarks and the Museum of Northern Arizona (Flagstaff) has a collection of these. Though the importance of marking one's work is being pushed by the Museum and by the Hopi Silvercraft Guild, there are still those who do not think signing their work is important to their recognition as artists.

Stamping

As with beads, the handmade stamps are all a little individualistic, while the machine-stamped versions are alike.

Wearmarks

Wearmarks are noticeable on any jewelry that the owner has worn regularly. Look for wearmarks on items such as concha belts, which would have received abrasion from counters and chairs. Check rings and bracelets for that "too shiny" look. Look for dings or dents which prove the jewelry may have been struck against a hard object, and for the obvious thinness of metal which has been worn in the same place for a long time.

Weight

Quality of Navajo jewelry can often be judged by its weight. The Navajo silversmiths often used all (or much) of the silver they had available because the Navajo prefer heavy silver.

After the 1800s, when trade and commercialism became more common, the silversmiths were given a certain amount of silver to work with and were paid per piece. During the period from 1870–1880, Navajo jewelry was much lighter, though there are arguments as to whether this was due to a shortage of silver or to the fact that there were so many beginners learning the craft at that time. The Navajo, if allowed to make jewelry as they wish, will go for heavy jewelry with bold designs.

THE MAKING OF INDIAN JEWELRY

Silver coins were the primary source of jewelry made by the Southwestern Indians. Before 1900, a silversmith had to melt down coins and cast them into an ingot because of the thickness and size of jewelry preferred by Southwestern Indians. He then hammered the ingot into a sheet and made a finished piece.

His work was hammered down as smoothly as possible with the tools available, and then it was polished with sand or ashes because sandpaper did not come along until much later. Old, unused jewelry often shows the marks left by polishing stones (before 1900).

JEWELRY OF VARIOUS TRIBES

Hopi (Southwest)

The Hopi learned to do silverwork after the Navajo and Zuni tribes. The majority of Hopi jewelry, as we know it today, was produced after the 1930s when a conscious effort was made to get the tribe to produce more silverwork and to develop an overlay style. Their quality is high and the Hopi designs are traditionally abstract. Hopi silversmiths generally do not use stones in their work.

Iroquois (Northeast)

Though the Navajo and Zuni are the best known silversmiths of all Indian tribes, the Iroquois Indians were also known to work with silver. Their silverwork began around 1800 when they hammered coins and ingots into sheets and decorated them with stamped designs.

Brooches, made of hearts, were often called the Iroquois National Badge. A design which incorporated the much-used heart with a crown was called "Owl" or "Guardian of the Night." Though brooches were very popular, dangling earrings were also popular and were worn by both male and female.

Lakes Area

The Lakes Area tribes made silverwork that was less lacy than that of the Iroquois tribe. The Menomini tribe made and wore hair decorations, earrings, bracelets, and combs of simple engraved or stamped designs.

Mandan (Plains)

The Mandan, as well as other Prairie tribes, used antlers to make bracelets. The antlers were made into strips, then engraved and soaked so that they could be bent into shape.

Navajo (Southwest)

It is said that Mexican silversmiths taught the Navajo Indians how to make jewelry, yet the Indians did not follow the Mexican style of filigree. The stamping designs used on Navajo jewelry are similar to Mexican designs on leatherwork, and even the swastika and arrow designs are attributed to Mexican influence.

Atsidi Sani was the first Navajo silversmith and his teacher was a Mexican blacksmith named Nakai Tsosi. Tsosi taught Sani ironworking and silversmithing techniques, although neither made jewelry. The Navajo had that idea and began making and wearing jewelry after their release from Bosque Redondo in 1868. Atsidi Sani taught at least nine other people his trade, including his son, Red Smith. His training provided a new way for his people to boost their economy and jewelry soon provided a surplus income, as well as necessary adornment.

Prior to 1880, decorations were applied by rocker engraving or cutting the design into the metal with a file. Before this time, a cold chisel was used, and, after 1885, stamping was done.

To stamp a design onto metal, a piece of a wornout file made of carbon was heated until it glowed, then was pulled from the fire and shaped by hammering. After the shape was achieved, the piece was reheated and allowed to slowly cool. After it was cool, the smith could file in final design details. Then the tool was cleaned and gently heated, and, once more, quenched. This process gave the piece the hardiness needed to keep it from bending, yet kept it soft enough to stop splitting or chipping when struck.

Navajos carved pieces directly into stone molds, as well as by hammering silver ingots. It took time to carve a design into a mold so this technique was not used often.

To make a good cast, a two-piece mold had to be made with a spruce hole and air vents. It also had to be coated with fine charcoal (or smoked) so that the hot metal would flow evenly into the design rather than stick in the deeper carved spaces. The piece was then filed and sanded until smooth instead of being flattened onto a sheet. This technique was used to produce buckles, bracelets, buttons, rings, najas (crescent-shaped pendants), and ketohs (bowguards, pronounced "gato").

Soldering is one of the hardest tasks to master when making jewelry, even for those jewelers of today who have modern torches and the help of chemical engineers who formulate fluxes. Indians had to make their own solder by combining silver filings with brass filings from old pans or cartridge cases. The mixture was then placed at the soldering point, along with borax (used as a sedimentary flux). The pieces were put into the red hot coals of a forge, just below the material's melting point. If the silversmith was lucky, the solder would work and the pieces would stick together. If not, additional heat was applied and the joint completed. If the pieces became oxidized, the process was begun over again.

Jewelry became so important to the Navajo that no proper Navajo Indian would feel "dressed" without it, and it became a sign of wealth. They often exchanged their jewelry for livestock, food, material or medical services.

By the turn of the century, lighter-weight pieces were being made by the Navajo for sale to those tourists now coming into the Southwest. The era of tourist trade had begun.

Northwest Coast

Northwest Coast Indians wore metal jewelry made of copper or silver. Tlingit silver bracelets were worn by shamans and incised with straight lines, geometric shapes, and the stylized animals which are instantly recognizable as Northwest Coast decoration. In the early nineteenth century, silver and gold replaced copper as the metal of choice because they were easier to obtain and to work with.

The Indians of this region had been metalworkers long before the arrival of the white man, and, although they used stone hammers and anvils, the results they achieved were not crude. Though earlier reports stated that Tlingits learned their jewelry-making techniques from Russians, upon further contemplation it is obvious that the skills the Indians had were already theirs and not learned from the "newcomers" to their land.

Tlingit history states that their first blacksmith was a Chilkat woman named Shukasaka. Her skill in metalworking had won her that name, which means "half man." These Indians used silver coins, brought to them by traders, as metal with which they made nose or finger rings. Money had no value to them, as did objects with no use. The only thing they could think to do with such things was to present them to one another as gifts. However, the words in the Tlingit, Haida, and Kwakiutl languages which mean silver are all variations on the English word "dollar."

Though Tlingits received praise for their copper and iron work, the Haida tribe was most proficient with silver, and they produced silver articles such as rings, earrings, bracelets, spoons, and napkin rings. Of all the jewelry, bracelets continue to be most popular. They are heavy and deeply carved, whereas Tlingit bracelets have bands of even width and are lighter in weight. Northwestern tribes commonly wear nose rings and other jewelry as symbols of status.

Before the turn of the century, white influences/motifs were as frequently used as native designs. For example, the American eagle was an oft-used motif. Haida eagles are generally more geometric than the realistic forms of Tlingit eagles. Whale designs done by Tlingits are distinctive and best recognized by their segmented, finger-like flippers which reveal the skeletal structure beneath their skin.

One Haida silversmith who has received attention is Charles Edenshaw. His career spanned 50 years and his style moved from an early split representation of a dogfish to the "classic style" reached in 1880. This latter style is recognized by less angular formlines, more fluid junctures, and more carefully planned negative spaces.

Plains

The Southern Plains tribes influenced Southwestern jewelry in that the concha belt, naja, and metal bridle were used extensively by them.

Conchas were originally hair pieces which were attached closely to the scalp, but the decoration grew until the hair plate often reached six feet long. When a man sat down, the hair plate was often pulled around his shoulder and across his lap, resembling a belt. Plains women often wore these ornaments as belts and let the extra length trail down to one side. The Navajo adopted the use of concha belts from the Plains, but changed the German silver to silver and applied Mexican-style decorations to the disks.

Naja decoration was constantly used by the Plains Indian on ear pendants, headstalls, and other items. When the Navajo made bridles, the construction was almost exactly the same as those used by the Plains Indians.

The Plains tribe wore their own metal decorative pieces by the beginning of the nineteenth century, using silver and brass until German silver was introduced in the 1860s. They worked with metal until the 1880s when such ornaments were readily available and the need to produce them diminished.

While the Navajo utilized some Plains ideas, it seems that the Plains Indians copied the Navajo idea of stamped designs on metalwork.

Seminole and Choctaw (Southeast)

Seminole and Choctaw silver jewelry is simple and consists mainly of brooches and pendants. The Seminole were also known to use watch chains as jewelry (though they seldom owned watches), but these chains were European and not made by the Indians.

Zuni (Southwest)

Frank Hamilton Cushing, the explorer and historian who lived with the Zuni tribe from 1879–1881, told of the Zuni's jewelry-making techniques. He said that draw plates, made from deer scapulae, were used previously by the Zuni to form silver and copper wire from silver and copper rods. The thinning, bending, stamping, and drawing of wire was done when the metal was cold because heat made the metal weak and crumbly.

The Zuni have also been carving stones and shells for hundreds of years and making jewelry from shell, jet, turquoise inlay, mosaic on shell, wood, stone, bone, and ceramics. Silver is merely a vehicle to hold turquoise with very little ornamentation. They try to make their pieces lighter, often by using twisted wire, raindrops, wire scallops, or stamping. For this reason, Zuni earrings are often long and dangly with pieces of stone or silver hanging from the wire. The Zuni decorations on their jewelry are lighter and finer than the Navajo, which has a massive look and feel to it.

Zunis excel in mosaic work and use jet, turquoise, coral, and shell in that type of work. They also carve small figures in their jewelry. Needlepoint, made with tiny, oval, pointed-end stones, is also made by the Zuni jewelry makers.

BIOGRAPHIES OF SOME INDIAN JEWELRY MAKERS

(There is some information within the chapter about the various jewelry makers of the tribes mentioned.)

Mike Bird (1946–)

Mike Bird, of the San Juan Pueblo, was self-taught and comes from an artistic family. His grandmother (Luteria Atencio) was a potter. Some of her work is owned by the Smithsonian. A weaver and embroiderer, his mother, Pablita Velarde, still shows at the Indian market.

Bird, like other traditional jewelers, has studied the ancient ways and incorporates what he has learned into his work. This work is evident in a necklace of his in the Millicent Rogers Museum (Taos, New Mexico.)

Bird uses the cross and heart symbols often in his work, but has also created pieces with carved animals or fish on them. He has generated prizes for his work at the Indian Market for petroglyph figural pins.

Cippy Crazy Horse, or Cipriano Quintana (1946–)

This Cochiti jeweler works in silver and is the son of Joe H. Quintana, a most productive and successful silversmith who was employed in 1939 (one of five from Cochiti). Crazy Horse, however, did not study silversmithing with his father. He did not learn his craft until an accident disabled him, and, unable to do much else, he tried his hand at silversmithing. Now he uses his father's work as an example and is making traditional silver jewelry.

Crazy Horse has regularly won awards for his jewelry in the eight years he has been entering his pieces at the Indian Market. He researches traditional styles which he uses in his necklaces, bracelets, concha belts, rings, and other pieces.

Crazy Horse uses homemade tools in his work, yet also employs the use of an acetylene torch, buffing wheels, and an assortment of other, more modern, tools.

Cippy Crazy Horse has won many awards for the clean aesthetic designs of his work, such as the 1987 Indian Market George C. West Memorial Award, as well as first place for his concha belt in the "Traditional Jewelry Without Stones" category.

Jake Livingston

This 1988 IACA "Artist of the Year" was born with a Zuni father and Navajo mother. His father, Jacob Halso Su, taught Livingston how to work with silver.

In 1969, Livingston left the Marine Corps, where he had earned three Purple Hearts, and went to work as an operating engineer and heavy equipment mechanic for the State of Arizona. In 1972, he started selling his work and was awarded Best of Show at the Gallup Ceremonial in 1974 for a reversible concho belt. He followed that award with Best of Show in 1975 for a four-sided gold necklace which sold for $60,000. Livingston has also won top awards at the Santa Fe Indian Market, the Heard Museum Show, the Museum of Northern Arizona, and others.

Charles Loloma (1921–)

A coral, lapis lazuli and gold bracelet made by Loloma was featured on the cover of an auction booklet for the American Craft Museum and sold for $10,000 at that auction. Loloma is credited with being the artist who created the first modern (ultra-contemporary) Indian jewelry. He and the generation of artists who are following him incorporate gold and semi-precious stones, rather than turquoise and coral, into their jewelry. (For more information on this artist, see biography in Art chapter.)

Preston Monongye (1927–1987)

Collectors have long praised this Hopi jeweler's work in silver and have rewarded his excellence with over 700 awards. A jack-of-all-trades, Monongye spent most of his adult life promoting Indian art both in America and internationally. He learned how to work silver from his uncle in the village of Hotevilla when he was nine years old. Later, he took a variety of college courses and served in the Army during the Korean war.

Angie Reano Owen (1946–)

A San Domingo jewelry maker, Owen does contemporary work mostly in mosaic on shell, yet adheres to the traditional way of making jewelry. She was born at the Santo Domingo Pueblo and grew up making jewelry, taught by her mother. Owen sold her first attempts at jewelry-making on the Plaza in Santa Fe, then her jewelry was bought by the Los Angeles County Museum Shop, as well as other museum shops.

Angie married Don Owen in 1969. He was recently coordinator of the annual Indian Market sponsored by the Southwestern Association on Indian Affairs. Owen encouraged his wife to research early Hohokam and Anasazi jewelry. Angie continues to study since having her work so well received.

Angie Reano Owen allows the natural shape of a shell or stone to design her jewelry. She just adds the mosaic geometrics that follow the curve and line of the piece. Owen's earrings trace the Hohokam sunburst style and the pendant styles.

The jeweler's work is in the Heard Museum in Phoenix, as well as in others, and she is making sure her techniques are passed on by teaching her son and daughter the art of making jewelry.

JEWELRY LISTINGS

Barrettes

Apache; beaded hide; 2½″ × 4½″ long; plum and white-colored beads in eight-point star/flower designs.   **$30–$50**

Navajo; silver and turquoise; sterling; 1½″ wide × 3″ long set with three, oval, blue-green cabochons; total wgt. 1¹/₁₀ ozs.   **$20–$40**

Belts/Belt Buckles

Hopi, silver belt buckle; sterling 2¼″ × 3³/₈″ with scroll and humpbacked flute player design; weight 2¾ ozs.   **$85–$125**

Navajo, belt; silver concho, comprised of seven stamped and engraved open-centered conchos, the open centered buckle stamp and repousse decorated buckle; 3¾″ × 3″; concho: 3³/₈″ × 4¼″; purchased early 1950s.   **$1600–$2000**

Navajo, belt; handmade silver concho belt w/turquoise stone in each concho; 41″; ca. 1885.   **$175–$250**

Navajo, belt; silver concho of nine stamped and repoussed; the open center buckle stamp and repousse decorated; purchased early 1950s at Frost Curio, Cody, Wyoming.   **$400–$600**

Navajo, Belt; silver and turquoise concho; sandcast; comprised of six spoked oval conchos, seven butterflies, a stamp-decorated buckle; all set w/oval spider web turquoise stones; conchos 2¾″ × 2⁵/₁₆″; butterfly 2″ × 1½″; buckle 3″ × 2¼″; purchased in the early 1950s.   **$850–$1000**

Navajo, buckle; "old pawn" sandcast turquoise and silver buckle; 3″ × 3½″; ca. 1935.   **$50–$80**

Navajo, buckle; large rectangular turquoise, coral, and silver buckle; initials "J.C." in coral; 3½″ × 3″; ca. 1940.   **$25–$35**

Silver belt buckles (3); two oval with stylized flowers and turquoise centers; one triangle decorated with a bear claw set in jet.   **$145–$200**

Zuni, belt; contemporary concho style/cluster, matched turquoise pieces.   **$2000–$3000**

Zuni, belt buckle; silver and petit point; 2½″ × 3½″ sterling set with approximately 116 blue slivers, signed W. Begay.　　**$110–$175**

Bola/Bola Ties

Bola, Zuni; "old pawn" inlay "Knife Wing" dancer bola tie; ca. 1935; 1½″ × 1″.　　**$55–$75**

Bola, Navajo; silver bola w/turquoise chip inlay and ironwood center; ca. 1965; 1½″ × 1″.　　**$15–$20**

Bola, Navajo; turquoise, silver, and coral chip inlay Peyote bird bola; signed Tommy Singer; ca. 1975; 2½″ × 1″.　　**$35–$50**

Bola, Navajo; unusual turquoise and silver bola tie w/heishe trim; ca. 1965; 2″ × 2″.　　**$35–$50**

Bola tie; large silver arrowhead-shaped bola tie set w/large turquoise stone; ca. 1970; 4″ × 2″.　　**$75–$95**

Bola tie; turquoise, silver, and coral "Eagle Dancer" bola tie; signed; ca. 1985; 4″ × 5″.　　**$170–$200**

Bola tie; turquoise, coral, and imitation bear claws; ca. 1986; 6″ × 2″.　　**$60–$80**

Bola tie; silver w/carved buffalo skull surrounded by silver; ca. 1965; 3″ × 2″.　　**$75–$125**

Bracelets

Beaded; wide, fully beaded bracelet w/multicolored geometric designs.　　**$45–$90**

Haida; rare hand-hammered copper bracelet w/totemic engraved designs; ca. 1930; 6″ × 1¼″.　　**$105–$150**

Hopi; silver and turquoise ladies 1¼″ sterling cuff set; "Shadow Box" style w/three graduated, sized, rectangular blue-green cabochons; ca. 1940s.　　**$65–$100**

Hopi; silver and multi-inlay; 1¾″ sterling cuff w/bird (eagle-parrot) designs on either side of inlaid disk in Apache "Gan/Mt. Spirit" dancer; signed by the Hopi Crafts Guild.　　**$110–$170**

Navajo; silver and turquoise; signed.　　**$95–$115**

Navajo; heavy silver bracelet set w/choice No. 8 spider web stone; ca. 1935; 6″ × 1½″.　　**$45–$70**

Navajo; early turquoise and silver "tourist" bracelet; ca. 1935; 6″ × 1″.　　**$30–$60**

Navajo; early silver "tourist" bracelet set w/unusual turquoise stone; ca. 1935; 6″ × 1″. **$30–$50**

Navajo; "old pawn" single-stone turquoise and silver bracelet; ca. 1935; 7″ × 1″. **$75–$100**

Navajo; ladies' silver watch bracelet set w/two turquoise stones; ca. 1965; 7″ × 1½″. **$35–$50**

Navajo; silver "slave" bracelet w/attached ring and set w/jet and mother-of-pearl stones; ca. 1986; 6″ × 6″. **$45–$70**

Navajo; silver and turquoise; sterling triangular three-wire shank set w/gem-quality blue Persian cabochon. **$100–$135**

Navajo; silver and turquoise watch bracelet; heavy sterling; ⁹/₁₆″ × ³/₁₆″ bangle set with a single, oval, green cabochon on each side of the opening; ca. 1930–40; attributed to Mark Chee. **$100–$140**

Navajo; silver and turquoise; heavy sterling wire shank set w/large (2½″ × 1⅞″) blue Morenci cabochon. **$250–$350**

Navajo; pawn silver, turquoise, and coral; triple-triangle wire sterling shank set w/two large, blue spider web and one blood-red branch cabochon; signed DHG. **$55–$105**

Navajo; silver, turquoise, and coral; sterling shank w/large leaf designs set w/five carved blue-green cabochons and one red branch; signed B.E. **$150–$250**

Navajo; large, three-stone turquoise and silver; 6″ × 2″; ca. 1970. **$75–$100**

Navajo; choice silver bracelet set w/five very rare No. 8 spider web turquoise stones; 7¾″ × ¾″; ca. 1965. **$175–$225**

Navajo; silver and turquoise ½″-wide sterling cuff w/stamped and repousse designs set with a single ¾″ long oval green cabochon; ca. 1930s. **$35–$65**

Navajo; crude sand-cast silver bracelet; 6″ × 1″; ca. 1930. **$45–$60**

Navajo; old three-stone T & S bracelet; ca. 1960. **$55–$75**

Navajo; heavy sand-cast silver bracelet set w/single turquoise stone; ca. 1940. **$60–$100**

Navajo; "old pawn" T & S cluster bracelet; ca. 1935; 7″ × 1″. **$25–$50**

Navajo; heavy sand-cast silver bracelet in Naja form and set w/large turquoise stone; 6″ × 2″; ca. 1970. **$65–$100**

Navajo; five-stone T & S bracelet; signed by Robert Ulibarri; ca. 1975; 6½″ × 2″. **$105–$175**

Navajo; choice "old pawn" w/large, natural turquoise stone; ca. 1975; 6″ × 2″.   **$55–$75**

Navajo; bracelet/necklace; sterling silver and turquoise. **$300–$350 set**

Preston Thompson (Winnebago); contemporary sterling silver bracelet w/natural high-grade turquoise spider webbed from Kingman mine in Arizona; won first prize in art show at Medical Center in Houston.
$1100–$1500

Silver; leaf decoration inset w/turquoise and red coral.   **$35–$60**

Silver-mounted turquoise set; three irregular-shaped turquoise; bead and leaf decoration.   **$75–$100**

Silver-mounted mother-of-pearl; set w/oval mother-of-pearl bead and stylized leaf decoration.   **$80–$100**

Silver; decorated with village scene; signed "R.H. Begay."   **$35–$55**

Silver with recessed center in polished turquoise; scalloped border; stamped on reverse "J.W."   **$55–$85**

Silver; set w/small turquoise and red coral swirl decoration. **$25–$40**

Silver; turquoise and red coral inlay.   **$32–$40**

Silver (two); set with red coral leaf scroll decoration and pierced bands.
$55–$80

Silver; eagle and star motif.   **$30–$45**

Silver; turquoise and red coral inlay.   **$32–$40**

Tlingit; hammered, sterling silver, carved totemic bracelet; marked Haines, Alaska; purchased during WWII.   **$700–$150**

Tlingit; very old, hammered, coin silver bracelet w/handcarved American eagle design; ca. 1900.   **$90–$160**

Zuni; silver, coral, and shell; sterling bangle with inlays of red coral and gold mother-of-pearl in floral-like, foliate, and pie wedge designs, signed T.K.W.   **$75–$110**

Zuni; choice turquoise and silver channel inlay "row" bracelet; ca. 1935; 6″ × ½″.   **$30–$50**

Zuni; silver and turquoise bracelet; sterling w/approximately 260 individual blue "channel"-style inlays, set in rosette designs; signed RB.
$110–$160

Zuni; fancy silver, turquoise and coral bracelet; ladies 1″ wide sterling cuff w/blue triangles surrounding other inlays of red, coral, and green malachite in a Cardinal bird perched on a leafy branch and floral designs; signed E & S Guardian (Esther and Sammy).   **$150–$225**

Zuni; silver and turquoise three-wire sterling shank set "Cluster" style; approximately 85 oval and round blue and blue-green cabochons; ca. mid–1940s.   **$125–$200**

Zuni; fine inlay Thunderbird bracelet w/inlaid eagle designs; ca. 1965; 7″ × 2″.   **$55–$80**

Zuni; fancy silver, turquoise, coral, and shell inlay; ladies sterling "spinner"/reversible w/red coral, jet, mother-of-pearl, and blue inlay Cardinal bird on one side, and blue inlay mother-of-pearl and coral Blue Jay on reverse; wgt. 4½ ozs.   **$175–$250**

Chokers

Choker-length solid turquoise nugget necklace; ca. 1970; 16″.   **$55–$75**
Malachite bead choker; ca. 1980; 18″.   **$50–$80**

Courtesy of Morning Star Gallery, Santa Fe, NM. Photo by Donald Vogt.

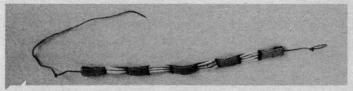

Nez Perce; formerly of Kober Collection; ca. 1870; (03496). **$500–$600**

Plains Indian; four rows of hair pipe bones interspersed w/leather dividers and red and blue trade beads; tiny cone and horsehair suspensions attached to a shell disk.   **$30–$60**

Santo Domingo; turquoise and pipestone choker; graduated-size brown stone interspersed w/green heishe and finished w/sterling beads and clasp.   **$25–$50**

Three different Indian chokers; ca. 1975.   **$10–$20**

Turquoise; small Lone Mountain turquoise nugget choker on heishe; ca. 1965.   **$15–$30**

Earrings

Hopi; silver; two pairs of sterling in geometric designs in overlay style.
                                                                        $30–$55

Navajo; earrings/necklace; silver w/inlaid birds.   **$75– $100 group**

Southwestern; turquoise, shell, and coral; "jaclas" w/contemporary silver and turquoise ear fasteners. **$100–$175**

Zuni; choice silver earrings w/row of inlaid turquoise, lapis, and shell in each; ca. 1985; 1½″ × ½″. **$25–$40**

Zuni; inlay "feather" earrings; ca. 1986; 1″ diameter. **$20–$40**

Zuni; choice T & S needlepoint earrings; ca. 1980. **$40–$80**

Zuni; silver and turquoise 3″ long sterling "dangles" w/incised blue-green cabochon and silver drum attached to each. **$40–$70**

Zuni; T & S needlepoint earrings; 3″ × 1″; ca. 1980. **$60–$80**

Zuni; silver and turquoise channel work w/turquoise set suspensions; 2⅜″ long. **$250–$350**

Zuni; choice silver earrings w/rows of turquoise, jet, and shell heishe; ca. 1986; 2½″ × ½″. **$25–$50**

Zuni; unusual silver earrings w/rows of turquoise inlays; ca. 1986; 1¾″ × 1″. **$25–$50**

Zuni; unusual-shape silver and shell inlay earrings; ca. 1986; 1½″ × ¾″. **$15–$20**

Zuni; choice turquoise and silver needlepoint earrings; ca. 1986; 2½″ × ¾″. **$25–$50**

Necklaces

Bead; five-strand, coral glass bead and silver bead necklace; ca. 1986. **$60–$90**

Beaded 30-strand; coral colored; ca. 1986; 28″. **$65–$90**

Apache; beaded hide medallion; decorated w/dark blue, red, sky blue, orange, clear lime, clear pink, and white beads in an eight-pointed star/flower design. **$25–$50**

Blackfoot; fully beaded loop necklace in red, white, and blue; ca. 1890; 24″. **$60–$80**

From the collection of Lahoma Haddock Goldsmith. Photo by Donald Vogt.

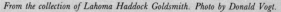

Cherokee; "tear" necklace (squash blossom) w/matching bracelet, given to collector to be worn "when you have tears to shed that you are not able to shed." **$150–$200**

From the collection of Lahoma Haddock Goldsmith. Photo by Donald Vogt.

Cherokee; made of rattlesnake vertebrae and trade beads, especially for the collection. **$75–$100**

Coral; three-strand tubular coral bead necklace; ca. 1930; 29″.

$45–$75

Crow; trade bead necklace made of mosaic glass beads, bear claws; strung on sinew; ca. late 1870s. $600–$700

Elk teeth and claws; large blue glass beads; ¼″ and strung on deerskin thong. $55–$75

From the collection of N. A. McKinney. Photo by Donald Vogt.

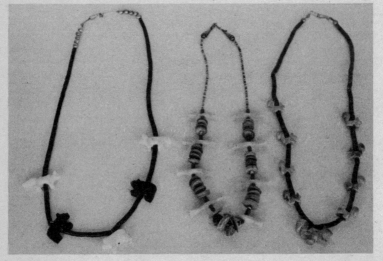

Fetish; bone birds, fossilized water lily disks, witches' wampum, and coral cylinders; middle to late 1800s. $175–$225

Fetish; serpentine, turquoise, abalone, pipestone, jet, mother-of-pearl, agate eagles, fish, various birds, squirrels, turtles, frogs, rabbits, bear, buffalo, and shell heishe; ca. 1980s (see photo above). $300–$400

Fetish; squirrel fetish necklace made of serpentine; ca. 1960 (see photo above). $100–$125

Fetish; serpentine and soapstone fetish necklace w/bears, foxes, and handmade silver beads w/serpentine heishe work; ca. early 1900s.

$125–$150

Five-strand; coral-colored, glass bead necklace w/silver beads and an old coin; ca. 1985. $35–$50

Group; group of necklaces including Job's tears (Cherokee) made of seed in light blue and gray; a Cherokee crynoids and raw turquoise stones; copper and shell bird necklace (Indians would cut telegraph wires in order to get copper to make necklaces). **$200–$500 ea.**

Heishe; turquoise, heishe, jacla, and coral beads in center; from Anadanko pawn shop; 20th centruy. **$300–$350**

Heishe; graduated pipestone heishe disks; ca. 1970. **$100–$125**

Heishe; ten strands of good quality shell heishe w/squaw wrap; ca. 1980; 30". **$85–$100**

Heishe and nugget necklace; ca. early 1900s; made of abalone, bone, jet, serpentine, and turquoise nuggets. **$150–$175**

Navajo; turquoise and silver squash blossom necklace; ca. 1960; 28".
$245–$300

Navajo; unusual silver squash blossom w/turquoise nuggets; 28" × 2"; ca. 1950. **$125–$175**

Navajo; six-strand tubular coral and turquoise nugget necklace; 26"; ca. 1980. **$75–$150**

Navajo; nine-strand shell heishe and turquoise nugget necklace; ca. 1940; 25". **$250–$350**

Navajo; 24" long, graduated size; handmade sterling w/handstamped designs. **$200–$245**

Necklace; squash blossom w/naja and single square-cut stone; handmade beads and squash blossoms; ca. 1920; probably made for a man because of its large and heavy size. **$3000–$3500**

Navajo; six-strand shell heishe and turquoise necklace; ca. 1930; 26".
$55–$80

Navajo; six strands of coral and turquoise beads; ca. 1986; 26".
$100–$150

Navajo; silver and turquoise squash blossom necklace; ca. 1910.
$3000–$4000

Navajo; silver, turquoise, and coral pendant necklace; sterling round, fluted and melon beads and mounting set w/two handcarved blue and one blood-red cabochon; signed E. w/fleur-de-lis overhead. **$60–$120**

Navajo; two necklaces; silver and turquoise squash blossom style; each w/turquoise set naja; 13" and 13¼". **$350–$500**

Courtesy of Robert W. Skinner, Inc., Bolton, MA.

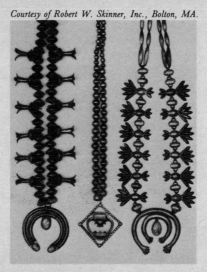

Navajo; silver and turquoise necklaces in squash blossom style; each w/turquoise set naja.   **$350–$450**

Necklaces; three different penshell heishe chokers; ca. 1965.   **$20–$40**

Pawn Santo Domingo turquoise Jacla; ca. 1910–30.   **$85–$135**

Pima; rare Pima rattlesnake vertebrae ceremonial necklace showing much use; ca. 1880; 29″.   **$135–$160**

Plains, three necklaces; a glass trade bead strand composed of numerous bead types, such as amber eight-sided wound, press-faceted, and clear wound melon, length 15½″; a Blackfoot fully beaded wrapped necklace over a trade cloth body w/ermine and rawhide wrapping, 16″ long, bead colors: crystal green and white heart reds; and a Crow bead-wrapped necklace, over a braided red wool body w/engraved German silver disc and dentalia shell suspensions, bead colors: white, crystal green and gold, black, sky blue, pink, and royal blue, 24″ long; provenance: The Science Museum of Connecticut.   **$600–$800**

Pueblo; made of turquoise and shell; 25″ long; "marriage/wedding" style; ca. 1900–30.   **$400–$550**

Pueblo; coral and jet fetish; single strand of 11 black bears w/red heartline inlays interspersed w/tube-type heishe and finished off in sterling cones and clasp.   **$175–$250**

Pueblo; shell fetish; single strand of handcut/carved serpentine, abalone, mother-of-pearl, and melon shell bears, birds of various sizes, and squirrels, all with black jet inlay eyes interspersed with mother-of-pearl heishe beads.   **$150–$275**

Pueblo; turquoise nugget and shell; five strands of vertically drilled green Persian interspersed with light brown heishe beads; "squaw wrapped" neck band.   **$130–$160**

Pueblo; three strands superfine ironwood and 14K gold heishi; ca. 1970; 16".   **$165–$200**

Santo Domingo; turquoise nugget; matching blue-green disks of irregular shapes, w/matching graduated-size heishe forming a portion of the neckpiece.   **$300–$395**

Santo Domingo; classic "T-bird" tourist necklace w/matching earrings; ca. 1935; 28" × 1½".   **$35–$50**

Santo Domingo; turquoise heishe w/silver beads; contemporary (ca. 1980); made in Santo Domingo Pueblo.   **$300–$350**

Santo Domingo; contemporary heishe necklace made of turquoise, serpentine, and pipestone by O. Crespin of the Santo Domingo Pueblo, New Mexico.   **$175–$200**

Santo Domingo; unisex mixed turquoise, serpentine, and pipestone heishi necklace; 22"; ca. 1950.   **$20–$30**

Silver; turquoise w/pendant drop stylized leaf decoration.   **$55–$70**

Silver; two turquoise drops with leap scroll drops.   **$40–$55**

Silver; beaded w/three turquoise drops.   **$35–$50**

Silver; one-of-a-kind necklace w/hinged body and black jet stones; ca. 1986.   **$55–$85**

Six-strand small turquoise nugget necklace on white heishi; 31"; ca. 1970.
                                                                                             $150–$200

Southwest; beaded necklace, 1" width; loom-style decorated w/cobalt blue, green, red, yellow, orange, sky blue, and lime-colored beads in geometric design.   **$10–$15**

Southwestern; shell and turquoise; composed of seven strands of brownish-white shell disc beads, interspersed w/coral-shaped red glass and turquoise disc beads and nuggets; pair of jaclas attached, each composed of graduated turquoise discs and white shell suspensions; 18½" long; attached pawn ticket: "no. 8504, 7-6-57, Louise James, Beeds, $98.00."   **$375–$425**

Trade beads; glass foil beads; early 1900s.   **$200–$300**

Trade beads; assorted trade beads, silver beads, and red Padre beads; ca. early 1900s.   **$125–$175**

Trade beads; assorted trade beads and silver beads; some Viennesse and some mosaic beads; ca. early 1900s.   **$150–$200**

Turned bone and glass bead; ³/₈" beads of clear green, blue, amber, white, and yellow w/three ¹/₂" bone tubes; tipped w/small brass cone bells; good condition.   **$45–$65**

Turquoise nugget and coral choker w/silver beads; 16"; ca. 1965.   **$85–$110**

Wampum; rare strand of Plateau clam shell wampum beads; ca. 1850; 36".   **$35–$50**

Zuni; silver, turquoise, coral, and shell; sterling squash blossom style w/inlays of blue-green, red, mother-of-pearl, tortoise shell, black jet, and abalone in individual horsehead design, ca. 1940–60.   **$325–$475**

Courtesy of Adobe Gallery, Albuquerque, NM. Photo by Donald Vogt.

Zuni; silver and turquoise bow squash blossom necklace; ca. 1916.
                    $1200–$1500

Zuni, fetish; two strands of handcarved abalone, pipestone, serpentine, mother-of-pearl, and shell birds, bears, and foxes by Quam; interspersed w/brown olive shell heishe; finished w/sterling beads, cones, and clasp.   **$175–$250**

Zuni; silver and coral squash blossom; all sterling w/six blossoms on each side interspersed with a central Naja (horseshoe-like pendant); all pieces set "cluster" style in matching blood-red color; signed Mary Marie.
                    $500–$800

Ornaments

Southwestern, three ornaments; silver and turquoise; Zuni; two cluster rings and a pair of turquoise and jet mosaic technique earrings.   **$75–$115**

Southwestern, two silver, coral and turquoise ornaments; Navajo; silver and coral squash blossom necklace, 16″ length; Zuni three-row turquoise and silver bracelet, 1″ wide.   **$350–$500**

Pendants

Hopi; silver pendant with chain; 1½″ diameter; sterling w/overlay-style Kachina mask design; signed with feather (Jackson Seklestewa).
   $30–$45

Hopi; silver pendant w/chain; perched eagle in overlay-style design; signed, hallmarked.   **$40–$70**

Navajo; silver, turquoise, and coral; signed Anson Joe A.   **$75–$115**

Navajo; silver and turquoise necklace, sand/tufa cast sterling pendant w/five geometric-shaped blue cabochons; weight 4½ ozs; signed WB.
   $125–$195

Navajo; sterling silver and turquoise in overlay style; set with a round blue Persion cabochon; signed Mary B. Smith.   **$30–$65**

Northwest Coast; pair of matched carved ivory animals used as pendants or earrings; ca. 1975.   **$150–$200**

Northwest Coast; ivory-carved pendant w/abalone inlay; ca. 1975; 3″ × 2¾″.   **$150–$175**

Northwest Coast; in form of Northwest Coast mask; marked "sterling, 1979, ss., 24/50, Beaverworks"; suspended on hand-wrought link chain; mask is 1½″.   **$140–$180**

Zuni; fancy silver and shell inlay multi-sided pendant; 3½″ long x 2½″ wide; sterling-paneled, plumb bob-like shape w/inlays of blue, red, white, and gold mother-of-pearl; jet, abalone, and turtle shell in Hummingbird, Blue Jay, Robin, and Cardinal designs; yeibichai and flowers inlaid on the surfaces of the surrounding mounting and more flowers and foliate designs above each bird; signed Jake and Irene Livingston.
   $700–$1350

Pins

Haida; carved agelite wolf pin signed John York; ca. 1950; 3″ × 1½″.
$55-$85

Navajo; silver and turquoise; cast, openwork, sterling flower-like design set with a blue-green cabochon. **$24-$35**

Navajo; silver and coral pin; sterling Naja (horseshoe-shaped) containing one oval red cabochon drop (pendant style). **$30-$60**

Navajo; silver and turquoise pin/pendant; sterling pinwheel w/hand-stamped designs and set w/oval green cabochon. **$20-$40**

Navajo; silver and turquoise pin; Tufa sandcast sterling; eight-pointed star/flower set w/blue cabochon. **$15-$35**

Navajo; "old pawn" silver pin set w/nine turquoise stones; ca. 1940; 4½″ diam. **$35-$55**

Zuni; large inlay turquoise, coral, jet and shell "Sunface" pin; ca. 1940. **$125-$150**

Courtesy of Jack Sellner, CAI.

Zuni; Old Pawn silver and turquoise pins. **$130-$225 ea.**

Rings

Hopi; fancy silver and coral; sterling in overlay style set w/large oval red cabochon; signed w/raincloud symbol (Victor Coochwytewa).
$75-$100

Navajo; fancy silver and turquoise; lady's; sterling w/large leaf design containing a single gem-quality, 1⅞″ × ½″ oval blue cabochon; size 7. **$75-$100**

Navajo; silver and turquoise lady's sterling w/handstamped designs containing single blue cabochon set "shadow box" style; size 6.   **$20–$40**

Navajo; silver and turquoise ring; man's sterling w/gem-quality blue Persian cabochon.   **$75–$100**

Navajo; fancy silver and turquoise ring; man's sterling set w/single gem-quality oval; 1⅛" × ½" Bisbee (Lavender Pit Mine-type) cabochon; size 10½".   **$35–$65**

Navajo; silver and turquoise ring; Hopi-style sterling full-bodied Kachina w/round blue cabochon eyes; signed J.C.T. (J.C. Tso), Gallup, 6/5/78.   **$25–$55**

Navajo; silver, turquoise, coral ring; five-prong sterling shank w/leaf designs set w/one each blue-green and pinkish-red cabochon; ca. 1940s–50s; signed George Toledo.   **$75–$125**

Navajo; ring/earrings; transitional coral and sterling silver; ring is shadow box design; earrings are needlepoint.   **$200–$250 set**

Courtesy of Naranjo's, Houston. Photo by Donald Vogt.

Preston Thompson (Winnebago); stamped and etched work.   **$400–$500**

Silver; set w/turquoise; signed "A.B."   **$35–$45**

Silver; incised bearclaw; set with turquoise.   **$30–$35**

Sterling silver; set w/irregular-shaped turquoise.   **$15–$20**

Zuni; fancy silver and turquoise; sterling set w/blue and blue-green inlays in Indian dancer design; signed.   **$100–$140**

Zuni; fancy silver, turquoise, and coral ring; sterling peacock w/blue, red, and gold mother-of-pearl inlays; signed Patsy Spenser. **$110–$150**

Sets

Navajo, necklace set; turquoise and silver choker w/leaf motif and matching earrings; ca. 1975; 18″.   **$55–$85**

Navajo; necklace and earring set; signed silver and jet set; 23″; ca. 1986.   **$35–$50**

Zuni, fancy silver, turquoise, coral, and shell necklace and earring set; sterling w/inlays of blue turquoise, red coral, jet, white and gold mother-of-pearl, serpentine, melon shell and abalone in bird and flower designs; signed Wesley & Ella Gia, Zuni, NM.   **$500–$850**

Zuni, three-piece turquoise, coral, and jet inlaid ''pipe tomahawk'' necklace and earring set; ca. 1986.   **$85–$100**

Zuni, necklace and ring set; handmade sterling link chain w/three rectangular plaques set w/matching blue-green needlepoint slivers; sterling ring similar in design.   **$175–$215**

Zuni; choice Zuni inlay ''sunface'' squash blossom necklace and earring set; ca. 1986; 25″.   **$190–$300**

Tie Bars

Silver; with an unusual large precious stone; ca. 1940.   **$10–$20**

Three; bag containing three old silver tie bars; one Zuni and two Navajo; ca. 1940.   **$35–$50**

Trade Beads

Beautiful black Venetian trade beads w/various color inlays; 24″; ca. 1840.
                    $60–$80

Choice large cobalt blue Peking glass trade beads; ca. 1880; 24″. **$100–$150**

Collection; large frame containing over 30 strands of rare Peking glass beads and other artifacts; 37″ × 23″; ca. 1880.   **$450–$650**

Glassed frame (cracked) of very old Venetian trade beads; ca. 1880; 18″ × 10″.
                    $325–$375

Huge, rare, Venetian chevron trade beads in various color inlays; ca. 1820; 24″.
                    $150–$200

Huge, tubular, yellow-core red ''chief'' beads; ca. 1820; 26″.   **$75–$150**

Huge, rare, long strand of cobalt blue Peking glass trade beads; ca. 1880; 24″.
                    $70–$100

Huge, tubular, cornaline de leppo trade beads w/yellow core called "chief" beads; 24″; ca. 1800. **$75–$125**

Huge and rare cobalt blue Peking glass trade beads; ca. 1880; 26″. **$175–$225**

Huge strand of ancient-faceted cobalt blue Russian trade beads; ca. 1880; 24″.
$85–$105

Jade green Venetian glass disc trade beads; ca. 1880; 24″. **$55–$80**

Jade green Peking glass trade beads; ca. 1880; 30″. **$95–$125**

Large cobalt blue and clear Venetian trade beads; ca. 1840. **$45–$75**

Large dark green Peking glass trade beads; ca. 1880; 22″. **$35–$80**

Large, old, Venetian cobalt blue trade beads showing much use; ca. 1880; 24″.
$40–$60

Large cobalt blue Peking glass trade beads; ca. 1880; 29″. **$45–$75**

Large black Venetian trade beads w/blue and white inlays; 24″; ca. 1820.
$75–$125

Large dark green Peking glass trade beads; ca. 1880; 22″. **$35–$50**

Long strand of beautiful cobalt blue Peking glass trade beads; ca. 1880; 28″.
$75–$100

Long strand of cobalt blue Peking glass trade beads; 38″; ca. 1920. **$145–$170**

Long strand of unusually long cobalt blue Peking glass trade beads; ca. 1890; 36″. **$35–$50**

Mixed black and inlaid Venetian trade beads; ca. 1840; 24″. **$55–$85**

Rare, solid black, Peking glass trade beads; ca. 1880; 32″. **$45–$75**

Rare, large, yellow-core cornaline de leppo "chief" beads; ca. 1840; 26″.
$75–$125

Rare blue "padre" or Father Kino beads from Arizona; ca. 1800; 22″.
$35–$70

Rare, medium-sized, green chevron trade beads; ca. 1840; 22″. **$50–$75**

Rare "dusty rose" Peking glass trade beads; ca. 1880; 24″ × 3″.
$145–$165

Rare strand of old mixed black and blue Venetian trade beads; ca. 1840; 22″.
$50–$80

Rare strand of round red yellow-core "chief" beads; ca. 1820. **$75–$150**

Rare strand of cobalt blue and clear Dutch glass trade beads; 30″; ca. 1800.
$100–$150

Rare old yellow Venetian trade beads w/multicolored inlays; ca. 1840; 22″.
$55–$75

Rare, huge, mixed-shape chevron trade beads; ca. 1800; 22″. **$275–$350**

Rare strand of large, faceted, Venetian vaseline glass trade beads; ca. 1860; 24″.   **$50–$75**

Riker mount containing an assortment of 65 old trade beads; ca. 1860. **$25–$50**

Riker mount containing eight large, old, green chevron beads and one blue one; ca. 1840.   **$20–$35**

Russian; mixed-size, faceted, cobalt blue trade beads; ca. 1820.
                                                                      $85–$125

Small long strand of cobalt blue Peking glass trade beads; ca. 1880; 33″.
                                                                      $55–$80

Strand of huge cobalt blue Peking glass trade beads; 30″; ca. 1880. **$125–$175**

Strand of large mixed Venetian trade beads; 24″; ca. 1840.   **$65–$85**

Strand of pristine-faceted cobalt blue Russian trade beads and a few gold ones; ca. 1800; 26″.   **$250–$350**

Strand of huge yellow trade beads w/colored diamond designs; 26″; ca. 1920.
                                                                      $75–$125

Strand of graduated chevron trade beads; ca. 1820; 30″.   **$75–$150**

Courtesy of Donna McMenamin, private collector. Photo by Donald Vogt.

Strung on sinew; burnt orange and black glass; unusual.   **$200–$250**

Ten strands of old blue tile or Crow trade beads; ca. 1880.   **$225–$275**

Unusual deep red and other old Venetian trade beads; ca. 1880; 24″. **$35–$50**

Unusual strand of mottled Venetian trade beads; ca. 1860; 22″.   **$35–$60**

Unusual faceted red Venetian trade beads; ca. 1900; 22″.   **$40–$60**

Unusual mixed-shaped, red Peking glass trade beads; ca. 1880; 24″. **$55–$80**

Unusual shape and design; mixed-color Venetian trade beads; ca. 1880; 24″.   **$55–$80**

Venetian black trade beads w/pink, white, and blue dot inlays; ca. 1820; 28″.
$75–$125

Very large, old, oval cobalt blue trade beads; ca. 1820; 24″.   **$55–$85**

Very large and unusual mixed Venetian trade beads; ca. 1880; 22″. **$45–$70**

Very unusual shape and color; old trade beads; ca. 1880; 29″.   **$55–$80**

Very unusual strand of swirled striped disc-shaped Venetian trade beads; ca. 1820.   **$55–$100**

Very large cobalt blue Peking glass trade beads; ca. 1880; 22″.   **$70–$100**

Very rare greasy yellow "Crow beads" along with a few red; ca. 1840.
$100–$125

Very large round cobalt blue Peking glass; ca. 1880.   **$70–$140**

Very large cobalt blue Peking glass trade beads; ca. 1890.   **$55–$75**

Very rare "dusty pink" Peking glass trade beads; ca. 1880; 28″.   **$75–$85**

Very rare red and blue glass beads w/beautiful white feather inlays; ca. 1840; 24″.   **$60–$100**

Very large oval cobalt blue and light blue Dutch trade beads; ca. 1800; 26″.
$75–$125

Watch Bands

Four ladies' turquoise and silver watch bands; ca. 1975.   **$45–$70**

Ring, earrings; Hopi; sterling silver.   **$150–$200**

Other

Courtesy of W. J. Arbuckle. Photo by Donald Vogt.

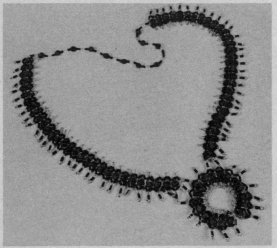

Birthing beads, Navajo; traditional birthing beads in juniper seeds, jet, and crystal; made by a medicine woman.　　　　　　　　　　**$25–$35**

Chain, Navajo; heavy, handmade, sterling silver chain; ca. 1940; 28″.
　　　　　　　　　　　　　　　　　　　　　　　　　$55–$70

Collar tips, Hopi; fancy silver and turquoise; set w/wedge-shaped inlay of mother-of-pearl and single green cabochon drilled bead.　　**$150–$180**

Group, Zuni; jewelry and combs including petit point and needlepoint designs.　　　　　　　　　　　　　　　　　　**$75–$100 group**

Hopi, silver watch tips; sterling w/large Kachina design in overlay-style; signed.　　　　　　　　　　　　　　　　　　　　**$30–$55**

Navajo, contemporary; grouping.　　　　　　　　　　**$10–$50 ea.**

Pill boxes, Southwest Navajo; silver set with turquoise.　　**$35–$80**

Wampum strand; large strand of clam shell wampum; ca. 1900; 40″.
　　　　　　　　　　　　　　　　　　　　　　　　　$35–$50

Wrist ornament, Navajo; sterling silver, leather mounted, tufa/sand cast in X-like design; ca. 3rd quarter 20th century.　　　　　**$70–$100**

Zuni, silver and coral cross; made by H. Itule; cross won 2nd prize ribbon Inter-Tribal Indian Ceremonial, Gallup, NM, 1974.　　**$140–$195**

Zuni, silver and petit point turquoise; sterling w/48 blue silver and round shapes; signed D. & V. Dewa (Don).　　　　　　　**$75–$125**

LEATHER

▼▼▼▼▼▼▼▼▼▼▼

INTRODUCTION

The North American Indians used animals for food, clothing, and shelter, making use of every part of the animal's body. They used the skins of buffalo, deer, elk, caribou, bear, and moose to make tepees, clothing, boats, shields, containers to hold food and medicines, and cradleboards for their infants.

To prepare skins for use required a lot of time and effort, for the skins would become hard, stiff, and smelly if not treated promptly and correctly. Though some Indians learned to treat the skins so skillfully that they became soft buckskin, others treated them just enough to keep them from spoiling. The men of the tribes in the Southwest and Northeast usually did this work, though in most other tribes the women handled the treating, cleaning, and preparation of skins.

The hides needed to be fleshed with tools, resembling chisels, which were often made from buffalo leg bones or gun barrels. Scraping the hide was accomplished by pulling a bent antler tool over the skin to plane and thin the skin. If the animal had hair (i.e., deer), its hair was removed with a tool that was curved, the end of which was made of metal or a blade of some sort. The scraping tool was used like a plane, pulling against the hide strongly, until the piece was free of hair.

Rawhide is used for parfleches, holy bags, saddlebags, moccasin soles, drumheads, and rattles. The Plains Indians used rawhide better than most other tribes because since they did little growing and were basically hunter/gatherers, they used hides for all purposes and virtually replaced pottery and wooden items. To make other items, such as tepees, bags, and moccasins, the rawhide is then softened.

Tanning the hide meant mixing a paste of brains and liver into the skin. A smooth stone is used to rub the mixture into all of the hide's pores. Then the hide is moistened and allowed to soak in water for a couple of days. It is then left to dry, then moistened again. Once more it dries and, again, is scraped with a rough stone which gives the hide and even, grainy appearance. It is again stretched, wrung out and dried, softened by stretching again, and, often, smoked so that it will remain soft. In most tribes a woman was judged by how good a tanner she was—she was considered industrious if she tanned well and lazy if she didn't.

Though many people interested in Indian artifacts have collected articles made of leather or rawhide, two of the first Americans to bring home articles from the various "modern" (as opposed to prehistoric) Indian tribes were the explorers Lewis and Clark.

The two men left on their long voyage in 1804, after a hurried education in the natural sciences, and were instructed to bring back examples of the natural resources of the region. They distributed peace medals to the Indians, as well as goodwill. In return, the Indians gave them articles from their lives which included a Mandan buffalo robe, presented to President Thomas Jefferson. The robe was painted with scenes of the Mandan and Minnetaree tribes fighting the Sioux and Arikara.

SOME LEATHER/RAWHIDE ITEMS

Boats

The Mandan Indians made circular boats which were made of bison skin lashed to willow frames. These paddle bullboats were used by these Indians for travel or to fish along the Missouri River.

Cases

A painted, cylindrical rawhide case was used to hold the Indian's headdress, feathers, whistles, and other ceremonial items. If the case belonged to a medicine man, it would hold herbs and fetishes. Though most of these sacred cases were painted, some tribes (such as those along the Columbia River) incised the decorations on their versions. The Western versions of these bags were painted with red paint mixed with wax as their final coating, while the Eastern versions might be varnished with a transparent yellow made from resin or buffalo gallstones.

Bows, bow cases, and quivers were made by the Hidatsa men and were often decorated with images of their conquests. Such scenes are virtually uninterpretable today because their meanings were known only to the makers. The small Hidatsa tribe not only made cases, but also the same kind of leather goods—parfleches, robes, pipe bags, moccasins, and shirts—that the other Northern Plains tribes did.

Medicine Bundles

Sacred to their owners, medicine bags often were filled with pieces of rock, feathers, a bit of trade cloth, animal bones, and other artifacts which held a special, mystical meaning to their owners. The power of a medicine bundle was different for each Indian. For some, it represented healing medicines; others used the powers tied up in their bundle for love, spiritual beliefs, or strength in battle.

Bundles were almost always the property of men, yet the women often made the containers in a fashion explained to them by the men who were to own them. Medicine bundles could be passed from one owner to another, with a great deal of ceremony, or could be kept within one family for generations.

Ceremonial bags/bundles were hung on tripods which were usually placed at the back of the lodge. Sometimes the man's shield, lance, and pipe were also hung on this tripod. When the weather was inclimate, the tripod was brought inside.

These bags, used in religious or medicinal rites, would belong to one owner who was instructed in the songs, ritual, and prayers associated with that bundle.

The Lakes area Indians (particularly the Winnebago tribe) made medicine bags from the whole skins of small animals, such as the otter, bobcat, squirrel, etc.

MEDICINE MEN

The Navajo tribe is in danger of losing the medicine men/women who have practiced since the beginning of history. Most who are practicing today are over 50 years old and have no one in line to take their place when they retire.

Some of the ceremonies the Navajo medicine men/women perform take 10 or more years to learn properly, and the young Navajos either have jobs or are going to school, leaving them little time to tutor with a medicine person.

Because the Navajo nation is concerned about losing the medicine men entirely, plans are underway to begin a program which will give a stipend to those interested in studying the ways of becoming a medicine man.

Parfleche

A light leather container, resembling a small suitcase, was made by the Plains Indians and decorated with brightly colored geometric designs. At first they were made because they were easily carried; later, they became status symbols. Not only were they traded, but often given as gifts. The parfleche is a symbol of the mobility of Indians who were once confined to one area (near shelter and water) because of their lack of domesticated animals. Once the horse was introduced to their environment, life for the Plains Indian was easier because he was able to move around. Early parfleches used fewer colors and less geometric designs than later ones, which were elaborately styled and extremely colorful.

Plains Indian women used the stiff rawhide of buffalo to make ceremonial robes, dresses, moccasins, leggings, and parfleches, which were used to hold dried meat and personal belongings. They decorated the leather with a sharpened, porous buffalo bone which was dipped in color (all the paints were made from natural ingredients).

Parfleches were decorated with triangles and other geometric designs, which were repeated aesthetically throughout. Sometimes these designs (handed down from mother to daughter) can be used to identify the artist. Designs on the parfleche were outlined in black and filled in with bright and rich colors, which had symbolic meaning. Among the Lakotas, red was the color of the sun; blue, the color of the moving spirit, the sky; and green, the color of the spirit of the Earth.

Tobacco or Pipe Bag

Leather containers designed to hold the pipe and tobacco Indians used during rituals and ceremonies were called pipe bags. The bags were often highly decorated and reflected the artistic ability of its owners.

Plains Indian decoration of pipe bags included porcupine quillwork, beadwork, or fringe, and is highly representative of the artwork of these tribes. Through study of this article, one can see the changes the Plains Indians underwent in the nineteenth century. Some are decorated with the horse, some with battle scenes, and you can even find some decorated with the American flag.

Shields

Thick rawhide was used as protection by the Indians because they discovered that the material, made into a shield, could stop the thrust of a spear or arrow. Jemez, Crow, Hopi, and other tribes decorated their shields with protective spirit designs or stories of the warrior who owned the shield.

The shields were constructed of three or four layers of shrunken rawhide to make them thick and strong. They were made by men who fasted and received their instructions from guardian spirits before attempting to make the shields. Sometimes a medicine man would make the shield, as well as conduct the ritual that went along with it. He would be paid an appropriate amount in horses, robes, or other goods. The shields were painted and decorated with feathers, animal skins, and/or red trade cloth.

The Plains groups used rawhide, while the Pueblo groups used rawhide with a removable animal hide cover, for their shields.

Tepees

The Plains Indians' tepees were the most decorated of all the Indians who used skin tents. Fifteen to twenty buffalo skins were used just to make an average-sized tepee (15'–20' across), while a large lodge (30' wide with 40' long poles) would require up to 50 skins.

The paintings on the sides of tepees were often ceremonial designs, paintings of warrior's exploits, or symbols which designated a medicine man/family.

BEADWORK

Almost all of the tribes that did beadwork also did netted beadwork which, in essence, were beads that were not sewn on material but, rather, were sewn to each other, making a solid beaded surface. This type of beadwork was used to cover solid rounded surfaces or would stand on its own as, for example, a large cape collar, such as those worn by the Mohave tribe. This type of decoration was used to identify everything from dresses and moccasins to bridles and gun holders.

Beadwork was done a number of different ways by the various tribes who used this type of decoration. The following is a sampling of how the different tribes used beadwork as a decoration on their leather items.

Assinoboin, Sarcee, and Blackfoot (Plains)

Assinoboin, Sarcee, and Blackfoot beadwork designs were geometric.

Blackfoot and Crow (Plains)

The Blackfoot and Crow used geometric spot-stitching beadwork designs until floral motifs became popular (about 1870). Crow forms were often triangular and sewn on red cloth.

Chippewa (Plains)

The Chippewa's beadwork was done a couple of different ways. The wood heddle separated the warps so that the beaded weft could be inserted. Other beadwork was done with a needle, thus producing either single- or double-weft weaving. Both styles were used by the Chippewa and the sewing style was also used by the Winnebago tribe.

Crow (Plains)

Adopted by Indians about 1800, beadwork was easier than quillwork and different tribes developed different styles. The Crows used geometrics.

Iroquois (Northeast)

The Iroquois used a unique method to accentuate their beadwork—they crowded the beads together and padded their designs in order to gain a raised effect. This type of beadwork was done mostly on velvet pieces, probably because velvet was easier to work with than tanned hides and made a nice background for the colorful beads these Indians used.

Micmac (Northeast)

Micmacs used delicate, double-curving forms, and, like other tribes, imitated European embroidery while combining that skill with their beadwork.

Nez Perce

The Nez Perce tribe made a four-tabbed, beaded leather bag which was widely traded. A similar bag was made by the Athabascan tribes.

Northeast, Lakes, and Northern Plains

These tribes used the method of laying strung beads in a design, then sewing them into place. They made shaded floral designs which decorated all kinds of clothing, bags, moccasins, and turbans. Northeastern beadwork gives the appearance of being lacy and stylized. Floral work is common among tribes such as the Penobscot, Iroquois, and Micmac.

Northwest Coast

Northwest Coast beadwork, though influenced by the styles of the Northern Plains, is distinctive in designs which one often sees repeated in their painting, sculpture, and rugs.

Plains Indians

The Plains tribes used a style of attaching their beadwork called "lazy stitch sewing." This form simply means that the beads were strung together, then attached to the garment at the ends of short lengths of beads (in other words: each bead was *not* individually fastened). "Pony" beads were larger beads, used from about 1800 on, while seed beads were smaller and popular during the period of approximately 1840 on.

Sauk and Chippewa (Plains)

These two tribes used bilateral symmetry in their bold style of beadwork.

QUILLWORK

Decorating with quills is a Native American art which pre-dates beadwork. Quills were taken from the porcupine and dyed different colors, then flattened out when pushed through the clenched teeth of the woman making the quillwork decoration. The effect of the decoration was one of flattened reeds which, when placed artistically, made a geometric or floral design on the garments they decorated. Decorating with quills demanded great dexterity. The quills were dyed, split, flattened, and sewn in many different techniques.

In the Cheyenne tribe, the craft of quilling was taught amidst great ritual and ceremony. If men saw the work while it was being done, it was said they would be deafened or gored by a bull. Symbols were used in quillwork, as in most other Indian arts. For instance, a star placed below the smoke hole of a tepee was a symbol for the sun, bringing blessings on all who entered the dwelling. Quillwork was still used after the white man brought beads to the Indian, but the Indians found it easier to work with the beads and quills eventually lost favor.

Described below are some of the ways different tribes used quillwork.

Cree (Plains)

The Cree Indians are credited with doing the finest quillwork in North America. The quills were woven into the work and pushed tightly together so that their design gives one the impression of long, flattened beadwork.

Huron and Iroquois (Northeast)

The Huron and Iroquois used a technique of embroidery, probably taught to them by French settlers. Moose hair was used to embroider moccasins, robes, boxes, and other items.

Northeastern and Lakes Indians

The Northeastern and Lakes region Indians applied quillwork to birchbark by pushing dyed quills through holes in the bark and bending their ends once through. Boxes of all kinds—rectangular, circular, oval, and square—were made by the Micmacs and other Northeastern tribes for sale to the Anglo traders.

Plains

Plains quillwork was geometric in design and was used to enhance clothing. Moccasins, breastplates, cradleboards, leggings, quirts, belts, and anything else which was made with leather was decorated by the Plains Indians with their fanciful quillwork.

LEATHER LISTINGS

Apache

Hat band; braided leather hat band w/beaded holders; ca. 1986; 28″.
$20–$40

Pouch; beaded hide, of rectangular form, yellow ochre paint decoration, tin cone suspensions on bottom; bead colors: royal blue, white, yellow, and white heart reds; 6¾″ long; attached note reads: "medicine bag, made by Apache Indians in Arizona, 1898"; minor bead loss.
$160–$200

Pouch; beaded hide, decorated w/concentric rosette motif on pink ground; fringed w/tin cone suspensions; 7″ long. $200–$400

Arapaho

Provenance: a Massachusetts historical society.
Courtesy of Robert W. Skinner, Inc., Bolton, MA.

Cradleboard cover; quill-wrapped parfleche decoration on a canvas body over a bentwood frame, quilled suspensions w/deer toe attachments at crown; frame 34″ long; extensive quill damage and fading.

$3100-$3500

Knife case; rectangular hide case w/geometric beadwork and containing an old knife; 9″ × 3″. $125-$200

Parfleche; rectangular, lidded rawhide box w/painted geometric designs; ca. 1985; 40″ × 22″. $95-$150

Parfleches; pair of beautiful matched rawhide cases w/geometric designs painted on both sides; ca. 1980; 24″ × 15″ ea. $300-$600

Courtesy of Canfield Gallery, Santa Fe, NM. Photo by Donald Vogt.

Possible bag; ca. 1875; made of beaded buckskin; 13″ × 23″.

$3500–$4500

Quiver; large hide quiver containing two old arrows; ca. 1880; 30″ × 5″.

$100–$150

Blackfoot

Courtesy of Canfield Gallery, Santa Fe, NM. Photo by Donald Vogt.

Parfleche; ca. 1875; 26″ × 15″.   **$4000–$5000**

Parfleche; rare, old, black-outline, rawhide medicine case w/long fringe;
ca. 1880; 15″ × 9″.   **$475–$575**

Rattle; very rare, painted, hide, medicine society ceremonial rattle.
$85–$150

Shield; contemporary, painted, rawhide shield w/trade cloth and feather drops; 30″ × 17″; ca. 1980. **$50–$100**

Cheyenne

Knife case; choice full-beaded, sinew-sewn knife case w/geometric designs; 9″ × 2″. **$175–$225**

Parfleche; rectangular rawhide case w/handle and geometric designs; ca. 1986; 12″ × 9″. **$125–$175**

From the William R. Nash Collection. Photo by Donald Vogt.

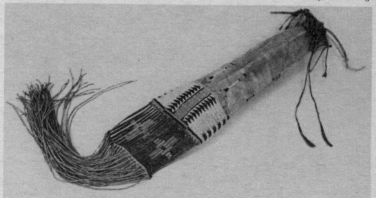

Pipe bag; beaded and fringed hide pipe bag, w/remains of yellow and blue pigment, stitched in pink and light and dark blue against a white beaded ground w/narrow strips around the top and down each side; broad panels containing checkered columns flanked by triangles on the front and back; the openwork section below w/pair of crosses in blue and (faded) yellow porcupine quillwork against a pale red ground; the hide fringe twisted; 39½″ long. **$2500–$3000**

Pouch; rare buffalo hide "peace medal" pouch w/circular green and white beadwork; ca. 1880; 4″ × 3½″. **$60–$100**

Pouch; rare rectangular rawhide pouch w/bead and quill decoration and tin cones; ca. 1800; 7″ × 5″. **$75–$100**

Cree

Bag; rectangular, fringed, Plains Cree hide bag w/beaded floral designs; ca. 1920; 14″ × 7″.   **$110–$125**

Pouch; small moosehide pouch w/beaded star on one side and a flower on the other; ca. 1920; 3″ × 3″.   **$20–$30**

Crow

Courtesy of Robert W. Skinner, Inc., Bolton, MA.

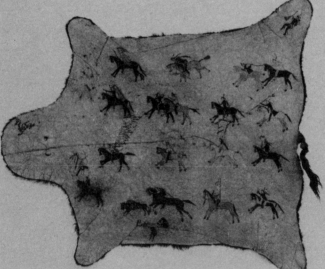

Buffalo robe; painted robe, native tanned multi-colored depictions on a subtle yellow pigment field of exploits such as hunting bear and buffalo and a variety of battles; details from scenes include dancer wearing otter skin turban w/roach and german silver ornamentation, wounded warrior w/scalplocks, split horn war bonnets, and two riders attacking a Crow warrior on foot; 56″ × 79″.   **$6250–$7000**

Knife case; choice hide case w/sinew-sewn, geometric beaded designs; 9″ × 3″.   **$180–$225**

Parfleche; rectangular rawhide container w/fringe and w/red and green painted designs; 13″ × 12″.   **$210–$300**

Parfleche; matched pair of blue-outlined, elk hide parfleche cases; ca. 1880; 28″ × 12″.   **$700–$1000**

Pouch; rare, small, hide medicine pouch w/geometric beaded design; ca. 1880; 3″ × 2½″.   **$125–$150**

Courtesy of Morning Star Gallery, Santa Fe, NM. Photo by Donald Vogt.

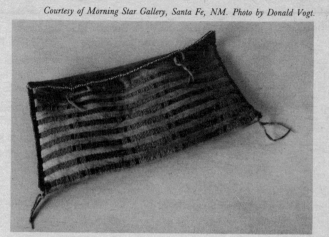

Tepee bag; ca. 1880.   **$675–$775**

Crow/Ute

Courtesy of Morning Star Gallery, Santa Fe, NM. Photo by Donald Vogt.

Mirror bag; beaded bag; ca. 1860.   **$6500–$7500**

Nez Perce

Bag; classic rectangular twined corn husk bag w/crisp geometric designs; ca. 1900; 18″ × 15″.   **$700–$900**

Bag; large, classic, rectangular, twined corn husk bag w/different geometric designs on each side; 18″ × 12″; ca. 1890.   **$275–$325**

Bag; rare, small, twined, corn husk belt pouch w/geometric designs; ca. 1890; 3″ × 3¼″.   **$65–$90**

Parfleche; choice rectangular rawhide container w/long fringe and painted decoration; ca. 1985; 16″ × 8″.   **$160–$190**

Pouch; early Nez Perce contour beaded pouch; ca. 1880; 7″ × 6″.
$95–$150

Pouch; old foldover corn husk belt pouch w/subtle geometric designs; ca. 1890; 5″ × 5″.   **$90–$125**

Sheath; large hide knife case w/beaded floral design; containing an old Sheffield knife; ca. 1920.   **$160–$200**

Northern Plains

Beaded pouch; geometric beaded medicine pouch; ca. 1890; 4½″.
$60–$80

Bridles; beaded, sinew-sewn beads on deerskin; extremely dry and brittle.   **$20–$40**

Northern Plains/Plateau, shirt; beaded and fringed hide shirt, decorated on the sleeves and on the front and back with four elongated panels containing geometric devices in green, translucent blue, red, and pink beadwork on a white ground; a circular medallion on the front decorated w/four tiny crosses in black, white, translucent red, and clear glass beads on a translucent green and white ground; ermine pelts and trade cloth suspensions on the sleeves; 27″ long.   **$4000–$4500**

Parfleches; group of parfleches (three-dimensional rawhide containers); ca. 1875.   **$1000–$3000**

Pouch; beaded peace medal pouch; ca. 1906; 4″ dia.   **$45–$90**

Northern Plateau

Belt; beaded; 43″ long and 1¾″ wide; sinew-sewn and decorated w/red w/white centers and yellow beads in connected square designs on a blue-beaded background.   **$100–$125**

Parfleche; large older parfleche; 20″ × 28″; red, dark blue, and yellow colors.   **$125–$195**

Northwest Coast

Hand drum; polychromed; hide stretched and nailed to bent wood frame, interior decorated w/stylized human face in red and black; 11¼" diameter. **$225–$350**

Mask; highly unusual hide-covered mask w/hair, paint, and abalone inlay; 10" × 7". **$200–$300**

Northwest Coast/Salish, drum; ca. 1890. **$5500–$6500**

Plains

Drum; round hide-covered hand drum and stick; drum has a painted eagle; ca. 1965; 15" × 3". **$35–$70**

Drum; small round hand drum w/faded paint decoration; ca. 1890; 10" × 2". **$85–$125**

Knife case; large, beaded hide knife case containing a fine old handmade knife; ca. 1920; 10" × 3½". **$75–$125**

Pair of hard sole moccasins and blanket strip. **$300–$400**

Parfleche; rectangular folded rawhide container w/painted designs; ca. 1900; 25" × 11". **$300–$400**

Parfleche; rectangular rawhide box w/geometric painted designs; ca. 1885; 6" × 3½". **$110–$140**

Pipe bag; beaded, hide; stitched on both sides and along edges with sinew-sewn beaded decoration on a yellow and red painted hide body; four forked tabs at opening, remnant twisted fringe; bead colors; sky blue, white, black, mustard and clear green, red, and sapphire blue, body length 12". **$500–$700**

Possible bag; beaded and quilled, trimmed w/tin cones and red horsehair suspensions; 36" × 26". **$1700–$2000**

Pouch; beaded hide, paint, bead and tin cone suspension decorated; brass button closure; 17½" long. **$225–$275**

Pouch; beaded; hide; painted overall in yellow ochre; bead-edged tab mouth; tin cone decorated suspensions on body and at bottom; bead colors: white, clear gold, white heart reds, cobalt, and pea green; length 10¾". **$275–$325**

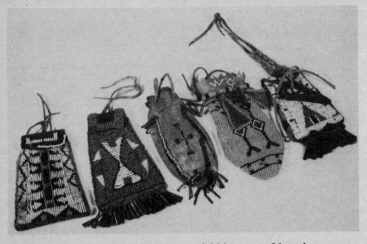

Pouches; five bead and quill decorated hide; most fringed; areas represented include Shoshonee, Santee Sioux, and Cheyenee.   **$275–$375**

Pouches; group of six beaded hide pouches, including three "strike-a-lights" trimmed w/tin cones and three small oval pouches; lengths are 4¼″ to 5½″; Provenance: Collected by Henry H. Wright, Second Lieutenant, 9th Cavalry, December 12, 1872, on frontier duty commander of detachment of Companies C and E, and Navajo Indian Scouts.
$1500–$1800

Six-piece group; consists of child's dyed quill-decorated hide vest; miniature bead-decorated hide cradleboard; three beaded hide dolls in native dress; and small pair of fringed high-top hide boots w/paint and tack decoration.   **$750–$950**

Sioux

Bow case; buckskin bow case and quiver w/porcupine quill trim and fringe; ca. 1890; 38″ × 6″.   **$200–$250**

Knife case; choice, full-beaded hide knife case w/classic sinew-sewn geometric designs; 7½″ × 7½″.   **$150–$200**

Knife sheath; beaded hide knife sheath w/bone-handled dagger; sheath has a waist band of tin cone dangles, w/red, blue, and green beads on white ground; the dagger made from an old file and has a short stag grip; ca. 1850–60; 10½″ long in 8″ sheath.   **$750–$1000**

Paint pouch; beaded bar design in red, pink, and blue on white ground; the original catalog label reads "Paint Pouch taken from Crazy Horse, Pine Ridge Reservation, South Dakota, 1878 from D.C. Blanchard," an Episcopal Missionary; 10½″ long without fringe, 3¼″ wide.   **$2450–$3000**

Parfleche; rectangular folded rawhide case w/geometric painted designs; ca. 1890; 25″ × 10″. $200-$300

Parfleche; rectangular rawhide container w/geometric painted designs in red, green, blue, and yellow; ca. 1890. $350-$500

Parfleche; rare rectangular lidded rawhide box w/painted black outline geometric designs; ca. 1890; 18″ × 10″. $500-$700

Parfleches; pair of parfleches; ca. 1875; 12″ × 22″. $3000-$4000 pr.

Pipe bag; quillwork is red and yellow; beaded buckskin; background is white w/green triangles trimmed in blue and blue crosses trimmed in red; ca. 1885; length 33″. $2500-$3000

From the William R. Nash Collection. Photo by Donald Vogt.

Pipe bag; quilled and fringed hide pipe bag, decorated on the front and back w/bright red quillwork panels containing geometric motifs in purple, yellow, and (faded) green; the short openwork section below wrapped in orange-red dyed quillwork and decorated w/row of small tin cone and red feather suspensions; remains of ochre, beaded trim along the sides; length 26½″. $2000-$2400

Courtesy of Robert W. Skinner, Inc.,
Bolton, MA.

Pipe bag; beaded and fringed hide pipe bag; small beaded and fringed knife sheath on the front, bag stitched on both sides and along edges w/geometric devices against a white ground; bead colors: apple green, bright blue, yellow, and white heart reds; the lower dyed, quill-wrapped hide openwork in a butterfly motif; hide fringe, dyed red horsehair, and tin cone suspensions; quill-wrapped hide suspension from bead-edged mouth; sinew-sewn; length, excluding fringe, 23¼". **$1500–$2000**

Pipe bag; beaded and fringed; stitched in dark blue, lime green, greasy yellow and white-heart reds on a white beaded ground w/geometric motifs on both sides; beaded linear pattern at mouth and down both sides; sinew-sewn; traces of green paint; 22½" long, excluding fringe (minor fringe loss). **$700–$900**

Pipe bag; beaded and fringed hide pipe bag, stitched on the front and back w/white beaded panels containing angular and arrowfeather motifs in green, light and dark blue, yellow, translucent red, and metallic beadwork; the lower openwork section bound in red, purple, and cream-colored porcupine quillwork (varnished?); 42" long. **$1500–$1800**

Pouch; round beaded hide pouch with other bead suspensions; ca. 1920; 9" × 3". **$25–$45**

Shield; contemporary rawhide shield w/painted decoration and turkey feathers; ca. 1980; 16" diameter. **$25–$45**

Sioux or Blackfoot, Awl case; beaded and colorful; ca. 1870. **$650–$800**

Ute

Courtesy of Morning Star Gallery, Santa Fe, NM. Photo by Donald Vogt.

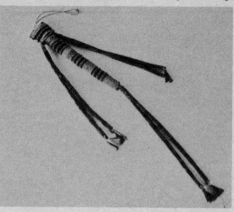

Paint bag; ca. 1870. **$3700-$4000**

Rifle scabbard; beaded and fringed hide rifle scabbard, decorated on the butt and point w/light blue beaded panels of terraced triangle and rectangle decoration in yellow, blue, and translucent red and green; remains of red trade cloth and purple-quilled trim; a leather shoulder strap, cloth bundle, and small animal's horn attached; 49½" long.

$4000-$4500

Wasco

Bag; rare net, beaded hide bag w/openwork diamond beaded designs and white bead fringe; ca. 1860; 6" × 3". **$55-$80**

Sally bag; rare old figured Wasco Sally bag w/"waterbug" designs; ca. 1840; 5" × 5½". **$150-$200**

Yakima

Bag; large full-beaded bag w/old time contour floral beadwork; 15" × 13"; ca. 1910. **$300-$500**

Bag; small rectangular hide bag w/fringe and floral designs; 9½" × 4"; ca. 1930. **$50-$75**

Bag; rectangular floral beaded bag w/fringe; ca. 1975; 11" × 12".

$70-$90

Gauntlets; large, high-top buckskin guantlets w/beaded elk and foliate motifs; 14" × 9"; ca. 1920. **$190-$250**

Courtesy of Canfield Gallery, Santa Fa, NM. Photo by Donald Vogt.

Parfleche; ca. 1890; 14″ × 28″.   **$4000–$5000**

Other

Athabascan, gun case; large hide gun case w/fine floral embroidered designs and fringe; 50″ × 7″; ca. 1920.   **$200–$500**

Belt; full-beaded; 28″ overall; light blue field w/floral and geometrical designs in green, brown, red, pink, and dark blue; sinew-sewn; beads missing in several places; metal buckle.   **$10–$15**

Belt; full-beaded man's; 41″ overall; blue, white, and red diagonal lazy-stitched designs; line of ¼″ brass spots runs down the center; good condition; metal buckle.   **$25–$40**

Chippewa, shield; Bear Society shield by Alfred Sky.   **$300–$400**

Comanche, cradleboard; doll size; beaded deerskin on painted wooden frame, bound by buckskin strings; homemade cloth doll included; the picket top vertical boards are loose; sinew-sewn lazy stitching; traces of yellow paint; 24″ long.   **$225–$300**

Deerskin; 9″ × 15″ panel decorated w/beads, porcupine quillwork, and feathers; sinew-sewn.   **$30–$50**

Deerskin panel; 7″ × 23″; decorated w/band of quilled fringe, tipped with hawkbells and dyed horse hair tassels; edged with ½″ band of blue, white, red, and green beadwork and four rows of red quillwork; sinew-sewn.   **$30–$55**

Drum; 4″ × 13″; painted w/designs of birds, animals, and snakes and marked "Pawnee Bill's Tom Tom."   **$60–$80**

Group of four items; includes a fully-beaded knife sheath, 5″ long; awl case, 7¾″ long; floral beaded bag, 9½″; and a pair of Blackfoot moccasins, 9½″ long.   **$550–$600**

Kootenai, parfleche; choice rawhide case w/long fringe and painted designs; ca. 1985; 12″ × 11″.   **$125–$175**

Mandan, pouch; unusual medicine pouch w/pony bead decoration; ca. 1870; 4″ × 4″.   **$75–$100**

Net bag; rare, rawhide w/deerskin rim; decorated w/light beadwork; pink and yellow beads; 7″ overall; good condition.   **$10–$15**

Possible bag; 10″ × 14″ beaded deerskin; 5½″ wide sinew-sewn beaded panel; geometric design in blue, white, red, and pink on a green field; matching design on flap; black cut glass bead work loop trim; further decorated w/yellow horsehair tassels in tin cone bells; good condition.   **$700–$900**

Potowatomi, bag; fine little net beaded hide "puzzle" pouch; ca. 1920; 5″ × 3″.   **$10–$15**

Quirts, miscellaneous group; wooden tacked handle; Cheyenne; ca. 1870.   **$2500–$3000**

Northern Plains; ca. 1880.   **$750–$850**

Crow, w/tacked decoration; ca. 1870.   **$1800–$2000**

San Felipe, shield; ca. 1860.   **$9500–$10,000**

Santee Sioux, pouch; round hide pouch w/Santee Sioux stylized floral beadwork; ca. 1920; 8″ × 4″.   **$55–$75**

Courtesy of Morning Star Gallery, Santa Fe, NM. Photo by Donald Vogt.

Sarcee, shoulder bag; beaded shoulder bag of Sarcee, Plains Indians; ca. 1860.   **$3750–$4000**

Shoshone, parfleche; ca. 1880; 13″ × 28″.   **$4000–$5000**

Courtesy of Morning Star Gallery, Santa Fe, NM. Photo by Donald Vogt.

Strike-a-lites, group; strike-a-lite made of saddle leather by the Kiowa tribe, ca. 1860. **$1650–$2000**

Strike-a-lite, Apache, formerly of the Kober collection. **$1500–$1750**

Beaded strike-a-lite, Apache (Chiricahua); ca. 1870. **$1250–$1500**

Skeletal bag, Apache, ca. 1890, formerly of the Guy collection. **$850–$1000**

Tlingit, bag; seal skin bag w/fur and w/beaded flowers; 10″ × 6″; ca. 1920. **$30–$50**

Tobacco bag; beaded, 6½″ × 14″ w/blue, white, yellow, and red beadwork points decorated w/tin cones and feathers; fairly brittle. **$30–$50**

MISCELLANEOUS
▼▼▼▼▼▼▼▼▼▼▼▼

INTRODUCTION

Some pieces just never seem to fit into a particular category, so we lump them together, whether or not they are related, into a category entitled "miscellaneous." However, these items are not unimportant, nor are they the rare, one-of-a-kind items that most avid collectors only see once or twice in a lifetime.

We hope that we have at least touched upon most items collected by the Amerind afficionado. If not, perhaps you'll find your favorite item, or an interesting piece of information, in this chapter.

GENERAL INFORMATION

Most tribes and their peculiarities have been covered in the other chapters of this book. However, there was certain information pertaining to miscellaneous items which I felt should be briefly mentioned.

For example, the Blackfoot men's society is called All-Friends Society. Out of the old groups, the Horns and the Brave Dogs are ones still in existence. They are the policemen of the tribe and enforce tribal law, as well as orders from the chief. Motokiks is the women's secret society. Four is the sacred number in their customs, which is based on the four directions (N, E, S, W) and the four seasons.

Medicine and Pipe Bundles and the Sun Dance Ceremony

This ceremony is put on by women, and in the old days it lasted a month or more because each society would have to go through its ceremonies. Often there would be a few medicine bags transferred during the ceremonies or some owners would open their bags to have a dance and give out tobacco.

Beaver bundles were transferred and cherished like medicine pipe bundles. A man in the tribe would be designated as main beaver man. He and his wife or wives would know all the birds and animals held in the bundle, all the songs needed for ceremonies associated with the beaver bundle, and all the legends and ceremonies.

Beaver men knew how the seasons change and could predict the weather. They kept track of time and the changing moon with sticks kept in their bundles. They were responsible for the Sun Dance and Holy Smoke ceremonies. The Beaver Bundle Dance was last performed in 1967. Today the knowledge of the ceremony is almost lost.

SOME MISCELLANEOUS ITEMS

Breastplates

Early breastplates (1855–89) were made from dentalium shells, while later ones were made from bones.

Bride's Suitcase

Called songo sivu, a bride's suitcase is made of the stems of the sungo tala, a tall reedy plant called sand grass *(Calamovilfa gigantea)* that grows near seeps in the dune areas about the Hopi mesas. Stems of the grass one-quarter of an inch in diameter are cut to length and pieced together w/cotton string to form a mat four feet or more in length.

This suitcase is used by the Hopi bride to hold a part of the wedding costume when she leaves the home of her groom's mother to return to her own mother's home. This wedding costume is called ova, which is the smaller wedding blanket.

Cradleboards

Cradleboards were used by the working women to carry their babies. The mother would be able to use her hands while the baby, wrapped in a soft cloth or hide, then put into a moss bag, would sleep, lulled by his/her mother's warmth, closeness, and rhythmic movements. When traveling, the strap on the back of the cradleboard was hooked over the saddlehorn. The cradleboard could also be hung from the branch of a tree while a mother worked.

Early Blackfoot cradleboard frames were made of willow branches. Later ones were sawed out of a board to the maker's desired shape. Once the frame was made, it would be covered with buckskin and beaded. The baby was kept in a bag with a hood attached to it which served as protection from the elements.

All types of cradleboards were made—some with a lining of fur, some with shells sewn on for the baby's amusement, and some made out of cloth. All had straps on their back to hang the cradleboard. Some tribes, such as the basketmaker tribes, made their cradleboards out of basketry materials. These cradleboards resemble their wooden and leather counterparts, though some may be slightly curved instead of flat (see Basket chapter for further information).

Calumet (Sacred Pipe)

The American Indians always used the calumet, a sacred pipe, in their important transactions. The pipe was usually made of red, black, or white marble, its head finely polished, and the quill, usually 2½' long, was made of a strong reed or cane and decorated with colorful feathers and locks of female hair. It was considered a symbol of peace and always respected as such. The Indian people strongly believed that if the pipe wasn't held in reverence, they would suffer a great misfortune as a result.

The calumet of war was distinguished by red feathers. It was presented and smoked when its owners were trying to determine what the weather should be, what to plant or what to eat; it was used to show hour, to strengthen peace, or to call for war. A ceremony, an age-old tradition which was as graceful and meaningful as Japanese tea ceremonies, was held whenever the calumet was used.

As with other possessions, the calumet was decorated and designed by the crafts people of the tribe. Carving and painting would decorate the pipe, along with hair, quillwork, and feathers. Once trade beads, coins, and tinklers became used by the Indians, they too were used to decorate the pipes.

The Plains Indians (Sioux, especially) used catlinite to make bowls, while the Comanche and Shoshoni tribes used a greenish material. The Iroquois used a brownish-black soapstone, and the Pueblos developed pottery or clay pipes with reed stems.

Effigies

Animal or human effigies were believed to *represent* the spiritual powers in which the Indian tribes believed. Effigies were not "idols," as some have believed, but instead were tangible representations of "God."

Effigies were used as hunting medicine (i.e., buffalo effigies for hunting the same) as well as for war or for curing illnesses. The effigies used for hunting could be as simple as a piece of stone shaped in the form of a buffalo or could be more elaborately carved to show the buffalo with bulging eyes and protruding tongue.

War medicines/effigies vary greatly. They could be feathers used to adorn war shirts or headdresses, carved human figures worn on necklaces, or war pipes decorated with human hair or feathers or carved with human figures or animals.

At victory dances, war effigies are used to reenact the occasion. One such dance stick (Hunkpapa) was sold recently (1987) at the Willis Henry Auction in Dedham, Massachusetts, for a world record amount (others like it are pictured in *Plains Indian Sculpture* by John C. Ewers). Most dance sticks are now owned by museums.

Medicine effigies included carved wooden bowls, spoons, human figurals, stomach kneaders, etc. Again, the effigies were carved with figures used to portray their strong medicine. Feasts were another occasion which gave the Indians an excuse/reason to carve effigy items such as spoons and bowls.

Ceremonial, witchcraft, and courting effigies were also made (i.e., the courting flutes). Ceremonial effigies included the Mandan evil spirit, Mandan and Hidatsa corn ceremony effigies, the snake effigy of the Hidatsa rain ceremony, the Thunder ceremonial effigies of the Nomadic Tribes, and Sun Dance Dolls of Crow, Shoshone, and Ute tribes.

Pipes

Effigy pipes were made by Plains Indians during the prehistoric era out of wood or catlinite. (Catlinite was the main substance used.) They were carved or adorned with sculptured figures.

Stones were polished, with the tools available, to a fine sheen and were chosen for their ability to endure heat without cracking. Pipestone (called catlinite in honor of George Catlin) was found near what is today, Pipestone, Minnesota.

The pipes took many different shapes and sizes—some with the smoking hole on the end, others with it in the middle. Most of the pipes we see today were made during the period from 1830 to 1910, with the majority of these being made in the 1880s. Animal effigy pipes can be found finely carved or made in a primitive style.

The Plains Indians even took their artistic talents a step higher and carved portrait pipes. As early as 1829, pipes carved to portray an individual's likeness have been found. The Plains Indians carved their own likenesses onto pipes, as well as those of white men they admired. One such pipe has a portrait of the civil chief of the Winnebagos cut upon its front. The pipe was given to Caleb Atwater (a negotiator at Prairie du Chien in 1829) and forwarded to the President, the chief requesting that the President put it under his looking glass.

Medicine Pipes

Though most are in museums or private collections, the few that are still owned by the tribes are relied upon to conquer illness or to give their people strength.

Medicine Pipe Bundles

In the Blackfoot tribe, the medicine pipe bundle was owned by a man and wife; a child, the third owner, wore the special topknot wrapping and fur headband which went with the bundle. Each time a bundle of this kind was opened, a ceremony was held with specific ceremonial songs.

The bundles came with a great deal of responsibility as they were sometimes passed from generation to generation. The owners had to take special care that nothing happened to their bundle and that the sacred ceremonies were followed carefully. If one family took over a sacred bundle from another, the family taking on the responsibility often gave up its best and most valued property (horses, cattle, money, etc.) to show its sincerity in taking on the responsibility.

The bundles were hung from tripods during the days when the families lived in tepees. When people started living in houses, the bundle would be hung by a nail on the outside of the house during the daytime and brought in again at night. Each time the bundle was moved, incense would be lit and prayers would be said.

Natoas Bundle

Holy women wear a Natoas bonnet, considered sacred, during the Sun Dance. A rawhide band holds large plumes and feathers. Generally, the Natoas is kept in a bundle and taken out only for ceremonies. Though there are very few bundles still held by Indians, there are, unfortunately, several which are held by museums or private collectors. Since these items are sacred, the American Indian people consider it a sacrilege when a Natoas bundle is opened up for display.

Twined Bags

Women in Great Lakes tribes (as well as Pacific Coast tribes) made bags out of twine and used them for storage and for carrying items. Fibers used came from the bark of a basswood tree as well as from brown buffalo hair. The sacred thunderbird and great cat were legendary figures used as motifs on such bags.

MISCELLANEOUS LISTINGS

Athabascan

Beadwork; rectangular floral beaded pin cushion; 4″ × 2″; ca. 1920.
$675–$700

Pillow; round moosehide pillow w/floral beadwork and "Alaska" in beading; ca. 1935; 15″ dia. **$40–$60**

Haida

Pipe; steatite pipe bowl in double bird form; rare; ca. 1870; 2″ × 2″.
$75–$100

Spoon; large, bent horn spoon w/totemic-carved handle and abalone inlays; 11″ × 3½″; ca. 1900. **$400–$600**

Spoon; rare, old, carved, mountain sheep horn ladle; ca. 1870.
$85–$110

Spoon; large, carved, mountain goat horn spoon w/many totemic carvings on the handle; 11″ × 2″; ca. 1900. **$300–$600**

Totem; argilite totems, approximately 8″ tall. **$800–$1000**

Hopi

From the William R. Nash Collection. Photo by Donald Vogt.

Bride's suitcase; called Songo Sivu; width 28″. **$1000–$1500**

Canteen; 6¼″ polychrome, Kachina design; stubbs for carrying strings are chipped. $100–$130

Iroquois

Bag; fancy beaded and sequined cloth bag; 7¼″ long × 7½″ wide; decorated on both sides w/lavender, clear dark red, sky blue, pony trader blue, green, yellow, orange, clear, and white beads in floral and foliate designs; ca. 1900. $65–$110

Bag; rounded beaded velvet bag w/beaded floral design on both sides; ca. 1880; 7″ × 6″. $30–$60

Courtesy of Morning Star Gallery, Santa Fe, NM. Photo by Donald Vogt.

Mask; corn husk mask. $1800–$2000

Rattle; turtle shell; 16½″ long; minor shell loss. $225–$450

Whimsey; large ornately beaded pin cushion w/horse and floral designs; ca. 1880; 10″ × 8″. $70–$125

Ketoh

Group; Santo Domingo bow guard; ca. 1950. $500–$750

Navajo bow guard; ca. 1940. $800–$1000

Navajo bow guard; ca. 1895. $1200–$1500

Ketoh, Navajo; bow guard; ca. 1920. $800–$1000

Bow guard; ca. 1940. $600–$800

Sandcast Navajo; ca. 1940. $800–$1000

Navajo

Courtesy of W. J. Arbuckle. Photo by Donald Vogt.

Beadwork; group of contemporary beaded pieces; includes belt, keychain, pen earrings; large earrings are porcupine quills; very colorful.

$200–$250 group

Buttons; pair of large silver and turquoise buttons; 1⅞″ diameter; sterling; each set w/one round blue-green cabochon. $50–$75

From the William R. Nash Collection. Photo by Donald Vogt.

Canteen; rare early hand-hammered silver tobacco canteen w/etched deer design on one side and triangles indicating the four directions on the opposite side; the silver stopper is attached by small link chain; 5″ × 3″. $500–$750

Courtesy of Canfield Gallery, Santa Fe, NM. Photo by Donald Vogt.

Head stall; silver horse headdress; ca. 1885; 18″ long.   **$3000–$4000**

Loom model.   **$175–$225**

Miniature rug, loom, and doll; 17″ × 13″ handmade tree branch loom containing a partially finished red, gold, black, and brown "eye dazzler" and a traditionally dressed seated figure.   **$45–$85**

Purse; handmade woven purse in gray, black, and maroon; contemporary.   **$50–$75**

Nez Perce

Bag; oval full-beaded bag w/different cut bead geometrics; one each side; 11″ × 8″; ca. 1910.   **$100–$150**

Bag; classic, rectangular, twined corn husk bag w/bright-colored geometrics and floral designs; 7¼″ × 7″; ca. 1910.   **$375–$500**

Bag; large, rectangular, twined corn husk bag w/bright-colored geometrics on both sides; ca. 1900; 18″ × 13″.   **$185–$225**

Bag; old beaded cloth; 12″ × 9″; decorated w/clear dark green, cobalt blue, and waxy yellow beads in a large floral and foliate design on an opaque beaded background.   **$125–$195**

Bag; huge rectangular, twined cornhusk bag w/crisp, bright-colored geometric designs on each side; 23″ × 16″; ca. 1880.   **$600–$1000**

Bag; rectangular, twined corn husk bag w/bright-colored geometric designs; ca. 1910; 10″ × 8″.   **$205–$250**

Bag; rare, round, twined corn husk "Sally bag" w/red and blue geometric designs; ca. 1890; 7½″ × 6″.   **$120–$150**

Bag; large, rectangular, twined corn husk bag w/different geometric designs on each side; ca. 1890; 18″ × 14″.   **$475–$550**

Bag; unusual round, twined, corn husk medicine bag w/colorful geometric designs; ca. 1880.   **$85–$125**

Cradle; rare full-size baby carrier w/contour beaded top and original board; 40″ × 12″; ca. 1890.   **$1000–$1800**

Cradle; miniature baby carrier w/beaded floral designs; ca. 1890; 10″ × 4″.   **$300–$500**

Corn husk bag; beautiful twined corn husk bag w/very colorful floral designs on one side and geometrics on the other; 11″ × 11″; ca. 1900.   **$300–$500**

Corn husk bag; twined, geometric polychromed decoration. **$110–$150**

Northwest Coast

Clan crest; polychrome decorated, carved and incised wood raven's head; concave base on tapering neck, abalone inlaid nostrils, beak, and eyes; traces of deep turquoise pigment over beak and eye grounds, crimson beak edge, and dark brownish-black pigment over crown and neck which is drilled for attachment and ornamentation; good patination; 5¼″ high, 4⅞″ long.   **$7000–$9000**

Dish; carved and painted cedar grease dish in beaver form w/abalone inlay, signed LaValle; ca. 1980; 4″ × 3″.   **$110–$200**

Horn spoon; in two sections; tenoned and horn pegged; elongated oval bowl tapering to a carved and incised totemic handle; abalone inlay accents; 10⅓″ long; minor bowl loss.   **$800–$900**

Mask; rare and unusual hide-covered mask w/abalone inlay and real hair; 10″ × 7″.   **$200–$300**

Spoon; large mountain sheep horn spoon w/simple circular designs on the handle; ca. 1880.   **$75–$125**

Paiute

Beadwork; pair of red and white beaded salt and pepper shakers; ca. 1940; 3″ × 2″.   **$50–$75**

Beadwork vase; geometric designs; ca. 1940.   **$35–$50**

Plains

Brass bells; antique pair of 25″ long, leather-mounted, dance-type bells; shows use, age, and tarnish. **$50–$100**

Fetish; round trade fetish in turtle form w/full-beaded back; 5½″ × 4″. **$75–$100**

Fetish; beaded hide, umbilical cord fetish; 46″ × 9″. **$55–$80**

Fetish; very rare, beaded hide, horse effigy fetish; 5″ × 5″. **$300–$350**

From the William R. Nash Collection. Photo by Donald Vogt.

Pipe; wood and stone pipe, composed of red catlinite elbow pipe head w/deeply grooved panels on the shaft and tall cylindrical bowl; the wood stem of rectangular section carved in high relief w/splayed turtle and three deer heads; inscribed in ink on the underside "Purchased from Crazy Horse, Oelrichs, S.D. Nov. 24th—92″; total length 35¼″. **$6000–$6500**

Spoon; bent horn spoon decorated w/geometric beadwork on the border; 9″ × 2″. **$145–$175**

Sioux

Breastplate; large, real bone breastplate w/Crow bead spacers and tin cones; ca. 1960; 40″ × 9″. **$150–$200**

From the collection of N. A. McKinney. Photo by Donald Vogt.

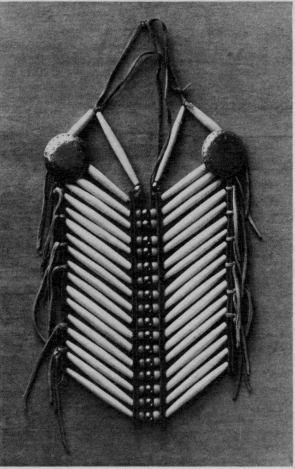

Breastplate; child's breastplate; heavy silver conchas w/stamped designs on leather w/silver beads, colored trade glass beads, and bone cylinders; ca. 1940; out of Oklahoma.   **$1500-$1800**

Fetish; hide umbilical cord fetish in turtle form w/beaded American flag design; 6″ × 3″.   **$200-$300**

Fetish; rare umbilical cord fetish w/fully quilled back in lizard form; ca. 1870; 7″ × 2″.   **$200-$400**

Courtesy of Canfield Gallery, Santa Fe, NM. Photo by Donald Vogt.

Fetish; umbilical fetish; beaded hide; late 1800s; turtle in green, dark blue, and white. **$400–$500**

Pipe; black stone "T" bowl w/red stone and pewter inlay and a tacked "cork screw" stem; 31″ × 5″. **$360–$400**

Pipe; red catlinite "T" bowl w/rectangular red catlinite stem; ca. 1890; 21″ × 4″. **$225–$275**

Pipe; red catlinite "T" bowl w/long wooden stem; ca. 1890. **$125–$200**

Tlingit

Amulet; old and interestingly carved fossil ivory or bone Shaman's amulet w/abalone inlay; ca. 1840; 2½″ × 1″. **$210–$230**

Bag; choice floral beaded "octopus" bag w/bead and red wool suspensions; 18″ × 9″; ca. 1920. **$450–$550**

Bowl; rare, large, ceremonial "seal" bowl w/shell and white bead inlay; ca. 1900; 15″ × 8″. **$1350–$1600**

Dish; small, carved, wooden seal dish w/abalone inlay; ca. 1920; 6″ × 1½″. **$55–$75**

Ivory pipe; carved ivory pipe in bird and shaman form, w/abalone inlays; ca. 1975; 3″ × ½″. **$150–$250**

Ivory; carved and painted four-figure ivory totem pole; ca. 1935; 6″ × 1″. **$45–$70**

Ivory; rare carving depicting a blanketed shaman w/abalone inlay on a wooden base; ca. 1900; 4″ × 2″.   **$200–$400**

Pipe; carved ivory pipe w/abalone inlay eyes; 4½″ × ½″; ca. 1850.
                                                      $75–$125

Pouch; round seal fur pouch w/beaded designs all around; ca. 1920; 3½″ × 4″.   **$50–$80**

Soul catcher; rare, fossil, ivory-carved totemic soul catcher; ca. 1870.
                                                      $100–$150

Spoon; small, black, mountain goat horn spoon w/handle fully carved in totemic designs; 6½″ × 1¼″; ca. 1870.   **$275–$375**

Spoon; black, carved, mountain goat horn spoon w/totemic designs, abalone inlay, and native copper reinforcement; 8″ × ½″ × 3″; ca. 1900.   **$350–$500**

Totem; carved and painted bone or ivory totem pole from Alaska; ca. 1940; 6½″ × ½″   **$65–$80**

Wasco

Bag; rare beaded wall pocket done in old beads; ca. 1860; 4½″ × 8″.
                                                      $55–$75

Pipe; rare, old, gray "T" bowl excavated on the Columbia River; ca. 1700; 4″ × 3″.   **$50–$100**

Pipe; excavated gray stone "L" pipe bowl from the Columbia River; ca. 1800; 1¾″ × 2½″.   **$55–$75**

Sally bag; rare, old, twined Sally bag w/bead and button decoration; 4″ × 4½″; ca. 1840.   **$60–$80**

Yakima

Bag; large, rectangular, hop string bag; ca. 1920; 16″ × 3″. **$65–$90**

Bag; rounded, small, rectangular cloth bag w/beautiful beaded flower; ca. 1920; 6″ × 5″.   **$45–$75**

Bag; twined hop string belt pouch, ca. 1920; 8″ × 7″.   **$75–$100**

Bag; "Sally" bag w/colored geometric corn husk decoration; ca. 1900; 10″ × 7″.   **$325–$500**

Bag; rare, old, double-sided, contour, floral beaded bag; ca. 1910; 9″ × 7″.   **$55–$80**

Bag front; large, rectangular, beaded bag front w/stylized floral beadwork; ca. 1920; 13″ × 13″.   **$150–$200**

Beaded set; hair holder, bola tie, and two buckles, all w/cut bead floral designs; ca. 1975. **$85–$125**

Zuni

Fetish; handcarved turquoise badger fetish w/fine detail; ca. 1970; 21½″ × 1″. **$75–$100**

Fetish; 6½″ high black grizzly bear w/turquoise eyes, red coral tongue, mother-of-pearl teeth and holding mother-of-pearl fish in one paw. **$175–$250**

Fetish; carved antler bear fetish w/turquoise eyes; ca. 1970; 4″ × 2″. **$60–$80**

Fetish; carved brown serpentine bear fetish; 2″ × 1½″; ca. 1940. **$30–$50**

Fetish; carved brown serpentine bear fetish; ca. 1975. **$20–$40**

Fetish; brown serpentine carved bear fetish; ca. 1975; 2″ × 1″. **$15–$20**

Fetish; carved stone bear fetish; ca. 1940; 2″ × 1½″. **$10–$25**

Silver and turquoise belt buckle set and keeper; sterling "ranger" set w/free form, hand cut, natural blue cabochons; signed A. Penketewa. **$40–$80**

Stone fetish; 1⅜″ × 3½″; green serpentine badger w/rawhide-wrapped mother-of-pearl arrowhead, olive shell heishe, red coral and blue turquoise on its back. **$80–$100**

Other

Ankle bells; large pair w/five 2½″ bells to the side. **$10–$15**

Bag, beaded; unusual pony beaded bag w/beaded drops; ca. 1900; 9″ × 3″. **$35–$50**

Beaded bolo tie, Apache; blue opaque and opalescent colors in barber pole-like and ten-pointed star/flower designs. **$15–$30**

Beadwork, Chippewa; beaded black velvet pillow cover w/floral designs; ca. 1910; 17″ × 18″. **$85–$100**

Belt; large sterling silver and turquoise concha w/five oval conchas; six butterflys and 3″ × 4¼″ buckle; set w/large ¾″ average turquoise stones; two in buckle; all set on 3″ wide, 41″ overall black leather belt; all hand silver work; fine condition. **$300–$450**

Belt; silver and turquoise concho; nine cast silver conchos, including buckle, set w/³/₈″ × ¹/₂″ blue spider web stones on black 36″ leather belt; fine condition.   **$310–$425**

Bookends; pair of cast iron "Indian chief" bookends; ca. 1930; 6¹/₂″ × 5″.   **$35–$50**

Breastplate, Crow; long hair pipe bones w/leather spacers and green faceted trade beads along w/dark blue trade beads; ca. 1880.   **$500–$750**

Breastplate; 92 hair-pipe bones w/central row of brass beads; brass beads and hair-pipe bones in the neck suspension; fringe on sides; a row of ten eagle claws divided by shell and brass beads is draped across the bottom of the breastplate; 29″ tall.   **$1200–$1500**

Breastplate; young girl's bone and bead breastplate; ca. 1965; 24″ × 2″.
                                                                            $20–$40

Ceremonial mask, Yaqui; Pascol Easter painted and carved mask w/horsehair.   **$55–$110**

Chest, Kwakiutl; very rare blanket chest from an old Alert Bay collection; decorated with totem poles on each end and a stylized eagle carved into the center of the front panel; ca. 1880; 20″ × 11¹/₂″.   **$375–$500**

Cigarette case; unusual pre–WWII fully beaded Lucky Strike cigarette case; ca. 1935; 3¹/₄″ × 2¹/₂″.   **$125–$150**

Coins; roll of 50 mixed-date U.S. Indian Head pennies; ca. 1900.
                                                                            $30–$35

Coins; bag containing 100 old assorted-date Indian head pennies.
                                                                            $45–$65

Cradle, Hupa; classic twined baby carrier w/dentellium shell suspensions; ca. 1880; 22″ × 7″.   **$175–$250**

Dance ankle bells; two pairs w/large 1¹/₂″ bells (six to a strap) and a pair of children's one-bell set.   **$30–$50**

From the collection of Gene and Linda Kangas. Photo by Gene Kangas.

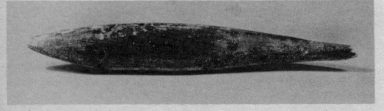

Decoy; prehistoric decoy of petrified ivory w/four hand-drilled holes for varied suspension under water.   **$200–$500**

From the collection of Gene and Linda Kangas. Photo by Gene Kangas.

Decoy; small fish decoy by Timothy Idlout, Northwest Territories; carved whale bone, moveable bone fins, lead weight.   **$200–$400**

Drum, Taos; classic Taos tourist drum w/eagle dancer painted on it; ca. 1950; 6″ × 5″.   **$10–$15**

Effigy piece; rare flint thunderbird ceremonial point; prehistoric.   **$60–$90**

Fetish, Pawnee; pony beaded hide fetish of triangular form w/trade bead-decorated fringe, net beaded body woven in concentric diamond motif; 3½″ long, excluding fringe; pony bead colors: violet-blue, greasy yellow, turquoise, pink, venetian glass trade beads.   **$700–$900**

Fetish, Kiowa; early beaded umbilical cord fetish, ca. 1890.   **$50–$125**

Hair feathers; cut legal feather hair drops.   **$20–$40**

Headdress; roach type w/tie strings.   **$25–$50**

Husk face mask, Woodlands; Cayuga, Husk Face Society, composed of bands of braided cornhusk and fringed mane.   **$350–$500**

Indian head pennies; bag containing 100 old Indian head pennies; ca. 1900.   **$20–$40**

Indian paint; native red and white painted stones and two small jars of trade vermillion.   **$5–$10**

Indian wedding post.   **$10–$15**

Miniatures; group of miniature fetishes by Lance Chema and Dan Quam are poised on miniature Indian rugs.   **$100–$250 ea.**

Needlepoint; needlepoint pictures which use Navajo symbolism; made for collector as gifts.   **$50–$60**

Painted skull; painted and decorated prairie bleached buffalo skull w/feathers; ca. 1985; 10″ × 20″.   **$75–$100**

Peace medal; John Tyler peace medal in silver and with a hold drilled to wear it; ca. 1841; 3″ dia.   **$225–$300**

Peace medal case; pony-beaded oval hide Peace medal case; ca. 1900.
$75–$125

Peace medal; silver Thomas Jefferson Peace medal w/hole drilled in it; ca. 1801; 3″ dia.   **$300–$400**

Peace medal; round silver Andrew Johnson Peace medal on bone bead choker; ca. 1865; 11″ × 5″.   **$250–$350**

Pipe; made to honor a Shawnee chief who was instrumental in establishing the Indian school at Chilocco; 62″ stem, 7″ bowl; made from birch poles.   **$90–$125**

Pipe bowl; small, catlinite.   **$40–$60**

Pipe; small carved stone "wine glass" cloud blower pipe from the Columbia River; prehistoric; 3″ × 1″.   **$60–$80**

Pipes; group of pipes; large one is woman's pipe; black one is pipe bowl; white one is made of deer antler.   **$35–$50**

Plaque; porcelain, handpainted plaque made by KPM Porcelains; of Indian attacking stagecoach.   **$450–$600**

Purse, Yurok; rare, carved, elk antler, dentellium money container from the lower Klamath River; ca. 1800; 4″ × 1″.   **$145–$180**

Silver medal; George Washington silver medal on real bone bead necklace; ca. 1780; 24″ × 1¼″.   **$200–$250**

Slave killer; large, classic, greenish slate slave killer from the Columbia River; ca. 1800.   **$400–$500**

Courtesy of Canfield Gallery, Santa Fe, NM. Photo by Donald Vogt.

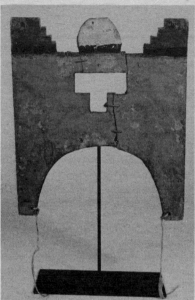

Tableta; Pueblo tableta from Rio Grande area; ca. 1910; 8″ × 9″.
                                                    $2000–$3000

Tomahawk; "U.S. Indian Scout" government issue; 17½″ long wood
handle finished with stag antler end; embossed U.S.I.S. between crossed
arrows.   **$400–$600**

Trade pipe; rare, old, white clay, Hudson Bay trade pipe; ca. 1870;
5″ × 2″ × 1″.   **$35–$50**

Two Indian bows; one Mohave; one Pomo; both polychrome decorated.
                                                    $325–$375

Whistle; Ghost Dance bone whistle w/quillwork streamer tipped with tin
cones and dyed horse hair tassels.   **$100–$150**

POTTERY
▼▼▼▼▼▼▼▼▼▼▼▼

INTRODUCTION

There is nothing more beautiful than a well-made piece of Indian pottery, and there are many potters throughout the United States, although the best-known potters come from the Southwest. The women and men involved in this age-old art learned their trade from members of the family or of the village where they lived. It is not something for which they went to school, nor do I know of a place which teaches the art of making Indian pottery.

It is because of that fact that Indian pottery is so innovative, yet so steeped in tradition that some of the designs used centuries ago are still being used today. It combines the Indians' love of the earth with their need to express themselves, and gives them a utilitarian bowl, pot or dish as a result. What could be more fulfilling?

What has amazed me during my research on the subject is that some of the ancient pottery brings less on the antique market than the modern pottery being currently made. In fact, at a recent (1987) Sotheby's sale of Indian art, interest in prehistoric pottery was light and many pieces were passed, while more recent "historic and later pottery" held the crowd's interest and sold well.

New potters are winning awards at annual crafts markets and exhibitions on a yearly basis and their work, as I said before, combines the old techniques with new ideas. Modern New Mexico and Arizona-area Indian women still hand-throw pottery, without the benefit of a wheel. They use a yucca leaf brush, with one end of it chewed into fibers. Acoma, San Ildefonso, Zuni, and Hopi mesas are still painting deer, birds, flowers, geometric designs, and identifiable symbols of their villages. Modern potters also now use new techniques, like selective firing, where the black carbon is burned away to reveal red clay.

Though there are few collectors today who can interpret them properly, there was much symbolism built into the decorative elements used in the pottery of the Zuni, Hopi, and San Ildefonso Indians (as well as others). For example, turkey tracks built into a Zuni design could indicate a wish for the turkeys to come back so that they could use their feathers for dance sticks, or a design that resembles bats wings can mean two rainbows. Each stroke of decoration meant something and no decoration was made just by chance.

For those collectors wishing to expand their knowledge of these symbols, there are many wonderful books which devote themselves exclusively to showing each sign and explaining its meaning. They are too numerous for this writer to explain in this chapter.

THE MAKING OF POTTERY

The process used to prepare the clay for making Indian pottery begins long before the potter's hands knead the clay and form it into shape. First, the potter travels to gather clay from deposits in the area (sometimes he/she must travel a great distance to find the right clay). Next, the clay is pulverized to a fine powder and cleaned (by sifting or tossing in a winnowing basket) to get out all the lumps and small rocks. After the cleaning is complete, the clay is stored until the potter is ready to use it. The final step, before use, is for the clay to be wettened and tempered. Water is added and the clay is kneaded on a dry, flat surface. While kneading, the potter tempers the clay with shells, sand, limestone, or plant fibers. The right amount prevents the clay from cracking during firing and drying.

The pottery techniques used by the American Indian are coiling, or modeling and paddling. Sometimes the two techniques are combined. Once the pot is "built," the drying, polishing, decorating, and firing techniques are basically the same. After the pot has been sun dried for a couple of days, it is smoothed with a flint chip or piece of bone (today's potters use a kitchen knife or scraper), then the pot is wiped with a wet cloth. If the pot will be decorated, it is necessary that the potter next apply a slip to the piece. A creamy mixture of colored clay and water is applied with a rag or rabbit's tail and is allowed to dry before the piece is polished with a small, smooth stone.

Firing is the trickiest part of the pottery-making process. It is during the firing process that a piece is either "finished" or broken. The great potter, Maria, used the firing process to cause the black-on-black surface indicative of her work. During this process, the fire is smothered with manure, giving the pottery a shiny black finish. If the fire is not smothered, but allowed to burn openly, the pottery will be red. After firing, the pottery is wiped so that the pieces will not flake or discolor.

Different types of decoration are applied by various tribes and these techniques have changed little during the centuries. Southwest potters (such as the Papago, who use sticks) paint their pottery. Corrugated pottery was a technique used in the prehistoric Southwest, though some of the contemporary potters are rediscovering this technique and enhancing it with their own variations. Other types of decorating include impressing designs, incising or scratching designs into an unfired pot or engraving the designs after firing.

The five basic pottery regions of the Amerind are: the Northern region, stretching from west of the Great Lakes to the Eastern Coast; the Central region, stretching from Georgia in the South to Michigan in the North, from Illinois in the West to the eastern border of Pennsylvania; the Southeast, encompassing all of Florida and that region along the coast which stretches to Delaware; the Gulf region of Louisiana, Mississippi, Alabama, part of Georgia, and the eastern border of Texas; and the Southwest, Arizona, New Mexico, part of Texas, Oklahoma, and the southern halves of Utah and Colorado.

The Northern Region potters (from tribes such as the Iroquois, Fox, Mandan, and Shoshoni) used angular incisions as designs in most of their pieces and the pottery color was mostly a gray-blue color mixed with beige. Cord marks, or cord-impressed designs, are commonly found on pottery made in this region.

In the Southeast region, the pottery is a lighter color and the decoration stamped or brushed. Tribes who were known to make pottery in this region include Cherokee, Creek, Apalachee, and Seminole.

The Central region (tribes such as Quapaw, Shawnee, and Winnebago) produced reddish pottery in various shapes and designs—such as the "head pots" of the middle Mississippi culture of Arkansas and the hunchback female effigy bottles made by the same culture.

The Choctaw, Caddo, Chickasaw, and Natchez tribes of the Gulf Region produced pottery with incised or engraved designs.

The Southwest potters are many and each is important when understanding the pottery of that region. Pottery is still made in the traditional way in the Southwest and one can find potters taught by their mothers, sisters, aunts, or grandmothers, the pottery of whom is well worth collecting.

The pottery culture in the Southwest is so strong that it can be divided into periods. The first, the Modified Basketmaker period (400–700), saw pottery like the Lino black-on-gray (unslipped) and the Abajo red-on-orange, while the Developmental-Pueblo period (700–1050) consisted of black-on-white pottery with painted designs. The Great Pueblo period (1050–1300) gave us hard, thin, highly polished pottery and the introduction of polychrome pottery. During the period from 1300–1700, the Regressive Pueblo period, polychrome pottery was developed further and mineral glaze paints were being used. Today's pottery ("modern" is from 1800–present) is made chiefly in the pueblo villages, with each area producing its own distinctive pottery products (i.e., Santa Clara's red and black pottery with impressed designs; San Ildefonso's black-on-black; and Acoma potters, who use a white to yellow-brown slip and whose typical patterns are geometrics and birds which look like parrots.

EXAMPLES OF POTTERY-MAKING TRIBES

Prehistoric pottery of the Amerind is more artistic than one would expect. Pottery effigies are almost abstract in form, highly polished pieces made out of whatever minerals (be it jaspar, terra cotta, or hematite, for example) the people had available to them.

Bowls and other vessels were sometimes footed and, more often than not, decorated. Their exteriors were incised by broad, curvilinear lines, sometimes showing designs of birds and other animals, sometimes being just a series of lines and circles. Beakers and bowls were adorned with bird, animal, and human effigies and designs differed with regions.

Anasazi (Southwest)

Anasazi Indians of the Southwest were cliff dwellers who populated the area around A.D. 1000 and created black-on-white, thin-line geometric abstractions on their pottery. (See information on Anasazi Indians in Artifacts chapter.)

Mogollan (Southwest)

The Mogollan people lived at approximately the same time as the Anasazi in the eastern part of southern New Mexico. Though the Hohokam were their neighbors in the west and the Anasazi were their northern neighbors, the Mogollan created their own type of pottery which we now recognize by the Mimbres art used as decoration.

Only five generations (between A.D. 1000 and 1150) produced black-on-white and polychrome pottery from the Mimbres Valley in New Mexico, most examples having geometric decoration. Many, however, portrayed human and animal figures which detailed what life was like at that time. The stories told by the decorations on this type of pottery tell us of birth, death, love, and even human sacrifice. Funerary pottery made by these people were placed over the dead person's face and then a hole was punched through the pot (as though the pot, too, was dead).

Archeologists have studied this fascinating culture, but are often frustrated by the fact that nearly every Mimbres site has been destroyed by looters.

San Ildefonso (Southwest)

The northernmost village of those pueblos using the rain bird design, San Ildefonso also has the noted distinction of making black-on-white wares in the same fashion for over seven hundred years. They never kept up with the trends other pottery-makers followed, instead adhering to their richly formal heritage.

Perhaps the cause of this unchanging atmosphere was the fact that their language (Tewa) was different than others in their region, thus they could not understand the newly conceived designs. Though they had a rather slow beginning, San Ildefonso potters are some of the best in North America.

Santa Clara

Though pottery-making goes on all year round, the heavy season is May to October, when potters beef up their stock for summer fairs/markets and for the tourist season. Sometimes a potter may work at his/her craft for eight to ten hours per day. Men, such as Ernest Tapia, Camilio Tafoya, Luther Guitterez, Joe Tafoya, and Joseph Lonewolf, have made their living at making pottery and have done as well at it as some of the more notable female potters.

Potters believe that their clay has a soul and that if you treat it right, it will treat you right. When a Santa Clara potter wants to gather clay for his work, it is often a family expedition. Pits are found on or near the reservation where the potters work, thus making that clay the type the pueblo will use. This also explains why some pottery is different colors than others.

Santa Clara potters use clay, tempering materials, and red paint for their creations. The place where the clay is obtained is called Na Pi' i we and is about a mile west of the pueblo, whereas the tempering material is obtained about seven to eight miles northwest of a village called Makawa oky.

After the clay dries in the sun for a couple of days, it is put in a washtub and water is added to cover it. The clay soaks for two to four days, during which time the potter draws off the excess water. After the excess water is drawn, clean water is added and the process repeated until the water runoff is clear. Once that step is accomplished, the potter will stir the clay until she/he removes the lumps and the mixture will pass through a sieve. Rocks and lumps are sorted out and discarded.

Now the potter will set up the amounts of clay she/he will need in the next several days. In a day or two, it is ready to be mixed with tuff or "sand," and broken pieces of unfired pottery may be added to the mixture in order to absorb some of the excess water. Temper or filler is usually volcanic tuff which, when combined with the clay mixture, will act as a binder to strengthen the body. It also serves to counteract shrinkage and facilitate uniform drying. Mixing the clay with tuff is hard and tiring work, usually done on the floor in the house. It is kneaded like bread dough, and, if wet, dried until it is the proper consistency for modeling.

Tools, such as modeling spoons, shaping and scraping tools, a mold, some water, and a lap board are some of the things a potter will gather when he/she is ready to mold.

Most vessels begin in the same manner—as a lump of clay, a little larger than a fist, that the potter models into the shape of a cone. The clay is held by the left hand and rotated. With his/her right fist, he/she punches a depression into the center, then enlarges the opening of that depression with the fingers of the right hand. The base is laid on the lap board, depression side up, and the potter takes a shaping spoon (kajape) and shapes the piece, making strokes parallel to the rim.

Scraping and thinning from the bottom of the base to the top, he/she finishes one area, then turns the piece and performs the process again on the next area. Rotating the vessel, he/she uses the wooden stick in diagonal moves, removes small amounts of clay from the exterior of the vessel, and works the entire surface until it is smoothed. The tools are kept moist by constant dipping into the water basin the potter keeps nearby. The vessel is built by adding successive rolls of clay to the piece, working as before, until the vessel is the desired shape and size.

Then it is time for smoothing and sanding (drying takes approximately two days, depending on the size of the piece and what the weather is like).

Sanding first thins the walls, removes any gouges or lines, then reduces the walls again. So much dust is created by this step that it must take place outside the house. In the past, pieces of bone or a sharp stone was used to smooth the surface. Once the exterior and interior are smooth, slipping is done and polishing begins. Polishing is done with smooth stones called, accordingly, polishing stones, and the process takes much precision and patience.

After the smoothing is done, the firing begins. The process the Santa Clara potters use is to keep the fire going under the pieces of pottery which need completion. The heat must be kept even and it is a job which takes the diligence of one who knows the importance of this final process. When the fire cools down, the pottery is carefully removed and the artist decorates the pot according to his/her style.

Santa Clara potters are well known in today's Indian collectibles market (whether that potter be alive or dead). Some of the families who are active in this art are the Guitterez family (Catherine, Denaria, Dolorita, Faustina, Laurencia, Luther, Margaret, Petra, and Pula), as well as Luther's daughter, Pauline Naranjo.

The Naranjo family also includes Barbarita, Veronica, Candelaria, Belah, Celestina, Christina, Elizabeth, Everesta, Flora (and her family), Isabele, Madeline, and Teresita. There are also a number of children coming along through the ranks who show great promise.

Helen Shupla and her husband, Kenneth, are known, as is the talented Tafoya family, such as Camilia Tafoya, his daughter, Grace Medicine Flower, and his son, Joseph Lonewolf, whose miniatures are among the finest made by the modern potters. One can also not forget Margaret, Madeline, Mida, and their families, as well.

Tesuque (Southwest)

Tesuque potters seemed to better comprehend the changes in pottery-making and concentrated on small decorative details, incorporating designs like the rain bird into a secondary design. Tesuque pottery reached its peak at the end of the nineteenth century and rapidly declined after that.

Zuni (Southwest)

The rain bird design is one of the most frequently used and most easily recognized of all Zuni pottery designs. Bird-like figures have been found on pottery dating back to the classical period of Mesa Verde pottery (approximately the thirteenth century), and were, at that time, pretty much geometric figures.

The rain bird figure was used by other pottery-making people of that region, with practically no change in the motif, and continued to be used in the Tularosa region on black-on-white wares. The red ware which succeeded the early black-on-white (Four-Mile polychrome) also used bird-like figures on the outsides of bowls. Jeddito black-on-yellow pottery had also used the bird symbol. Though Four-Mile polychrome wares lasted until the fifteenth century, they disappeared shortly after that and the Hopi yellow wares were a result of the Jeddito black-on-yellow. Before the coming of the Spaniards, Sikyatki polychrome pottery came into popularity and spread over the whole Pueblo region.

Zuni pottery underwent a change in the type of glaze used by approximately 1700, when the potters favored a dull and flat look to their pots. The "rain bird" design first came into evidence at this time and is divisible into several distinct features. The center of the design is a single coil, representing the bird's head and beak, and, below this coil, its crest. On either side of this design is a stepped outline which encloses two solid figures—the body and the wings.

Through the study of Pueblo pottery design, one can discern many minute and individualized changes in this design, yet the basics are the same whether one calls the design a bird, a chicken, a turkey, or, its rightful name, "the rain bird."

The symbolism of designs found on Indian pottery may be disputed, but intellectually speaking, anyone who has studied the Amerind must come to the conclusion that all decoration meant something to the decorator (the Indian was never without myths and stories); thus, the rain bird figure, which existed on so much of the pottery made in the Southwest, was a significant one.

Other pottery-making groups, such as the Hopi, Acoma, Laguna, Santa Ana, San Ildefonso, Tesuque, Cochiti, Zia, and Santo Domingo peoples, all used a form of the rain bird design (most made very small, if any, changes in the design).

SPECIAL POTTERY

Effigy Pottery

Effigy pottery articles, most of which were made by women, were only a small portion of the articles that Indian men used in religious ceremonies. They were also traded to other tribes, sometimes carried great distances, and were highly prized by their owners.

Ollas

Large water jars (ollas) were used in the Southwest to carry liquids. Indian women would balance these large jars on their heads and carry them to the spring or well and back. The potters often competed to see who could make the thinnest, finest, largest and most beautifully decorated ollas.

Storytellers

Storyteller figurines, made famous through the work of potter Helen Cordero (1915–) and well-publicized by knowledgeable Southwestern galleries, such as the Adobe Gallery in Albuquerque, New Mexico, owned by Alexander Anthony, Jr., have become an integral part of Pueblo pottery. These figures, originally modelled after Cordero's grandfather and his storytelling techniques, have shown up at major auctions, galleries, and Indian markets, winning prizes and commanding four- and five-figure prices. They are folk art in the purest native American form.

Though figurative pottery has been a part of Indian pottery since the beginning of Indian history, storytellers are a "new" form initiated by Cordero, but which has its basics in Cochiti figural pottery. Figures, such as the "portraits" of Anglo professionals developed by Cochiti potters in the late 1800s, were made to "tease" the white man, and their forms often took the shape of sheriffs, cowboys, priests, circus entertainers, and even Italian opera singers. Louis Naranjo and Ivan Lewis reproduced such caricatures in recent years, and they have even updated their humorous versions of Anglos to include those in bikinis and tourists in shorts, carrying cameras.

Cordero began making her storytellers in the 1950s, combining the ancient seated figure with outstretched legs, head thrown back and mouth wide open, with tiny figures seated or climbing on the figure, their faces showing either rapture or fear (depending on the story she was depicting). She was 45 years old, her children grown, and she needed to make extra money. She never realized what an impact she would make on the art of pottery.

When asked by a folk art collector to make larger examples of the figures she had begun making, she modelled one after Santiago Quintana, her grandfather, who was a storyteller of such expertise that he always had children begging him for a new tale. Quintana was not unknown—either in the Cochiti pueblo or by historians who had listened to the old man who wanted to make sure "they got it right." He is quoted in many volumes of ethnographic works and was photographed and quoted by Edward S. Curtis in *The North American Indian* (1926).

Almost instantly Cordero's storytellers won prizes at the New Mexico State Fair and the Santa Fe Indian Market. She was asked to give demonstrations at universities and national monuments, was included in exhibits both in the United States and abroad, and had her work on display at major Indian art shops and galleries throughout the country. Her work has even appeared on the cover of *National Geographic* (November, 1982).

Her business exploded and Cordero was producing many different kinds of storytellers, including a kneeling version. This version was made after one of her customers got down on his hands and knees and begged her to make him a storyteller. She did, and the storyteller was on his knees, as was her collector.

Originally potters who made storytellers were from the Cochiti pueblo. Now the number of artisans making these figures has risen to above a hundred and they come from many other pueblos (i.e., Jemez, Acoma, Nambe, Isleta, and San Felipe). Each pueblo has an unmistakable style of pottery and their storytellers are as unique as their pottery.

We have included only a handful of biographies of storytellers, trying to highlight those who are innovative or award-winning. As with other types of pottery, there are many more who follow in the tradition of master storyteller potter, Helen Cordero, and we believe it is a folk art which collectors of Indian art should keep an eye on.

CORDERO FAMILY

Helen's family has followed her lead, and nowadays her son, George (1944–), daughter, Tony, and grandchildren Tim (1963–), Buffy (1969–), and Kevin Peshalakai (1964–), also make storytellers. We were fortunate enough to see examples of both Helen's and Buffy's storytellers at the Adobe Gallery in Albuquerque.

TONY DALLAS (1956–)

Mudhead storytellers are the trademark of Hopi potter Tony Dallas. His mother-in-law, Lucy Suina (1921–), another storyteller potter, introduced him to the art of making pottery in 1982.

His clown storytellers are unique in that Cochiti potters are enjoined against making and selling clown and kachina figures. Dallas's mudhead storytellers usually hold a bowl and the little mudheads that crawl all over the larger figure are very "active."

LOUIS AND VIRGINIA NARANJO (1932–)

Naranjo is a well-known name in pottery, but the Cochiti pottery husband-and-wife team of Louis and Virginia are well known for their nativities and storyteller figures. They have even been original enough to make animal figures in the storyteller style. Virginia won an award for one of her turtle storytellers in 1973 and both she and Louis have won many other awards since that time.

ROSE PECOS (1956–) AND SUN RHODES

The husband-and-wife team of Rose Pecos and Sun Rhodes are Jemez storyteller makers whose figures are made in the Navajo style. The boys who listen to the storyteller wear cowboy hats and are a more realistic size in comparison to the adult around whom they gather. The girls often hold Navajo wedding baskets or cradleboards, and detailing on their clothing is in the Navajo style.

ADA SUINA (1930–)

Also of the Cochiti pueblo, Ada has won prizes for her storytellers, nativities, and drummers since she began making them in 1976. Her work is extremely fine and the faces on her figures large and distinctive. Ada has passed her talent on to her four daughters who have also begun to win prizes with their pottery figures.

MARY E. TOYA (1934–)

Toya is one of the Jemez pueblo and has earned the distinction of making the largest storyteller, which holds 115 children. The children hold pots, baskets, bags, dolls, balls, and drums, and the figure stands 18″ high. It took Mary Toya six months to make this masterpiece.

Toya also is known for having seven daughters following in the storyteller pottery-making tradition. She has won prizes for almost every kind of pottery, and not only has she made the largest storyteller, but also some of the smallest as well.

BIOGRAPHIES OF SOME INDIAN POTTERS

Karen Kahe Charley (Hopi)

As a child, Charley was allowed to play with clay while her mother modelled pottery, but she didn't begin taking the art seriously until returning to the reservation in 1983, after living and working elsewhere for almost ten years. She and her husband, Jim, had traveled around the Midwest while he worked as an ironworker.

Charley's mother, Marcella Kahe, taught her daughter in the same manner that Marcella's mother had taught her. The orange-red color in Charley's pottery is a family secret that other Hopi potters have not yet imitated. Charley has shown her work at the Santa Fe Indian Market, Pueblo Grande in Phoenix, and at the Tulsa Indian Arts Festival.

Tony Da (San Ildefonso)

One of the few male traditional potters, Da was well known for his innovative work in the field of pottery. Da was the grandson of the grand dame of pottery, Maria. Since his untimely death, Da's pottery has skyrocketed and looks to become increasingly collectible.

Lucy Lewis (Acoma)

Born at Sky City during the 1890s, Lewis did not go to school, but instead grew up on the mesa in the Indian way and was influenced in pottery by her great aunt, Helice Vallo.

Lewis married Toribio Luis (or Haskaya) in the late 1910s and has nine children alive today. The oldest son, Ivan, is a Cochiti storyteller potter. His wife, Rita, and children Dolores, Emma, and Andrew, also make pottery.

Dr. Kenneth Chapman, artistic director of the New Mexico Museum, showed Lucy ancient pottery when Laura Gilpin took Lewis to Santa Fe in 1958. Chapman had also influenced Maria and Julian.

Lucy received the Indian Arts Foundation award, as well as the Maria Martinez award for the fine-line decorated pottery she made, and she was the first at the Acoma pueblo to show her work. She has also won numerous other awards and has received world recognition for the Mimbres designs which are so popular in Acoma pottery. Her pieces are highly collectible.

Charles Loloma (Hopi)

(See Loloma's biography in the Art chapter.)

Maria Montoya Martinez (San Ildefonso)

Born at the San Ildefonso pueblo, this unassuming, yet great, artist lived there until her death when she was well into her nineties. Because of the lack of well-kept records, her birth date is not exact, but believed to be approximately 1887. She died in 1980.

Maria's pottery debut was at the 1904 World's Fair, but it wasn't until she married her husband, Julian, in 1913, that she began working on making the black-on-black pottery which became her claim to fame. In 1919, Julian developed the black-on-black pottery by smothering the flames of their firing process with dried manure. The pair soon demonstrated their skill at the Museum of New Mexico.

Julian worked at the Museum as a janitor and the couple spent a great deal of time there, studying the ancient ceramics held in the storerooms of the Museum. Anthropologists Kenneth Chapman and Edgar Hewett encouraged Julian and Maria to experiment with painting on their black-on-black pottery. Maria made and polished the pottery forms, while Julian painted the designs.

When they returned to the San Ildefonso pueblo, Maria passed on some of her skills to the other women of the village and began selling her pottery. At that time, Julian and Maria were excited to get $.75 to $1.25 per piece! As their pottery skills increased, the pueblo's economy was bettered.

After Julian's death, Maria's daughter-in-law, Santana, worked with her and decorated the pottery. From 1953–1971 (when he died), Maria's son, Popovi Da, decorated her pottery. He was also responsible for collecting her pottery and that collection is now on display at the Popovi Da Studio of Indian Art at San Ildefonso. Her grandson, Tony Da, held the promise of a brilliant career, but died an early death in an auto accident. The potter outlived her husband and three of her four sons.

Maria traveled with her pottery, meeting presidents, movie stars, and other famous people, yet she lived like any other pueblo woman, wearing traditional clothes and trying not to acknowledge her many accomplishments. Her concerns were always for her people and her pueblo.

Maria's works have been shown all over the world and have been demonstrated at almost every world's fair from 1904 to her death. In the 1930s, she toured the country for the U.S. government. She was also awarded numerous prizes and awards for her accomplishments (such as two honorary doctorates—one from New Mexico State University in 1971, the other from Columbia College in 1977), and her pottery is held by museums all over the world. Maria's pottery is one of the best drawing cards an auctioneer has when holding an auction of Indian items.

Nampeyo (Hopi) (1856–1942)

Nampeyo was also called "the old lady." She lived on the Hopi First Mesa in Northern Arizona. When archeologists uncovered the prehistoric village of Sikyatki, three miles away from where Nampeyo lived, her husband (a worker at the archeological site) brought home some pottery pieces to show her. Nampeyo sought, and received, permission to recreate some of the ancient designs on her own pottery.

Soon she was making variations on the designs and was credited with creating a new pottery expression. She taught her daughters, granddaughters, and great-granddaughters her art and they have a hard time meeting the demand for their work today.

Joy Navasie

Also known as the "frog woman," Navasi uses the ancient Sikyatki style of decorations on her pots and paints them on almost pure white slip.

Margaret Quintana (Cochiti)

This contemporary potter is of Cheyenne/Arapaho heritage and grew up in the southern Cheyenne community of Watonga. She works with micaceous clay to form Cochita-style storytellers. She learned the art form after marrying her husband, Paul, and moving to the Cochiti pueblo.

Quintana began learning how to work with red Cochiti clay in the early 1980s. Interest in mica began when she saw it in the Sangre de Cristo Mountains in Taos. Her work is featured in the Millicent Rogers Museum and in 15 Taos galleries.

Dextra Quotskuyva (Hopi) (1928–)

A Hopi potter who learned her trade from her mother, Dextra did not make her first pot until she was 39 years old (1967). She uses organic and mineral paints, yucca leaf brushes, and polishing stones, just as her great-grandmother, Nampeyo, did.

Margaret Tafoya (Santa Clara)

A Santa Clara potter whose trademark is polished blackware, Tafoya uses bear paws frequently in her work and believes that they are good luck because "the bear always knows where the water is."

POTTERY LISTINGS

Acoma

Animal; 4¼" polychrome owl; signed Joyce L. (Leno). $20–$30

Animal; black-on-white turtle; signed Hailstorm. $10–$15

Basket; classic pottery basket w/braid handle; ca. 1930; 4" × 3".

$20–$40

Bowl; 3¼" × 4"; black-on-white w/serrated and fineline designs; signed Lucy M. Lewis, Acoma, NM. $95–$125

Bowl; done by John Aragon; 10" diameter × 3¼" high. $600–$800

Bowl; 1" × 1¼"; polychrome w/deer and heartline designs; signed R. Chino. $20–$30

Canteen; 1⅝" × 2"; polychrome; Mimbres-like armadillo design; signed Joyce L. (Leno). $15–$25

Canteen; 1⅝" × 2"; polychrome w/Mimbres-like bear design; signed Joyce L. (Leno). $15–$25

Fancy jar; 8" × 10"; polychrome w/black and dark orange on white colors in deer, bear, moose, and rams w/heartlines, owls, flowers; fineline, serrated and geometric; signed M. Antonio. $250–$500

Figurine; 8" deer figurine made by M. Antonio. $400–$600

Figurine; 8¾" high; polychrome owl w/black and orange on white colors; signed E. (Eva) Histia. $100–$175

Jar; 7" × 9"; polychrome w/black and orange on white colors in fineline terraced and geometric designs. $40–$80

Jar; 6¾" × 8¾"; polychrome w/black and sienna on white in large bird, X-like flora, foliate, fineline, terraced and linear designs; signed B.L. Cerno. $150–$215

Jar; 3½" × 3½"; black-on-white with Mimbres-like humpback flute player and fineline designs; signed R.C. $40–$65

Jar; 9" × 10"; polychrome w/black and orange on white colors; signed R. Aragon. $195–$235

Jar; 1½"; polychrome; signed LV. $10–$15

Jar; 11″ × 9″; polychrome w/brown and sienna on white colors; signed Salvador.   **$125–$160**

Jar; 4⅛″ × 4½″; polychrome w/dark brown and orange on white colors in featherlike, terraced, fineline and geometric designs; signed RLC, Acoma, NM.   **$25–$50**

Jar; 1⅜″; black-on-white; signed LV.   **$15–$20**

Jar; 8½″ × 9″; polychrome; black and orange on white colors in large bird, curvilinear, and fineline designs; scalloped "pie crust" rim; signed R.S., Acoma, New Mexico.   **$185–$245**

Large jar; 10¼″ × 10″ polychrome w/black and orange on white; signed Eva Histia.   **$225–$325**

Miniature seed jar w/fineline designs; signed Rose; ca. 1975; 2¼″ × 2¼″.
                                                                                                         $20–$40

Olla; unusual, large, fineline design; 15″ × 9″; ca. 1950.   **$90–$150**

Olla; classic olla signed M. Torovio; ca. 1975; 8″ × 7″.   **$85–$115**

Olla; polychrome olla w/turkey or bird design; 12″ × 12″; ca. 1900.
                                                                                                $5000–$6000

Plate; ³⁄₁₆″ × ⅞″ diameter; black-on-white; signed D.R.   **$20–$40**

Pot; black-on-white w/fineline design; ca. 1890; 12″ × 9″.
                                                                                                $2200–$2500

Pot; done by John Aragon; 6½″ diameter × 5½″ high.   **$395–$450**

Pot; black-on-white w/triangle design; signed J.R.D.A.; 8″ × 6″; ca. 1985.   **$125–$200**

Pot; done by Lucy Lewis; 6½″ diameter × 4½″ high.   **$900–$1000**

Courtesy of Canfield Gallery, Santa Fe, NM.
Photo by Donald Vogt.

Pot; polychrome; ca. 1910; 12″ diameter.   **$2000–$3000**

From the Hadden/Saylor Collection. Photo by Donald Vogt.

Pot; done by Sandra Victorino; 10½″ diameter × 8½″ high.
$1350–$1500

Vase, 4½″ height; black on white "wedding" style with fineline designs; signed Lucy M. Lewis. **$75–$100**

Vase; 8½″; polychrome, black and orange on white in modern bird, geometric, fineline and terraced designs; signed, Acoma, New Mexico.
$40–$85

Anasazi

Bowl; fine black-on-white; prehistoric; 8″ × 3½″. **$130–$160**

Pitcher; corrugated pitcher, approximately A.D. 1100. **$600–$800**

Rare Rugas-area pottery bowl in excellent condition; prehistoric; 9″ × 5″.
$125–$200

Apache

Bowl; very small painted bowl signed C. Bogulas; ca. 1986; 1″ × 1½″.
$20–$40

Jar; finely painted pottery jar w/geometric and curvilinear designs; signed C. Bogulas; ca. 1986; 1¼″ × 1″. **$20–$30**

Olla; miniature olla signed C. Bogulas; ½″ × ¾″; ca. 1986. **$15–$25**

Olla; choice miniature olla done by C. Bogulas; ca. 1986; ¾″ × ¾″.
$25–$50

Olla; western Apache olla measuring 14″ high; geometric design; ca. 1880–90. **$1200–$1500**

Plate; finely painted; signed C. Bogulas; ca. 1986; 1¼" diam. **$20–$40**

Turtle; miniature turtle w/very fine painting by C. Bogulas; ca. 1986; ¾" × ¾". **$15–$30**

Turtle; unusual pottery miniature turtle w/woman and baby riding on top; by C. Bogulas; ca. 1986; 1¼" × 1". **$20–$30**

Vase; miniature wedding vase w/fine painting by C. Bogulas; ca. 1986; ¾" × ½". **$20–$30**

Casas Grande

Bowl; 3½" × 6"; prehistoric; polychrome w/black and sienna on gray colors in concentric circles and terraced designs; ca. A.D. 12–1300.
$20–$40

Choice miniature painted pottery olla; ca. 1970; 2½" × 2". **$15–$30**

Classic excavated human effigy pot in seated position; prehistoric; 8" × 8".
$150–$200

Classic polychrome two-faced human effigy pot; prehistoric; 8" × 8".
$150–$250

Effigy pot; classic polychrome prehistoric human effigy pot; 8" × 5".
$125–$200

Effigy pot; excavated classic parrot effigy pot; prehistoric; 9" × 9".
$100–$200

Jar; 7" × 7"; four-color polychrome w/black, white, and sienna on buff colors in an encircling snake design; signed Felix Ortiz. **$40–$80**

Jar; classic human effigy pottery jar; 6" × 6". **$30–$50**

Large and choice signed olla w/polychrome geometrics and curvilinear motif; ca. 1986; 14" × 13". **$275–$400**

Olla; red and black olla w/geometric designs; signed Saccora Sandoval; 11" × 10"; ca. 1985. **$250–$300**

Olla; large classic olla w/polychrome curvilinear designs; prehistoric; 12" × 8". **$150–$200**

Olla; huge, fantastic pottery olla signed Felix Ortiz; museum quality piece; ca. 1985; 17" × 14". **$300–$400**

Olla; curvilinear and geometric designs; signed Felix Ortiz; ca. 1986; 14" × 12". **$200–$300**

Olla; classic fish effigy olla; 9" × 9". **$55–$75**

Olla; classic style parrot motif olla; 10" diameter. **$35–$70**

Pottery jar; 7" × 7"; polychrome w/black and white on buff colors in spotted and striped lizard designs; signed Felix Ortiz. **$60–$90**

Prehistoric pottery jar; 7″ × 7″; Ramos polychrome w/black and dark red on buff colors; ca. A.D. 12–1300; repaired w/minor restoration.

$65–$110

Prehistoric bowl; 5½″ × 8½″; polychrome w/black and sienna on orange in concentric circles, geometric and serrated designs; ca. A.D. 12–1300.

$85–$110

Water jar; classic design pottery water jar; 9″ × 9″. $35–$50

Chaco

Bowl; black-on-white pottery bowl w/checkerboard designs on the inside; prehistoric; 9″ × 4″. $115–$150

Bowl; small black on white bowl w/geometric designs; prehistoric; 6″ × 2″. $80–$125

Cochiti

Courtesy of Jack Sellner, CAI.

Figurine; storyteller; 4½″ high; 7 babies; by Felecita Eustace.

$250–$350

Figurine; 1¾″; polychrome; ''storyteller'' w/one baby; signed Mona H. Cochiti. $25–$40

Figurine; figure of sheriff; this type of pottery started in the late 1880s when the Indians had fun ''spoofing'' the white man; piece was made by Louis Naranjo of the Cochiti Pueblo; ca. 1983; 19″ high.

$1500–$1800

Ho Ho Kam

Bowl; glazed black pottery bowl; prehistoric; 5″ × 2″.   **$25–$30**

Pot; excavated cooking pot w/fingernail design; prehistoric; 7″ × 3″.   **$20–$30**

Rare small pottery olla w/red painted circular swirl motif; prehistoric; 3″ × 3¼″.   **$50–$70**

Hopi

Bowl; 4″ × 5″; polychrome w/dark brown and red on orange; signed S. (Sunbeam) David.   **$30–$55**

Bowl; 3⅝″ × 7″; four-color polychrome stylized modern parrot, feather, geometric and linear designs; signed Fawn.   **$110–$175**

Bowl; 2½″ × 8½″; polychrome w/dark brown and sienna on yellow colors in a large bird, feather-like, and rectangular panel design; signed Alice Adams, Tewa Village, First Mesa, Polacca, Arizona.   **$60–$85**

Bowl; classic round pottery bowl w/bird designs; ca. 1940; 5″ × 3″.   **$50–$75**

Bowl; 10″ × 6″ pot; by Rondina Huma; polychrome; both sides are identical; decorated on the bottom all the way around; symbols represent kiva steps, lightning, wind, and all the elements.   **$5000–$5500**

Bowl; done by Zella Adams; ca. 1950; 7½″ diameter × 2¼″ high.   **$350–$500**

Bowl; small pottery bowl w/faded designs; ca. 1940; 5″ × 2¼″.   **$20–$40**

Bowl; 2½″ × 3¾″ black on yellow w/serrated and triangle designs; signed A. Dashee, Walpi.   **$20–$40**

Fancy jar; 6″ × 6½″; polychrome w/dark brown and sienna on creme colors; signed Alice Adams, Tewa Village, First Mesa.   **$110–$160**

Jar; 5½″ × 6″; redware w/black bird, feather-like, sworl, and terraced designs; signed S. (Sunbeam) David.   **$75–$110**

Jar; 6¼″ × 5½″; polychrome w/dark brown and sienna on orange colors in large panels w/linear, sworl, feather-like, and geometric designs within each; signed S. David (Sunbeam).   **$85–$130**

Jar; 4½″ × 6″; polychrome w/dark brown and sienna on white colors; featherlike, fineline, and geometric designs; signed with a frog (the Frog-woman, Joy Navasie).   **$300–$500**

Jar; 5½″ × 5½″; black on red with sworl, terraced, feather-like, and concentric circle designs; signed S. (Sunbeam) Davis.   **$65–$95**

Jar; 4½″ × 5″; polychrome w/dark brown and sienna on yellow colors in geometric, fineline, concentric circle, and serrated designs.   **$25–$50**

Jar; 3¾″ × 4″; dark brown on yellow colors in horizontal banded, scalloped, and fineline designs. **$20-$40**

Jar; late historic/early contemporary period; 5″ × 6½″; polychrome w/dark brown and sienna on yellow colors in concentric circle, curvilinear, geometric, and linear designs. **$300-$450**

Miniature pottery jar; signed J. Sahu; ca. 1975; 3½″ × 3½″. **$20-$40**

From the Hadden/Saylor Collection. Photo by Donald Vogt.

Seed pot; done by Dextra Quotskuyva; 4¾″ × 3″ high. **$800-$1000**

Courtesy of Norman Y. and Bernice M. Harris, private collection. Photo by Donald Vogt.

Seed pot; Stella Huma; 12″ wide × 3½″ high. **$3000-$3500**

From the Hadden/Saylor Collection. Photo by Donald Vogt.

Seed pot; done by Featherwoman (Sylvia) and measures 5″ diameter × 3³/₄″ high.   **$595–$650**

Tiles (4); 4⁵/₈″ × 4⁵/₈″; polychrome w/dark brown and red on orange in a modern, stylistic parrot design; signed A. (Alice) Adams. **$40–$60**

Vase; 7¹/₂″ high; polychrome w/dark brown and sienna on creme colors in large, modern, stylistic, parrot symbol designs; signed Patricia Yava Honie.   **$55–$85**

Vase; 7¹/₂″ × 4³/₄″; polychrome, "cylinder" type, dark brown and sienna on yellow in large bird and flower design; ca. mid–20th century.
$100–$125

Courtesy of Jack Sellner, CAI.

Vase; rare cylinder vase in polychrome; 8″ high.   **$250-$300**

Work done by Gary Nampeyo (Tom Polacca's son), contemporary Hopi potter.
        $1200-$1800 ea.

Courtesy of Broken Arrow Indian Arts and Crafts, Taos, NM. Photo by Donald Vogt.

Works done by Tom Polacca, a contemporary Hopi potter.   **$3000-$3500**

Jemez

Bowl; 1½" × 2¼"; five-color polychrome; signed Rebecca T. Gachupin.   **$12–$20**

Bowl; 3½" × 4"; four-color polychrome w/dark brown, sienna, white on buff colors in feather, fineline, serrated, and linear designs; signed Dolores Toya.   **$25–$45**

Figurine; 10" polychrome "storyteller" with babies; signed Lupe Loretto Lucero.   **$375–$525**

Figurine; 3¾" × 4"; four-color polychrome "storyteller" w/dark brown, sienna, and tan on buff colors holding four "babies"; signed A. Shije.
                                                                  $60–$95

Jar; 3" × 4"; buff on sienna "seed"-type with feather, fineline, sworl, and hook-like designs; signed C.G. Loretto.   **$40–$55**

Jar; 6½" × 6"; four-color polychrome w/black, sienna, and taupe on buff colors; signed Ponca Fraqua.   **$60–$120**

Jar; 4" × 4¾" polychrome w/brown and sienna on buff colors in feather-like, sworl, geometric, terraced, and linear designs; signed C.G. Loretto.   **$40–$80**

Jar; 5¼" × 5"; four-color polychrome w/dark brown, sienna, and beige on buff in curvilinear, scalloped, feather-like, and serrated designs; signed J. Gachupin.   **$60–$95**

Vase; 9¼" × 5"; polychrome w/black, sienna, and buff colors in feather, terraced, fineline, curvilinear, serrated, and geometric designs; signed G. Madalena.   **$50–$75**

Vase; 1½"; polychrome; signed VG.   **$15–$25**

Vase; 2¼"; polychrome; "wedding" type; signed C.T.   **$10–$20**

Vase; 7½"; polychrome w/dark brown and sienna on buff colors; signed V. Sando.   **$60–$90**

Maricopa

Bowl; black on sienna with wavy and serrated linear designs; 3⅝" × 4⅞".   **$25–$45**

Bowl; 3¾" × 7"; highly polished redware; signed Nina Bill.   **$30–$65**

Pot; pot w/whirling log design which is now called swastika, but was used by Indians much earlier than WWII; made by Mary Juan; ca. 1920s–30s; 9″ tall, 7″ diameter. **$900–$1200**

Vase; 5″ high; amphora-like shape, black on red colors in sworl designs. **$15–$30**

Vase; 6″ high; black on sienna; ''wedding'' style w/sworl designs.
$30–$60

Navajo

Classic black pottery w/rope design rim; ca. 1935; 7″ × 4″. **$30–$50**

Pot; ''Whirling Rainbow Goddesses''; by Lucy Leuppe McKelvey; 13″ diameter × 8″ high. **$2700–$3000**

Pot; ''Masks of the Nightway''; by Lucy Leuppe McKelvey; 12½″ diameter × 7″ high (see photo above). **$2400–$2800**

Pot; ''Arrow People''; by Lucy Leuppe McKelvey; 6¾″ × 11″ (see photo above). **$1800–$2200**

San Ildefonso

Courtesy of Robert W. Skinner, Inc., Bolton, MA.

Blackware bowl; rounded body with matte painted stylized decoration on shoulder, inscribed on the base; "Marie and Santana;" 5¼" diam.
$650–$750

Blackware jar; tapering globular body, painted on the shoulder w/matte black stylized bear paws; inscribed on base "Maria Popovi" (see photo above).
$700–$900

Blackware jar; flaring sides, rounded shoulder, tapering neck; matte painted reversed crown and leaf decoration; inscribed on base "Marie and Santana"; 6¼" diameter, 4¼" high (see photo above). **$700–$800**

Bowl; 2⅜" × 4½"; blackware; "seed"-style, signed Tahn-Moo-Whe, '73.
$150–$275

Bowl; rare 2⅜" × 3¾"; redware w/sgraffito Avanyu (water serpent) designs; signed DA (Tony Da, Maria's grandson).
$700–$900

Courtesy of Robert W. Skinner, Inc., Bolton, MA.

Jar; blackware jar, w/flaring sides, rounded shoulder, and tapering neck; polished "gun metal" body w/matte black-painted decoration of geometric, crosshatched, and curvilinear devices; inscribed on base "Marie."
$2100–$2500

Jar; 2½" × 3¾"; highly polished blackware; signed Tahn-Moo-Whe, '74. **$70–$100**

Jar lamp; rare; 10⅜" x 12¾"; highly polished black-on-black w/foliate, cloud, and rain symbols repeated four times around neck and shoulder; ca. 1925; attributed to and made by Maria and Julian Martinez. **$1575–$1825**

Large bowl; 11" × 17½"; four-color polychrome w/black, taupe, and sienna on buff colors; signed Carlos "Sunrise" Dunlap. **$1000–$1500**

Older bowl; 4½" × 6½" polished black-on-black bear paw and terraced wedge-like designs; ca. post–1946; signed Marie & Santana. **$900–$1200**

Pot; black-on-black; signed Marie; ca. 1925; 6" × 6". **$125–$250**

Pot; 2⅜" × 4½"; blackware: "seed"-style, signed Tahn-Moo-Whe, '73. **$150–$275**

Superfine buff on red pottery jar; serpent designs; signed Helen Gutuierez; ca. 1976; 6" × 4". **$50–$100**

Santa Clara

Animal; 2¼" × 2½"; five-color polychrome raccoon; signed Margaret & Luther. **$35–$75**

Bottle; polished black square pottery bottle; ca. 1935; 4" × 3".

$65–$85

Bowl; 1½" × 1¾"; "pumpkin"-style blackware; signed Leona Baca. **$20–$30**

Bowl; ⅞" × 1½"; black-on-black designs, signed Birdell. **$25–$35**

Bowl; black pottery bowl measuring 3½". **$50–$60**

Bowl; black pottery duck bowl; ca. 1945; 12" × 7". **$65–$85**

Bowl; 4" × 6½"; black-on-black Avanyu (serpent) design; signed Nicolosa. **$100–$150**

Choice, carved, red, miniature pottery seed jar w/flute player, signed Haungooah; 1½" × 1½"; ca. 1977. **$90–$125**

Clown; 1¼"; four-color polychrome "baby Koshari" with corn stalk hair; signed Margaret and Luther. **$20–$30**

Figurine; rare miniature pottery child signed by Margaret and Luther; ca. 1955; 2" × 1¼". **$85–$115**

Jar; 4¼" × 3½"; blackware w/carved designs; signed Stella Chavarria. **$75–$125**

Jar; 1"; black-on-black designs; signed Sylvia. **$10–$20**

Jar; 7″ × 6″; highly polished black-on-black with a large Avanyu (water serpent); signed Nicolosa.   **$125–$195**

Jar; 2½″ × 2¾″; blackware w/sgraffito (incised) butterfly and flower designs; signed Goldenrod.   **$100–$160**

Jar; 4″ × 4″; blackware with carved designs; signed Stella Chavarrea.   **$85–$140**

Large wedding vase; 13½″ high; blackware w/bear paw designs; signed Nicolasa.   **$275–$350**

Melon seed pot; done by David Baca; 4½″ × 3″ high.   **$450–$600**

Polychrome red pottery jar (miniature); signed Santanita Suazo; ca. 1975; 3″ × 2½″.   **$35–$50**

Pot; miniature red and buff pot; signed M. Naranjo; ca. 1975.

$55–$75

Rare black-on-black; 8″ × 3″.   **$85–$125**

Rare, carved, red pottery seed jar w/quail design and signed Mae Tapia; 1½″ × 1¾″; ca. 1978.   **$65–$100**

Seed jar; carved red Huungoah seed jar; ca. 1976; 2″ × 1½″.

$215–$250

Turtle bola tie; black pottery tips; unusual; by Florence Naranjo; 3″ × 1″; ca. 1950.   **$50–$75**

Vase; black-on-black pottery vase; 4″ × 4″; ca. 1930.   **$40–$75**

Vase; highly polished, tall, black pottery vase; ca. 1940; 9½″ × 6″.

$55–$80

Vase; 8½″ high; highly polished black-on-black with Avanyu (water serpent) design; signed Nicolasa.   **$100–$135**

Santo Domingo

Dough bowl; for working and kneading the dough; ca. 1870s; 17″ diameter × 10″ deep.   **$6500–$7000**

From the collection of Joyce Williams. Photo by Donald Vogt.

Jar; large (16½" by 11½", w/14" at shoulder); ca. 1900.   **$5000-$7000**

Jar; black on cream colors; ca. 1910; 11" × 11".   **$2000-$2500**

Vase; old style vase; 4" × 3"; ca. 1920.   **$20-$40**

Seneca-Iroquois

Bowl; 3½" × 3¾"; polychrome w/black, yellow, and natural colors in rectangular-shaped vertical designs; ca. 1940s.   **$30-$50**

Figurine; 12½" high; kiln-fired polychrome w/black, white, yellow, dark blue, light blue, and faded blue colors in a long-haired male figure wearing a Western hat, athletic jacket, jeans and moccasins; by Peter B. Jone.   **$75-$95**

Southwestern

Five-piece group; includes a polychrome-painted San Ildefonso blackware triangular jar, inscribed on base "Santana"; a polychrome paint-decorated Santa Clara redware jar, inscribed on base; blackware bowl, sizes range: 3¼" to 6" in diameter; roughness to lot.   **$125-$250**

Five-piece group; two whimsical Santa Clara blackware pieces in the form of a canoe and corner fireplace; a San Ildefonso paint-decorated blackware bowl, inscribed on base "Florence Naranjo", diam. 3¾"; and a paint-decorated Santo Domingo handled cup, 4⅝".   **$225-$275**

Two pieces; rectangular tile painted w/black linear and crosshatched designs over a creamy gray slip; attached old paper label "made by Taos Indian, Mexico"; 4½″ × 6″; and an Acoma canteen round body w/polychrome paint decoration. 7″ dia.   **$300–$500**

St. Johns

Bowl; polychrome w/painted designs inside and outside; prehistoric; 12″ × 5″.   **$200–$300**

Bowl; polychrome bowl w/swirl design on the inside; prehistoric; 7″ × 3½″.   **$100–$150**

Choice polychrome pottery bowl w/geometric painting inside and out; prehistoric; 11″ × 6″.   **$125–$250**

Zia

Dough bowl; ca. 1900; 17″ diameter × 10″ deep.   **$4000–$5000**

Large jar; 6¾″ × 7″; polychrome w/dark brown and sienna on dark buff colors in large bird, rainbow-like, terraced, and geometric designs; signed Julia Saiz.   **$75–$100**

Large older jar; 12″ × 16″; polychrome w/dark brown and sienna on creme colors; ca. late 1930s; attributed to Gloria or Helen Gachupin.
                    $550–$750

Large dough bowl; 5⅛″ × 11¼″; polychrome w/dark brown and sienna on cream in terraced design with pointed tips, scalloped and linear designs; signed Teodora Galvan.   **$110–$175**

Olla; geometric design; trios polychrome; Zia Pueblo; ca. 1880; 12″ diameter × 9½″ high.   **$4000–$4500**

Olla; 8″ × 8″; ca. 1875.   **$2000–$2500**

Pot; polychrome; ca. 1910–1920.   **$3750–$4000**

Zuni

Bowl; kiva bowl, ca. 1880.   **$5500–$6500**

Canteen; ca. 1880; 13″ × 14″.   **$4500–$5000**

Ceremonial fetish jar; 1⅜″ × 1⅝″; covered w/ground blue turquoise having three carved animals attached to the exterior and one in a bed of corn meal placed inside.   **$50–$90**

Ceremonial jar; 4½″ × 7¼″; ground turquoise-covered pottery vessel containing four hunting fetishes; four more fetishes of the same type "feeding" on the sacred corn meal at the bottom.   **$300–$500**

Courtesy of Jack Sellner, CAI.

Fetish jar; rare ceremonial fetish jar; 5¼″ × 9¼″; ground turquoise-covered pottery vessel containing eight rawhide thong-attached serpentine, jet, and pipestone hunting fetishes ranging in length from 3″ to 3½″. There are two more fetishes of the same type "feeding" on the sacred corn meal at the bottom. All of the fetishes are of the hunting type, i.e. have arrowheads and bits of turquoise and coral tied to their backs. **$350–$600**

Jar; rare ceremonial fetish jar; 5¼″ × 9¼″; ground turquoise-covered pottery vessel containing eight rawhide thong-attached serpentine, jet, and pipestone hunting fetishes ranging in length from 3″ to 3½″. **$450–$650**

Jar; broad rounded body and tapering neck raising from well-defined shoulder; solid-painted concave base appears incised at point where it meets body; decoration of dark brown and red design motifs and four "heart-lined" deer over a creamy white slip; 9¼″ dia. (two longitudinal cracks in neck, one w/appearance of native repair/reinforcement). **$1000–$1200**

Jar; small pottery jar w/black and red geometric designs; ca. 1880; 3″ × 3″. **$20–$40**

Olla; rain bird design; ca. 1880; 12½″ diameter × 10½″ high. **$4500–$5500**

Other

Bear; a bear representation done by both Ernest and Marion Rose (they were divorced so will not be doing anymore pottery together); fineline etching. **$700–$800**

Bear fetish done by Red Starr (Sioux) w/turquoise inlays all around and turquoise eyes. **$400–$500**

Bowl, black; contains 15 Indian boiling stones which were heated in a fire and dropped into a bowl, boiling the water and, thus, cooking the food. **$20–$40**

Bowl, pink; contains large glass trade beads, brass hawkbells and beadwork. **$10–$15**

Courtesy of Adobe Gallery, Albuquerque, NM. Photo by Donald Vogt.

Figure, mudhead; piggyback mudhead (clown); adult and child; by Jim Fred of Hopi Third Mesa; contemporary; 14″ tall. **$1500–$2000**

Figure, mudhead; piggyback mudhead made in 1930s; 27″ tall; by Otto Pentewa of the Hopi Third Mesa. **$7000–$7500**

Figurine, Rivera; fineline black-on-white "Anasazi man"; pottery signed Rivera–85. **$100–$150**

Gila, large prehistoric bowl; 5½″ × 9″ polychrome w/black-on-white *interior and exterior* and sienna bottom in swirl, dots within squares, fineline, fret, and terraced designs; ca. A.D. 1300. **$450–$600**

Courtesy of Norman Y. and Bernice M. Harris, private collection. Photo by Donald Vogt.

Group; all done by Joseph LoneWolf (most famous miniature potter). He started in 1971–72 and is now in his mid 50s. His works are considered classics. "Certain Success" is one of aquatic, land, and bird creatures of Mimbres period being hunted. **$4000–$5000**

"Rocky Mountain Mule Deer" is as described. **$1700–$1900**

"Monarch Butterfly," black background w/red and white decoration. **$6000–$8000**

"The Hummers" is a species of hummingbird known as Allen's Hummingbirds. **$2250–$2600**

Isletta, four Kachina figures; 3½″ to 4½″; including a Cholawitze (fire god), flower/laguna corn-type, and others; signed Zuni (Fred & Maggie). **$140–$170**

Miniature seed jar; Margaret & Luther; w/polychrome animal designs signed by the makers; ca. 1970; 2″ × 1½″. **$65–$90**

Miniature; Joseph LoneWolf; tiny carved red "pottery gem"; signed and numbered 124C. **$475–$550**

Miniature; group of contemporary miniature pottery pieces, all 1″ to 3″ tall. **$5–$20 ea.**

Miniatures; Joseph LoneWolf; group of three by the miniature potter; "Praise be to all Creatures." **$3200–$3500**

"The Hockey Players." **$2750–$3000**

"Bear." **$3300–$3500**

Miniatures; group of miniature pottery pieces done by contemporary potter Thomas Nastaway. **$200–$250 ea.**

Miniatures at the Kiva/Steve Cowgill. Photo by Donald Vogt.

Miniatures; group of pottery done by members of the Naranjo pottery family; pieces by Geri Naranjo (mother). **$90–$600 ea.**

Her daughter, Monica Naranjo (age 10). **$30–$40 ea.**

Pieces done by Geri's son, Kevin (age 14). **$75–$200 ea.**

Miscellaneous; Art Cody pieces include red pot w/fish and ivory inlay for eye, feather design; 1½" × 1½". **$800–$1000**

Green fetish of a bear, special clay used, 1¼" × 1¼". **$750–$850**

Mimbres figures of a grasshopper, cricket and frog. **$900–$2000**

Niadi, bowl; rare miniature painted pottery bowl by the famous potter, Niadi; ca. 1970; 1¾" × ¾". **$85–$100**

Ohio Valley Mound Builders, pot; effigy pot. **$80–$100**

Owl; done by Margaret and Luther Guitterez; the owl won 1st prize at the Gallup Ceremonial in 1974 and is 10" high, 8" at its widest point. **$3950–$4200**

Papago, olla; small brown-on-buff olla; ca. 1950; 6″ × 4″.   **$45–$65**

Pima, olla; 19″ story jar showing horses, men, ducks/chickens; ca. 1890.   **$3000–$4000**

Plate; Maria and Popov (son of Maria, artist w/great talent, governor of pueblo six times, and father of Tony Da); 11½″ diameter; water serpent design.   **$11,000–$14,000**

Plate; Santana and Adam (Maria's daughter-in-law and son—Adam was the potter, Santana the designer); 8″ diameter; water serpent design.
$1500–$1800

Platter; Maria & Santana; 15″ feather platter; ca. 1942.   **$4000–$5000**

Pot; Maria Martinez, design by Santana (daughter-in-law); Maria was the mother of the modern pottery movement; this piece was done ca. 1946–53 and is 7½″ wide and 5″ high.   **$8000–$10,000**

Pot; Maria Martinez and husband, Julian; ca. 1926–35; 10″ wide × 7½″ high.   **$9000–$10,000**

Pots; done by Blue Corn; the black piece is done in checkerboard sort of matte glaze w/mica in it.   **$2000–$2400**

Polychrome has a feather design.   **$2250–$2500**

Sculptures; Tony and Patty Padella; unique sculpted pottery figures; buffalo dancers, buffalo maiden, and buffalo figure which is entitled "Plains Laziness"; Padellas are from Santa Clara Pueblo; large dancer, 11¼″.
$1400–$1600

Smaller dancer, 9″.   **$1200–$1400**

Buffalo maiden.   **$1200–$1400**

Buffalo figure.   **$395–$450**

Sikyatki, dish; rare and beautiful brown-on-buff pre-Hopi pottery dish; prehistoric; 8″ × 3½″.   **$125–$150**

Storytellers; the master potter of storyteller figures is Helen Cordero; this piece is ca. 1965, the second year she was making the figures;
$7500–$8000

Also an example of a storyteller made by Buffy Cordero, Helen's 17-year-old grand-daughter (1988).   **$750–$800**

Taos, jar; 7¼″ × 9″; micaceous clay cooking jar w/"pie crust" rim.
$450–$600

Tera Humara, pot; old pottery olla used for making an Indian alcoholic drink; ca. 1880; 16″ × 13″.   **$125–$250**

From the collection of David L. Atteberry. Photo by Donald Vogt.

Teseque, figures; rain gods; pueblo is north of Albuquerque.   **$50–$100**

Tonto, bowl; large basin bowl w/black-on-cream curvilinear designs on the inside; prehistoric; 15″ × 17½″.   **$225–$300**

Courtesy of Norman Y. and Bernice M. Harris, private collection. Photo by Donald Vogt.

Vase; done by Grace and Cammillio Medicine Flower, vase has butterfly design incised w/colors; 5″ × 3″.   **$3000–$3500**

Dragonfly piece; done by Camillio Tafoya, and the small pot w/membries figures (see photo above).   **$2000–$2500**

Rain dancer plate; 4″ diameter, done by Joseph LoneWolf (he is now 87 years old and is Grace Medicine Flower's father, the brother of Christine Naranjo and Margaret Tafoya) (see bottom photo on p. 326).

$1500–$2000

Wedding vases; three miniature wedding vases done by Joyce Cisneros Gallegos; 2″ × 2″; 2½ × 4″; and 3″ × 5½″.　　**$400–$500 group**

Wingate; black-on-red pottery bowl w/painted circular swirl motif; prehistoric; 12″ × 6″.　　**$120–$200**

Yuma, figure; standing male figure, painted overall w/red linear decoration over an ochre slip; coiffure and facial features in black; wearing blue and white glass bead earrings and choker; 5¼″ tall; repaired.

$400–$600

TOOLS AND WEAPONS
▼▼▼▼▼▼▼▼▼▼▼▼

INTRODUCTION

All Indian tribes made the most of whatever natural elements they had available, whether it be wildlife, plants or certain types of soil. They were attuned to using whatever Mother Earth had to offer.

When a large animal was killed for food, its fur/hide was used for clothing, the inner organs (i.e., bladders) were often used as vessles for liquids and the bones were made into tools. Pointed pieces of bone made awls, daggers, or engravers for pottery. Indian women used slimmer pieces of bone to make needles which they used to draw sinew through leather or to poke holes in rawhide or fur in order to sew the pieces together. Needles were used by Lakes and Northeast tribes for webbing snowshoes. Pins were even made from the penis bones of small animals, such as the raccoon. The Southwest tribes used bone pieces to make weaving tools. Some have serrated edges while others are notched near the end.

Tribes which lived near the coast, or by a body of water, would use bones to make harpoons or projectile points for fishing. Some, like the Ingalik tribe, barbed their bone points to make pronged fish spears. The larger animal bones, such as buffalo shoulder blades, were used to make hoes by the Plains tribes. That bone could also be used to make knives. The Menomini, and other tribes, made deer and bear scapulae into scoops or spoons of varying sizes.

The scrapers the women used to take the flesh off a hide were often made from toe bones (bear or dog) which were easily held by placing one's fingers in the joints. Other scrapers, made from deer legs by the Southwestern tribes, were engraved and decorated.

Deer, elk, or caribou antlers were used to make spear throwers, harpoons, clubs, celts, wedges, spoons, purses, figurines, jewelry, combs, effigy figures, and handles. The Northwest Coast tribes made use of the bones of whales and were able to fashion a wide range of tools and objects from the large bones.

Once the white man invaded the North American Indian's territory, weapons changed. Arrowheads began to be made from iron and brass and a knife could be found to have a brass blade and an antler handle. Tomahawks were made when a piece of hot strap iron was hammered around a rod to form an eye. They were often used as a hand ax and carried in battle because, once fired, a musket was worthless until re-loaded, yet a tomahawk could be used at close range.

In general, the shape, size, and material of tools and weapons changed drastically with the advent of civilization. However, it must be noted that the pride of the North American Indian has caused most tribes to hold onto the old ways and you will still find artisans, leatherworkers, potters, jewelers, and basketmakers who continue to use the tools their ancestors did.

TOOLS AND THEIR MAKERS

Cooking Utensils

Kettles date back to the Tetons' earliest contact with the white man. The Brules were noted by Prince Maximilian to have used iron kettles as early as 1834. These iron pots were often ordered from trading posts or captured from Army camps which the Indian had raided.

All of the round-bottomed, cast-iron kettles used by the Tetons were similar looking, but varied in size from one to five gallons. They would either have three short legs or none. Commonly traded were sheet-iron kettles, which were factory made and collected by such tribes as the Ogala.

Skillets were also commonly traded and the Indians appeared to have preferred those with long handles because they were easier to use when cooking over an open fire. Old skillets were often cut up and used for arrowheads.

Craftwork Tools

All tools were made by hand. Flint knives and sharp-edged stones were used for cutting, pointed pieces of bone were awls (used to make holes for stitching), and sinew was used as thread.

Gardening Tools

In the Southeast, it was common for Indian tribes to make tools from shells. Whole conch shells were hafted as picks and hoes.

Gardening tools were also used by the Eastern Indians. Their hoes were made of chipped stone, as were projectile points. Spades and post-hole diggers were hoes made with a straight edge instead of a rounded one.

A corn planter, which was a long, pointed stick or a long-shaped rock or shell attached to a wooden pole, was used by the New England tribes to help them plant their main crop.

To fertilize the soil, fish were buried in each hill. Especially nutritious for the soil was the horseshoe crab, which would be chopped to bits before being used as fertilizer. The corn first introduced to New England grew to three times its size with this fertilizer.

Leatherworking/Sewing Tools

As with other tools, the early leatherworking and sewing tools of the Plains Indians were soon replaced with more modern versions once trading was firmly established in the West.

Awls were used since the earliest times Indians worked on leather and are still in use today. Crooked awls were made exclusively for Indian trade during the 1800s and were proven to be more functional because of the two 90° bends in the shank's center.

Florida tribes made needles from thin pieces of shells and also used shells to make chisels and plummets. Hide scrapers were made from elk horn or antler by the Plains Indians until about 1880, the time when elk became extinct in that area. Fleshing tools were made from old gun barrels by the Tetons by cutting off the barrels and hammering the ends flat. Scissors were used by nearly all the Plains Indian women and were much like what we might buy in a store today.

Needles were also commonly traded and used in sewing beads onto cloth or in sewing the cloth itself—they were even packaged as "beading needles" by such companies as the Brabant Needle Company of England.

Another tool developed solely for Indian use was the quill flattener. In the old days, when an Indian woman prepared to decorate with quills, she would use a smooth object to flatten them. The nineteenth century brought about the advent of a tool to flatten quills which was deeply curved at both ends and forged around the middle.

Pottery and silver thimbles came about when the sewer realized that thimbles did, indeed, help to push the needle where the finger could not. Potters and silversmiths realized the marketability of such a product and began to make them for friends and relatives. They soon began to be sold, as had just about every other Indian craft, to the white man.

Meat Carving Tools

Carving a cow on the Blood Reserve in the 1920s was done much the same way the Indians carved buffalo years before. The women in charge of the task would begin by sharpening their ax and knives.

Then, the first cut would be made by bringing the ax into the backbone, and, by chopping away, she would bring the carcass away from the spine. She would then cut a one-piece loin that was about 4' long. This was the favorite cut of meat because it was very tender (i.e., "tenderloin").

The shoulder ribs were considered a special man's meal, which, cooked over an open fire in the tepee, were eaten right away. The other ribs were often smoked so they could be saved for later meals.

Metalworking Tools

The earliest metalwork tools were made in copper by the Lakes area tribes (ca. 3000 B.C.). The Lake Superior region supplied those tribes with pure copper nuggets or copper veins which were found in rocky areas. Tools and weapons, such as spears, arrows, knives, and celts, were made from copper by the Indians of the Old World Copper Culture (ca. 3000 B.C.).

Mortars and Pestles

Mortars and pestles were made from soapstone quarries by the New England tribes.

Spoons

The Yurok and Hupa tribes made spoons from antlers which only the men and guests were allowed to use to eat acorn meal mush. The women of those tribes used mussel shells as their spoons. The spoons were a distinct style, with jagged-edged handles.

Weaving Tools

Weaving tools used by the Navajo include wood battens, pins, combs, and sacking needles.

Woodworking Tools

Woodworking tools such as the ax, pick, whetstone, hatchet, and celt were used by New England Indians to make house poles, bed planks, platforms, and other wooden items.

WEAPONS

Armor

The Northwest Coast tribes made suits of armor from tiny wood slats which they pieced together. With these suits, the Indians would wear wonderfully carved and painted wooden helmets.

Blow Guns and Darts

Cherokee and Iroquois Indians used blow guns and darts against their enemies. These items are rarely found today.

Bows

The bows made by the Mohave tribe were wooden and were often decorated. Bows used in New England were characteristically five to six feet long and made of ash, oak, witch hazel, and hickory.

Clubs

There were a few kinds of war clubs made by the New England tribes. The hatchet club was a chipped stone, such as granite, quartz, basalt or pegmatite, which was attached to a piece of wood with sinew. A ball-headed club (rare) was made from a glacial cobble, attached to a bent piece of wood which wrapped about the center. A pronged war club, wooden with a rounded knob, would have a triangle of stone imbedded in the ball. This type of club could also be made from a small birch tree by cutting it about 30″ from the ground and sharpening the roots into lethal prongs. Seal clubs, made on the Northwest Coast, were of yew woods and were used to kill seals or otters, as well as halibut and salmon.

As with all other wooden implements made by Indians of the Northwest Coast, carving and decoration was done on each piece, a favorite subject being the efficient hunter, the sea lion.

Daggers

Northwest Coast weapons were often elaborately and beautifully crafted and, because of that fact, often became family heirlooms.

Daggers made by Tlingits in the late eighteenth century were skillfully made from iron and copper and so beautifully decorated that Europeans were impressed with the Indian's ability to produce them.

Artists such as Kuch-Kee-Ees (Black Wolf of Klukwan) made daggers or swords and gave them names, such as Killer Whale Dagger. The carving on these pieces is bold and almost geometric, and historians are still baffled by the techniques which may have been used.

Tlingit warriors were the chief owners of such weapons.

Firearms

Weapon making was very important to the Sioux, which makes it easy to understand why the use of iron caught their attention before 1840. Iron was far superior than the flint and bone they had used for weapon making in the past, and they replaced their lithic blades with those made of iron as quickly as they could.

Most of the iron weapons the Indian used were commercially produced by the white man, though he fashioned some of his weapons using tools bought from traders. The Indian agencies and trading posts during that period all had blacksmiths working on or near the premises and they all worked with the Indians, repairing pieces, shodding horses, and making items such as traps, axes, fish and muskrat spears, and hoes.

The Tetons first traded for guns during the winters between 1799 and 1802 and, by 1804, were well acquainted with guns. Zebulon Pike, the explorer, estimated in 1804 that there were approximately 100 guns owned by the Tetons, who at that time numbered approximately 2000.

Fur trading companies (American and Canadian) sold what came to be known as the "Northwest gun." They were made in a standard pattern from 1750 to approximately 1900—being a light, smooth-bore fusil stocked to the muzzle. A Northwest gun that was typical of what was being purchased by the Tetons was the Barnett Northwest gun, manufactured in England.

After the turn of the century, traders were freely bringing firearms up the Missouri River and selling guns such as the Jacot and Lacy rifles. The Smithsonian holds a Hudson's Bay Company Northwest gun dated 1876 which was taken from Sitting Bull's band in 1881 at Fort Buford when they surrendered.

The Plains tribes soon began using "trade" rifles, which had deadly accuracy but were double the weight of a Northwest gun. Some of the companies selling "trade" rifles to the Indians from approximately 1836–1880 were the Pierre Chouteau, Jr., Co., the Edward K. Tryon Co. of Philadelphia, and the Henry E. Leman Co. (also of Pennsylvania).

When the Indian Wars began, Indians were using all types of rifles, acquired in many different ways. Sitting Bull surrendered a Winchester Model 1866 carbine when he returned to the United States in 1881. Indian police carried Whitney-Kennedy lever-action rifles in the late 1870s, which were marked "USID," as well as some Model 1877 Remington-Keene bolt-action carbines. The Ogala chief, Young-Man-

Afraid-of-his-Horse, carried a .45–70 carbine, while the Ogala warrior, Red Dog, carried a Sharps buffalo rifle.

Revolvers came into Indian hands after the Civil War. More than 200 Colt, single-action, .45 caliber revolvers were captured by the Tetons at Little Big Horn in 1876.

The Indian police were issued the last revolvers used by the Tetons.

Fishing Tools

Early archaic fishing tools were plummets with spears attached to the ends of the weights to catch the fish. Harpoons were also used. These were made of bone and used primarily to catch larger fish (i.e., sea bass, bluefish, sturgeon, and seal). The Northwest Coast Indians decorated their harpoons and clubs with abalone inlay and engraving.

Poles, halibut hooks, and lures were all made of wood and used by Indian fishermen. The halibut hooks made by Northwest Coast Indians were often so decorative that one wonders whether the maker grieved when the hook was lost with the fish. Two pieces of wood and a bone barb would be lashed together, and the hook was extremely efficient in doing the job of hooking the halibut, though its appearance belied that fact. Halibut hooks were often decoratively carved with birds (ravens) or animals, such as bears.

Knives

Green River knives were named for the Green River in Massachusetts and made by the John Russell Factory in Greenfield, Massachusetts (the company was founded in 1832). The butcher knives and carving knives this company made were sold wholesale to trading posts throughout the West for $1.50 to $3.50 per dozen and, in turn, the trading posts retailed the knives for $.50 to $1.50 each. The John Russell Company filled a void in American marketing with their knives because most blades that had been sold in this country up to that time were made in Sheffield, England. The long butcher knives, which backwoodsmen carried and considered a necessary part of their equipment in the early West, impressed the Shawnee Indians so much that they called the frontiersmen the "Long Knives."

Though the knives made by the Green River factory were mainly used for skinning, the user of the blade would often sharpen and shape it to his liking, sometimes so much so that its original shape was completely altered and often obliterated the "Green River" name which was hand-stamped on the blade.

The Plains Indians sometimes took the blades out of their knives and fastened them to the end of a lance or on their gunstock war clubs, and collectors can find a number of examples of Green River knives which were used in this fashion.

The knives became so well known by trappers, frontiersmen, and Indians that phrases were coined using the knives' name (i.e., "up to the Green River" could mean stabbing someone with the knife by plunging it so far into the body that the blade went in "up to the Green River" name stamped on it, or it could mean that a trapper with an Indian squaw who was considered "up to the Green River" would think himself very fortunate). After 1836, approximately 60,000 of these knives were sent west each year and, by 1840, the American-made knives dominated a market once held by the English factories in Sheffield.

The Russell-Harrington Cutlery Co., the result of a 1935 merge between the original John Russell Co. and the John Harrington Co. of Southbridge, Massachusetts, still produces butcher knives and other kitchen cutlery.

Quivers

New England quivers were made of leather, bark or wood, and bow strings were often made of moose sinew.

Spears

Spearing fish or lobster was often the easiest way to bring fish home for supper for New England Indians. For example, lobsters were speared with a two- to three-foot long shaft.

During the summer, when the water was low, a stone wall would be built in a drop in the stream bed and a sieve of sticks made, onto which the fish would tumble. They also used nets which were made of hemp and other fibers and attached to a long, split stick.

TOOL AND WEAPON LISTINGS

Tools

Awl case; band design beaded case, fringed; 14″. $40–$60

Awl case; fully beaded in salt and pepper decoration with tin cones; 12″ long. $40–$60

Ax; stone ax w/leather-wrapped handle; 14″ long. $75–$110

Eastern Plains, saddle; woman's saddle composed of a wood frame stretched with hide; 22″ long. $45–$60

Eastern Woodlands, crooked knife; curving blade joined to pie crust-edged, shield-shaped handle; carved and incised w/two busts of men wearing hats and inscribed ''I End X OT AT NARRQ WD, AEP, NS, M OF M, 1923.''   **$225–$300**

Haida, mountain goat horn spoon; carved in two sections and joined together; 11″ long.   **$350–$450**

Haida, spoon; horn spoon with killer whale design carved on handle; 2¾″ × 10½″.   **$60–$80**

Halibut hook; carved halibut hook showing good wear, in the form of a bird; 6″ × 12″.   **$475–$525**

Iroquois, mortars; two carved wood mortars; show good patina. **$40–$60**

Metal ax; with wood handle; 21″ × 9″.   **$15–$25**

Navajo, cooking pot; characteristic color and form; 6″ high.   **$35–$50**

Navajo rug loom weaving; ten pieces—combs/brushes, spindle, combs, wool/yarn shears, batten, carrying bag.   **$80–$140**

Northwest Coast, needle case; carved in form of a sea otter with trade bead inserts; 1″ × 3½″.   **$110–$150**

Northwest Coast, spoon; mountain goat horn spoon; 7″ length; showing age and use; ca. 1900.   **$85–$115**

Northwest Coast, spoon; steer horn carved with a raven and a wolf on the handle; 4¾″ × 10½″.   **$300–$400**

Northwest Coast, spoons; carved spoon showing good patina; 14″ × 3¼″; some bug damage.   **$300–$400**

Northwest Coast, stone hammer; rare hand hammer; bird (raven?) image tops classic phallic form; collected in the 1880s; nick near the base; 7⅝″ high.   **$2200–$2500**

Northwest Coast, stone hammer; hand hammer; T-shaped maul of type used by early Tlingit and Haida; weathered nicks; 4¾″ wide by 4½″ high.
                                                                    $450–$500

Plains, Maul; stone w/hide-wrapped handle; 15″ × 3½″.   **$25–$45**

Plains, stone maul; head and handle encased in hide; 6¼″ × 15½″.
                                                                    $130–$160

Sioux, awl case; fully beaded in scatter design; 8″ long.   **$35–$50**

Southwest, stone maul; w/handle; 4″ × 15½″.   **$80–$100**

Spoon; horn spoon carved w/snake design; 11½″ long.   **$25–$35**

Squaw ax; hand-forged head with makers mark and original handle; 6½″ × 20″.   **$250–$350**

Tlingit, spoon; horn spoon; heavily carved sea monster on back with abalone shell inserts; 4″ × 14″.   **$350–$450**

Trade ax; hand-forged head with a trace of the maker's mark; 6¼″ × 14¼″.   **$25–$50**

Wood tool; wood handle w/lead or pewter inlay; 9″.   **$35–$50**

Tools/Weapons

Blackfoot, quirt; classic antler quirt w/brass tacks and good patina; ca. 1890; 18″ × 3″.   **$200–$300**

From the William R. Nash Collection. Photo by Donald Vogt.

Club, Eastern Great Lakes; wood club w/recessed grip; shaft of rectangular section incised on one side w/zig-zag arrow column containing small triangular arrow points; a rectangular column containing concentric triangles and diamonds on the reverse; the large ovoid head w/remains of burnishing; a row of notches along the back; 21½″ long.

$1000–$1200

Eight arrows; group of eight old Plains Indian arrows; ca. 1870; 28″.

$250–$325

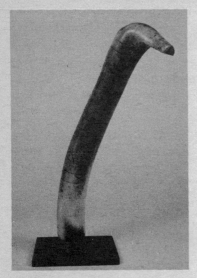

Courtesy of Canfield Gallery,
Santa Fe, NM.
Photo by Donald Vogt.

Hide scraper, Northern Plains; ca. 1850s; made of elk antler, incised decorations; 14″ long. **$1500–$2500**

From the William R. Nash Collection. Photo by Donald Vogt.

Hide scraper, Plains; approximately 12″ long, w/metal plate attached by leather strip; ca. 1850. **$300–$400**

Knife; rare and beautiful B.C. green jade knife; ca. 1800; 6½″ × ¾″. **$145–$200**

Knife; Sheffield knife w/silver-tipped deer hoof handle; 12″ long.
$20–$30

Lance; colorful, 9′ long wood lance w/long, saber bayonet blade; probably captured by the Army; brass tack and water paint decoration, w/ermine fur and brass bell tails; colors still fairly strong, but aged.
$1500–$1800

Northwest Coast, halibut hook; carved in two pieces, in the form of an animal in transition to human form on one arm, steel barb protruding from other; lashed together w/cedar bark strips; 12½″ long; collected pre–1884.
$600–$800

Plains, bow case and quiver; rare North Plains hide bow case and quiver w/beaded and fringe decoration and containing a bow and seven arrows; ca. 1880; 45″ × 8″.
$1100–$1500

Plains, club; large stone club w/rawhide-wrapped handle decorated w/quill work; ca. 1870; 23″ × 5″.
$60–$100

Plains, club; large black egg-shaped stone club w/pewter inlays and a full beaded handle; ca. 1870; 25″ × 6″.
$325–$500

Plains, knife case; hide knife case w/beaded American flag designs and containing an old knife; 24″ × 3″.
$175–$250

Plains, war club; rare gunstock war club w/file-brand design, brass tacks, and a hand-forged iron blade; ca. 1870; 23″ × 11″.
$1500–$2000

Plains, war club; large pipe tomahawk w/file-brand designs, brass tacks, and a hand-forged iron blade; 23″ × 11″; ca. 1870.
$900–$1200

From the collection of Lahoma Haddock Goldsmith. Photo by Donald Vogt.

Sewing, Acoma; group of pottery thimbles.
$5–$10

From the collection of Lahoma Haddock Goldsmith. Photo by Donald Vogt.

Sewing, Alaskan; group of sewing objects by Alaskan Indians, including thimbles, pincushions, cutting stone (decorated w/walrus—jade is used for sharpening needles). **$15–$50 ea.**

From the collection of Lahoma Haddock Goldsmith. Photo by Donald Vogt.

Sewing, Apache; group of Apache thimbles (silver one is Spider Lady) and pin holders; all made by one man who died when working on the unfinished Four Winds thimble. **$15–$20 ea.**

Sewing, Apache; wedding ring and thimbles w/same design.

$15–$100 ea.

Sewing, Cherokee; pincushion in shape of duck; hostess would keep it threaded at a quilting bee and send it "swimming" across the table to the sewer who needed it. **$25–$35**

Sewing, Chippewa; thimble holder made of sweetgrass. **$3–$8**

Sewing, Choctaw; thimble holder from Lyons Indian Store in Tulsa, Oklahoma. **$3–$8**

Sewing, Cousahatta; thimble holder. **$10–$15**

Sewing, Hopi; commercial kachina thimbles bought from a catalog. **$10–$15**

Sewing, Hopi; two-armed and four-legged demon thimble in silver. **$25–$35**

Sewing, Houma; thimble holder made of Spanish moss by Houma tribe of Louisiana. **$10–$15**

From the collection of Lahoma Haddock Goldsmith. Photo by Donald Vogt.

Sewing, Mohawk; scissor holders and thimble holders; the small one is the oldest and made for Simmons SBC thimble. **$10–$15**

Sewing, Navajo; thimble made by Mrs. Jim Long. **$10–$15**

Sewing, Northern Skagit; silver thimble and ivory thimble; made to be used as necklace by Jay Bowen, Northern Skagit Indian. **$50–$75**

Sewing, Ottawa; thimble holder made of birchbark and porcupine quills. **$10–$15**

From the collection of Lahoma Haddock Goldsmith. Photo by Donald Vogt.

Sewing, Seminole; pincushions, dress ornament, and thimble; ca. 1970.
$25–$50

Sewing, Seneca; cornhusk thimble holder. $15–$20

Sewing, Sioux; miniature moccasin thimble holder. $10–$15

Sewing, thimble; kachina thimble made by Jay Bowen; pewter is applied. $25–$35

From the collection of Lahoma Haddock Goldsmith. Photo by Donald Vogt.

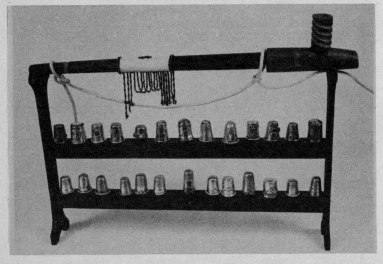

Sewing, thimbles; group of miscellaneous Indian thimbles. $5–$15 ea.

Sewing, thimbles; trade thimbles; three from Minnesota; one believed to be from the Sparrow Mines in Oklahoma.　　　　　　**$10–$15 ea.**

Sewing; clay thimble holder, horsehair thimble holder, and blanket tape measure; ca. 1930s.　　　　　　**$20–$30 ea.**

Sioux, deerskin knife scabbard; full-beaded, sinew-sewn, trimmed w/beaded fringe and hawk bells; 12" long; blue and green designs and trim on greasy yellow background.　　　　　　**$100–$150**

War Items

Arrows; 12 in lot; six w/metal points; traces of feathers.　　**$110–$160**

Plains, ceremonial war club; 11" full-beaded shaft; 6" pipestone head; chipped at one end; bound w/beaded rawhide.　　　　　　**$70–$110**

Plains, club; stone-headed w/16" rawhide-covered shaft; 20" long; good condition.　　　　　　**$30–$50**

Weapons

Apache, quiver; rawhide bow case and arrow quiver, w/cut leather fringe, strap from the same rawhide, the separate bow case once attached to the quiver with thongs; each approximately 30" length plus fringe; showing some wear, soiling from use by the warrior; the front panel of the quiver is decorated with a five-pointed "Texas"-type star w/interior embellishing, as if inspired by the ranger badge; probably 1900s or earlier; some sinew and thread stitching.　　　　　　**$250–$350**

Armband, Plains; pair of beaded.　　　　　　**$75–$100**

Armband, Plains; pair of quill.　　　　　　**$55–$75**

Arrows (4); all with wood shafts and iron arrowheads; from 24" × 26½" long.　　　　　　**$160–$200**

Bow; flattened wood bow showing good patina; 1½" × 46".
　　　　　　$100–$150

From the William R. Nash Collection. Photo by Donald Vogt.

Bow, Plains; sinew-backed bow 39½″ long; sinew-strung; little sinew wrapping at bow tips and grip; light color remains on bow; pale green on sinew face; some red and blue at grip; back has some symbols which may relate to ranch where Indian lived; piece of old decorative ribbon tied to one end.   **$400–$500**

Club; stone war club; egg-shaped stone w/rawhide-covered handle.
                                                              $25–$45

Club; dance; fully beaded handle with catlinite head; 21½″ × 4¼″.
                                                            $80–$100

Collection of over 300 projectile points in a design of four flying ducks, all contained in large frame; prehistoric.   **$200–$500**

Cree, knife case; beaded front panel on buckskin case; 3½″ × 10¾″.
                                                          $110–$200

Crow, knife case and knife; 15″ × 5″.   **$70–$100**

Eastern Woodland, knife; classic crooked knife w/wood handle; 8½″.
                                                           $70–$100

Great Lakes, club; early ball-head club w/carved human hand holding the ball head, the haft decorated w/raised grip band and resisters of carved XXXX's, crowsfeet, and diamond markings; 16″ long.   **$200–$300**

Great Lakes, tomahawk; engraved blade, haft has brass decoration; 18″ × 5″.   **$700–$1000**

Harpoon collection; five (5) harpoons w/ivory heads and two hide ropes, all mounted on a frame; rare; ca. 1860.   **$600–$800**

Holster; Dodge City-made holster; for a Colt S.A. w/7½″ bbl.; the front stamped with the maker's name, S.C. Gallup & Co., Dodge City, Kansas; active there around 1878 (prior location at Pueblo, Colorado) from 1870s; the back belt loop scratched with marking "Texas Ranger 1885" by an unknown hand.   **$185–$225**

Iroquois, knife; crooked knife w/carved handle; 10″ × 1¾″.   **$80–$100**

Iroquois, pair of knives; crooked knives; ca. 1900–10.   **$70–$100**

Iroquois, war club; hide-covered club w/turtle painted design; 27″ long.
                                                                                $50–$75

Knife case, Crow; full-beaded knife case w/classic geometric designs; ca. 1920; 8″ × 2½″.   **$160–$200**

Knife case w/knife; fully beaded knife case w/tab; white background, with a box design line; 16″ × 5″.   **$160–$200**

Knife; tacked knife case w/knife; 11″ × 4″.   **$10–$20**

Modoc, bow; wood bow w/painted geometric designs; 41″ × 2¾″.
                                                                                $100–$150

Northwest Coast, wood and iron dagger; hand-wrought blade w/swagged and raised median rib on one side, flat on the other; bound to carved hardwood handle w/rawhide, twined cedar and fiber; abalone inlaid pommel in the form of a finely carved and incised wolf's head w/flaring nostrils, delineated trachea, and bared abalone teeth; old wooden ear loss; excellent patination overall; 20½″ long.   **$17,000–$20,000**

Pistol; Colt 1861 Army pistol, serial #134493.   **$150–$200**

Pistol; Colt Special Edition, 1/500, "Butterfield Overland Dispatch," .44 caliber, 2 cylinders, serial #201099.   **$200–$300**

Plains, war club; oval stone head w/beaded and fringed rawhide-covered handle; 21″ × 3″; ca. 1880.   **$250–$350**

Quill case, Plains; beaded with horsehair rattles.   **$55–$90**

Rifle; Gallagher carbine; early production, patented July 17, 1860; sling ring and bar on left side; serial #13275.   **$250–$300**

Sioux, club; stone club with hide-covered handle and horsehair trim; 30″ × 4½″.   **$150–$200**

Sioux, knife case; hide case, multicolored geometric beadwork; 3″ × 20″.
                                                                                $180–$225

Sioux, knife case; hide case with multi-colored geometric beadwork; 10½″ × 2½″.   **$70–$100**

Sioux, knife case; parfleche case w/painted geometric designs; 11″ × 3″.
$140–$180

Sioux, knife case; beaded case w/geometric designs; sinew-sewn; 12″ × 2½″.
$130–$160

Tlingit, knife; bone knife carved with raven head handle; 2″ × 10½″.
$60–$80

Woodlands (Penobscot), bow; double compound "made by Gabriel Paul, Penobscot Chief, Old Town, Maine, 1933."
$200–$300

WOODEN ITEMS
▼▼▼▼▼▼▼▼▼▼▼

INTRODUCTION

As I have said before, the Amerind was capable of utilizing everything Mother Earth gave him. He used the grasses on the ground to weave blankets and clothing, and to teach him how to grow foods. The animals around him gave him food, clothing, and shelter. The sea gave him food and he used the shells which held his food to make utensils, tools, and ornamentation. The trees which gave him shade on a sunny day also served to make a number of things.

The way the Indians used the bark of trees and the wood from trees was sometimes ingenious, always useful, and, as shown by those tribes on the Northwest Coast, could also be used to create art. In this chapter we describe a small portion of those items made with wood by the American Indian tribes.

ITEMS MADE OF WOOD

Back Rests

Back rests were made by the Plains tribes. They were made of horizontal slats of wood wound into an inverted cone shape and attached to a tripod, made of poles, by a loop at the top of the backrest. Furs were often thrown over the backrest to make it comfortable for the person sitting against it.

Bark Art

The Chippewa tribe perfected the decorative art of drawing pictures on bark. On it, they told the story of a ceremony or of a birth, and it became a way of preserving the history of the tribe. Transparencies of these birch bark designs are made by the Chippewa woman's teeth—she bites her design into the wood. The design is shown clearly when held up to the light.

The Midewiwin (the Grand Medicine Society) information was recorded on a scroll-like piece of bark. Designs were pressed into the bark with the point of a bone, then the designs were rubbed with vermillion (a natural red dye) so that the impressions could be clearly seen.

Baby Carriers

Each tribe had its own style of baby carrier. The Northwest Coast made coffin-like boxes which the parents often chose to decorate.

Wooden slats made up the "bed" of Apache baby carriers and, at the crown, was a wooden hoop that tended to act as an umbrella to keep the elements out of the baby's face. One would imagine that that wooden hoop which made a half-circle over the baby's head would also be a safety device. If the carrier were to be dropped, the hoop would protect the baby's head.

Eastern tribes made their baby carriers of flat boards, with a footrest at the base and a faceguard on the sides.

Bowls

Bent corner bowls made by the Northwest tribes were used for food. Early examples were made from birch bark, but nineteenth century pieces were usually made of yellow or red cedar.

Characteristic of these bowls are their undulating rims—high at the ends with dipping sides. The sides of these bowls were bent by steaming the wood until it became flexible. Once carved with an adze and shaped with a knife to form the high-ended form, the sides were joined to a red cedar base.

These bowls come in all sizes, from individual containers to great feast dishes which may be as long as twenty feet.

They are decorated, painted, carved or embellished with shells, and their sides are joined in any number of ways, including pegging, lacing, lashing or fitting with tenons and scarfs. Brass tacks and shells were a popular form of decoration used around the rims of these bowls.

Boxes

The Northwest Coast tribes made boxes which served as storage, cooking utensils and also coffins. Some were painted and carved, some trimmed with shellwork, and, still others, just painted.

The sides were connected to the box in a rather unique way—they were sewn with spruce root. Thicker wood boxes would have the ends joined with small wooden pegs. The woods used by the Northwest Coast tribes to make these boxes were straight-grained red and yellow cedar, spruce, yew, and other woods. They were split with a wooden or antler edge, adzed to a particular thickness or thinness, and shaved with a knife to achieve a flat surface.

Canoes and Boats

The Chippewa tribe, the largest and strongest of the Great Plains, were the ones who developed the birch bark canoe into one of the country's major means of transportation at that time.

Dugout canoes, made from one piece of wood, were popular forms of transportation for New England Indians. Canoes and paddles made by the Northwest Coast Indians are as decorative as they are useful. The early models are characterized by a low bow, while later ones have an upswept bow.

Detail in the geometric painting of these canoes is extremely important and mimics the work done on Northwest Indian masks. The animal's head is painted toward the front, or bow, of the canoe and its hindquarters are depicted on the stern. The paddles are decorated as well, and the colors used are mainly black and red. Wooden dugouts and bark canoes made by the Indians of old are not much different than the modern versions.

Birch bark canoes made by the Eastern forest Indians were made by stripping the bark off the birch trees which grew around the Great Lakes. First, a tree was felled. Great care was taken to choose a tree which was tall and straight, with no knots, and a tough, firm bark. Then the tree was examined for damages, and, if the tree was indeed perfect, the tree length was marked off at approximately 18' and an incision was made lengthwise so that the bark could be stripped from the tree. Once the bark was properly stripped, it was flattened by use of a torch which was carefully applied to the surface of the bark. If the bark was discovered not to be large enough, another tree's bark could be added, for bark is easily sewn and patched.

When the framework was prepared and had the proper shape, it was covered by the bark. The framework for the canoe was usually cedar, but any other straight-grained green wood could be used (because long pieces were split out). The gunwales, ribs, and sheathing were made from these long pieces and the interior sheathing was thin and three or four fingers broad. Ribs, 1½" thick, were bent outside (the *natural* outside of the wood) to prevent splitting and breaking. To enable the wood to bend, the wood was boiled in a large steaming box; once bent, it had to be tied. The canoe's top shape was decided by the gunwales, which were made carefully and turned upwards at each end. Then, crossbars divided the canoe into four equal sections.

Once the canoe was ready to be constructed, Indians formed a framework by driving stakes into the ground. The spot was made even and smooth before the bark was placed in the framework and the gunwales and end pieces attached. Then the V-shaped rear and bow boards were squeezed in to fit the gunwale angle. Once they were in place, the shape of the canoe was defined. Basket splints were then placed edge-to-edge in the canoe to line the inside and protect the exterior bark from abrasion. After the ribs and thwarts were secure, the canoe was taken from the frame, turned over, and the seams sealed with pitch. Once the pitch was dry, the canoe was ready to be personalized with decoration and then used on lakes or rivers.

Headdresses and Masks

Northeast Coast Indians were masters when it came to carved and decorated wooden objects. Dancing headdresses were made of a cylindrical frame. Down the back hung a long panel of ermine skins and the front would be an incredible plaque of hardwood, painted and decorated (usually with abalone). The frontlet (or plaque) is said to represent a mystical creature, and, on Haida and Tlingit headdresses, the frontlet is often framed by rows of orange and black feathers with a band of iridescent green and black mallard head-skin across the forehead.

The dance which the headdress is made for can be done on many different occasions (i.e., to welcome visitors, and those visitors will, in turn, do their own dance). In the Kwakiutl tribes, the dance is done before a figure appears and is masked as a crest of the headdress dancer. This figure becomes possessed, then flees the house.

Other masks made by the Northwest Coast tribes vary in form, shape, and purpose, and may be used to celebrate times of change (i.e., birth, death, or marriage). The Skhwaikhwey mask is owned by one person and is passed on to that person's descendents. It is used in the cleaning ritual of the Salish.

The Kwakiutl tribe uses a Goomokwey mask, made of wood and cedar bark. Goomokwey is the chief of the undersea world and whoever gains his favor is rewarded with wealth and prestige. The Thunderbird, a favored subject of the Kwakiutl, is used in a dance which celebrates the power of ancestors who had contact with supernatural beings.

Bark Houses

East of the Mississippi most Indians lived in wooden houses rather than the leather/rawhide tepees of other Indians. Iroquois and many Algonkin (or Algonquin) tribes made "great houses" of bark and poles. These buildings were very long (more than 100') and narrow (15'-20'). Holes were made in the ceilings to let smoke from fireplaces escape.

In the early days, before the advent of the ax, the Indians would get the wood for their houses by burning down what they needed. Before proceeding to build, the "construction crew" would decide how big the house was to be, then proceed to collect corner posts, supporting poles, rafters, and the bark (usually elm) which would be applied to the outside of the building.

Bunks were built on the inside of the building to comfortably house its inhabitants, and storage platforms would be built above these beds, to be used for storing corn and other foods. Doors to the lodge were usually made of bearskin pelts which would be tanned and attached to the jamb posts by thongs.

Indian settlements in the East were made up of a number of these buildings, sometimes stockaded to keep their inhabitants safe.

Maple Sugaring Items

Sap dishes were made to be placed under maple sugar trees. These dishes, usually made from elm or birch bark, would be scraped smooth and bound with strips at each end. Sometimes a bark "cone" would be filled with snow and topped with maple syrup as a treat for the children.

Bark containers were made from white birch, elm, chestnut, basswood, ash, cedar, fir, and spruce. When the sap was flowing in the spring, the tree would be stripped by making two circular cuts on the trunk, then making a third cut, which connected the two others lengthwise. A sturdy stick was used to pry the bark from the tree.

Water pails would be made out of this bark by first soaking the bark in hot water to make it easier to fold. Then four corners were folded up and a handle put in the middle. Sometimes these "pails" were even used for boiling.

Mortars

Wooden mortars made by New England Indians were often up to 25″ long. A log would be hollowed out to create a mortar and the Mohegans were known to carve their mortars on the outside. The interior would be burned hollow and the mortar scraped from the sides.

When used to crush kernels, the force of the pestle would push the smaller pieces to the top of the mortar, while the larger ones stayed on the bottom.

Spoons

Wooden spoons made by the Northwest Coast Indians were usually of alder, maple, or yew and they resembled ladles. Though most are plain and useful, other spoons are decorated or embellished with carving, painting, and inlay.

Northeastern tribes used wooden spoons and bowls made from the burls of trees, burnt and scraped until they were just a thin shell. These serving vessels were often used by everyone in the tribe. Though there were many made, few still exist because wood does not hold up well when buried in cold New England soil.

Totem Poles

Totem poles are the work of Northwest Coast Indians whose wood carvings were truly the best and most dramatic of any of the North American Indian tribes. The Haida tribe was unequaled as totem pole carvers. However, there are hundreds of different type poles which have crumbled beyond salvaging. The Haida culture itself began to collapse in the mid–1870s when its people began to die by the thousands after contracting European diseases, diseases to which they had previously not been exposed.

Totem poles were made hundreds of years before European contact, yet the art of pole carving grew slowly because only the wealthiest and most powerful families in the village could afford to have them made. Once the tools used to make these poles were more modernized, they became easier to make and their use spread. Totem pole carving was also encouraged by the unexpected flow of material goods into small villages.

Two distinct types of poles were carved: memorial poles, to honor past leaders, and house poles, decorative posts installed within the house itself. Some villages raised many poles and, upon entering the village, there appeared to be a forest of poles, while others raised only a few or none at all. The oldest memorial poles were simple, uncarved shafts which were topped by single carved figures. The house posts probably came after the memorial posts, and were used in supporting the house roof and to display the lineage crests of the homeowners. They were not erected to memorialize the dead, but rather to record the family history. Their carvings are more detailed, and they are more complex and broader than memorial posts.

Heraldic poles, or true totem poles, are free-standing storytelling poles. The poles tell of mythical and historical pasts by carving one figure on top of another and painting them brilliantly. It publicly displays important tales of renowned ancestors and, naturally, the better the carver, the more impressive the pole.

The most commonly depicted characters on poles are the raven, portrayed as a male; the eagle, its curved beak turning back to the face; the thunderbird, a larger eagle with outstretched wings and ears resembling horns; the grizzly, with a large open mouth and long, narrow tongue (sometimes biting a frog which it holds in its hands); a wolf, similar to a grizzly, but thinner, with a more narrow snout and more pointed teeth; a beaver, always upright with its paws holding a stick; frogs, used as space fillers, having broad, toothless mouths and big eyes; whales, with flat faces, rounded teeth, and circular blow holes above the foreheads; and numerous others. Human beings are also depicted on totem poles and may have animal or bird characteristics.

Some well known Kwakiutl totem pole carvers include Mungo Martin; Charles James; Bill Reid; Douglas Cranmer; Robert Davidson, and others who are not as well known. The totem pole carvers were well-respected members of the community and their "signatures" were often the strippling on the pole.

WOODEN ITEM LISTINGS

Cree

From the collection of Phyllis Ellison. Photo by Gene Kangas.

Decoy; bundled stick goose decoy. $75–$150

From the collection of Gene and Linda Kangas. Photo by Gene Kangas.

Decoy; field goose decoy; these were not intended to float, but were stuck in snow or mud.   **$250–$500**

Crow

Dance wand; fully beaded in blue, pink, and white; 21″ × 2½″.
                                                         $25–$45

Quirt; carved wooden quirt w/bead decoration and braided rawhide ends; 37″ × 1″.   **$70–$100**

Rattle, Kit Fox Society; belonged to "Plenty Coups"; ca. 1880.
                                                     $2000–$2500

Haida

Bowl; carved and painted feast dish w/trade bead inlays around top; ca. 1930; 11″ × 5″ × 3″.   **$105–$150**

Paddle; small paddle w/black and red old-time painting of a shark on each side; 30″ × 4½″.   **$100–$150**

Speaker's staff; 19th century of carved alder; age crack at right foot and at back of head; 23″ long.   **$1350–$1600**

Totem pole; bird, clan hats, and bear figure in polychrome house paint; ca. 1920; signed "Vancouver, Canada" and store name on back; 12½″ high.   **$100–$150**

Wood clapper; carved w/two Shaman masks, one on each side; show old paint and good patina; 10″ long. $275–$325

Iroquois

Mask; miniature carved and painted "false face" mask; signed LaValle; ca. 1965; 4″ × 2½″. $60–$80

Mask; unusual miniature "false face" Society mask; signed LaValle; ca. 1975; 5″ × 3″. $75–$100

Kwakiutl

Carving; unusual totemic wood carving depicting two house posts w/animals on top; signed Don; ca. 1965; 9″ × 8″. $65–$95

Carving; classic carved and painted carving of a masked Shaman; 9½″ high. $200–$250

Dish; contemporary carved wooden frog dish w/lid on back; 9″ × 7″.
                                               $110–$175

Rattle; rare, carved, and painted ceremonial rattle; ca. 1930; 15″ × 6″.
                                               $475–$700

Totem pole; finely carved depicting an eagle atop a beaver; ca. 1970; 22″ × 4″. $105–$200

Navajo

Cradleboard; wood, hide, and silver decorated; 29½″ long × 9″ wide, solid wood boards w/hide-thong ties and two, old, hand-stamped and repousse design buttons. $100–$150

Handmade wood and wool loom; 9½″ × 9½″ w/partially finished rug in place. $30–$70

Nootka

Canoe; carved and painted model wooden canoe w/mast and paddles; ca. 1986; 9″ × 2½″. $20–$40

Canoe; large, carved wooden model canoe painted black along w/mast and two paddles; 31″ × 6″; ca. 1985. $80–$130

Northwest Coast

Courtesy of Robert W. Skinner, Inc., Bolton, MA.

Bowl; of flaring rectangular form, w/stylized totemic face motif at each bowed end, linear incised decorations on sides, rim decorated w/inset row of cowrie shells, subtle red and black pigment on end design; 14¹⁵/₁₆″.
$1200-$1500

Bowl; carved, wooden food bowl with facing eagles at each end; fine mellow patina; one beak is abraded; 15³/₄″ long × 4″ high.
$425-$500

Carving; wall plaque; designed and carved by Ward Howard Lane; 23½″ × 18″.
$80-$110

Carving; Kwakiutl, face mask; 21″ × 18″; restored.
$550-$700

Carving; wood painted and carved Makah boat; 17½″ × 4″. **$15-$25**

Carvings; pair of signed, carved and painted eagle design wall plaques; ca. 1986; 7″ × 4″.
$85-$100

Carving; colored, wooden eagle head wall hanging; signed RY; ca. 1985; 11″ × 8″.
$50-$75

Carving; carved, wooden killer whale; signed RY; ca. 1987; 15″ × 11″.
$35-$50

Club; large fish killing and gaffing club; ca. 1900; 17″ × 2″. **$50-$75**

Comb; finely carved w/raven and frog and w/abalone inlay; 3½″ × 1½″; ca. 1975.
$150-$200

Dish; carved, wooden frog bowl w/abalone and shell inlays; signed LaValle; 9″ × 3½″; ca. 1975.
$250-$300

Dish; carved to represent a seal; decorated with bone, beads, and abalone; 12″ × 6″ × 4″. **$550–$700**

Dish; fine rectangular food dish; sloping sides carved stylized head, sides and tail of beaver; mellow patina; inside shows much evidence of cutting and chopping; small age crack at one end; 9¼″ wide × 18½″ long.
$1400–$1600

Dish; fine carved and inlaid wooden raven dish; signed LaValle; ca. 1975; 9″ × 4″. **$100–$150**

Frontlet; carved and painted "bird beak" frontlet; ca. 1880. **$100–$150**

Frontlet; finely carved and inlaid animal head effigy frontlet; signed LaValle; ca. 1975; 3½″ × 3″. **$175–$200**

Mask; miniature carved, painted, and inlaid mask; signed LaValle; ca. 1975; 3½″ × 3″. **$110–$150**

Mask; miniature carved and painted mask; signed LaValle; ca. 1975; 3½″ × 2″. **$65–$100**

Mask; Makah house mask; carved and painted; 31½″ × 21″.
$500–$700

Mask; miniature carved and painted wood mask w/abalone inlay; signed LaValle; ca. 1975. **$40–$80**

Mask; carved, contemporary face mask with human hair, copper ring in nose, painted with mirror inlay. **$225–$325**

Mask; large, carved and painted cedar mask; signed LaValle; 10″ × 9″.
$150–$250

Mask; miniature carved and painted wooden mask w/abalone inlay; signed LaValle; 4″ × 3″. **$75–$100**

Mask; rare, miniature, carved and painted ceremonial mask; signed LaValle; ca. 1980; 3″ × 2″. **$60–$75**

Mask; Kwakiutl moon mask by Tony Hunt; 19″ × 19″ × 5″.
$220–$300

Paddle; small, beautifully painted and carved wooden paddle; 32″ × 4″; ca. 1880. **$105–$130**

Paddles; cedar wood Haida killer whale ceremonial paddles; ca. 1900; 17″. **$775–$1000**

Pipe; carved in kneeling human form w/long metal bowl; 3″ × 2½″; ca. 1975. **$100–$200**

Pipe; carved, wood pipe with shell inlay; 9″. **$80–$100**

Courtesy of Robert W. Skinner, Inc., Bolton, MA.

Rattle; polychrome, carved in two sections in the form of raven in flight w/man reclining on his back, w/frog being pulled from his mouth by a kingfisher bird; the belly of rattle/raven is decorated w/sharply hooked nose hawk; two-ply twined fiber-wrapped handle; 14″ long.

$4500–$5500

Rattle; finely carved rattle in form of killer whale; good patina; 11″ × 5″; wood splitting at handle and at mouth. **$700–$900**

Rattle; painted wood; 9½″ long; polychrome "fish" w/drilled and hammered copper disks suspended on rawhide from the mouth; sealskin-wrapped handle. **$135–$175**

Speakers staff; long, carved, painted, and inlaid; signed LaValle; 46″ × 2″; ca. 1975. **$450–$800**

Totem Pole; carved w/voracious bear seated on an oval base and holding a human figure in his forepaws, surmounted in turn by five incised potlatch rings and a hawk at the top, holding a totemic mask in its talons; red, green, and black painted details; 20⅝″. **$750–$1000**

Passamaquody

Box; round birch bark; figural decoration around the body; floral design scratch-etched into the lid; 7″ diameter. **$60–$110**

Firkin; round birch bark w/floral and geometric etched pattern decoration, bottom w/crack, lacking lid; good size; approximately 13″ diameter; 8″ high.   **$150–$225**

Salish

Carving; large, carved killer whale; signed Aleck; 26″ × 12″; ca. 1985.
$125–$150

Mat creaser; old, carved mat creaser in bird head form; ca. 1870; 6¾″ × 3″.   **$175–$225**

Tlingit

Bowl; carved, wooden bowl in form of a seal w/abalone shell inlay; 7″ × 15″.   **$350–$500**

Bowl; small wooden grease dish in frog form; 2½″ × 4½″. **$90–$125**

Carving; carved and painted grease dish in seal form; ca. 1910.
$50–$75

Seal bowl; Tlingit/Haida; wooden food dish, carved to represent a seal; 6″ × 15½″.   **$350–$500**

Totem pole; model totem pole; ca. 1900; wasco over wolf figure; soft blue-green, red, and black print; fine aged patina; 12½″ high. **$195–$250**

Totem pole; old pole w/four bears climbing up and one on top, all being chased by a canine; 52″ × 10″; ca. 1890.   **$750–$1000**

Wand; carved, wooden raven wand; concave back typical of 19th century work; wonderful old patina.   **$725–$900**

Woodlands

Basket; covered birch bark basket trade cloth top; handle missing; 9″ × 6″.   **$60–$80**

Birch bark containers (2); w/peeled back decoration.   **$150–$250**

Bowl; heavy, small Eastern Woodlands burl bowl w/handles; ca. 1870; 7″ × 3″.   **$110–$130**

Bowl; burled wood utility bowl of flaring form; rectangular openwork handles; 19¼″ long; 14½″ wide.   **$1600–$1800**

Container; made of birch bark; cylindrical form; decorated overall w/geometric designs, floral motifs, hunter, moose, and a deer; 13″ high.   **$275–$350**

Cup; carved burl cup w/carved handle and a deer in bas relief on the bottom; ca. 1870; 2″ × 4¾″.   **$60–$90**

Ladle; broad, shallow round bowl; tapering handle; terminates in a stylized hook; 12″ long.   **$125-$200**

Moose call made from birch bark; Northeast Woodlands; 18″ × 5½″.
                                                                        $35-$70

Spoon; carved, broad oval bowl w/handle terminating in stylized resting water fowl; 9″ long.   **$375-$425**

Other

Courtesy of Donna McMenamin, private collector. Photo by Donald Vogt.

Box, Northeast; birch bark box decorated w/red, blue, and green painted designs; probably used for storage.   **$400-$500**

Box; folded bark storage box; bentwood rim attached w/string; fine utilitarian object; 11″ × 14″.   **$100-$150**

Courtesy of Jack Glover, Sunset, TX. Photo by Donald Vogt.

Box; owned by Quanah Parker; heavily carved with eagles on both ends as well as on top; painted w/white, blue, yellow, and red.

Courtesy of Jack Glover, Sunset, TX. Photo by Donald Vogt.

Cane; belonged to Geronimo; beaded in blue background w/white, green, and red designs; provenance stated in owner's papers.

Carving, Wasco; ancient stone fish effigy carving w/drilled holes for use as a pendant; ca. 1700; 4¾″ × 1¼″. **$25–$50**

Carving; wall plaque w/Indian chief head carved in relief; 6″ × 5″; ca. 1940. **$20–$30**

Ceremonial mask; Yaqui Indian; Pascol Easter painted and carved mask w/horsehair. **$55–$110**

Chippewa, canoe; large model birch bark canoe made exactly like a large one; ca. 1910; 26″ × 5″. **$35–$55**

Container; old, oval porcupine-quilled container w/three bands of spruce root windings forming the height 3″; the top band being the rim of the cover; the top of the box w/X cross design with triangles and diamonds; some quill loss, but good for mid–19th-century example of quillwork.
$150–$200

Cradleboard; by Armenia Miles, first prize Navajo fair 1985 (Arts and Crafts). **$110–$150**

From the collection of David L. Atteberry. Photo by Donald Vogt.

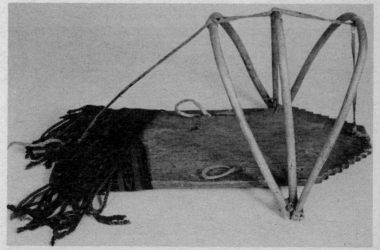

Cradleboard, Santo Domingo; cradleboard w/sash for securing child to board; measures 15″. **$200–$300**

From the collection of Gene and Linda Kangas. Photo by Gene Kangas.

Decoy; fish decoy from a reservation near Lake Simcoe, Ontario; wood stained white w/burned spots, gills, eyes and mouth; metal fins and tail.   **$75–$150**

From the collection of Gene and Linda Kangas. Photo by Gene Kangas.

Decoy; pike spearing decoy by Frank Gensio, Stockbridge, Wisconsin; used on Lake Winnebago; natural cedar w/copper fins.   **$350–$500**

From the collection of Gene and Linda Kangas. Photo by Gene Kangas.

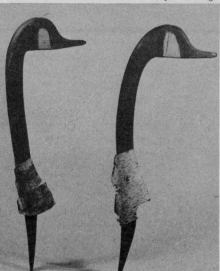

Decoys; two stick-up Canada goose heads; two-piece head and neck construction; bottoms wrapped w/natural birch bark to resemble the white chest of a goose; Prince Edward Island, Canada.   **$200–$400 ea.**

From the collection of Gene and Linda Kangas. Photo by Gene Kangas.

Decoy, Shinnecock; heron decoy; Long Island, NY; relief-carved wings, two wooden legs; these large birds were hunted for food and feathers.
                                                                    $6000–$10,000

From the collection of Gene and Linda Kangas. Photo by Gene Kangas.

Decoy, Micmac; stick-up sea gull; hollow construction; a large and rare decoy. **$8000–$12,000**

Hopewell, carved figure; male effigy 4½″ tall and book and letter on Hopewell pipes. **$25–$45**

Hopi, five polychromed figural wooden carvings; contemporary; of Apache Gan dancers, each wearing ceremonial headdress and carrying dance wands; minor areas of repair; average height 16″. **$400–$500**

Makah, house totem; carved and painted wood totem in form of eagle; 34″ × 36″; some damage. **$200–$250**

Mask; crooked mouth false face mask w/black, red, and white paint; 7½″ × 6″. **$60–$80**

Micmac, box; quill decorated, birch bark; of domed rectangular form, paneled wood lining, geometric design motif of dyed porcupine quills (quill and binding loss); 5⅜″ × 4½″ × 4″. **$275–$375**

Osage, dance rattle; turtleshell w/5″ painted wooden handle, tipped w/turtle head; 9½″ overall size; good condition. **$30–$50**

Pipe, Athabascan; rare, carved wooden pipe w/carved stem and brass trim; ca. 1880; 7″ × 1¼″. **$30–$50**

Plains, dance wand; wand carved w/horse head; painted and brass tacks; showing file burn marks and good patina; 30½″ long. **$275–$325**

Quilled box; mid–19th century; spruce root banded lid with top quilled in a diamond and chevron design; showing some losses and age; oval; 6″ × 3½″ × 3″ high.   **$170–$220**

Totem pole; carved and painted model wooden totem pole; ca. 1930; 11″ × 2″.   **$25–$30**

THE MODERN
ARTIST/ARTISAN

▼▼▼▼▼▼▼▼▼▼▼▼▼

Though most antique collectors shy away from those items made from the 1950s until today, Indian art collectors are beginning to realize the value of the work today's Indian artists are producing. In most cases, today's Amerind artists, jewelers, potters, leather workers, kachina carvers, basketmakers, and blanketweavers have learned their art from their parents, grandparents or other family members. There are few instances where the artist uses totally modern tools in his/her work and even fewer where the Indian is not celebrating his/her own heritage through his/her art or craft. Because of that reason, the work being produced today is highly collectible and should be recognized as part of this book.

Throughout the previous chapters, I have detailed various artists/artisans whose work has come to light and whose names are known. There are many more who have not been mentioned because of lack of information and there will be many new faces in the years to come.

The cultural center of Amerind arts and crafts in today's United States is in the Southwest, though the Northwest Coast Indians are still producing fine, carved wood pieces, such as totem poles, and an occasional blanket may still be ordered from a craftsperson who has retained the art. The Northeast, though never as strong as the Southwest in crafts, does not produce any items of note. Yet, there are artists living throughout the Northeast who are producing art which people believe comes from the Southwest (i.e., Jamie Reason). In the South, you may still buy a Seminole doll or clothing made in the Seminole patchwork style.

The reason for the Southwest's continued prominence in the world of art may be that it supports its artists and craftspeople by giving them the opportunity to sell their wares to the public and by celebrating their heritage through ceremonials, shows, sales, auctions, and direct sales through trading posts. Prizes are given for the art produced by the younger Indians and it encourages them to stay in their field, to produce the best basket, jewelry, pottery, etc., that they can. It also provides an income which can be as high or low as they wish (depending on their talent and how much work they wish to put into their art).

The Gallup ceremonial, held once a year in August, is known for being "the place to be" to get your art seen. Every year new blue-ribbon winners come from the ceremonial and offer collectors the chance to buy their wares (complete with ribbons attached). Competition for these new winners is intense and collectors consider it a "feather in their cap" to add a first-prize-winning basket or other item to their collection.

Other ceremonials are held all over the Southwest and West throughout the summer and can provide a season's entertainment for those collectors who want to run the circuit. Other such ceremonials include the Indian Hills Pow-Wow (Tehachapi, California), Prescott All Indian Pow-Wow (Prescott, Arizona), Chin-Qua-Pin Pow-Wow (Woodland Park, Colorado), Indian Market and Mountain Men Rendezvous (Page, Arizona), Plains Indian Pow-Wow (Cody, Wyoming), Intertribal Pow-Wow (Oakland, California), Hopi Craftsman Exhibition (held for well over 50 years in Flagstaff, Arizona), Taos Pueblo Pow-Wow, (Taos, New Mexico), and many, many others.

The young artists are supported by the Indian Art Foundation in Albuquerque, New Mexico, who provide assistance in marketing, consumer education, and funding sources. The craftspeople are also represented in a catalog published by the Indian Arts and Crafts Association. Members are listed, with their addresses, as craftspeople, collectors, or retailers, and the booklet proves to be quite useful when you are trying to find new avenues to explore or new craftspeople to study.

Auctioneers who specialize in Indian items usually have a few of the newer pieces of art available for sale and make it their business to know something of the artist, because that is the best way to make a sale. It is also a practice of dealers who specialize in American Indian art to know something of the people who make the items which they sell. Of all the dealers we visited throughout the Southwest, I believe there was only one who did not represent any of the new artists.

The trading posts always have work by contemporary artists, though each post is different and it takes some time and energy to explore them before you find the articles you desire. Often the store will have a catalog available for customers, and it might save time and energy to write to them before making a trip to ask them whether they represent the Indian artist you are interested in collecting.

Publications, such as *The Indian Trader, American Indian Art* magazine, and the new (and very beautiful) *Native Peoples* magazine, published by the Heard Museum, are extremely helpful in getting collectors in touch with new artists and their wares. *The Indian Trader* makes it a point of doing features on prize-winning artists or artisans who work in an unusual manner, while *American Indian Art* concentrates on those represented in museums.

If you happen to be lucky enough to buy from the artists/craftspeople directly, make sure you get their signature on the piece you are purchasing because it will make it easier to identify later and will add to its value. As I have explained earlier, most baskets were not signed, making it difficult to identify their makers, but jewelry, pottery, and other crafts have been identified for many years and have, therefore, increased tremendously in value.

One last thought: since antique Indian items are among the hottest collectibles in the antiques world right now, some of them might be out of your price range . . . which gives you another reason to patronize the younger and upcoming artists—their work is still easy on the pocketbook!

Happy collecting!

Appendixes

APPENDIX A:
DEALER LISTINGS

▼▼▼▼▼▼▼▼▼▼▼

Gunther Adams
Rangeley, ME

Adobe Gallery
Alexander Anthony, Jr.
413 Romero N.W. (Old Town)
Albuquerque, NM 87104
Specializing in art of the
Southwest Indian.

Donna Ash
IGLS Fine Art, Inc.
Route 101
Amherst, NH 03031

*Broken Arrow Indian Arts
and Crafts*
222 North Plaza
Taos, NM 87571

Cameron Trading Post
Cameron, AZ

Wanda Campbell
Indian Art Unlimited
Route 1
Carmi, IL 62821

Canfield Gallery
414 Canyon Road
Santa Fe, NM 87504

Timothy C. Duran, Director
J.J. Brookings & Co.
330 Commercial Street
P.O. Box 1237
San Jose, CA 95108

Enbee Collectibles
San Diego, CA

Jack Glover's Wild West Museum
Sunset, TX 76270

Larry Gottheim
Fine Early Photographs
33 Orton Avenue
Binghamton, NY 13905
Publisher of photographic
brochure.

Joe Grandee, Artist
Dallas/Fort Worth, TX

Randy R. Lubow
North Palm Beach, FL 33408

Many Horses Gallery
Contemporary Fine Arts
of the Southwest
7140 N. La Cienega Boulevard
Los Angeles, CA 90069

Miniatures at the Kiva
222 N. Plaza
Taos, NM 87571

Morning Star Gallery
Santa Fe, NM 87501

*Naranjo's World of
American Indian Art*
4621 Montrose, Suite 210
P.O. Box 7973
Houston, TX 77270

Old Town Antiques
Eleanor Maher/Joan Gough
2108 Charlevoix Street N.W.
Albuquerque, NM 87104

Randy Sandler
Cincinnati Art Galleries
635 Main Street
Cincinnati, OH 45202

Susan Sheehan, Inc.
52 East 76th Street
Third Floor
New York, NY 10021
American prints.

Two Star Collection
P.O. Box 90075-243
Houston, TX 77290
Specializing in American Indian
items.

Zaplin-Lampert Gallery
651 Canyon Road
Santa Fe, NM 87501
Specializing in nineteenth- and
twentieth-century American
paintings, watercolors,
drawings, and prints. Also
available are native American
Indian artifacts.

APPENDIX B:
AUCTIONEER LISTINGS

▼▼▼▼▼▼▼▼▼▼▼

Col. Doug and Debbie Allard
P.O. Box 460
St. Ignatius, MT 59865

James O. Aplan
HC 80, Box 795
Piedmont, SD 57769

Dunning's Auction Service, Inc.
755 Church Road
Elgin, IL 60123

*The Fine Arts Company of
Philadelphia, Inc.*
2317 Chestnut Street
Philadelphia, PA 19103

Garth's Auctions, Inc.
2690 Stratford Road
Box 369
Delaware, OH 43015

C.E. Guarino
Box 49
Berry Road
Denmark, ME 04022

Ted Hake
Hake's Americana and
Collectibles
P.O. Box 1444
York, PA 17405

Frank C. Kaminski Co.
P.O. Box 29
Stoneham, MA 02180

Joy Luke
Fine Arts Broker and
Auctioneer
The Gallery
300 E. Grove Street
Bloomington, IL 61701

*Bob, Chuck & Rich Roan, Inc.,
Auctioneers*
Box 118, RD #3
Cogan Station, PA 17728

Judy Robinson Gallery
3500 Columbia Parkway
Cincinnati, OH 45226

Jack Sellner, CAI
P.O. Box 1113
Scottsdale, AZ 85252
Yearly Indian auctions.

Robert W. Skinner, Inc.
Route 117
Bolton, MA 01740

Von Reece Auctioneers
6605 Live Oak Drive
Austin, TX 78746

APPENDIX C:
COLLECTOR LISTINGS

▼▼▼▼▼▼▼▼▼▼▼▼

Winona Joan Arbuckle
TX

David L. Atteberry
3974 Lost Creek
Dallas, TX 75224

Gloria and Steve Cowgill
Taos, NM

Phyllis Ellison
Savannah, GA 31401

Lahoma Haddock Goldsmith
Okmulgee, OK

Jack Glover (author/sculptor)
Sunset, TX 76270

Hadden/Saylor
Albuquerque, NM

Norman Y. and Bernice M. Harris
CA

Gene and Linda Kangas
Painesville, OH

N.A. McKinney
TX

Donna McMenamin
Houston, TX

William R. Nash
Tulsa, OK

Helen Pringle
Aledo, TX

Jamie Tawodi Reason (artist)
New York/Vermont/London,
England

Joyce Williams
Okmulgee, OK

BIBLIOGRAPHY

▼▼▼▼▼▼▼▼▼▼▼▼

Antiques and the Arts Weekly, February 5, 1988, "Lost and Found Traditions—Renwick Gallery Show on View Thru March 6," pp. 1-3.

———, February 12, 1988, "Ethnographic Art to be Sold at Hesse Galleries February 20," pp. 100-101.

———, February 12, 1988, "Navajo Rug Exhibition Opening in Lexington," p. 35.

———, September 25, 1987, "It's Westward Ho at the Springfield Art Museums," p. 20.

Appleton, LeRoy H. *American Indian Design and Decoration*, Dover Publications, New York, 1971.

Arden, Harvey. "The Fire that Never Dies," *National Geographic*, September, 1987, pp. 375-403.

Arizona Highways, July, 1972, "The Story of the Gallup Inter-Tribal Indian Ceremonial."

———, June, 1973, "Hopi Kachina Artist Alwin James Makya."

———, June, 1973, "Basket Making in Arizona by Don Dedera."

———, June, 1973, "Asmar—Interprets Southwestern Indian Ceremonies and Life."

Arnold, David L. "Pueblo Artistry in Clay," *National Geographic*, Vol. 162, No. 5, November, 1982.

Art and Antiques, March, 1988, "America's Top 100 Collectors," pp. 49-81.

Babcock, Barbara A., and Monthan, Guy and Doris. *The Pueblo Storyteller*, The University of Arizona Press, Tucson, 1986.

Bataille, Gretchen M., and Sands, Kathleen Mullen. *American Indian Women: Telling Their Lives*, University of Nebraska Press, Omaha, 1984.

Beidler, Peter G., and Egge, Marion F. *The American Indian in Short Fiction*, an annotated bibliography, The Scarecrow Press, Inc., Metuchen, NJ and London, 1979.

Bennett, Edna Mae, and John F. *Turquoise Jewelry of the Indians of the Southwest*, Turquoise Books, CO, 1973.

Bennett, Kathleen Whittaker. "The Navajo Chief Blanket—A Trade Item Among Non-Navajo Groups," *American Indian Art Magazine*, Winter, 1981, pp. 62–68.

Brose, David S., Brown, James A., and Penney, David W. *Ancient Art of the American Woodland Indians*, Harry N. Abrams, Inc., New York, 1985.

Brown, Dee. *Bury My Heart at Wounded Knee*, Bantam Books, New York, 1961.

Brownell, Charles De Wolf. *The Indian Races of North and South America*, Hurlbut, Scranton and Company, Philadelphia, 1865.

Bunzel, Ruth L. *The Pueblo Potter: A Study in Primitive Art*, Dover Publications, New York, 1972.

Canby, Thomas Y. "The Anasazi: Riddles in the Ruins," *National Geographic*, Vol. 162, No. 5, November, 1982.

Catlin, George. *Letters and Notes on the Manners, Customs and Conditions of the North American Indians*, Dover Publications, New York, 1973.

Chavez, Denise. "Words of Wisdom," *New Mexico Magazine*, December, 1987. Vol. 65, No. 12, pp. 72-78.

Cirillo, Dexter. "Back to the Past: Tradition and Change in Contemporary Pueblo Jewelry," *American Indian Art*, Spring, 1988, Vol. 13, No. 2, pp. 46–63.

Clark, Carol. "Charles Deas," *American History Illustrated*, pp. 19–33.

Clark, Ella E.. *Indian Legends of the Pacific Northwest*, University of California Press, CA, 1953.

Clark, Jackson. "The 1988 IACA Artist of the Year," *The Indian Trader*, November, 1987, Vol. 18, No. 11, pp. 4–5.

Culin, Stewart. *Games of the North American Indians*, Dover Publications, New York, 1975.

Currier, William T. *Currier's Price Guide to American Artists 1645-1945 at Auction*, Currier Publications, Brockton, MA, 1987.

Dallas, Sandra. "Triumph on a Loom," *Americana*, June, 1988, Vol. 10, No. 2, pp. 54–57.

Densmore, Frances. *How Indians Use Wild Plants for Food, Medicine and Crafts*, Dover Publications, New York, 1974.

Dockstader, Dr. Frederick. "A Capsule View of the Hopi," *The Indian Trader*, March, 1988.

Drimmer, Frederick, ed. *Captured by the Indians, 15 Firsthand Accounts, 1750-1870*, Dover Publications, New York, 1961.

Durrell, Pat. "Collecting Trade Beads," *The Indian Trader*, October 1987, Vol. 18, No. 10, pp. 4–5.

Elliott, Malinda. "Collectors Find Hidden Gold," *New Mexico Magazine*, January, 1988, Vol. 66, No. 1, pp. 50–54.

Elliott, Mark, "Basic Techniques in Beading," and "Material and Techniques of Beadwork," *The Indian Trader*, October, 1987, Vol. 18, No. 10, pp. 14–15.

Erdoes, Richard, and Ortiz, Alfonso. *American Indian Myths and Legends*, Pantheon Books, New York, 1984.

Ewers, John C. *Plains Indian Sculpture—A Traditional Art From America's Heartland*, Smithsonian Institution Press, Washington, D.C., 1986.

Falk, Peter Hastings. *Who was Who in American Art*, Sound View Press, Madison, CT, 1985.

Fielding, Mantle. *Dictionary of American Painters, Sculptors and Engravers*, Modern Books & Crafts, Inc., CT, 1974.

Fleming, Paula Richardson, and Luskey, Judith. *The North American Indians in Early Photographs*, Harper and Row, New York, 1986.

Frank, Larry. *Indian Silver Jewelry of the Southwest, 1868–1930*, New York Graphic Society, Boston, 1978.

Gillman, Carolyn. "The Way to Independence: An Exhibition at the Minnesota Historical Society," *American Indian Art*, Spring, 1988.

Gustafson, Eleanor H. "Museum Accessions," *The Magazine Antiques*, October, 1987.

Harsant, Wendy J. "The Otago Museum, Dunedin, New Zealand: The North American Indian Collection," *American Indian Art*, Spring, 1988.

Hassrick, Royal B. *The George Catlin Book of American Indians*, Promontory Press, NY, 1977.

Holm, Bill. "A Wooling Mantle Neatly Wrought: The Early Historic Record of Northwest Coast Pattern-Twined Textiles—1774–1850," *American Indian Art Magazine*, Winter, 1982, pp. 34–47.

Hothem, Lar. *Collecting Indian Knives (Identifications and Values)*, Books Americana, Inc., Florence, AL, 1986.

———, *North American Indian Artifacts*, 3rd Edition, Books Americana, Inc., Florence, AL, 1984.

Hungry Wolf, Beverly. *The Ways of My Grandmothers*, William Morrow and Company, New York, 1982.

Jacka, Jerry D. "Innovations in Southwestern Indian Jewelry: Fine Art in the 1980s," *American Indian Art Magazine*, Spring, 1984, pp. 28–37.

Jacka, Lois, and Tanner, Clara Lee. "Moments with Maria," *Native Peoples: The Journal of the Heard Museum*, Winter, 1988, pp. 24–29.

Jacobsen, Anita, *Jacobsen's Sixth Painting and Bronze Price Guide*, Vol. VI, published by Anita Jacobsen, 1983.

James, George Wharton. *Indian Blankets and Their Makers*, Dover Publications, New York, 1974.

————, *Indian Basketry*, Dover Publications, New York, 1972.

Kahn, Brenda Norrell. "Margaret Quintana, Mistress of the Storytellers," *The Indian Trader*, December, 1987.

Kazin, Alfred. "Southwestward—The Great American Space," *American Heritage*, April, 1987, pp. 53–61.

Keating, Bern, and Harbutt, Charles. "Today Along the Natchez Trace Pathway Through History," *National Geographic*, November, 1968.

Kent, Kate P. "Pueblo Weaving," *American Indian Art Magazine*, Winter, 1981, pp. 32–45.

Kimball, Richard. "Up to the Green River—The Knife that Won the West," *The Indian Trader*, May, 1988.

————, "The Great Tree of Peace," *The Indian Trader*, March, 1988.

Kopper, Philip. *The Smithsonian Book of North American Indians Before the Coming of the Europeans*, Smithsonian Institution Press, Washington, D.C., 1986.

Kramer, Fran. "Crystal Ball Gazing," *Antique Review*, February, 1988, p. 27.

Kroeber, A.L. *Handbook of the Indians of California*, Dover Publications, New York, 1976.

Lamar, Howard R., ed. *The Reader's Encyclopedia of the American West*, Harper and Row, New York, 1977.

Laxalt, Robert, and Woolfitt, Adam. "New Mexico, the Golden Land," *National Geographic*, September, 1970.

LeFree, Betty. *Santa Clara Pottery Today*, University of New Mexico Press, Albuquerque, 1975.

Looney, Ralph, and Dale, Bruce. "The Navajo Nation Looks Ahead," *National Geographic*, December, 1972.

Mallery, Garrick. *Picture Writing of the American Indians, Vol. I and Vol. II*, Dover Publications, New York, 1972.

Mariette, Kim Rosea. "Why Indians Painted Their Horses," *American West*, February, 1988, Vol. XXV, No. 1, pp. 72–75.

McCoy, Ronald. "Apache Rawhide Playing Cards," *American Indian Art Magazine*, Summer, 1984, pp. 52–59.

McCullough, David. "Frederick Remington," *American History Illustrated*, February, 1988, Vol. XXII, No. 10, pp. 26–39.

McKay, Gary. "Connoisseurship-Consuming Interests," *Ultra, The Texas Lifestyle Magazine,* January, 1988, Vol. XVII, No. 5.

Meilach, Dona Z. *Ethnic Jewelry—Design and Inspiration for Collectors,* Crown Publishers, NY, 1981.

Mera, H.P. *Pueblo Designs,* Dover Publications, New York, 1970.

Meredith, Roy. *Mr. Lincoln's Camera Man: Matthew B. Brady,* Dover Publications, New York, 1946.

Miller, Pamela Stanley. *Authentic American Indian Beadwork and How to Do It,* Dover Publications, New York, 1984.

Moeser, Vikki. "Lost and Found Indian Traditions," *The Indian Trader,* December, 1987.

Navajo School of Indian Basketry, *Indian Basket Weaving,* Dover Publications, New York, 1971.

Naylor, Maria, ed. *Authentic Indian Designs,* Dover Publications, New York, 1975.

New Mexico Magazine, November, 1987, "Santa Fe Creators," Vol. 65, No. 11, pp. 43–49.

O'Kane, Walter Collins. *The Hopis: Portrait of a Desert People,* University of Oklahoma Press, OK, 1953.

Page, Jake. "Inside the Sacred Hopi Homeland," *National Geographic,* Vol. 162, No. 5, November 1982.

Parker, Arthur C. *The Indian How Book,* Dover Publications, New York, 1975.

Perry, Erma. "Stephen Laurent: An Authority on the Abenaki Indian History," *Grit,* November, 1987.

Plett, Nicole. "The Best of the Westerns," *Southwest Profile,* Vol. II, No. 2.

Raycraft, Don and Carol. *Collector's Guide to Country Store Antiques,* Collector Books, Paducah, KY, 1987.

Reichard, Gladys A. *Weaving a Navajo Blanket,* Dover Publications, New York, 1974.

Rhodes, Lee. "Conceived in Beauty—Executed w/Dignity," *Arizona Highways,* July, 1972.

Ripp, Bart. "Eleven Indian Painters Created a Treasure at Maisel's," *Indian Trader,* March, 1988.

Sagel, Jim. "Frank Waters," *New Mexico Magazine,* February, 1988, Vol. 66, No. 2, pp. 52–57.

Sayers, Robert. "Symbol and Meaning in Hopi Ritual Textile Design," *American Indian Art Magazine,* Winter, 1981, pp. 70–77.

Sides, Dorothy Smith. *Decorative Art of the Southwestern Indians*, Dover Publications, New York, 1961.

Smithsonian Magazine, August, 1987, "At the Renwick, American Traditions."

Sneve, Virginia Driving Hawk. "Remembering Minnehaha," *Country Living*, August 1986, pp. 72–74.

Snodgrass, Jeanne O. *American Indian Painters—A Biographical Directory*, Museum of American Indian, New York, Heye Foundation, 1968.

Stafford, Kim R. "A Few Miles Short of Wisdom," *American West*, February, 1988.

Starline, Marjorie. "Karen Charley, Traditional Hopi Potter," *The Indian Trader*, March, 1988, Vol. 19, No. 3, p. 19.

Stuart, George E. "Mounds: Riddles From the Indian Past," *National Geographic*, December, 1972.

Sturtevant, William C., ed. *A Seminole Sourcebook*, Garland Publishing, Inc., 1987.

Sutton, Jacqueline E. "Following the Santa Fe Trail," *Gift Reporter*, February, 1988, pp. 22–25.

Tanner, Clara Lee. *Indian Baskets of the Southwest*, University of Arizona Press, 1983.

The Antique Traveler, January, 1988, "Indian Territory Sold at the Turn of the Century," pp. 6, 13.

The Indian Trader, August, 1987.
"The Folk Art Carvings of Johnson Antonio—The Making of a Bisti Carver," Vol. 18, No. 8, p. 4.

———, October, 1987, Vol. 18, No. 10.
"The History of Glass Beads," pp. 6–81.
"Wampum—An Early Medium of Exchange," pp. 10–11.
"From Quillwork to Beadwork," p. 20.

———, December, 1987, "The Plight of the Navajo Medicineman," Vol. 18, No. 12, pp. 4–5.

———, January, 1988, Vol. 19, No. 7.
"Indian Art Enjoying a Second Renaissance," pp. 3–4.
"The Meanings Behind Decorative Symbols used in Indian Art," p. 6.
"The Beauty of California Mission Basketry," pp. 7–9.
"The Diamond Rattlesnake Basket," pp. 9–11.
"The Calumet: A Sacred Pipe used for Rituals of Peace and War," pp. 15, 18.

————, February, 1988, "A Brief Description of the Pow-Wow and its Origins."

————, March, 1988, Vol. 19, No. 3.
"Southern Plains Museum Features Works by Tony Jojola," p. 21.
"Wampanoag Historian Traces Forefather's Lives," p. 15.
"Masayesva Selected Poster Artist for Festival of Native American Arts," p. 11.
"Newlands Outline: A New Regional Style Rug," pp. 3-4.

Theran, Susan. *Official Price Guide to Fine Art*, House of Collectibles, New York, 1987.

Thompson, Laura, and Joseph, Alice. *The Hopi Way*, United States Indian Service, 1944.

Titiev, Mischa. *The Hopi Indians of Old Oraibi: Change and Continuity*, University of Michigan Press, Detroit, 1972.

Tully, Lawrence N. *Flints, Blades and Projectile Points of the North American Indian*, Collector Books, Paducah, KY, 1986.

Turano, Jane Van N. "Sotheby's Winter Sale of American Indian Art," *Maine Antique Digest*, February, 1988.

Viola, Herman J. *Exploring the West*, Smithsonian Books, Washington, D.C., 1987.

Weinstein, Robert. "Silent Witnesses," *Photo Bulletin*, Ray Hawkins Gallery, Los Angeles, CA.

Wheeler, George M. *Wheeler's Photographic Survey of the American West 1871-1873*, Dover Publications, New York, 1983.

Whiteford, Andrew Hunter. *North American Indian Arts*, Golden Press, New York, 1973.

Whitt, Jennie. "The Art of the Plains Indians," *The Indian Trader*, June, 1983, Vol. 14, pp. 5-10.

Wild, Peter. "N. Scott Momaday: Gentle Maverick," *American West*, February, 1988.

Wright, Barton. "Kachina Carvings," *American Indian Art Magazine*, Spring, 1984, pp. 38-45, 81.

————, *Kachinas: A Hopi Artist's Documentary*, Northland Press, Flagstaff, with the Heard Museum, Phoenix, 1973.

Wright, Robyn K. "The Burke Museum: Northwest Coast Collection," *American Indian Art*, Spring, 1988, Vol. 13, No. 2, pp. 32-37.

Yenne, Bill. *The Encyclopedia of North American Indian Tribes*, Bison Books, 1986.

Zuend, Pat. "Michael Paul, Colville Indian Storypole Carver," *The Indian Trader*, November, 1987, Vol. 18, No. 11, pp. 9, 11, 13.

INDEX

▼▼▼▼▼▼▼▼▼▼▼▼

ABOUT THE AUTHOR

▼▼▼▼▼▼▼▼▼▼▼

A dealer for almost ten years, Dawn Reno has also written for many antiques, regional, and national publications such as *Vermont Woman*, *USAir*, *The Lion*, *Country Living*, and many others. She is also the author of *Collecting Black Americana* and *The Jenny Books*, a series of children's books.

Ms. Reno is currently at work on a book on American country collectibles and a novel about the world of antiques.

Today, Dawn lives in northern Vermont with her husband, Robert, daughter, Jennifer, and stepson, Bob.

The HOUSE OF COLLECTIBLES Series

☐ Please send me the following price guides—
☐ I would like the most current edition of the books listed below.

THE OFFICIAL PRICE GUIDES TO:

☐ 753-3	American Folk Art (ID) 1st Ed.	$14.95
☐ 199-3	American Silver & Silver Plate 5th Ed.	11.95
☐ 513-1	Antique Clocks 3rd Ed.	10.95
☐ 283-3	Antique & Modern Dolls 3rd Ed.	10.95
☐ 287-6	Antique & Modern Firearms 6th Ed.	11.95
☐ 755-X	Antiques & Collectibles 9th Ed.	11.95
☐ 289-2	Antique Jewelry 5th Ed.	11.95
☐ 362-7	Art Deco (ID) 1st Ed.	14.95
☐ 447-X	Arts and Crafts: American Decorative Arts, 1894–1923 (ID) 1st Ed.	12.95
☐ 539-5	Beer Cans & Collectibles 4th Ed.	7.95
☐ 521-2	Bottles Old & New 10th Ed.	10.95
☐ 532-8	Carnival Glass 2nd Ed.	10.95
☐ 295-7	Collectible Cameras 2nd Ed.	10.95
☐ 548-4	Collectibles of the '50s & '60s 1st Ed.	9.95
☐ 740-1	Collectible Toys 4th Ed.	10.95
☐ 531-X	Collector Cars 7th Ed.	12.95
☐ 538-7	Collector Handguns 4th Ed.	14.95
☐ 748-7	Collector Knives 9th Ed.	12.95
☐ 361-9	Collector Plates 5th Ed.	11.95
☐ 296-5	Collector Prints 7th Ed.	12.95
☐ 001-6	Depression Glass 2nd Ed.	9.95
☐ 589-1	Fine Art 1st Ed.	19.95
☐ 311-2	Glassware 3rd Ed.	10.95
☐ 243-4	Hummel Figurines & Plates 6th Ed.	10.95
☐ 523-9	Kitchen Collectibles 2nd Ed.	10.95
☐ 080-6	Memorabilia of Elvis Presley and The Beatles 1st Ed.	10.95
☐ 291-4	Military Collectibles 5th Ed.	11.95
☐ 525-5	Music Collectibles 6th Ed.	11.95
☐ 313-9	Old Books & Autographs 7th Ed.	11.95
☐ 298-1	Oriental Collectibles 3rd Ed.	11.95
☐ 761-4	Overstreet Comic Book 18th Ed.	12.95
☐ 522-0	Paperbacks & Magazines 1st Ed.	10.95
☐ 297-3	Paper Collectibles 5th Ed.	10.95
☐ 744-4	Political Memorabilia 1st Ed.	10.95
☐ 529-8	Pottery & Porcelain 6th Ed.	11.95
☐ 524-7	Radio, TV & Movie Memorabilia 3rd Ed.	11.95
☐ 081-4	Records 8th Ed.	16.95
☐ 763-0	Royal Doulton 6th Ed.	12.95
☐ 280-9	Science Fiction & Fantasy Collectibles 2nd Ed.	10.95
☐ 747-9	Sewing Collectibles 1st Ed.	8.95
☐ 358-9	Star Trek/Star Wars Collectibles 2nd Ed.	8.95
☐ 086-5	Watches 8th Ed.	12.95
☐ 248-5	Wicker 3rd Ed.	10.95

THE OFFICIAL:

☐ 760-6	Directory to U.S. Flea Markets 2nd Ed.	5.95
☐ 365-1	Encyclopedia of Antiques 1st Ed.	9.95
☐ 369-4	Guide to Buying and Selling Antiques 1st Ed.	9.95
☐ 414-3	Identification Guide to Early American Furniture 1st Ed.	9.95
☐ 413-5	Identification Guide to Glassware 1st Ed.	9.95

☐ 412-7	Identification Guide to Pottery & Porcelain 1st Ed.	$9.95
☐ 415-1	Identification Guide to Victorian Furniture 1st Ed.	9.95

THE OFFICIAL (SMALL SIZE) PRICE GUIDES TO:

☐ 309-0	Antiques & Flea Markets 4th Ed.	4.95
☐ 269-8	Antique Jewelry 3rd Ed.	4.95
☐ 085-7	Baseball Cards 8th Ed.	4.95
☐ 647-2	Bottles 3rd Ed.	4.95
☐ 544-1	Cars & Trucks 3rd Ed.	5.95
☐ 519-0	Collectible Americana 2nd Ed.	4.95
☐ 294-9	Collectible Records 3rd Ed.	4.95
☐ 306-6	Dolls 4th Ed.	4.95
☐ 762-2	Football Cards 8th Ed.	4.95
☐ 540-9	Glassware 3rd Ed.	4.95
☐ 526-3	Hummels 4th Ed.	4.95
☐ 279-5	Military Collectibles 3rd Ed.	4.95
☐ 764-9	Overstreet Comic Book Companion 2nd Ed.	4.95
☐ 278-7	Pocket Knives 3rd Ed.	4.95
☐ 527-1	Scouting Collectibles 4th Ed.	4.95
☐ 494-1	Star Trek/Star Wars Collectibles 3rd Ed.	3.95
☐ 088-1	Toys 5th Ed.	4.95

THE OFFICIAL BLACKBOOK PRICE GUIDES OF:

☐ 092-X	U.S. Coins 27th Ed.	4.95
☐ 095-4	U.S. Paper Money 21st Ed.	4.95
☐ 098-9	U.S. Postage Stamps 11th Ed.	4.95

THE OFFICIAL INVESTORS GUIDE TO BUYING & SELLING:

☐ 534-4	Gold, Silver & Diamonds 2nd Ed.	12.95
☐ 535-2	Gold Coins 2nd Ed.	12.95
☐ 536-0	Silver Coins 2nd Ed.	12.95
☐ 537-9	Silver Dollars 2nd Ed.	12.95

THE OFFICIAL NUMISMATIC GUIDE SERIES:

☐ 254-X	The Official Guide to Detecting Counterfeit Money 2nd Ed.	7.95
☐ 257-4	The Official Guide to Mint Errors 4th Ed.	7.95

SPECIAL INTEREST SERIES:

☐ 506-9	From Hearth to Cookstove 3rd Ed.	17.95
☐ 504-2	On Method Acting 8th Printing	6.95

TOTAL	

SEE REVERSE SIDE FOR ORDERING INSTRUCTIONS

FOR IMMEDIATE DELIVERY

VISA & MASTER CARD CUSTOMERS
ORDER TOLL FREE!
1-800-638-6460

This number is for orders only; it is not tied into the customer service or business office. Customers not using charge cards must use mail for ordering since payment is required with the order—sorry, no C.O.D.'s.

OR SEND ORDERS TO

THE HOUSE OF COLLECTIBLES
201 East 50th Street
New York, New York 10022

POSTAGE & HANDLING RATES

First Book $1.00
Each Additional Copy or Title $0.50

Total from columns on order form. Quantity_____ $_____

☐ Check or money order enclosed $_____ (include postage and handling)

☐ Please charge $_____to my: ☐ MASTERCARD ☐ VISA

Charge Card Customers Not Using Our Toll Free Number Please Fill Out The Information Below

Account No. _____ Expiration Date_____
(all digits)
Signature_____

NAME (please print)_____PHONE_____

ADDRESS_____APT. #_____

CITY_____STATE_____ZIP_____